The Critical Turn in Tourism Studies

In today's increasingly complex tourism environment decision-making requires a rounded, well-informed view of the whole. Critical distance should be encouraged, consultation and intellectual rigour should be the norm amongst managers and there needs to be a radical shift in our approach to educating future tourism and hospitality managers and researchers.

This edition intends to move the debate forward by exploring how critical tourism inquiry can make a difference in the world, linking tourism education driven by the values of empowerment, partnership and ethics to policy and practice. This volume is designed to enable its reader to think through vital concepts and theories relating to tourism and hospitality management, stimulate critical thinking and use multidisciplinary perspectives. The book is organised around three key ways of producing social change in and through tourism: critical thinking, critical education and critical action. Part 1 focuses on the importance of critical thinking in tourism research and deals with two key topics of our academic endeavours (i) tourism epistemology and theoretical and conceptual developments; (ii) research entanglements, knowledge production and reflexivity. Part II considers 'the University as a site for activism' by mapping out the moral, academic and practical role of educators in developing ethical and responsible graduates and explores the student experience. Part III attempts to provide new understandings of the ways in which social justice and social transformation can be achieved in and through tourism.

This timely and thought provoking book, which collectively questions tourism's current and future role in societal development, is essential reading for students, researchers and academics interested in tourism and hospitality.

Irena Ateljevic is Assistant Professor at Wageningen University, The Netherlands.

Nigel Morgan is Professor of Tourism Studies at Cardiff School of Management's Welsh Centre for Tourism Research at the University of Wales Institute, Cardiff.

Annette Pritchard is Professor of Critical Tourism Studies and Director of the Cardiff School of Management's Welsh Centre for Tourism Research at the University of Wales Institute, Cardiff.

Routledge advances in tourism
Edited by Stephen Page
London Metropolitan University, UK.

.

The Critical Turn in Tourism Studies

Creating an academy of hope

**Edited by Irena Ateljevic, Nigel Morgan
and Annette Pritchard**

Routledge
Taylor & Francis Group

LONDON AND NEW YORK

First published 2012
by Routledge
2 Park Square, Milton Park, Abingdon, Oxon OX14 4RN

Simultaneously published in the USA and Canada
by Routledge
711 Third Avenue, New York, NY 10017 (8th Floor)

Routledge is an imprint of the Taylor & Francis Group, an informa business

British Library Cataloguing in Publication Data
A catalogue record for this book is available from the British Library

Library of Congress Cataloging in Publication Data
The critical turn in tourism studies/edited by Irena Ateljevic, Nigel
Morgan and Annette Pritchard.
   p. cm.
   Includes bibliographical references and index.
   1. Tourism–Study and teaching. I. Ateljevic, Irena. II. Morgan, Nigel.
   III. Pritchard, Annette.
   G155.7.C75 2011
   338.4′791–dc22   2011005259

ISBN: 978-0-415-58552-1 (hbk)
ISBN: 978-0-203-80658-6 (ebk)

Typeset in Times New Roman
By Wearset Ltd, Boldon, Tyne and Wear

This book to dedicated to Tina Ateljevic, Derek and Carole Morgan, Phyllis and Ernest Pritchard and Shannay Angharad – you fill us with hope and love.

Contents

Figures, exhibits and tables

Figures

Exhibits

Tables

Contributors

Nazia Ali was awarded her PhD in tourism studies from the University of Bedfordshire (England) in 2008. Nazia has published in areas relating to tourism, worldmaking, identity, migration and reflexivity. She is currently positioned within the Division of Tourism and Leisure at the University of Bedfordshire.

Irena Ateljevic obtained her PhD in Human Geography in 1998. Since then, her research perspective shifted from (post)modern critical theory and pessimistic observation of structural socio-spatial inequalities to critical praxis and action research that can contribute to more just and hopeful futures in the context of an increasingly distressed, divided and unsustainable world. Dr Ateljevic is deeply committed to hopeful scholarship and caring action that awakens the power of individual agency.

Claudia Bell is senior lecturer in sociology at the University of Auckland. Her teaching and research specialties are national identity formulation and international tourism. Her published books and articles include work on landscape tourism, nation branding, World Expos, town promotion, rural identity, backpacking, outsider art and contemporary artists.

Kellee Caton is a cultural studies scholar who currently holds an assistant professorship in the Department of Tourism Management at Thompson Rivers University. Her work focuses on the role of tourism in ideological production, the lived experience of travel, and epistemological and pedagogical concerns in tourism research and education.

Senija Causevic is a Senior Lecturer in International Tourism Management at London Metropolitan University. Senija's research interests include peace and tourism discourse, i.e. tourism role in the normalisation of social relationships in the post-conflict societies; social justice and tourism; nationalism, and contested heritage and tourism, critical theory and emancipatory knowledge.

Daniel R. Fesenmaier is Professor, School of Tourism and Hospitality Management, Temple University and Professor, MIS Department, Fox School of Business, Temple University. He is also Director of the National Laboratory for Tourism and eCommerce for the School of Tourism and Hospitality

Management, Temple University. He has co-authored a number of monographs, including *Assessing and Developing Tourism Resources* and *Searching for the Future: Technology and Change in Destination Marketing*, co-edited several books including *Travel Destination Recommendation Systems: Behavioral Foundations and Applications*. Dr. Fesenmaier is co-founding editor of *Tourism Analysis*, and currently is Editor, *Journal of Information Technology and Tourism*.

Alexander Grit's research focuses on hospitality space, politics and the potentialities for new connections. This is actualised in research into home exchange experiences, museum spaces and hospitality art projects. He is Academic Dean at Stenden University Qatar, a University which specialises in Hospitality and Tourism Management.

Freya Higgins-Desbiolles is a lecturer in tourism with the School of Management of the University of South Australia. She is a critical theorist who is committed to social justice and has forged fruitful links with people of 'host' communities impacted by tourism, NGOs agitating for more just forms of tourism and tourism operators using tourism to share stories of injustice and alternative visions of possible futures.

Anne-Mette Hjalager is CEO at Advance/1. Advance/1 is involved in contract research in issues such as tourism and other service industries, regional development and policy and management. Predominantly, the research takes place in collaboration with universities in Denmark and abroad. Anne-Mette Hjalager has published widely, and in recent years particularly on issues related to innovation in tourism. She works with Dr. Janne Lidburd and colleagues at the University of Southern Denmark on the development of the INNOTOUR.com platform, a tool for education, research and business development.

Keith Hollinshead is a transdisciplinary/adisciplinary researcher who inspects the symbolic inheritances and traditions of established and emergent populations. English by birth, Australian by experience, he studies the cosmological clashes that accompany the late explosion in travel and mobility. He is currently Professor of Public Culture at the University of Bedfordshire.

Nathalia E. Jaramillo is Senior Lecturer, School of Critical Studies in Education, Faculty of Education, University of Auckland, New Zealand.

Teresa Leopold is a Senior Lecturer in Tourism and Events Studies at the University of Sunderland. Her research interests span from power relations within the social construction of communities and socio-cultural aspects of events and festivals to the political economy of tourist migration and critical thinking in tourism and event curricula.

Janne J. Lidburd is an Associate Professor and Director of the Centre for Tourism, Innovation and Culture at the University of Southern Denmark. She is a cultural anthropologist and her research interests are in the field of sustainable tourism development. She has published on national park development, heritage tourism, open innovation and Web 2.0, tourism education, tourism crisis communication, NGOs and accountability. Dr Lidburd has conducted a number of research projects relating to competence development for tourism practitioners and tourism educators. Dr Lidburd served as Chair of the *B.E.S.T. Education Network* (2005–2010) and is a steering committee member of the *Tourism Education Futures Initiative.*

Paul Lynch is Reader in Critical Hospitality Studies in the Department of Management at the University of Strathclyde. His research interests include small firm entrepreneurship, networks and networking, hospitality and space, advanced qualitative research methods. He is co-editor of *Hospitality & Society.*

Peter McLaren, formery Professor of Urban Schooling, Graduate School of Education and Information Studies, University of California, Los Angeles, is now Professor, School of Critical Studies in Education, Faculty of Education, University of Auckland, New Zealand.

Heather Mair is Associate Professor in the Department of Recreation and Leisure Studies at the University of Waterloo in Ontario, Canada. Her interests include rural tourism development, sport and community development, qualitative methodologies as well as critical approaches to tourism and leisure research.

Nigel Morgan PhD is Professor of Tourism Studies at Cardiff School of Management's Welsh Centre for Tourism Research at the University of Wales Institute, Cardiff. A strong proponent of advocacy scholarship, he was one of originators of hopeful tourism and has written extensively on tourism, social justice and citizenship, creative destinations and place reputation stewardship. Nigel is an editorial board member of several leading international journals including *Place Branding & Public Diplomacy, Hospitality & Society* and *Vacation Marketing* and is Joint Research Notes Editor of the *Annals of Tourism Research.*

Jan Mosedale is Senior Lecturer in Tourism, Hospitality and Events at the University of Sunderland. His research interests lie in the analysis of multiple forms of economic practices across space, focusing on tourism commodity chains as well as non-capitalist exchanges. Jan is editor of *Political Economy and Tourism: A Critical Perspective* and co-editor for the *Current Developments in the Geographies of Leisure and Tourism* book series.

Chaim Noy teaches at the Sapir College (Israel), where he gives courses and seminars on critical and political aspects of tourism – specifically in/to Israel. His research is multidisciplinary and focuses on performance studies, discourse and narrative studies, (auto)mobility, gender and qualitative research methods.

Annette Pritchard is Professor of Critical Tourism Studies and Director of the Cardiff School of Management's Welsh Centre for Tourism Research at the University of Wales Institute, Cardiff. Annette has a long-standing interest in places, representations, identities and transformative tourism enquiry and was one of the originators of the hopeful tourism perspective. She has published 15 books and is currently an editorial board member of the *Journal of Tourism and Cultural Change* and *Tourism and Hospitality Research* and Joint Research Notes Editor of the *Annals of Tourism Research.*

Lisa Schwarzin coordinates the Initiative for Transformative Sustainability Education at Wageningen University, where she is currently completing her MSc in Leisure, Tourism and Environment. Lisa has a keen interest in facilitating and conducting research into processes of transformative learning for societal change in both formal and non-formal education settings. She is also co-founder of an international sustainability learning institute that promotes human development and innovative action, and is soon to be established in Croatia.

Pauline J. Sheldon is Professor Emeritus at the School of Travel Industry Management, University of Hawaii. Her interests include sustainable tourism policy, corporate social responsibility, tourism economics, tourism education, and research methods in tourism. She is President of the International Academy for the Study of Tourism and co-founder of the Tourism Education Futures Initiative (TEFI).

John Tribe is Professor of Tourism at the University of Surrey. He has authored books on philosophy, strategy, economics, education, research and environmental management and his research concentrates on epistemology, education, and sustainability. He is Editor-in-Chief of *Annals of Tourism Research* and Co-Chair of the UNWTO Education and Science Council and was the tourism expert reviewer for the last UK national Research Assessment Exercise (RAE).

Foreword

Dialectical thinking and critical pedagogy – towards a critical tourism studies

Peter McLaren and Nathalia E. Jaramillo

As staunch advocates and international practitioners of critical pedagogy, we have over the years been making a case for an approach to research and practice that is grounded in dialectical reasoning. If we take seriously the assertion of Marx, Hegel and other philosophers of praxis that the world in which humanity is presently ensepulchured functions dialectically, then it makes eminent sense to construct a dialectical understanding of such a world. Concomitantly, if we wish to transform such a world, to undertake a critical praxis in which dialectical thought plays a fundamental role in the intermediation of the contradictions that inform it becomes a prime imperative. The editors and contributors to this new edition of *The Critical Turn in Tourism Studies* are alert to such an understanding, and are mindful of the challenges and difficulties in conducting research in the new global playing field turned battlefield in which the very survival of humanity is being played out.

The current crisis of global capitalism that haunts the planet is neither the work of a cabal of hedge fund hucksters nor the prehensile tail of the banking industry sweeping away the eleemosynary poor cluttering the horizon in their casas de carton/cardboard houses. The crisis is built into the very capitalist structure itself. We are sickeningly aware that the phrase 'the development of underdevelopment' still retains as much analytical and heuristic value today as it did when it became a popular slogan 40 years ago. This phrase underscores the nature of the process whereby economic development in the so-called First World characterised by social inclusion is internally related to simultaneous underdevelopment (or what we call 'overexploitation') in the so-called Third World, accompanied by massive social exclusion (Harvey 2003). This is, as Fredric Jameson notes, a situation that demands to be understood dialectically: 'This is not simply an unfortunate combination of circumstances but rather a genuine dialectic, in which the positive and the negative are dependent on each other and evolve simultaneously and by interaction' (2009: 574).

The dialectical system underscored here can be described in more general terms as 'the structural necessity for capitalism to create a reserve army of the unemployed and to exclude whole sections of society (or here, in globalisation, whole sections of the world population)' (Jameson 2009: 576). As a doughty dialectician of the political unconscious, Jameson turns to the opposition between work and unemployment that characterises the history of capitalism and reveals that the positive term, work, has not one but two opposites: 'the reserve army of the unemployed and those – aged, infirm, as well as the famous lumpens – who are not available even for the seasonal or boom-condition employment for which the reserve army is destined to be drawn upon' (2009: 580). But what term will now oppose the term, 'the unemployable'? The missing fourth term in Jameson's actantial system, which will allow us to fill in the blank that appears opposite the term 'unemployable', and which is implicitly identified in Marx's Capital, is what Jameson calls the 'formerly employed' (2009: 580). What we are seeing as part and parcel of today's epidemic of transnational capitalism are 'the working populations once active in vital industries which have now ceased to function, and around whose idle factories the veterans of dead labor live on with their families' (2009: 580). Mapping this situation globally, we are seeing

> First and Second World workers hesitate between the status of a reserve army (should new industries and possibilities start up in their immediate vicinities) and that of the formerly and now permanently unemployed situation of people whom 'development' has permanently passed over.
>
> (2009: 580)

This situation, of course, has been accelerated by neoliberal capitalism's

> tireless quest for ever cheaper labor: abandoning the former workers of the Mexican maquiladoras who assumed the tasks of former US factory workers and moving to China, where already recently built factories are being closed in view of even lower-paid labor elsewhere in Southeast Asia.
>
> (2009: 580)

As educators, we are interested in how global capitalism is dialectically interwoven with underdevelopment, and how this process is related to the production of knowledge, specifically in school systems and how such school systems teach us how to think, to research, and to develop our methodological skills that often leave us degage and docile. As we understand it, prior to the ascendency of neoliberal capitalism, the primary mission of mass schooling was to create the deep character of the nation state by legitimising the superiority of elite culture, transcoding the culture of the ruling class with the culture of the nation state so that both were essentially seen as 'natural' symmetrical reflections of each other. Schools were important mechanisms in the invention of the identity of the modern nation state in the era of industrialisation and played an important role in developing the concept of the citizen (a concept always contested by many groups, including conservatives, liberals and radicals). However, schools today (since the mid-1980s) are discernibly shifting their role from building the nation state and creating democracy-minded citizens to serving the transnational corporations in their endless quest for profits. The nation state, it appears, is losing its ability to control capital by means of controlling the transnational corporations.

Schools that were once an important political entity that had a public code-setting agenda in creating conventional rules and regulations to be followed by each citizen are fast becoming part of the private sector bent on creating consumers within the capitalist marketplace. As society abandons its outmoded historical garb and takes on new forms, the perpetuity of the existing social order is increasingly called into question. In today's global capitalist society marked by the process of deregulation, the state is playing a decreasing role in setting the everyday agenda of our lives. However, as Zygmunt Bauman (1999) so presciently expounds, this in no way means that we are experiencing a decline of regulation, only the retreat or self-limitation of the state. So-called non-political forces – those associated with financial and commodity markets – are now the dominant forces of indoctrination and code setting within our market society.

We have embraced negative freedom (the freedom to choose) as the absence of restraints imposed by the legislative/regulating power exercised by political authority. There exists, however, two sets of constraints to the freedom to choose noted by Bauman (1999) – that are determined by the agenda of choice (i.e. the range of alternatives available to the chooser) and the code of choosing itself (i.e. the rules that tell the chooser on what grounds preferences should be given to some items over others). Modernity was marked by the law-giving and law-executing state legislating often preselected choices that would be made available to the chooser (i.e. legislation limited abstract choices from the range of practical possibilities by increasing punitive sanctions on certain choices). The main vehicle for setting the code of choosing was education, which Bauman describes at length as follows:

> Education is an institutionalized effort to instruct and train individuals in the art of using their freedom of choice within the legislatively set agenda. Education is to supply the choosers with orientation points, the rules of conduct, but above all with the choice-guiding values, that is with the ability to tell the right reasons for according preference from the wrong reasons, and the inclination to follow the first while avoiding the second. Education is aimed at inducing individuals to internalize the norms which are henceforth to guide their practice. If the legislation sets the agenda by dividing the abstractly possible choices into such as are allowed to be made and other which are prohibited and punishable—education performs its code-setting function by further dividing the set of available/permitted choices into such as are desirable/advisable/proper and such as are unwelcome/inadvisable/inappropriate.
>
> (1999: 73)

Of course, progressives, conservatives and radicals fight to this day for the type of legislation that they each feel should set the agenda for our schools but such a fight seems to be increasingly futile for a number of reasons. Given the refiguring of the roles of the state and its extant political institutions (including education), their function in agenda and code setting is being attenuated significantly, if not outright abandoned. If we conceive of neoliberal capitalism and its sacerdotal policy of deregulation as separating power from politics (we are using politics here in a limited sense of the context of electable, representative institutions), then the non-political forces that have now stepped in to assume the role once defined by the state are those sworn to defend corporatisation and privatisation – i.e. financial and commodity markets. This process was set in motion in the mid-1980s when the increase in foreign direct investment outpaced the rise in world exports, that is, when the total output of transnational corporations outside their home countries overtook the volume of world exports in manufacturing. This marked corporate power as a major rival to state power.

Today the problem is not that of the absence of values nor their sheer plurality but a question of agency. Bauman puts it thus:

> Were not the agenda-setting task abandoned by territorial state authorities, it would anyway be ineffective; the hub of the present-day crisis of political process is not so much the absence of values or confusion caused by their plurality, as the absence of an agency effective enough to legitimate, promote, install and service any set of values or any consistent and cohesive agenda of choices.
>
> (1999: 74)

Clearly, public education is delimiting its agenda-and code setting role, giving this function over to corporate rule as the hedge funds, finance capital and betting on the stock market dictate the future of public schooling and overdetermine the demise of public schooling. The state is now focusing on the direct rule over certain social categories – patriotism and terrorism – while the forces of the market are viewed increasingly as a god-given process. Reason and rationality do not apply the same way as they did when the state set the agenda for choice. The corporate worldview is one of seeing the world as a menu for consumers and the media are set in place to create the necessary modes of desire to power these acts of consumption. Whereas within the modern industrial state the code was directed towards a steady state ideal premised on the accretion and accumulation of achievements, the prevalent code of choosing in today's consumer society is serviced by the media as episodic experiences and pleasures. This code endorses the desire to desire and legitimises the choice of certain objects of desire over others. As Bauman (1999) notes, the transformation we have undergone from political citizens to market consumers has not given us an increased number of choices nor a greater capacity for negotiating the code of choosing; what is has given us is the distinct illusion that we have more choice since the processes of agenda- and code-setting has been made more invisible (and since the code itself is embedded in the production of desire).

As consumer citizens, we experience our unfettered obedience to the code as a product of our own desires rather as a set of desires manufactured by the marketplace, as a commandment from above. The sources of our unfreedom are occulted and imputed to an extra-social domain. Here, hegemony is secured by our consent to this process as we are clearly 'manufactured' to believe there is no alternative to the way we organise our lives to overcome necessity. But this unfreedom is not experienced as oppressive. On the contrary, we feel safe and 'at home' when we are consuming commodities. Bauman writes:

> The state of unfreedom is endemically ambivalent. This makes that much easier the task of all powers, the task of eliciting discipline and obedience to its commands: the bossiness of pastoral power always hovers on the brink of oppression, but all to often tends to be gratefully received, perhaps even eagerly sought, by the flock – as the reliable warrant of safe and secure daily routine.
>
> (1999: 79)

But, as Bauman underscores, all unfreedom is a condition of heteronomy, and never autonomy. It is always 'a state in which the acting person is an agent of somebody else's will' (1999: 79). Real freedom, writes Anne Fairchild Pomeroy, 'is not freedom from society but the freedom provided for one another by and through our social being' (2004: 168). We are only autonomous when we comprise the rules that guide our behaviour. This reminds us of Kant's (1784) dictum that individuals already possess the necessary intellect but need the courage to think without the direction of another. For Paulo Freire, educators enter into relations of oppression when they take away a subject's right to conscious awareness and remove their right to transform the world. According to Freire, any true liberatory education:

> must possess a basic aim: to make it possible for human beings, through the problematizing of the unity being-world (or of human beings in their relations with the world and with other human beings) to penetrate more deeply the *prise de conscience* of the reality in which they exist. This deepening of the *prise de conscience*, which must develop in the action which transforms reality, produces with this action an overlaying of basically sensuous knowledge of reality with that which touches the *raison d'etre* of this reality. People take over the position they have in their *here* and *now*. This results (and at the same time it produces this) in their discovering their own presence within a totality, within a structure, and not as 'imprisoned' or 'stuck to' the structure or its parts.
>
> (1982: 107, cited in Au 2007)

Our collaborative existence as consumers has produced a closure on meaning through the very activity of opening up our desire to consume market commodities by means of a default set of blinders created by a capitalist imaginary that provides the formula or criteria of choice. There exist autonomous societies in themselves and for themselves. The difference between the two societies is, Bauman remarks, the difference 'between the presence or absence of the awareness of autonomy and the degree to which that awareness has been institutionalised in the day-to-day operation of society' (1999: 80). The taking of collective responsibility for the human origin of society makes a society autonomous for itself since being self-consciously critical of autonomous society is an awareness of the historicity of society and its inbuilt mortality and a tacit admission that autonomous societies cannot claim immunity from scrutiny and critique. True autonomy, therefore, means accepting our mortality, perpetually questioning and re-examining our judgments. It means situating autonomy as a political struggle where politics 'is an effective and practical effort to subject institutions that boast de facto validity to the test of de jure validity' (1999: 84). Citing Castoriadis, Bauman writes, 'accepting mortality means denying any lasting grounds and immortal/eternal/extemporal foundations to de facto validity of institutions and significations' (1999: 83). The challenge for *de jure* validity requires critical reflection. This is a type of autonomous thinking that 'derives its resolve from the refusal to leave any thought-construct, including its own explicit or tacit presumptions, outside its critical brief' (1999: 85).

Richard Quantz (in press) has examined critical reflection (or the lack thereof) of U.S. high school students and identified interaction patterns between teachers and students in learning situations in high school classrooms that are modelled after solving puzzles. He distinguishes three types of knowledge produced in these problem-solving scenarios: conventional knowledge or action, technical knowledge or action and meaningful knowledge or action. He associates conventional problem solving with modern industrial societies in which schools were designed to provide students with the rules and conventions to solve particular problems via rule-based reasoning. Knowing the rules of the democratic state was the most important goal and this was often taught by means of a textbook–assignment–recitation pattern. With the advent of consumer society and the replacement of Western high culture with transnational corporate culture (which relies on well-trained technical workers), the focus has moved away from conventional thinking to technical thinking. What this ultimately excludes, of course, is critical reflection, or producing knowledge from real-life problems or what Quantz (in press) calls 'meaningful action'. Meaningful action does not always take place in situations where relevant knowledge is available or where people are aware what the right choices and actions might be. Meaningful knowledge does require some knowledge of technical reasoning but it requires as well the ability to interpret and critique – to make moral choices and to commit to some action even when relevant knowledge is not available. It requires larger patterns of understanding and reasoning – and it requires us to create and recreate its own foundations and goals as it goes along. Given the abandoning of political institutions such as schools by the state, the focus has been on technical problem solving as a means-ends reasoning that involves selecting from available rules those that will help individuals achieve a particular given end. This move from conventional thinking to technical thinking, to a type of bottom-line thinking, shifts away from state and local guidelines to bottom line ends and ultimately embraces the new heteronomy of corporate culture. And it makes meaningful knowledge and action – or what Bauman (1999) calls autonomous thinking – less a part of the school experience than ever before. If we need to make the public sphere capable of creating autonomous individuals and autonomous society by subjecting institutions that boast de facto validity to the test of *de jure* validity, what type of critical reasoning is required at this urgent historical juncture? We argue that this requires a type of dialectical thinking developed by Marx. Here we make a distinction between Understanding and Reasoning (Pavlidis 2010), arguing that in order to create a pedagogy and praxis of meaningful knowledge we need to move from understanding to critical reasoning.

All movement is the negation of what is. As Anne Fairchild Pomeroy (2004a) notes, what is, might not be, and what is not yet, might be. Likewise, Periklis Pavlidis (2010) reminds us that thought is always in motion; as a form of critical action, it moves from the sensuous concrete (the surface of the object) to abstract concepts (the essential relations governing it) and then from abstract concepts to the surface of the object again based on the knowledge of its essence gleaned by means of verifying the internal affinities of those essential relations.

The first stage of the cognitive process is Understanding. The second stage is Reason. In the activity of Understanding, concepts seem autonomously generated, unchanging, static, and given whereas in the activity of Reason, concepts are seen as fluid, developing and interlinked. Thinking as Understanding begins with sensuous knowledge – empirical knowledge presented through the senses—which can be considered concrete in the sense that it perceives the object in its entirety and uses the object to contemplatively ground its concepts. We learn that a certain object exists but we don't know much about its various aspects and properties and the relationships among them because these properties are seen as inert, systematised and unconnected. We don't know about the history or internal relations associated with the object, only its phenomenal nature, its external and formal traits. We cannot capture its quiddity. Understanding disrupts the sensual form, separating out its various aspects, an activity marked by division and abstraction. Once these are separated out, Understanding abstractly moves from the individual idiosyncratic object to general, common and fixed features of the object. This is what Karel Kosik (1976) refers to as the 'psuedo-concrete'. Abstracting and generalising from this particular empirical data always remains tied to or dependent upon this data. Ollman writes that

> the process of abstraction provides the indispensable first step in getting the thinking process started. We can only think in parts and about parts of one sort or another. Marx believes, therefore, that everyone abstracts and that we learn how to do it 'appropriately' – that is, in ways that allow us to function in the culture in which we live – during the process of socialization and particularly when acquiring language. Once the work is done, however, most people come to treat the culturally determined units of thought that result from the process of abstraction now embedded in language as reflecting absolute divisions in the real world. Not so Marx.
>
> (2003: 186)

One of the problems with remaining at the level of Understanding is that we fall prey to what Pomeroy calls 'misplaced concreteness' which is 'to allow oneself to be ruled by abstractions and to allow oneself to be ruled by abstractions is to commit the fallacy of misplaced concreteness' (2004: 157). It is to deny our processual, dialectical being. In fact, Pomeroy warns that

> capitalism is lived misplaced concreteness, except that in this case, mistaking the abstract for the concrete is no accidental error and the neglect of awareness of the degree of its abstraction is no mere oversight. The logic of the valorization of value absolutely requires it.
>
> (2004: 157)

She adds further: 'capitalism is a production of the world as valorized nonbeing' (2004: 160). The fallacy of misplaced concreteness is at the heart of alienation under capitalism. Pomeroy expands on this condition:

> And so capitalism, by taking its abstractions to be the whole story, disregards that dialectical relationality of each to its other that we can the natural ecosystem, rapes and devastates the natural world, uses nature as its storehouse and dumping ground, foreshortens our vision of the wealth of possible relations offered to us by nature and culture. By consciously misplacing the abstract for the concrete, it does not look to the necessary connectedness of all, but to the independence of each as a value: the common capitalist substance of all natural objectsis their disconnection and their disconnection is the mistaken abstraction from their necessary concrete relatedness.
>
> (2004: 158)

Reason, on the other hand, deals with the concepts generated in the act of Understanding, and of course is dependent upon the process of Understanding, by goes further than Understanding by exposing the internal contradictions of a developing object, transforming the object by reconnecting what was separated and divided into a totality of organically linked properties. It is, in other words, zetetic and critical. As Bertell Ollman notes,

> for Hegel, the thing under examination is not just the sum of its qualities but, through the links these qualities (individually or together in the thing) have with the rest of nature, it is also a particular expression of the whole.
>
> (2003: 40)

It shifts the tetonic plates of thought. Reason enables the links between these contradictions through a synthesis that serves as a living conceptual system, one that notes the object's difference from itself, and its evolution and transformation into something else. Reason, therefore, is not simply an attempt to subtilise but to restore the wholeness of the object, its internal unity, and in the process comprehend the inner driving force of its evolution (Pavlidis 2010). Thus the object reemerges as something concrete – not a sensuous whole but a conceptual whole (Pavlidis 2010). Reason helps us to recognise that 'in the concrete, each actual entity right here, right now is the locus of the relationality of all being. Without this absolutely unique e-valuation, without this particular conspiracy of objective datum, there is no concrete process' (2004: 161). Pomeroy recognises further that 'there can only be processively the dialectical dependence of the general on the particular and vice versa' (2004: 161). Tragically, in the case of capitalism, 'every aspect of reality becomes a form of appearance of social average labor time' (2004: 161).

This process of dialectical thinking follows the work of Paulo Freire (2000) that stipulates a detailed investigation by means of student-generated themes of the limit situation or obstacles or contradictions and negations that impede the process of humanisation. Students react to such actual and possible limit situations by probing into the structures of society in order to overcome those obstacles by transforming the structural impediments facing them. Ira Shor (1980) has built problem-solving activities build on Freire's (problem-posing) approach which involves students undertaking life descriptions (observations of taken-for-granted objects), diagnosis (coding/decoding, socio-historical, interpretive and value-based analysis of the social roots of the object of investigation) and resolution or reconstruction (moving from a decodification or contextual analysis of the object to a structural perception of it, leading to the creative re-imagining or reconstruction of the object). In his book with Shor, Freire argues states that:

> [W]hat we do when we try to establish a cognitive or epistemological relationship with the object to be known, when we get it into our hands, grasp it, and begin to ask ourselves about it, what we really begin to do is to take it as a *totality*. We then begin to split it into its constituent parts ... In a certain moment, even though we may not have exhausted the process of splitting the object, we try to understand it now in its totality. We try to *retotalize* the totality which we split! ... The moment of summarizing has to do with this effort of retotalizing of the totality we divided into parts.'
>
> (Shor and Freire 1987: 161)

Clearly, as Wayne Au (2007) points out, Freire worked within a dialectical materialist epistemology that attempted to posit a dialectical relationship between the objective world and our subjective understanding and knowledge of that world. In other words, Freire understood we are not only in the world but with the world, in the sense that our reality is always a social world (there is no longer an 'I think' but a 'we think', and that we can exercise choice in the world and choose to transform the world (Freire 1982). Freire's dialectical materialist epistemology operated within his concept of *conscientização*:

> Only when we understand the 'dialecticity' between consciousness and the world – that is, when we know that we don't have a consciousness here and

the world there but, on the contrary, when both of them, the objectivity and the subjectivity, are incarnating dialectically, is it possible to understand what *conscientização* is, and to understand the role of consciousness in the liberation of humanity.

(Davis and Freire 1981: 62, as cited in Au 2007)

Freire understands 'consciousness as consciousness *of* consciousness' (Freire 1973: 107, as cited in Au 2007), and that '*Consciousness is intentionality towards the world*' (Davis and Freire 1981: 58, original emphasis, as cited in Au 2007).

Of course, this is but a thumbnail sketch of the workings of a dialectical reasoning, something that was much more complex in the writings of Marx. While Marx accepted the relational framework that housed his views, he opposed the role that Hegel gave to ideas and their concept. Marx refused to accept the independent development of ideas, linking them to material relations. But Marx definitely remains indebted to Hegel for his own philosophy of internal relations:

Operating with philosophy of internal relations taken over from Hegel – and never criticized by Marx in all his discussions of Hegel – Marx considers all of reality as an internally related whole whose aspects can be mentally combined in a variety of ways and, therefore, into a multiplicity of different parts. To be sure, where boundaries get drawn is based, to some degree, on the real similarities and differences found in the world, but equally important in affecting these decisions are the aims, needs, and interests of the party doing the abstracting.

(Ollman 2003: 186)

It is this dialectical method that enables us to study capitalist society in its totality, as distinct from the positivism that reigns supreme within the social sciences and enables us to examine the world by means of abstract Understanding and not critical Reasoning. But critical Reasoning, to be truly transformative, must not just remain at the level of comprehending the social totality as a conceptual whole. It must also involve engaging in the transformation of that totality through critical praxis. Here we need to recognise that concepts are more than tropes, more than experiential narratives, and they must be generated dialectically by means of engaging in the world protagonistically. Anna Stetsenko captures this dialectical relationship between the self and the social when she writes:

Understanding that people always contribute to social practices, rather than merely participate in or sustain them, places activities that allow individuals to purposefully transform the world at the very core of the self. That is, the self appears as made up of real-life processes and as oriented toward real-life practical tasks and pursuits of changing something in and about the world (including in oneself as part of the world). In other words, the self appears as an activity and instrument of transforming the world, as an

instrument of social change.... That is, this notion conveys that social productive activities in the world are not reifications of the self but the 'real
work' in which the self is born, constructed and enacted. Therefore, to con-
ceptualize the self as a leading activity is to emphasize that it is constituted
by the ways in which we 'do' and perform, rather than have, a self, and,
moreover, by what we do about the world (thus transcending ourselves), as
we engage in activities that contribute to changing something in and about
the world. In this sense, the self can be also described as an embodiment of
a meaningful life project...

(Stetsenko 2008: 529)

Like Pavlidis, Ana Stetsenko (2002; 2008) argues for a dialectical reasoning
as a path to becoming conscious of and transcending the limits in which we can
make ourselves, in externalising, historicising and objectifying our vision of liberation, in treating theory as a form of practice and practice as a form of theory
as we contest the psychopathology of everyday life incarnate in capitalism's
social division of labor. Here we need to examine how our thinking is contingent
on the discourses and communities that grant them value. But discourses and
concepts don't shape the world in isolation from the forces of capitalist production and class struggle. To change the world requires liberatory praxis. Knowledge production is fundamental to praxis, to reading the world and the world
dialectically. But such a reading must take place through acting in and on the
world as protagonistic agents of struggle. Here we need to emphasise that practice serves as the ultimate ground for advancing and verifying theories as well as
for providing warrants for knowledge claims. These warrants are not connected
to some fixed principles that exist outside of the knowledge claims themselves,
but are derived by identifying and laying bare the ideological and ethical potentialities of a given theory as a form of practice. Dialectical reasoning approaches
these relationships and practices and tries to examine their contractions when
seen in relation to the totality of social relations in which those particular relations and practices unfold.

The revolutionary critical pedagogy that we are supporting is directed at
understanding the world dialectically as an effect of multiple antagonisms whose
conditions of possibility are intensified by the contradiction between labor and
capital. Dialectical thinking in this regard is attentive to the movement of the
world's totality and how this totality is uncovered by human beings, and how, in
our understanding of this multi-layered totality, we develop a particular ontological openness towards being and becoming. Reality is seen as a structured, self-
forming whole. Here, cognition of a fact or set of facts is, according to Kosik
(1976: 23) 'the cognition of their place in the totality of this reality.' Kosik
expands here on the concept of dialectical thinking and is worth quoting at
length:

In distinction from the summative-systematic cognition of rationalism and
empiricism which starts from secure premises and proceeds systematically

to array additional facts, dialectical thinking assumes that human cognition proceeds in a spiral movement in which any beginning is abstract and relative. If reality is a dialectical, structured whole, then concrete cognition of reality does not amount to systematically arraying facts with facts and findings with findings; rather, it is a process of concretization which proceeds from the whole to its parts and from the parts to the whole, from phenomena to the essence and from the essence to the totality. It arrives at concreteness precisely in this spiral process of totalization in which all concepts move with respect to one another, and mutually illuminate one another. Neither does further progress of dialectical cognition leave individual concepts untouched; such cognition is not a constructed once and for all but is rather a spiral process of interpenetration and mutual illumination of concepts, a process of dialectical, quantitative–qualitative, regressive–progressive totalization that transcends abstractness (one-sidedness and isolation).

(1976: 23)

Marx understood social life as shaped by dialectical contradiction, specifically the historically produced internal relations of capital and labor that constitute capitalism. With internal relations, one element of the relation cannot exist without the other. If the internally related opposites cease to exist, this occurs only because the entire relation has been abolished. All dialectical contradictions are internal relations, a relation of two opposing entities that could not exist, continue to exist, or have come into existence in the absence of their other (Allman *et al.* 2005). The opposites could not be what they are or what they are to become outside of this relation. A dialectical contradiction – the fundamental one of capitalism is capital–labor – is an internal relation that is an antagonistic relation: the existence of each opposite is variously constrained or hampered by virtue of the fact that it is in a necessary internal relation with its opposite, and both are attempting to occupy the same space. However, one of the opposites, despite these limitations, actually benefits from the relation. It is in the interest of this opposite – often referred to as the positive – to maintain the relation. In relation to the capital–labor relation, it is in the interest of capital to maintain the relation. The other opposite – the negative – although it can better its circumstances temporarily within the relation, is severely limited by its relation to its opposite because the positive continually uses it to its own advantage, to the point of near devastation (although for the positive to continue to exist, it cannot follow through with the abolition of the negative).

Labor is the negative pole in the capital–labor relation. It is in the interests of the negative pole – in our example, labor – to abolish the capital–labor relation (Allman *et al.* 2005). In this case, the negative opposite does not cease to exist, but it does cease to exist in the position of the negative, the inferior, opposite due to its existence within an internal relation/dialectical contradiction. Often these internal relations lead to a type of dichotomised thinking (Allman 2007) that arises from and reproduces the fragmented and partial consciousness of social totality, and consequently blocks revolutionary class consciousness, sometimes under the guise of 'enlightened false consciousness'. Dichotomised thinking yields understanding that is distorted because it fails to perceive the components of dialectical contradictions as related, and internally so. Consequently, we experience and simultaneously make sense of related opposites (such as capital versus labor) as if they are discrete or separate from each other – a circumstance that serves the interests of the capitalist class. In order to struggle against such fractured and partial thinking, it is necessary to learn to grasp the fundamental relations of social life as dialectical – a whole constituted by opposing elements that cannot be changed without affecting the terms themselves between which the relation holds (Allman 2007). What a critical pedagogy underwritten by dialectical thinking attempts to cultivate is a philosophy of internal relations that leads to a profoundly historical and developmental way of conceptualising social life, a way of conceptualising how the opposing elements of social life are related over time and reshaped by their own dialectical laws of motion. Dialectical thinking is accomplished through what Raya Dunayevskaya, following her understanding of Marx and Hegel, referred to as 'absolute negativity' as the seed of social transformation.

Peter Hudis (2005: 8–9) notes that the genius of Hegel was that he was fully aware that negation is dependent on the object of its critique. In other words, ideas of liberation are impacted, in one way or another, by the oppressive forms that one tries to reject, and that negation per se does not totally free one from the negated object. But unlike the postmodernists that centuries later followed him, Hegel believed that there was a way for negation to transcend the object of its critique. He therefore introduced the notion of 'the negation of the negation.' Hudis makes clear that the negation of the negation, or second negativity, does not refer simply to a continuous series of negations – that can potentially go on forever and still never free negation from the object of its critique. Hegel instead argues for a self-referential negation. By negating itself, negation establishes a relation with itself – and therefore frees itself from dependence on the external object. According to Hudis (2005), this kind of negativity, second negativity is 'absolute,' insofar as it exists without relation to another outside itself. In other words, negation is no longer dependent on an external object; it negates such dependency through a self-referential act of negation.

According to Hudis (2005), Marx did not dismiss the concept of the 'negation of the negation' as an idealist illusion but instead appropriated the concept of the self-referential negation 'to explain the path to a new society'. Marx (1967) understood that simply to negate something is still leaves us dependent upon the object of critique, in other words, it merely affirms the alienated object of our critique on a different level. As Hudis and other Marxist humanists have point out, that has been the problem with revolutions of the past, they remained dependent upon the object of their negation. The negation of the negation, however, creates the conditions for something truly positive to emerge in that absolute negativity is no longer dependent on the other. Here is how Hudis (2005) puts it in his own words, using the example of communism:

Communism, the abolition of private property, is the negation of capitalism. But this negation, Marx tells us, is dependent on the object of its critique insofar as it replaces private property with collective property. Communism is not free from the alienated notion that ownership or having is the most important part of being human; it simply affirms it on a different level. Of course, Marx thinks that it is necessary to negate private property. But this negation, he insists, must itself be negated. Only then can the truly positive – a totally new society – emerge.

According to Hudis, Marx believed that labor or human praxis can achieve the transcendence of alienation but what was need was a subjective praxis connected with a philosophy of liberation that is able to illuminate the content of a post-capitalist society and project a path to a totally new society by convincing humanity that it is possible to resolve the contradiction between alienation and freedom. We can't resolve such a contradiction within the social universe of capital and capital's value form of labor. In Hudis' (2005) terms, we need to concretise 'Absolute Negativity as *New Beginning*, rather than repeating the truths of an earlier era that no longer have the power to seize humanity's imagination.'

Anne Fairchild Pomeroy (2004b) uses the concept of absolute negation in her discussion of the work of Raya Dunayevskaya, the founder of the Marxist humanist tendency in the United States. The first negation occurs when we negate our status as objects of history, when we refuse to be commodities in the service of neoliberal capital, when we shout a resounding 'no' to serving as wage labor for capital. I am *NOT* wage labor. Here, the emphasis is on the *NOT*. This is similar to the dialectical method of Marx, moving from the concrete to the abstract through Understanding. When we become self-conscious of our act of negating our role as wage labor for capital, that is, when we become more educated and self-reflective about it, then we then are participating in a second negation, and this is greatly facilitated by the kind of self-reflexivity taught by critical educators, and is similar to moving from the abstraction we referred to as Understanding back to the concrete through a type of thinking that we have called Reason. Here, understanding our relationship to capital through a dialectical method can help individuals reflect upon the refusal of their status as capitalist labor; it can help individuals come to see the positive content of their original act of negation, recognise that capital is dependent upon their labor-power, and thus help them acknowledge their own power through acts of self-determination. I *AM* not capital. The emphasis in this instance is on the *AM* (Pomeroy 2004b).

Individuals in this second negation, through the movement of understanding towards reason, are able to become more critically self-conscious about their power as subjects of history. In Pomeroy's (2004b) terms, individuals recognise themselves as the one with the power to say no, as the very source of the negation, and thus they become through this recognition the subject of the movement of history itself. In other words, they come to understand themselves as agents of history. In this case, individuals come to recognise themselves through the abstraction of Understanding as the source of the valorisation of capital – they see themselves and those like themselves as sources of profits for the rich. But moving from abstract Understanding to concrete praxis they come to understand that they, too, are the very source of capital's undoing. A critical understanding gives substance to the notion that individuals have the capacity to alter what it is about their world that they no longer want to be – slaves to capital. They begin to take charge of their own creative capacities and realise it is possible to build a future outside of capital's value form, outside of the social universe of capital and value production itself. But this future can only come into being when their refusal is joined by the refusal of others, in a collective movement to fight capitalism at its roots. When individuals realise the power of their acts of negation but simultaneously understand this negativity as their positivity, then they realise that it is through their great refusal that ideas are produced anew (Pomeroy 2004b).

Students begin to realise that mere acts of negation by means of Understanding are inadequate to changing the world. What is needed is the second negation, the movement from the abstract to the concrete, to transforming the object. But acts of negation that move beyond mere acts of negation are those that negate the negation itself, and this occurs when we recognise the positivity of acts of negation as negativity. We are all beings of negativity. We are dialectical beings and our self-determination is our absolute right. The negation of the negation is the return of human beings to themselves, as we recognise that capitalism is that which enslaves the negative, it requires the subservience of this critical self-consciousness, of the I *AM* not wage labor. Here we find the freedom to create organisational forms that will enable us to live outside of capital's value form, here we find the freedom in our particular acts of struggle that we also recognise is absolute freedom, because negation is the source of all movement. We recognise that there is no freedom that does not simultaneously will the freedom of the other, and that as Pomeroy (2004b) notes, our form of being becomes the Absolute Idea (in Hegel's terms), that is, our simultaneous individual and universal realisation that I am the movement of the real, that my own self-consciousness takes on the burden of freedom, of responsibility of sociality. Stetsenko captures dialectical this relationship between knowledge and practice as follows:

> In my elaboration of this view, knowledge (including its theoretical forms) does not merely reflect the world. Instead, knowledge embodies past practices, at a given point in history and in a given sociocultural context, to only momentarily reflect these past practices through the lenses of future goals in what essentially are continuously expanding and unbroken cycles of 'practice-theory-practice' .... In this sense, thought and knowledge (including theory and concepts) entail action from which they spring and for which sake they exist. Thought and knowledge therefore appear as practical acts in the world because they always come out of active transformative practices and always return into them, serving as but a step in carrying out these

practices and having their grounding, their mode of existence, and their ulti-mate relevance within these broader transformative practices. The famous Lewin's expression about theory being practical can and needs to be expanded with the notion that there is nothing more theoretical than a good practice.'

(2008: 531)

One of the precautions we would invoke at this point in our discussion of dia-lectical analysis is falling into what Reitz (2000) calls, in reference to the aes-thetic ontology of Herbert Marcuse, 'Romantic negation' – a concept rooted not in the dialectical transcendence offered by historical materialism but rather a dualism grounded in the emancipatory potential of the aesthetic dimension which is incapable of overcoming contradiction.

Marx's answer was not resistance via a radical aesthetics but rather a very systematic de-mystifying philosophical and social analysis – that is, a dialect-ical and materialist philosophy. Marcuse's radical aesthetics and that of other Frankfurt School theorists don't really provide a dialectical ground for forward motion. In this sense, much of critical theory is essentially circular, comprised of a polar reciprocity, or a frozen paradoxical juxtaposition. This, Reitz argues (2000), is really a pseudo-dialectics. Against the self-reflexive logic of the aesthetic-ontological approach of the Frankfurt School, Marx's dialectical understanding of capitalist social relations raises the problems and possibil-ities of intervention against material relations of oppression and alienation and not just shifting from one pole of a contradiction to the opposite. The first thing we need is a dialectification of consciousness, that is, comprehending, after Hegel, that only the oppressed have the power to recognise the dialectic of interdependence that binds the subjectivity of the master to the subjugated condition of the servant. There is a social power imbalance that prevents the master from recognising the truth of this condition but disposes the servant toward it. We need to examine our social location through our own doing and the doing of others and this 'reciprocal doing' must be objectively framed and structured. We need to embrace, therefore, a dialectical and materialist epi-stemology of oppression that will enable us to see social structure in ourselves and ourselves in the social structure. For the working class, critique is not only a debate between abstract theses, an ideological battle against false conscious-ness but part of a historical battle against oppression and exploitation – a battle against dominant economic, educational, legal and cultural systems. It is about organised social struggles that can educate us all as a society about ali-enation, exploitation and power. We must, in other words, refuse to allow the dialectic to become an ahistorical aesthetic/ontological form. We must under-stand the struggles that have led to standards of criticism in ethics, logic and in art, science and the social sciences so as to develop our own criteria of judgment.

Kevin Anderson (2010) notes a similar problem with theorists such as Hardt and Negri who subscribe to a Foucauldian notion of biopower that stipulates that, since power is everywhere and nowhere, it need not be resisted only at its pinnacle but at any point. According to Hardt and Negri (2004), a global multitude of the powerless – a heterogeneous web of workers, migrants, social movements, and non-governmental organisations – is now in place as a web of resistance to capital that can effectuate transformation even without a unified philosophical approach. Here, Anderson notes that Hardt and Negri remain trapped in the pre-Hegelian split between immanence and transcendence by rejecting all forms of transcendence in favor of remaining on the plane of immanence and trusting in the self-activity of the multitude. Thus, according to Anderson (2010), Hardt and Negri

> cut themselves off from … the dialectical notion that a liberated future can emerge from within the present, if the various forces and tendencies that oppose the system can link up in turn with a theory of liberation that sketches out philosophically that emancipatory future for which they yearn.' In other words, there exists a 'deep hostility toward any notion of conceptualizing dialectically an alternative to capitalism.

While for Marx, the working class was immanent or internal to capitalism, the working class needs to fight not only for a bigger share of the pie, but to overcome capitalism itself, therefore becoming a force of the future in the present, a force of transcendence.

A transformative pedagogy for a critical tourism studies must attempt to create an explicit connection with a philosophy of liberation that projects the path to a totally new society. It must, in other words, not simply exist at the plane of immanence, but also possess a Promethean side that points towards a transcendence of the given. So long as the gap persists between subjects of revolt and the philosophy that illuminates the content of a post-capitalist society, humanity will remain unconvinced that it is possible to resolve the contradiction between alienation and freedom. Peter Hudis puts it thus:

> Therefore, the task before us is not to repeat what we already know – the centrality of the Subject – or even worse, to reduce the concept of Absolute Negativity as New Beginning to mere confirmation of the Subject's creative powers. What is needed is to *begin from the Absolute* by explicitly spelling out the vision of the new society that is found in the *philosophies* of Hegel, Marx and Marxist-Humanism in strict relation to today's subjects of revolt. Then and only then will we be in the position to meet the challenge of this era: concretizing Absolute Negativity as *New Beginning*, rather than repeating the truths of an earlier era that no longer have the power to seize humanity's imagination.
>
> (Hudis 2005: 10)

Hudis' comments are apposite here if only to remind us that dialectics, left on its own, cannot be its own foundation. As Octavio Paz reminds us, dialectics cannot be its own foundation because by its very nature it denies itself the moment it affirms itself. It is perpetual rebirth and perpetual death. If the will to power is continually threatened by the return of the Same, dialectics is similarly threatened by its own movement: every time it affirms itself, it denies itself. In order not to cancel itself out, it needs some sort of ground, some principle prior to movement. If Marxism rejects Spirit or the Idea as its foundation, and if matter also cannot be its foundation, the Marxist is trapped in a vicious circle.

(1967: 120)

Clearly, there must be something supersensible, an original principle and reality, in which a radical negativity, a dialectics of praxis, can be built. Dialectics must be guided by the principle of autonomy, and the drive towards total freedom, guided by a philosophy of praxis and a vision of a new society of freely associated producers. Paz contrasts reactionary violence with revolutionary violence as follows:

When man [sic] is confronted with a state of affairs that is unjust he rebels. This rebellion begins as a naysaying and gradually becomes a consciousness: it becomes a critique of the existing order and a determination to bring about a new just, rational, universal order. Criticism is followed by action: waging revolution demands the invention of a technique and an ethic. Revolutionary technique views violence as an instrument and power as a lever. It transforms human relations into physical objects, mechanisms, or forces. Reactionary violence is passionate: it takes the form of punishment, humiliation, vengeance, sacrifice; revolutionary violence is rational and abstract: not a passion but a technique. If violence becomes a technique, a new ethic is needed to justify or reconcile the contradiction between force and reason, freedom and power.

(1967: 186)

If a critical pedagogical approach grounded in a dialectical analysis of social life is to be revolutionary, it must move beyond the 'technique' of reactionary violence and become grounded in an ethic of social justice for the poor and dispossessed, one that can inform us about ways in which social life can be both organised and administered in a manner that can transcend the limitations of bourgeois individualism. This calls for a direct or participatory democracy to be developed within local communities and workplaces and in larger institutional formations of the state. This also situates tourism studies within a problematic that exceeds liberal ideology and its focus on legal and political perspectives, because such ideologies have proven to be fraudulent. They are fraudulent largely because they are anti-dialectical and remain at the level of abstract talk about abstract freedom, something Pomeroy points out as a form of 'living misplaced concreteness' (2004a: 168).

The idea of this new society is already implicit in the dialectic of negativity that characterises the struggle of workers from practice to theory, and from theory back to practice. In other words, such knowledge is immanent in the workers' drive for total freedom (Hudis 2010). Freire (1978; 1981) believed that it wasn't a prerequisite to acquire a critical consciousness in order to struggle for social justice. Quite the contrary. Critical consciousness was the outcome – not the precondition – of struggle. It is in the act of struggling that educands become critically conscious. Critical educators need in my view to make what is implicit in the educands' experiences explicit by linking their spontaneous development of a critical or socialist consciousness to a larger, more comprehensive theory and philosophy of revolution (Hudis 2010). In other words, critical educators can hasten the outcome of mass struggle.

A critical tourism studies requires a necessary class consciousness, which is grounded in self-affirmation and self-appropriation. Here, solidarity with the subaltern, the proletariat, is key because

> they are the ultimate representation of human bondage occurring within capitalism, their essential poverty is capital's private property. Therefore, class consciousness is human consciousness – the consciousness of this bondage (capitalism's bondage of the of the human essence and human potential) is the key to real freedom. The liberation from wage labor (the liberation of the proletariat), is, therefore, the liberation of all human life for itself.
>
> (Pomeroy 2004a: 190)

To achieve the kind of creativity necessary in overcoming capitalism, we need to actualise our essential being. But this does not mean we are reduced to what we all share in common as a human species. It means that we can only be ourselves in relation to others. As Pomeroy writes:

> It is the actualization of our essential being but this essence does not reduce us to commonality, it frees us for the full development of our individuality. It is the actualization of our absolute difference from each other but such difference does not separate us from one another because it arises as our gift to one another. It is actualization of our uniqueness but such uniqueness is not self-centered because each achievement is a relational-ization of and for the whole.... A genuine dialectical unity is achieved finally for human life because we are beings-in-relation to one another, this is not just self-appropriation and self-affirmation as freedom for myself, but the freedom that I gain by appropriating my own creative ability is also an act of freeing others. Only when I feel the solidarity of myself and all others will I really feel the suffering of the other as (necessarily) my suffering.
>
> (2004a: 191)

What is important to grasp in Pomeroy's remarks is that dialectical thinking relies on novelty and while capitalism involves a reification of the past, dialectical thinking necessarily orients itself to 'the potentiality of the future', to non-conformal propositions of an anticipatory nature that consider the 'not yet'

(2004: 184). Dialectical thinking can help us envision a future in which there 'is no antithesis between the social and the individual because processive human being is aware of arising from a social nexus as a configuration of and contribution to this nexus' (2004: 187).

This can only occur if critical tourism studies sets its sights on the autonomy of thought of which Bauman speaks, which is only possible by utilising dialectical thinking guided by philosophy of praxis and grounded in an analysis of the self and social life from a relational understanding of the totality of capitalist relations. Only then can we endeavor to create a truly autonomous society not only *in itself* but *for itself*, which means a society that understands that its own freedom is dependent upon the freedom of others.

In closing, if we have any further suggestions for the future direction of critical tourism studies, including (even especially), those studies informed by socialist perspectives, we would urge tourism studies to begin a dialectical shift in its geopolitics of knowing, understanding and reasoning – what Catherine Walsh calls a 'critical border positioning' – and take seriously the contributions of indigenous knowledges as a way of intervening in the colonial horizon ensepulchured in structures of domination – economic, political, social, cultural and epistemic. We would encourage an epistemological revolution that can enable a de-linking from the un-dialectical paradigms or 'paradogmas' of Western concepts of identity, which have for over five centuries participated in acts of epistemological genocide (epistemicide), and a move towards a radically different social contract from that of the neoliberal capitalist state. Instead of identity politics based on Western concepts of the nation state, the focus of critical tourism studies should be on 'identity in politics' (Walsh 2010). The notion of identity in politics takes seriously the historicity of identities delinked from the notion of the nation state. Here we take notice of the Constituent Assemblies both in Ecuador and Bolivia in 2007–2008, and the contributions of the National Confederation of Indigenous Nationalities of Ecuador (CONAIE), writers such as Catherine Walsh, Walter Mignolo, Nelson Maldonaldo-Torres, Lewis Gordon, Ramon Grosfoguel, Anibal Quijano, Enrique Dussel, Sandy Grande, Linda Tuhiwai Smith and Graham Smith, whose political projects have explored the limitations of multiculturalism and advanced the transversal axioms of interculturality and plurinationality that have contributed to rethinking concepts of the nature, justice, coexistence, as well as the state, society and social life through multiple logics, cosmologies and life systems in their pluriversal forms – all of which have the potential to lead to a new social contract outside of the neoliberal model that is currently ravaging the planet. The issue here is not to replace the hegemonic epistemologies grounded in western modernity with the logics and civilisatory frames of indigenous communities – which would be an essentialist quest for authenticity – but to think with epistemological frames of indigenous peoples that do not originate with the uni-national structure of the modern nation state (Walsh 2010). This does not mean that we adopt or romanticise all Indianist ways of knowing and reject everything that white-mestizo intellectuals have contributed to the struggle for social justice, but that we begin to rethink concepts such as 'the common', 'community' and 'communalism' from the perspective of interculturality (co-thinking, co-existing, and co-living grounded in principles of co-dependence, complementarity, and relationality) rather than from the perspective of a domesticated multiculturalism (a recognition of different cultural logics, rather than a thinking with such logics, and an inclusion of different cultures into a model that is already dominated by liberal, modernist conceptions of the state and capitalist social relations of production). Interculturalidad is a 'model constructed from below and is based on territorial and educational control, self-sustainable development, care of the environment, reciprocity and solidarity, and the strengthening of communal organisations, languages, and cultures' (Meyer *et al.* 2010: 393). This term reminds us that 'our activism must be embedded within, and never separate itself from, the multivoiced hemispheric conversation on resistance, hope, and renewal' (2010: 397). Here, centrality is given to concepts such as Pachamama or Mother earth, to ancestral knowledges as well as to technological and scientific knowledges, and to the notion of buen vivir (sumak kawsay), which is a term that comes from the indigenous peoples of the Andean region, and the Aymara people in particular, that refers to harmony and equilibrium among men and women, among different communities, and among human beings and the natural environment – what Catherine Walsh (2010) refers to as 'notions, logics, practices and modes of living grounded in collective well-being and the mutual dependence of all beings (human and otherwise).' Buen vivir is grounded in the notions of the collective and co-dependency, 'and the complementariety and relationality that both necessarily entail' (Walsh 2010).

Embracing this new geopolitics of knowing means rethinking Western notions of socialism itself, especially those models that still work within the dominion of the capitalist marketplace (as in market socialism) and its founding logics and systems of intelligibility.

Any socialism for the twenty-first century needs to adopt a pluriversal approach and take seriously the epistemic perspective/cosmologies/insights of subalternised peoples. Walsh (in press) argues that interculturality 'engages a knowledge and thinking that is not isolated from dominant paradigms or structures' because 'by necessity (and as a result of the historical process of coloniality) this logic "knows" these paradigms and structures.' The ancestral and community-based knowledges that we are discussing are not hybrid knowledge constructions but the development of new epistemological frameworks 'that incorporate and negotiate both indigenous and westernised knowledges, consistently maintaining as fundamental the coloniality of power and the colonial difference to which they have been subject' (Walsh, in press). This logic 'does not seek inclusion in the Nation State as it stands but instead conceives of an alternative construction of organisation, society, education, and governance in which difference is not additive or constitutive' (Walsh, in press). Walsh (in press) writes that a critical border positioning recognises 'the capacity of social-ethnic movements to enter in/to work within and between the social, political, and epistemological spaces previously denied them and to reconceptualise these spaces in ways that contest the persistent re-coloniality of power, knowledge, and being and look towards the creation of an alternative civilization, a kind of strategical confrontation with the subalternising conditions established by coloniality itself.'

The struggle for socialism should not be limited to Western/European responses to liberalism and capitalism alone, but rather – as noted in Walter Mignolo's (2010) analysis of Aymara sociologist Félix Patzi Paco's work regarding Indian/indigenous conceptualisations of the 'communal' – should include the views of those who continue to suffer under the expansion of Western civilisation while recognising that their perspectives in response to colonisation may not fully overlap with communist/Marxist responses to capitalism. An inclusion of indigenous perspectives within revolutionary critical pedagogy should recognise that 'the left of European genealogy of thought (and the same genealogy in modern/colonial states) doesn't have the monopoly to imagine and dictate how a non-capitalist future shall be' (Mignolo 2010: 148). Instead, following the insights of Patzi Paco, Mignolo (2010) attests that indigenous systems do not have the same political pillar or economic management pillar as those of Western, capitalist systems or colonial systems and, therefore, take on a different perception of justice, collective rights, and change.

Critical tourism studies would benefit from embracing the concept of comunalidad. Comunalidad is an Oaxacan concept that serves as a type of cosmovision and deals with 'the complex intertwining of history, morality, spirituality kinship and communal practices' (Meyer *et al.* 2010: 387). Out of this concept is cultivated the concept of reciprocity. Solidarity is a selective and individuated term and does not speak to relations of equality as it is essentially a one-way, unidirectional relation that is by and large temporary. The concept of reciprocity, by contrast, is a set of practices that requires the other or others to make an equivalent response and it is meant to be a permanent relation and inclusive of all members of the community (Myer *et al.* 2010: 389). A critical tourist studies grounded in a global comunalidad – would be open to a relational (i.e. dialectical) understanding of human development.

And finally, a critical approach to tourism needs to expand the issue of tourism beyond questions of management and governance, to that of reclaiming the world for humanity. Technological revolution and the market will not be enough to solve the growing environmental challenge and alleviating the problem of ecological decline and overcoming necessity. Tourism inquiry, as well as tourism as a social practice, must be rethought from the standpoint of those who exist at the bottom of the global capitalist hierarchy, if we are to prevail in the continuing wars over scarce resources. Whether we support models of eco-communalism, eco-socialism or the new sustainability paradigm, it is clear that critical tourism studies underwritten by a social justice agenda will require more than lifestyle change but a concerted critique and transformation of the unbridled barbarism of capitalist social relations. This edition of *The Critical Turn in Tourism Studies* reflects a new school of thought that takes issues of methodology and practice seriously by locating tourism as both a social practice and an ethical and political project dedicated to creating conditions of equality, sustainability and human freedom. Critical discourse analysis, critical qualitative methods, critical ethnography, critical race theory, critical media literacy, standpoint epistemology, post-colonial critique, critically conscious language and literacy research and critical policy analysis are only a few of the approaches available. But whatever theoretical and analytical models we choose to explore the social practice of tourism and tourism research within the hydra-headed domains of global capitalist society, we will benefit greatly from an approach grounded in dialectical thought.

References

Allman, P. (2007) *On Marx: an introduction to the revolutionary intellect of Karl Marx*, Rotterdam, The Netherlands: Sense Publishers.

Allman, P., McLaren, P. and Rikowski, G. (2005) 'After the Box People: the labor-capital relation as class constitution and its consequences for Marxist educational theory and human resistance,' in P. McLaren, *Capitalists and Conquerors: a critical pedagogy against empire*, Lanham, MD: Rowman & Littlefield.

Anderson, Kevin (2010) *Overcoming Some Current Challenges to Dialectical Thought: U.S. Marxist Humanists.* August 18. Retrieved from: www.usmarxisthumanists.org/articles/overcoming-some-current-challenges-to-dialectical-thought/.

Au, Wayne (2007) 'Epistemology of the Oppressed: the dialectics of Paulo Freire's theory of knowledge', *Journal for Critical Education Policy Studies*, 5 (2) (November). Retrieved from: www.jceps.com/index.php?pageID=article&articleID=100.

Bauman, Zygmunt (1999) *In Search of Politics*, Sanford, CA: Stanford University Press.

Davis, R. and Freire, P. (1981) 'Education for Awareness: a talk with Paulo Freire', in R. Mackie (ed.), *Literacy and Revolution: the pedagogy of Paulo Freire*, New York: The Continuum Publishing Company, pp. 57–69.

Freire, P. (1973) *Pedagogy of the Oppressed*, New York: Seabury Press.

Freire, P. (1978) *Pedagogy in Process: the letters to Guinea-Bissau*, New York: Seabury Press.

Freire, P. (1981) *Pedagogy of the Oppressed*, New York: Continuum.

Freire, P. (1982) 'Extension or communication' (trans. L. Bigwood and M. Marshall), in *Education for Critical Consciousness*, New York: Continuum, pp. 93–164.

Freire, P. (1985) 'Dialogue is not a chaste event', Compiled by Paul Jurmo, The Center for International Education, School of Education. Hills House South. University of Massachusetts, Amherst.

Freire, P. (2000) *Pedagogy of the Oppressed*, New York and London: Continuum.

Hardt, Michal and Negri, Antonio (2004) *Multitude: war and democracy in the age of empire*, New York: Penguin.

Harvey, David. (2003). *The New Imperialism*, Oxford: Oxford University Press.

Hudis, Peter (2005) 'Marx's critical appropriation and transcendence of Hegel's theory of alienation', presentation to Brecht Forum, November.

Hudis, Peter (2010) 'The critical pedagogy of Rosa Luxemburg', paper prepared for the Encuentro Internacional del Pensamiento Critico: Marxismo y Educacion Popular. Morelia, Michoacan, Mexico, 9–11 December 2010.

Jameson, Fredric (2009) *Valences of the Dialectic*, London and New York: Verso.

Kant, Emmanuel (1784) 'An answer to the question: what is Enlightenment?' Retrieved from: www.english.upenn.edu/~mgamer/Etexts/kant.html.

Kosik, Karel (1976) *Dialectics of the Concrete*, Holland: Reidel Publishing Company.

Marx, K. (1967) *Capital* (volume 1, trans. S. Moore and E. Aveling, ed. F. Engels), New York: International Publishers.

Meyer, Lois, Kirwin, Julianna and Toober, Erin (2010) 'An open-ended closing', in Lois Meyer, and Benjamin Maldonado Alvarado, *New World of Indigenous Resistance: Noam Chomsky and voices from North, South, and Central America*, San Franciso: City Lights Books, pp. 383–389.

Mignolo, Walter D. (2010) 'The communal and the decolonial', *Pavilion*, 14, pp. 146–155.

Ollman, Bertell (2003) *Dance of the Dialectics: steps in Marx's method*, Urbana and Chicago: University of Illinois Press.

Pavlidis, Periklis (2010) 'Critical thinking as dialectics: a Hegelian–Marxist approach', *Journal for Critical Education Policy Studies*, 8 (2) (December): 74–102.

Pomeroy, Anne Fairchild (2004a) *Marx and Whitehead: process dialectics, and the critique of capitalism*, Albany, New York: State University Press of New York.

Pomeroy, Anne Fairchild (2004b) 'Why Marx, why now? A recollection of Dunayevskaya's power of negativity', *Cultural Logic*, 7. Retrieved from: http://clogic.eserver.org/2004/pomeroy.html.

Quantz, Richard (in press) *Ritual Critique for a New Pedagogy: education, politics and public life*, London and New York: Routledge.

Rancier, Jacques (1989) *The Nights of Labor: the workers' dream in nineteenth century France* (trans. John Drury), Philadelphia: Temple University Press.

Rancier, Jacques (1991) *The Ignorant Schoolmaster: five lessons in intellectual emancipation* (trans. Kristin Ross), Stanford: Stanford University Press.

Reitz, Charles (2000) *Art, Alienation and the Humanities: a critical engagement with Herbert Marcuse*, Albany, New York: State University of New York Press.

Shor, I. (1980) Critical Teaching and Everyday Life, Boston: South End Press.

Shor, I., and Freire, P. (1987). A Pedagogy for Liberation: dialogues on transforming education, South Hadley, Mass.: Bergin & Garvey Publishers.

Stetsenko, A. (2002) 'Vygotsky's cultural-historical activity theory: collaborative practice and knowledge construction process', in D. Robbins and A. Stetsenko (eds), *Vygotsky's Psychology: voices from the past and present*, NY: Nova Science Press.

Stetsenko, Anna (2008) 'Collaboration and cogenerativity: on bridging the gaps separating theory–practice and cognition–emotion', *Cultural Studies of Science Education*, 3: 521–533.

Walsh, Catherine (2010) 'Decolonial thinking and doing in the Andes: a conversation by Walter Mignolo with Catherine Walsh: a propos of her book *Interculturalidad, Estado, Sociedad*', Luchas (De)Coloniales de Nuestra Epoca/Interculturalism, State, Society. (De)Colonial Struggles of our Times, part 1. *Reartikulacija*. Retrieved from: www.reartikulacija.org/?p=1468.

Walsh, Catherine (in press) 'Interculturality and the coloniality of power: an "other" thinking and positioning from the colonial difference', in Ramon Grosfoguel, Jose David Saldivar and Nelson Maldonado (eds), *Unsettling Postcoloniality: coloniality, transmodernity and border thinking*, Durham, NC: Duke University Press.

Acknowledgements

We said in the acknowledgements of the first edition of this book that no text is ever purely the result of three people's efforts and this second edition is no different. Once again we would like to thank all our contributors for agreeing to be part of this project of hope. We would also like to express our gratitude to our editors at Routledge for their assistance and guidance throughout the process, particularly the book series editor, Stephen Page, for giving us the opportunity to return to our academy of hope book project. We owe a special debt of gratitude to Lisa Schwarzin for all her painstaking editorial work on the manuscript – you know we could not have done it without you! Finally, the three of us owe so much to so many wonderful and beautiful people – our families, our friends and our colleagues – that to attempt to name you here would be an invidious task. Please forgive us and accept our simple thank you for inspiring and supporting us in this and all our efforts.

Irena Ateljevic
Croatia

Nigel Morgan
Cardiff

Annette Pritchard
Cardiff
1 February 2011

Introduction

Creating an academy of hope: an enquiry–learning–action nexus

Annette Pritchard, Nigel Morgan and Irena Ateljevic

> It is in the power of everybody with a little courage, to hold out a hand to someone different, to listen, and to attempt to increase, even by a tiny amount, the quantity of kindness and humanity in the world. But it is careless to do so without remembering how previous efforts have failed, and how it has never been possible to predict for certain how a human being will behave. History, with its endless procession of passers-by, most of whose encounters have been missed opportunities, has so far been largely a chronicle of ability gone to waste. But next time two people meet the result could be different. That is the origin of anxiety, but also of hope, and hope is the origin of humanity
>
> (Zeldin 1994: 471–2)

A story of hope

This book presents the latest thinking around hopeful tourism, a new and unfolding transformative perspective in tourism enquiry (see Pritchard *et al.* 2011). Hopeful tourism scholarship is a values-led, humanist perspective that strives for the transformation of our way of seeing, being, doing and relating in tourism worlds and for the creation of a less unequal, more sustainable planet through action-oriented, participant-driven learnings and acts. It connects critical and interpretive tourism scholarship with the values of the emergent perspectives of the dynamic feminine (Hill 1992; Judith 2006), transmodernity (Ghisi 2006; 2008) and worldism (Agathangelou and Ling 2009) and advocates critique, education and action for planetary justice and responsibility – the enquiry–learning–action nexus in the title of this chapter.

In the introduction to the first edition of this book we described the hopeful tourism project as 'a commitment to tourism enquiry which is pro-social justice and equality and anti-oppression: it is an academy of hope' (Ateljevic *et al.* 2007: 3). That edited collection was the first hesitant iteration of the hopeful tourism perspective and since then it has achieved 'a measure of success in enrolling people, ideas and inscriptions' (Tribe 2010: 12) and gathered momentum through a growing body of publications (e.g. Pritchard *et al.* 2011; Richards *et al.* 2010; Sedgley *et al.* 2011). The hopeful tourism knowledge network has attracted scholars in the tourism academy who espouse interpretative and critical approaches, particularly those among them who seek to disturb its hegemonic ontologies which exert so much influence on how its knowledge is performed, created and disseminated (Ren *et al.* 2010). In many ways, the network has become a loose coalition of like-minded people brought together by their shared desire to challenge the dominant way of understanding and being in the tourism world, not by dismissing it but by engaging it to demonstrate that it offers but one perspective. Those of us who are firmly aligned with such thinking contend that tourism enquiry, education and practice need 'a story of hope ... the kind of hope that employs all of our efforts in creating a mature vision of what's possible' (Judith 2006: 14). Here, by way of introducing the second edition of this book, we take a moment to reflect on how that vision is evolving.

Why does tourism need hope?

We live in uncertain times. Unquestionably now seems to be an appropriate time to dispute the hegemonic neo-liberal ways of producing and disseminating tourism knowledge (Ayikoru *et al.* 2009) and to call on responsible tourism intellectuals to engage understandings which directly relate to the challenges of creating a just and sustainable planet (e.g. Higgins-Desbiolles 2006; 2008; Cole and Morgan 2010; Pernecky 2010). As Peter McLaren and Nathalia Jaramillo remind us in their essay which is the foreword to this volume:

> A critical approach to tourism needs to expand the issue of tourism beyond questions of management and governance, to that of reclaiming the world for humanity. Technological revolution and the market will not be enough to solve the growing environmental challenge and alleviating the problem of ecological decline and overcoming necessity. Tourism inquiry, as well as tourism as a social practice, must be rethought from the standpoint of those who exist at the bottom of the global capitalist hierarchy, if we are to survive the continuing wars over scarce resources.

To engage in critical tourism research that is values-led and embraces the knowledge of multiple worlds and ways of knowing connects our scholarship with new thinking in fields as diverse as sustainability studies, evolutionary biology, neuro-cognitive science and child development research (Holling and Gunderson 2002; Judith 2009; Rifkin 2009). New perspectives are emerging across many disciplines and research fields – from relativity theory in physics and the findings of depth psychologists, to new approaches in anthropological and ecological studies – as constant revision redefines how we understand our universe and our human race. For example, scholars in global change, resilience and sustainability studies are seeking conceptualisations and models which integrate the earth system, human development and sustainability based on a widely shared view that 'the challenge of sustainable development is the reconciliation of society's development goals with the planet's environmental limits over the long term' (Clark and Dickson 2003: 8059). At the same time, researchers in economics (Scott-Cato 2009; Scott-Cato and Hillier 2010), urban studies and economic geography (Huggins 2003) and destination marketing (Morgan *et al.* 2011) are re-evaluating orthodox definitions of competitiveness based on growth and accumulated wealth and advocating measures of a place's success based on its relevance, community cohesion, quality of life, capacity for creativity and stewardship of culture, traditions and environment.

Such revisionism and reflection is particularly pertinent as never before in human history have so many cultures, belief systems, and new scientific discoveries emerged and interacted so quickly. Our contemporary moment is calling into question much orthodoxy and the dominant ways of being in and understanding the world and its business, governance and institutional structures increasingly seem flawed. Consumer confidence is fragile in many of the world's more economically developed economies and despite the end of the Cold War, the world remains a hostile place and there are many threats to peace, of which global inequalities, political instability and transnational violence are just three. Moreover there loom more gradual, menacing global threats to which most of us pay only periodic attention – those linked to human pressures on our planet's natural resources, resulting in climatic change and food, water and energy shortages (Hall 2010).

Some commentators suggest that such signs of institutional and environmental stress signal the end of the neoliberal industrial age as we know it, while others call this era the age of globalisation, the information age or the age of the knowledge or experience economy; yet others see signs of a new transmodern age of planetary responsibility. Many are describing our era as one of regime change, system flip or paradigm shift. This period may yet prove to be one of generational economic and social transformation during which people, communities and places will need to find alternative ways of living and working. This sense that our world is at a tipping point environmentally, socially, culturally, economically and perhaps intellectually provides the context which has given birth to our academy of hope.

'Hope' is such a key word for this book and the wider hopeful tourism network. The antonyms of hope are fear and despair and clearly there is much to fear in today's world – at an individual, community and global level. We are faced by confrontations across cultures, religions and worldviews and we fear for the sustainability of our planet. The majority of the readers of this book will be students and academics and most, especially those early in their careers, will be anxious about their employment prospects and job security and many may have to sacrifice personal intellectual agendas to secure tenure or promotion. People fear for the future everywhere and at every level. At the most basic level of human survival, more than half the world's population lives on less than $2.50 a day, at the same time, inequality continues to rise in richer countries and our existing institutions and practices have 'brought us straight to the cliff edge of rapidly diminishing natural resources and unpredictable climate change' (Abdallah *et al.* 2009).

How we define and mark success has (at least in the West) centred on economic growth indicators such as collective GDP levels and individual material wealth. But such markers seem increasingly ill-suited to the times in which we live. Over the past half century people in more developed economies have seen their wealth levels increase significantly but there has been no concomitant rise in life satisfaction or happiness levels. More and more people are recognising the need to broaden and deepen our measures of success to focus on that which makes life worth living, notably a sense of contentment with who we are, our relationships with others and a sense of meaning and purpose in life. Following the findings of a provocative 2009 study conducted by two Nobel prize-winning economists, Joseph E. Stiglitz and Amartya Sen at the behest of French President Sarkosy, countries such as France, Canada and the UK are now adopting new assessment tools that incorporate a broader concern for human welfare which goes beyond simply economic growth.

Nic Marks, statistician and founder of the Centre for Well-Being at the independent think-and-do-tank the New Economics Foundation, argues that his evidence-based research demonstrates how people worldwide value happiness, love and well-being ahead of material wealth and that fundamentally they aspire to peace and hope (www.happyplanetindex.org). As he says elsewhere, when Dr Martin Luther King wanted to mobilise people behind the civil rights movement in the 1960s, he didn't tell them that he had a nightmare vision of the future but that he had a dream of hope for it (www.ted.com/talks/lang/eng/nic_marks_the_happy_planet_index.html). Fear paralyses people; it does not inspire them to action. But hope directs us to the possibilities for positive transformative action. The origins of the word hope are obscure and it is a complex concept which can be discerned, not only in the utopian writings of philosophers such as Marx and Hegel and in the establishment of hopeful utopias, but across the full gamut of human culture. The last thing to be released from Pandora's jar, hope continues to play a major role in most contemporary faiths and religions and has connotations of spiritual truth, coming to humanity as a spiritual gift.

In our contemporary world our engagement with hope and love seems very limited and yet we should remember that both are central to all social justice movements (hooks 2000). Of course, we are not attempting to present hopeful tourism as some model for the accomplishment of social justice. But we do believe that it represents an unfolding vision, a perspective, a way of knowing the world and a set of methods, which could play a part in prompting syncretic growth and co-transformative learning (Pritchard *et al.* 2011). Tourism needs a new compass to set it on a path towards mindful development and learning. We believe that hopeful tourism can contribute to this by focusing on what truly matters to humanity and the planet. Crucially, however, rather than being a passive hope of dreams and longings, hopeful tourism is an active hope that visualises an idea and formulates a plan to accomplish its ends. It looks forward to change with confidence; it is about moving *towards* something rather than moving *away* from something else; it is a collective vision of what is possible, an organising principle for co-transformation. This second edition of *The Critical Turn in Tourism Studies* thus 'reflects a new school of thought that takes issues of methodology and practice seriously by locating tourism as both a social practice and an ethical and political project dedicated to creating conditions of equality, sustainability and human freedom' (McLaren and Jaramillo, this volume).

John Tribe argues that tourism enquiry's philosophical foundations have 'remained stubbornly underdeveloped' in a world rooted in neo-liberal market ideologies and values where the tourism industry has become a 'runaway' phenomenon, ill-managed and barely controlled (2009: 3–4). By deciding to momentarily step outside of this world and to question its dominant philosophies and ontologies, the contributors to this book are themselves committing transgressive and potentially transformative acts. These are ideas which tourism researchers have consistently shied away from as too few have truly pushed the field's paradigmatic boundaries. And yet the continued conceptual development of tourism as a field of enquiry depends on the exploration of new paradigms and perspectives, because when we push ourselves away from dominant and taken-for-granted thinking we open up possibilities of seeing ourselves and our multiple worlds anew.

Defining hopeful tourism

A number of new perspectives have emerged in the social sciences, which attempt to provide understanding of our transitory times and hopeful tourism connects strongly with three of these – the dynamic feminine (Hill 1992; Judith 2006), transmodernity (Ghisi 2006, 2008) and worldism (Agathangelou and Ling 2009). Guided by consensual practices of cooperation, reciprocity, interdependence, activism and support, the paradigmatic shift promised by transmodernity and the dynamic feminine resonates with the ideas of leading feminists such as bell hooks (2000) and her work on the envisioning of love ethics and Gloria Steinem (1993) and her writing on the circularity paradigm (see Ateljevic *et al.* 2007: 4–5). Judith describes the dynamic feminine as a participatory movement, founded on civil rights and a unity of body and mind and the planet and culture.

In rejecting patriarchal values of control and domination, both the dynamic feminine and the transmodern paradigms offer collective empowering, egalitarian and respectful visions for women and men where civil rights are fundamental and the sacred re-evaluated. Transmodernity is a new global consciousness which recognises our interdependencies, vulnerabilities and responsibilities to each other, to the natural world and to the planet (Ateljevic 2009; Ghisi 2006; 2008; Rifkin 2005). Hopeful tourism strongly connects with the empowering and egalitarian values of the dynamic feminine and transmodernity; indeed its naming took inspiration from bell hooks' 2003 book *Teaching Community: a pedagogy of hope*, which offers insights into how to create critical education arenas that dismantle oppression across racial, ethnic, gender, class and nation lines and work towards socially just communities. Hopeful tourism also resonates powerfully with Agathangelou and Ling's (2009: 1) worldism perspective and its focus on:

the multiple relations, ways of being, and traditions of seeing and doing passed to us across generations. More than a postmodern sense of 'difference', worldism registers the entwinement of multiple worlds: their contending structures, histories, memories, and political economies in the making of our contemporary world.

Just like these three emergent perspectives, hopeful tourism presents an unfolding vision that is committed to co-transformative learning, social justice and the universality of human rights. We have elsewhere defined hopeful tourism and summarised its 13 key tenets, starting with ontology, epistemology and nature of knowledge, moving through values and ethics, methodology, aim, action, control, voice and researcher positioning, training and credibility and ending with research dissemination (Pritchard *et al.* 2011). Hopeful tourism has at its heart co-transformation, especially of relationships between the researcher and the researched – no longer subjects or even participants in projects, but wherever possible, collaborators in tourism storying (e.g. Dunkley 2007; Richards *et al.* 2010; Sedgley *et al.* 2007). This places significant demands on the researcher as it centralises the emotional, spiritual and ethical responsibilities its researchers have to their co-creators of tourism knowledge and creates multiple entanglements (Ateljevic *et al.* 2005). This transformation also creates alternative discourses of research credibility, beginning with the ontological matters of being, becoming and meaning and foregrounding trustworthiness, participatory consciousness and resonance.

Hopeful tourism strives for co-created, co-transformative learning, impacting the self and others. In contrast to the scientific rational approach it is values-led rather than value-free, it embraces the oneness and integration of mind, body and spirit found in non-western wisdom traditions (e.g. Bishop 2005; Tuhiwai Smith 2005; Fox 2006) and is empowering and participant-driven. It seeks to disrupt the hegemony of the field's intellectually detached western research traditions and emphasises multiple relations, ways of being, and traditions of seeing and doing. Crucially hopeful tourism does not simply turn its back on the dominant way of understanding and being in the tourism world but offers an alternative perspective, one which envisions a tourism industry that values syncretic, mindful growth not mindless development (Morgan *et al.* 2011: 10) and an academy that embodies the connections of multiple worlds to speak truth to power not to excuse it.

An increasing number of voices are critical of many western higher education institutions' embrace of market-values and of their failure to address social conscience, ethics, sustainability and concern for the world's disenfranchised populations in their curricula (Ciancanelli 2007; Corbyn 2008). This is particularly true of many business schools (home to most tourism academics) who have failed to engage with fundamental questions concerning wealth distribution, the environment, workers' rights, equality issues and business ethics, which could help provide answers to the very real and pressing problems our world faces (Dunne and Harney 2008). As a perspective guided by ethics, values and responsibility, hopeful tourism has an activist edge and while it aims for co-transformation in and through enquiry and practice, it is important to recognise that it plays a role in the classroom and that learning and education are also transformative acts (e.g. hooks 2003; McLaren *et al.* 2010). Hopeful tourism seeks to engage democratic and emancipatory learning agendas, transforming the traditional hierarchical character of much pedagogic practice (Brookfield 1995) and valuing multiple worlds and knowledge experiences in the classroom (Biggs and Tang 2007). Such scholarship encourages researchers to reflect on their role in promoting education as personal transformation (Molesworth *et al.* 2009) and to centralise student agency, empowerment and active participation (Angus *et al.* 2001; Hyman 2000).

The story of the book

Although it is an emergent perspective, hopeful tourism is already beginning to transform enquiry, education and practice. For example, scholars are engaging with disability and citizenship (Richards *et al.* 2010; Small and Darcy 2010), older people and advocacy (Sedgley *et al.* 2011), justice and peace (Higgins-Desbiolles 2010; Pernecky 2010), human rights (Cole and Eriksson 2010), education and knowledge production (Ren *et al.* 2010), inequality (Cole and Morgan 2010) and destination reputation stewardship (Morgan *et al.* 2011). As we will see in the coming chapters by scholars (more and less) associated with the new hopeful tourism perspective, it challenges educators and researchers to disturb hegemonic socio-political tourism practices, to prepare ethical tourism professionals and academics and to agitate for human dignity, human rights, and justice.

While hopeful tourism scholarship focuses on critical thinking, education and action for a just and sustainable world, this is not to underplay the longevity of analyses of the causes of inequality and injustice in tourism and how they relate to wider international systems of political and economic dependency relations (e.g. de Kadt 1979 and Harrison 2001). The underlying causes of inequity relating to unjust global systems, unfair international trade agreements, the workings of transnational corporations, and the neoliberal capitalist system have long been the subject of enquiry (see Cole and Morgan 2010; Hall and Brown 2006). However, while we fully acknowledge previous contributions to this debate, hopeful tourism scholars try to move the discussion forward in a number of new ways. To identify and critique injustice is one task but to understand multi-faceted problems and to seek transformations is quite another undertaking.

For ease of navigation the book is divided into three parts, focusing on the three entanglements of hopeful tourism: critical thinking, critical pedagogy and critical action. Taken as a group, the book's contributors draw on a range of disciplines and case-studies to provide unique perspectives on these three dimensions of hopeful scholarship, although such division is artificial of course, since thinking and teaching are both forms of critical action. The disciplinary perspectives of its contributors include sociology, cultural studies, media studies, geography, anthropology, history, and tourism and hospitality management and they illustrate their arguments with international case studies drawn from countries including Argentina, Bosnia and Herzegovina, Canada, Denmark, Israel, the Netherlands, New Zealand, the UK and USA. While discussion of the power dynamics of international, institutional and personal politics are embedded in the book, Part I examines critical thinking and innovative methodologies in tourism and Part II explores ways in which we can bring the values and aspirations of hopeful scholarship into our classes and examines critical education as a transformative act.

Finally, Part III consists of a series of chapters that consider the confrontation of injustice and inequalities through critical action. Here, the contributors urge us to see power relations through new lenses, to appreciate their complexities and to demand change. In fact, this is true of all of the chapters in the book in different ways as their authors go beyond examining the problems to ask 'what can be done' and 'is there another way'? Moreover, what is profoundly attractive about these contributors is that they are all 'critical'. Although they might not all conform to your view of critical scholarship or share your ontological vision, our hope is that some of the work in this book resonates with your experiences of the research process as the contributors range from postgraduate students to established professors with many years of experience as teachers, researchers and writers. What binds them together is their desire to examine critically the purpose of their academic practice and their willingness to ask whether orthodox tourism knowledge serves social justice or whether it confirms hegemonic practices and social relations. In the face of global conflict and uncertainty, we all need to (re)discover the power of our agency and our own processes of becoming. We hope that the following chapters will demonstrate that there are alternatives to dominant ways of understanding and being in the tourism world and that this orthodoxy increasingly requires questioning.

References

Abdallah, S., Thompson, S., Michaelson, J., Marks, N. and Steur, N. (2009) *The Happy Planet Index 2.0*, London: New Economics Foundation.

Agathangelou, A. M. and Ling, L. H. M. (2009) *Transforming World Politics: from empire to multiple worlds*, Oxford: Routledge.

Angus, T., Cook, I., and Evans, J. *et al.* (2001) 'A manifesto for cyborg pedagogy', *International Research in Geographic and Environmental Education*, 1 (2): 195–201.

Atelejevic, I. (2009) 'Transmodernity: remaking our (tourism) world?' in J. Tribe (ed.), *Philosophical Issues In Tourism*, Bristol: Channel View, pp. 278–300.

Atelejevic, I., Pritchard, A. and Morgan, N. (2007) 'Editors' introduction: promoting an academy of hope in tourism enquiry', in I. Ateljevic, A. Pritchard and N. Morgan (eds), *The Critical Turn in Tourism Studies: innovative research methodologies*, Oxford: Elsevier, pp. 1–11.

Ateljevic, I., Harris, C., Wilson, E. and Collins L. (2005) 'Getting "entangled": reflexivity and the "critical turn" in tourism studies', *Tourism Recreation Research*, 30 (2): 9–21.

Ayikoru, M., Tribe, J. and Airey, D. (2009) 'Reading tourism education: neoliberalism unveiled', *Annals of Tourism Research*, 36 (2): 191–221.

Biggs, J. and Tang, C. (2007) *Teaching for Quality Learning at University* (3rd edition), Berkshire: McGraw Hill/The Society for Research into Higher Education.

Bishop, R. (2005) 'Freeing ourselves from neocolonial domination in research: a Kaupapa Maori approach to creating knowledge', in N. K. Denzin and Y. S. Lincoln (eds), *The Sage Handbook of Qualitative Research* (3rd edition), London: Sage, pp. 109–139.

Brookfield, S. (1995) *Becoming a Critically Reflective Teacher*, San Francisco: Jossy-Bass.

Ciancanelli, P. (2007) '(Re)producing universities: knowledge dissemination, market power and the global knowledge commons', in D. Epstein, R. Boden, R. Deem, F. Rizvi and S. Wright (eds), *World Yearbook of Education 2008: geographies of knowledge, geometries of power: framing the future of higher education*, New York and London: Routledge.

Clark, W.C. and Dickson, N. (2003) *Sustainability Science: the emerging research program*, PNAS 100(14): 8059-8061.

Cole, S. and Eriksson, J. (2010) 'Tourism and human rights', in S. Cole and N. Morgan (eds), *Tourism and Inequality: problems and prospects*, Oxford: Cabi, pp. 107–125.

Cole, S. and Morgan, N. (eds) (2010) *Tourism and Inequality: problems and prospects*, Oxford: Cabi.

Corbyn, Z. (2008) 'Did poor teaching lead to crash?' *Times Higher Education*, 25 September: 5.

de Kadt, E. (1979) *Tourism: passport to development?* Oxford: Open University Press.

Dunkley, R. A. (2007) 'Collected tales of Thanatourism experience', unpublished Ph.D., University of Wales Institute, Cardiff.

Dunne, S. and Harney, S. (2008) 'Speaking out: the responsibilities of management intellectuals: a survey', *Organization*, 15 (2): 271–282.

Fox, K. (2006) 'Leisure and indigenous peoples', *Leisure Studies*, 25 (4): 403–411.

Ghisi, L. M. (2006) 'Transmodernity and transmodern tourism: a keynote presented at the 15th Nordic Symposium in Tourism and Hospitality Research: *Visions of Modern Transmodern Tourism*', Savonlinna, Finland, 19–22 October.

Ghisi, L. M. (2008) *The Knowledge Society: a breakthrough towards genuine sustainability*, India: Stone Hill Foundation.

Hall, C. M. (2010) 'Crisis events in tourism: subjects of crisis in tourism', *Current Issues in Tourism*, 13 (5): 401–417.

Hall, D. and Brown, F. (2006) *Tourism and Welfare: ethics, responsibility and sustainable well-being*, Wallingford, CABI.

Harrison, D. (2001) 'Introduction', in D. Harrison (ed.) *Tourism in the Less Developed World: issues and cases.* Oxford, CABI, pp. 1–22.

Higgins-Desbiolles, F. (2006) 'More than an "industry": the forgotten power of tourism as a social force', *Tourism Management*, 27: 1992–1208.

Higgins-Desbiolles, F. (2008) 'Justice tourism: a pathway to alternative globalisation', *Journal of Sustainable Tourism*, 16: 345–364.

Higgins-Desbiolles, F. (2010) 'Justifying tourism: justice through tourism', in S. Cole and N. Morgan (eds), *Tourism and Inequality: problems and prospects*, Oxford: Cabi, pp. 195–212.

Hill, G. (1992) *Masculine and Feminine: the natural flow of opposites on the psyche*, Boston: Shambala.

Holling, C. S. and Gunderson, L. (eds) (2002), *Panarchy: understanding transformations in human and natural systems*, Washington, DC: Island Press.

hooks, b. (2003) *Teaching Community: a pedagogy of hope*, New York: Routledge.

hooks, b. (2000) *All About Love: new visions*, New York: Harper Collins.

Huggins, R. (2003) 'Creating a UK competitiveness index: regional and local benchmarking', *Regional Studies* 37 (1): 89–96.

Hyman, R. (2000) 'Research pedagogy and instrumental geography', *Antipode*, 32 (3): 292–307.

Judith, A. (2006) *Waking the Global Heart: humanity's rite of passage from the love of power to the power of love*, Santa Rosa, CA: Elite Books.

McLaren, P., Macrine, S. and Hill, D. (eds) (2010) *Revolutionizing Pedagogy: educating for social justice within and beyond global neo-liberalism*, London: Palgrave Macmillan.

Molesworth, M., Nixon, E. and Scullion, R. (2009) 'Having, being and higher education: the marketization of the university and the transformation of the student into consumer', *Teaching in Higher Education*, 14 (3): 277–287.

Morgan, N., Pritchard, A. and Pride, R. (2011) 'Tourism places, brands and reputation management,' in N. Morgan, A. Pritchard and R. Pride (eds), *Destination Brands: managing place reputation* (3rd edition), Oxford: Butterworth-Heinemann.

Pernecky, T. (2010) 'The being of tourism', *The Journal of Tourism and Peace Research*, 1 (1): 1–15.

Pritchard, A., Morgan, N. and Ateljevic, I. (2011) 'Hopeful tourism: a new transformative perspective', *Annals of Tourism Research*, 38 (3), forthcoming.

Ren, C., Pritchard, A. and Morgan, N. (2010) 'Constructing tourism research: a critical enquiry', *The Annals of Tourism Research*, 37 (4): 885–904.

Richards, V., Pritchard, A. and Morgan, N. (2010) '(Re)envisioning tourism and visual impairment', *The Annals of Tourism Research*, 37 (4): 1097–1116.

Rifkin, J. (2005) *The European Dream: how Europe's vision of the future is quietly eclipsing the American Dream*, New York: Penguin Group.

Rifkin, J. (2009) *The Empathetic Civilization: the race to global consciousness in a world in crisis*, New York: Tarcher/Penguin.

Scott-Cato, M. (2009) *Green Economics: theory, policy and practice*, London: Earthscan.

Scott-Cato, M. and Hillier, J. (2010) 'How could we study climate-related social innovation? Applying Deleuzian philosophy to the transition towns', *Environmental Politics*, 19 (6): 869–887.

Sedgley, D., Pritchard, A. and Morgan, N. (2007) 'Insights into older women's leisure: voices from urban South Wales', *World Leisure Journal*, 49 (3): 129–141.

Sedgley, D., Pritchard, A. and Morgan, N. (2011) 'Tourism and ageing: a transformative research agenda', *The Annals of Tourism Research*, 38 (2): 422–436.

Small, J. and Darcy, S. (2010) 'Tourism, disability and mobility', in S. Cole and N. Morgan (eds), *Tourism and Inequality: problems and prospects*, Oxford: Cabi, pp. 1–21.

Steinem, G. (1993) *Revolution from Within*, USA: Gloria Steinem.

Tuhiwai Smith, L. (2005) 'On tricky ground: researching the native in the age of uncertainty', in N. K. Denzin and Y. S. Lincoln (eds), *The Sage Handbook of Qualitative Research* (3rd edition), London: Sage, pp. 85–109.

Tribe, J. (2009) 'Philosophical Iissues in tourism', in J. Tribe (ed.) *Philosophical Issues in Tourism*, Bristol: Channel View, pp. 3–25.

Tribe, J. (2010) 'Tribes, territories and networks in the tourism academy', *The Annals of Tourism Research*, 37 (1): 7–33.

Zeldin, T. (1994) *An Intimate History of Humanity*, London: Vintage Books.

Part I

Critical tourism research

Annette Pritchard

Today the tourism research field is characterised by tremendous growth and increasing fragmentation. There has been an explosion in the number of tourism-related programmes offered by higher education institutions, and the number of tourism-related journals has grown from a dozen in the 1970s to around 150 today, over half of them established in the last decade alone. Yet despite this growth much tourism scholarship continues to pursue narrow empirical studies at the expense of theoretical or conceptual writing. After half a century of sustained tourism enquiry our field still neglects its ontological, epistemological and methodological shortcomings. As a consequence, tourism scholarship has remained on the margins of many of the philosophical debates which have energised the wider social sciences during that time. Moreover, tourism is typically found in business and management schools, where critical reflections on the market economy are all too rare and whose leading researchers continually eschew key social, political and ethical questions in favour of technical, problem-solving research. While on the surface tourism enquiry thrives, it faces a yawning philosophical gap.

It is incumbent on tourism researchers to bridge this gap and to push tourism's ontological and methodological boundaries much more rigorously. The four chapters which comprise this part of the book each take on this task in different ways and each evolves the hopeful tourism scholarship project. While this part of the book is focused on the research issues of positionality and critical emotionality (Ali), performance, voice and narrative (Noy), reflexivity (Mair) and the post-disciplinary terrain which stretches before critical tourism scholars (Hollinshead), there is clear overlap with the other parts of the book. This reflects hopeful tourism scholarship's agenda to promote knowledge-based critique in conjunction with education and action for planetary responsibility – the research–education–action nexus. Thus, the following four chapters also discuss how the critical tourism studies academy of hope endeavours to energise self-reflexive and emotionally literate learners and professionals (Ali), confront the blurring of academia and political activism (Noy), scrutinise how engaging in critical and reflexive research can sharpen our consideration of grassroots power relations (Mair) and consider postgraduate activist and intellectually open curricula (Hollinshead).

Nazia Ali opens this suite of chapters with discussion of tourism enquiry's putative engagement with critical emotionality. Building on the theoretical stances of reflexivity as an emotional process, she focuses on her ethnographic engagements with the Pakistani community in her doctoral fieldwork – people she considered as her 'own'. Her chapter describes how she moved through revolving outsider and insider spaces of the research setting and how she empathised with her informants' living in-between the hyphens of a British and Pakistani ethnic identity. This account is followed by Chaim Noy's examination of how tourism discourses and practices are used for political objectives in Occupied East Jerusalem and how he shifted into an activist academic position. Noy employs performance, voice and narrative as his conceptual framework to interrogate the powerful colonial discourses of tourism – concepts which are readily critical due to the notion of plurality which they imply. His chapter eloquently demonstrates how, even when there is seemingly one dominant voice, if we listen carefully we can discern other often silenced, subversive and resistive narratives. This chapter is followed by Heather Mair's examination of the practical implications of becoming a critical tourism researcher and her reflections on nearly a decade of research with an activist edge with small Canadian communities. She considers the opportunities and obligations inherent in advocacy scholarship and asks, 'how can we ensure that tourism development and research comes closer to its emancipatory potential?' This look to the future is taken up by Keith Hollinshead as he aptly rounds off Part I. In a wide-ranging essay which urges us to embrace hybrid forms of post-disciplinary knowing, he discusses the shifts in the social sciences resulting from the loosening of the grip of universalism and generalisability and reflects on the implications for tourism of the new pluralist reinterpretations of human, cultural, psychic and political life.

1 Researcher reflexivity in tourism studies research

Dynamical dances with emotions

Nazia Ali

Introduction

This chapter examines the dynamics of emotions in tourism studies research in the context of reflexivity. The focus is upon the experience of various emotions during interpretive ethnographic fieldwork, rather than researching emotions per se. This process is commonly referred to, from a sociological perspective, as the 'emotion-alization of reflexivity' (Holmes 2010: 139). The '*emotionalization of reflexivity*' emphasises the importance of emotions in research encounters with informants and consequently the influence of these emotions upon the researcher's life. Therefore, the premise of this chapter is to build on the theoretical stances of reflexivity as an emotional process and contribute to the emerging study, in the field of tourism studies, of critical emotionality in reflexive research agendas. The current work extensively focuses upon my emotional interpretive ethnographic engagements with people and populations I considered as my 'own' — the Pakistani community. This concept of 'own' was previously critically explored in the *2nd Critical Tourism Studies Conference, Split: Croatia* (Ali 2007) to understand the emics and etics of studying people and populations with whom I perceived to share a similar ethnic (Pakistani), religious (Muslim) and racial (Asian) identity (see Ali 2007 and Ali 2010 for reflexivity and identity-making/remaking/demaking in interpretive ethnography). This chapter interprets the emotions that surfaced as a consequence of my interactions with research informants and my emotional reactions to their responses while conducting the fieldwork.

The study of emotions in qualitative research, i.e. interpretive ethnography, challenges positivistic/scientific notions on the production of knowledge, which claim to be objective and rational. Matthews *et al.* (2004: 3) argue that scientifically objective investigations are at risk of producing 'emotionally illiterate' researchers incompetent of identifying, expressing, understanding and assimilating their emotions in their studies. On the contrary, linking emotions with intelligence in knowledge production, or what is commonly referred to as 'emotional intelligence' (EI) (Goleman 1995) undermines this scientific distinction between 'heart' and 'head'. Goleman (1995: 43) draws upon the work of Yale psychologist Peter Salovey to explain the concept of emotional intelligence, which is, to mention but a few important tenets, about '*knowing one's emotions*' (self awareness); and '*recognising emotions in others*' (empathy). The notion of emotional intelligence is further advanced by Mayer and Salovey:

> Emotional intelligence is the ability to perceive emotions, to access and generate emotions so as to assist thought, to understand emotions and emotional knowledge, and to reflectively regulate emotions so as to promote emotional and intellectual growth.
>
> (1997: 5)

The notion of emotional intelligence is also reflected in the Critical Tourism Studies Academy of Hope, which encourages its associates or critical thinkers to create 'critical turns', which are informed by emotionally intelligent academic endeavours to fuel self-reflexive – emotionally literate – students/professionals, as well as to engage themselves in emotionally intelligent and self-reflexive academic endeavours, all with the aim to, hopefully and courageously, make a difference in the worlds of tourism.

Theoretical and conceptual issues

Defining reflexivity

Reflexivity is more often than not linked with qualitative inquiry whereby the researcher is aware of her/his presence in the construction of knowledge, and in the conduct of research, the fieldworker scrutinises and exposes her/his subjectivities as a result of interactions with the researched (Hertz 1997; May 1998; Nightingale and Cromby 1999; Denzin and Lincoln 2000; Lincoln and Guba 2000; Willig 2001; Holliday 2002). Willig identifies two forms of reflexivity: (1) the personal; and (2) the epistemological:

> *Personal reflexivity* involves reflecting upon the ways in which our own values, experiences, interests, beliefs, political commitments, wider aims in life and social identities have shaped the research. It also involves thinking about how the research may have affected and possibly changed us, as people and as researchers. *Epistemological reflexivity* requires us to engage with questions such as: [...] How could the research question have been investigated differently? [...] Thus, epistemological reflexivity encourages us to reflect upon the assumptions (about the world, about knowledge) that we have made in the course of the research, and it helps us to think about the implications of such assumptions for the research and its findings.
>
> (2001: 10, emphasis in original)

Of particular relevance to this work is 'personal reflexivity', because my reflexive practice concentrated predominately upon ways in which the research process moulded my ethnic (Pakistani) identity and the altering states of emotions experienced during interpretive ethnography.

Describing emotions

Emotions can be 'negative' (e.g. sadness); 'positive' (e.g. happiness); 'passive' (e.g. empathy); 'active' (e.g. alarmed); 'obstructive' (e.g. frustration); 'conducive' (e.g. impressed); 'low power' (e.g. embarrassed); and, 'high power' (e.g. triumphant) (Scherer 2005: 720). According to Lupton (1998), emotions emerge through social and cultural interactions and entanglements with people, places and spaces. Thus, it can be argued that the research setting, for qualitative fieldworkers, is an intensively and interactively emotional domain, both socially and culturally, because such situational experiences impact upon 'ways of seeing the world' under study (McLaughlin 2003: 67). Different emotions are stimulated as a result of various occurrences, which are self-consciously defined by individuals. For instance, shame (public or private), guilt (linked to failure), pride (feelings of self-satisfaction) and embarrassment (related to shame) are referred to by Lewis (2000: 629–631) as 'self-conscious emotions', which direct the individual to focus upon her/himself rather than the event that produces the particular emotion/emotions. Subjectivity in defining emotions coincides with the existentialist interpretation of human emotions, as Sartre (1957: 28) states; 'I myself choose the meaning they (emotions) have'. However, there is no agreement as to what actually constitutes an emotion, as comprehensions, definitions and descriptions overlap.

Emotions in qualitative research

Many social scientists who advance the paradigm of the *sociology of emotion* – developing a theory of emotion in the discipline of sociology (Turner and Stets 2005) – have argued for greater recognition of the position of emotions in qualitative inquiry (Hochschild 1998; Bondi 2005; Holland 2007; Holmes 2010). The magnitude of emotions experienced by researchers are juxtapositions of academic, personal and professional identities and subjectivities, which need to be accounted for in the research process (Holland 2007). Researchers cannot escape the emotional encounters, experiences and expressions in their investigations because as Bondi (2005: 232) states, 'emotions are integral to research relationships'. During the collection of data the fieldworker twists and turns through a 'kaleidoscope of emotions', which can comprise of positive occurrences (e.g. laughter, happiness, love, longing and happy memories) and/or negative happenings (e.g. tears, grief, anger, and fear) (Bourne 1998: 92). Hedican (2006: 18) provides an account of how he was drawn into responding to grief following the premature death of a pre-fieldwork acquaintance and prominent member of the north Canadian Aboriginal village, Elijah Redbird:

> Elijah's death affected me in a very profound way, filling me with feelings of intense sadness and remorse, yet my academic training left me largely unprepared to deal with the emotional consequences of such an event.

Reflexivity and emotions

The acknowledgement of emotions in fieldwork has been viewed as central to developing reflexive practice in post-positivistic research (Rosenberg 1990; Bourne 1998; Gray 2008). However, Gray (2008: 936) argues, 'emotion in the practice of reflexivity tends to be overlooked' by fieldworkers locating themselves in the research situation. Moreover, Holmes (2010: 139) asserts, the 'sociology of emotions seems to similarly lack emotionality' and 'theories of reflexivity do not adequately attend to emotions' (2010: 140). Nevertheless 'emotionalisation of reflexivity' has not been completely disregarded in qualitative thought, practice and writings, especially in terms of the role played by emotions in the construction of knowledge (Williams and Bendelow 1998; Mauthner and Doucet 2003; Holland 2007). Williams and Bendelow (1998: xv) observe the symbolic link between 'head' and 'heart', whereby emotions are an '"indispensable faculty" for the acquisition of human knowledge'. Furthermore, our emotional reflexive responses to our respondents, shadowed with our ontological and epistemological assumptions, influence the process of data analysis (Mauthner and Doucet 2003). This interrelationship between reflexivity, emotions and construction of knowledge is illuminated by Holland (2007: 195), who states that 'emotions are important in the production of knowledge and add power in understanding, analysis and interpretation.'

Tourism studies and emotionality in research

In tourism studies research, emotions have been examined in various contexts and are a central theme in the Critical Tourism Studies conferences (Carlisle-Gaye 2007; Dunkley 2007; Everett 2007). The importance of recognising and writing about emotions is central to producing rich text on researcher experiences in the field. Tucker (2009) offers a postcolonial worldmaking interpretation of the emotion of shame during her field work in Göreme, Central Turkey. Shame for Tucker (2009: 453) produced moments of awkwardness and discomfort as she became aware of her position as 'both colonizing researcher (helping to make or define the world) and a colonising tourist (consuming and perhaps further appropriating a locality captured by and through tourism).' Cohen (2010: 28) further notes that emotions perform a key role in developing and identifying relationships with others, especially when the fieldworker is confronted with physical and emotional hardship:

> Mutual challenges to the body that were shared with my participants afforded common reference points upon which sympathy, empathy, trust could develop in our relationships .... (T)he emotions I experienced in the field undoubtedly influenced how I perceived, interpreted and attributed meanings to others' experiences.

Researching emotions in interpretive ethnography

Background to research philosophies and principles

In this part of the chapter I discuss how the research methodology chosen was to a certain extent, responsible for the dynamical dances with emotions experienced in this research. The main aim here was to identify research philosophies and principles that would enhance interpretive and reflexive practice and thought. The research design was dominated by the post-positivistic paradigm. Post-positivism emerged to scrutinise and criticise the use of positivistic theory in sociology (Glesne 2006), which is criticised for overlooking 'meanings' people attach to their behaviours (Lincoln and Guba 1985). Hence, the anti-scientific study of society can be referred to as 'post-positivism', which is often viewed as an opposite of positivism (Guba and Lincoln 1989; Denzin and Lincoln 1994; 2000; Holliday 2002). Researchers addressing ontological, epistemological and methodological shortcomings in tourism research are calling for fieldworkers to employ post-positivistic modes of enquiry (Decrop 1999; Riley and Love 2000; Tribe 2001; Hollinshead 2004a, 2004b, 2004c; Phillimore and Goodson 2004). For instance, Riley and Love (2000) observe the need for tourism research to diverge from 'positivistic' modes of enquiry to 'post-positivistic' paradigms to produce interpretive and reflective accounts of tourist behaviours.

Post-positivism is philosophically, theoretically and methodologically 'interpretative', comprising of research perspectives such as interpretivism, critical theory, constructivism, postmodernism and feminism (Guba and Lincoln 1989; Denzin and Lincoln 1994, 2000; Holliday 2002). The philosophical perspective at the root of my research was 'interpretivism' or 'interpretive' methodology. Hughes (1990: 89) argues fieldworkers adopting interpretive theoretical and philosophical stances in post-positivistic studies are an essential part in the construction of meanings, because: 'experiences of others can be grasped through the apprehension of their inner meaning.' In view of the post-positivistic research paradigm and interpretive philosophy, my study adopted a qualitative methodological approach, aiming to understand 'how social experience is created and given meaning' (Denzin and Lincoln 1994: 4).

Studying emotions in a interpretive ethnography inquiry

I did not set out to research my emotions during my interpretive ethnographic study, but found it to be intertwined with the practice of reflexivity. The pre-, during and post-research reflexive inspections were shadowed by my emotions and those imposed onto me by the informants, which at first overwhelmed me but then learned to appreciate during the PhD journey. Before conducting interpretive ethnography, the emotions I encountered were an amalgamation of anxiety, fear, hope, enthusiasm, enjoyment and positivity. While in the field, the emotions that emerged were a mixture of anger, empathy, envy, frustration, happiness and shame. After the collection of data and during the write-up of my thesis a concoction of admiration, empathy, gratitude, longing, relief and sadness surfaced. Whatever the stage of the research (e.g. before, during and after data collection) emotions seep into the study and cannot be ignored, neglected or suppressed (Bourne 1998; McLaughlin 2003; Bondi 2005; Hedican 2006; Holland 2007; Gray 2008). The emotional dances encountered were a consequence of my interactions with research participants; responses of respondents to certain questions asked; and, my position as an insider and/or outsider.

To examine researcher reflexivity and subsequently the emotions emerging from reflexive analysis I kept a personal research journal, extracts of which are used in this chapter to illustrate the dynamic emotional twists and turns faced when inspecting individuals and groups I considered as my 'own'; with whom I perceived to share a similar ethnic identity. By calling the research population, the Pakistani diaspora, my 'own' I personalised the emotions confronted as I was unable to distinguish between my positions as a fieldworker 'in' the research setting and as a non-fieldworker on the 'outside'. I experienced a blurring of researcher locations, moving through revolving outsider and insider spaces of the research setting. During the collection of data I encountered numerous situations which produced feelings of belonging to a community, family or group. These feelings of being an insider amongst people and groups I considered as my 'own' were intertwined with the emotions of empathy and happiness. Despite this, I also had many outsider moments, especially relating to aspects of my diasporic Pakistani ethnic identity that contradicted with those of the informants. The sentiments of being an outsider amongst a community I viewed as my 'own' were entangled with the emotions of envy and shame.

Collecting emotions for reflexive analysis

The 'emotionalisation of reflexivity' was studied at three stages in the research process, first pre-research, second during research and third post-research. The pre-research phase refers to the five months (November 2002 to April 2003) before conducting the study, the during research phase includes 26 months (April 2003 to June 2005) of data collection and analysis, and the post-research phase (September 2005 to June 2006) marks the end of data collection, the continued interpretation of findings, and the moment I left the research setting permanently. The main data collection techniques used were casual conversations, semi-structured interviewing, and systematic lurking. The data was collected in various research environments, such as the local community centre, at a women's group, in local restaurants, at the workplace of participants and in the home of informants. The interpretive ethnographic findings were analysed using thematic analysis, as a means to organise data for interpretive scrutiny (Holliday 2002). This thematic analysis was based on Blum's (1997) procedure of identifying main themes and sub-themes for data analysis. For example, the main theme of 'identity' included a sub-theme referring to 'locations of theme', which in turn held the sub-sub theme 'Pakistan/Britain'.

The focus of the interpretive ethnographic enquiry was to understand the significance of ethnic identity in tourism journeys of the United Kingdom Pakistani diaspora. Luton in south-east England was selected as the research location, a place where Pakistani migrants settled in early 1960s as a result of demand for labour in the manufacturing industries (Luton Borough Council 2003). Since 1971 Pakistanis have been the largest group of immigrants (Luton Borough Council 2003) and constitute 9.2 per cent of the town's population (National Statistics 2001). The research sample comprised of 24 informants; 10 were first-generation Pakistanis born in Pakistan; 12 were second-generation Pakistanis born in the UK to parents born in Pakistan; and 2 were third-generation Pakistanis, i.e. children of the second-generation. This chapter draws upon data collected in a variety of fieldwork interactions that were reflected upon in my personal research journal and from which surfaced many different emotions.

Findings and discussion of emotions

The emotional reflexive accounts presented here are considered in view of pre-research, during research and post-research stages of my interpretive ethno-graphic inquiry. The pre-research stage discusses the emotions of anxiety and hope; the during research period presents the emotions of empathy and shame/embarrassment; and the post-research phase examines emotions of envy and admiration. 'False names' are used to ensure confidentiality and anonymity, and responses marked with an asterisk (*) refer to extracts from interviews that were conducted in Punjabi or Urdu and later translated to English. The presented find-ings regarding the emotionalisation of reflexivity are limited to my subjective interpretations and the impact of the emotions upon me rather than the particip-ants. Thus this study disregards the dynamical emotional dances experienced by the research informants as a consequence of their interactions with myself and participation in the interpretive ethnographic inquiry.

Pre-research emotionalisation of reflexivity

Before conducting the actual fieldwork I took the 'Who am I?' test,[1] as a means to examine my position as an insider and/or outsider in my interpretive ethno-graphic study. This test illustrated that *I am*: (1) Pakistani, (2) Muslim, (3) British, (4) an ethnic/racial minority, (5) a Punjabi and Urdu speaking person, (6) a second-generation Pakistani born to first generation Pakistani migrants to Britain, (7) a student, (8) a researcher, (9) a female, (10) researching my 'own' community'. Furthermore, it showed that *I am not*: (1) participating in return visits to Pakistan, (2) born in Pakistan, (3) wearing the traditional dress outside my home, (4) a practising Muslim, (5) wearing the *hijab*, (6) married, (7) living amongst a Pakistani community, (8) a 'member' of the Pakistani community in Luton, (9) a migrant, (10) researching my 'own' community. By conducting the 'Who am I?' test I was emotionally moulding my research study before I under-took any field work. However, it is not uncommon for researchers to be shaped by their emotional assumptions before data collection and in turn generate emo-tions about their participants (Holland 2007).

On the one hand the 'Who am I?' test made me very anxious at the prospect of investigating tourism participation in the UK Pakistani diaspora because I felt like a 'cultural incompetent'. Anxiety was accompanied by feelings of nervousness, stress and worry because the *I am not* part of the 'Who am I?' test positioned me as an outsider. It is not uncommon for researchers to feel a sense of anxiety and even exhaustion at the beginning of their work because their emotions are likely to be in a state of confusion (McLaughlin 2003). On the other hand, the 'Who am I?' test provided me with the hope of being an insider, which was intertwined with feelings of confidence and optimism. I wrote the following entry in my personal research journal:

> I am feeling VERY nervous about doing this research because I am not sure how the Pakistani community in my work will respond to me. I don't want them to dislike me because I have not travelled to Pakistan ... I am REALLY stressed about this – but there is nothing I can do ... it is impossible for me to go to Pakistan now ... I worry whether I have chosen the right area to research, I worry about the impression I will make on my research informants, I worry about worrying about all this ... But I am hopeful ... I am hopeful that I will learn more about myself and also learning [*sic*] about the Pakistani community beyond my home environment ... I am confident that what [*sic*] my grandparents and parents have equipped me with enough knowledge and socio-cultural skills to work with Pakistani informants for this study ... so I am not totally culturally incompetent ... and optimistic that parts of my diasporic Pakistani ethnic identity will make me an insider and that all will work out ... hopefully ... yes, I am happy ... well for the time being...'
>
> (Personal research diary entry: 14 January 2003)

During research emotionalisation of reflexivity

As the fieldwork progressed many emotions surfaced as a result of research meetings with participants and responses given by informants to various questions. During research emotionalisation of reflexivity was also attached to the interplay between insider/outsider moments and the negotiation (and re-negotiation) of my diasporic Pakistani ethnic identity. There was little constancy of insider/outsider moments in a given situation; the positions were continuously altering and subsequently I was sliding from negative to positive (or vice versa) emotions. The emotions that were particularly prevalent during the actual conduct of the study were empathy and embarrassment (stemming from shame). Empathy is a feeling directed at our participants, which reflects the Weberian concept and practice of *Verstehen*. 'Verstehen' as an interpretative act is understood to be consistent with interpretive comprehensions of social phenomena (Schutz 1967; Fielding 1993; Schwandt 1994, 2000). 'Verstehen' entails 'placing oneself in the position of other people to see what meanings they give to their actions' (Abercrombie *et al.* 1994: 477). However, Kleinman and Copp (1993:

27) suggest that as researchers we believe that we 'should feel what participants feel', thus questioning whether 'true' empathy is occurring in research settings.

There were aspects of the informants' lives that I was able to seek empathy with such as encounters with racism and living in-between the hyphens of a British and Pakistani ethnic identity. I noted the following in my personal research journal:

> I keep hearing from both first-generation and second-generation Pakistani research participants making reference to racism ... as they are speaking to me I am thinking about my own encounters with racism, mostly when I was in primary school and when we first moved to an area in London (in 1982) where my family was a racial minority, and the children from our 'whit' 'neighbours called out 'Paki' to us or 'go back to your own country' ... it was very upsetting for me, so I really empathise with the research inform- ants when they talk about the impact of racism on their lives ... yes it has happened to me and I know how it feels ... so my head tends to nod and I have a sympathetic gesture on my face ... my emotions and feelings begin to show.
>
> (Personal research journal entry: 6 March 2004)

When I commenced data collection, a sense of shame shadowed me because of not having visited my ancestral homeland Pakistan on a regular basis. I had only been to Pakistan once when I was 4 years old and had no recollection of my trip. While this emotion of shame was also relevant before data collection, it then had much less intensity, because it was very much controlled by me (a private observation of shame), whereas, during the research it was controlled by the research participants (a public observation of shame). The fact that I had not travelled (much) to 'my' homeland Pakistan was frowned upon by the research participants. This was viewed as a deficiency in my diasporic Paki- stani ethnic identity and I was considered an outsider. The emotion of being ashamed extended to embarrassment, a form of 'emotional dissonance', which is closely linked to ethnographic research, when identity is entangled with emotions (Down *et al.* 2006). This is illustrated in the following personal journal entry I made a few hours after a casual conversation with a local Pakistani man.

> I had to speak in Punjabi. Mr Haq was amazed to hear I was carrying out research and it being a PhD. I asked Mr Haq 'where do you travel to the most?'* What I interpreted as a very sarcastic response from the tone in his voice he replied 'where do you think Pakistani people go to ... China?... Pakistan of course.'* I felt like I had asked him a wrong or taboo question, which left me feeling intimidated and embarrassed ... I felt Mr Haq had little regard for my topic, let alone for me, from which surfaced such negat- ive emotions as anger and sadness.
>
> (Personal research journal entry: 31 May 2004)

Post-research emotionalisation of reflexivity

Once my fieldwork was completed and I was confined to interpreting (and re-interpreting) the ethnographic data, I decided to consider the emotionalisation of reflexivity in the post-research period. McLaughlin (2003: 76) stresses the importance of 'de-briefing' and 'reflecting' on emotional parts of the research as a means to overcoming 'emotional blindness'. Overall, the 26 months spent in the field were an intensively emotional time for me, which I had not anticipated when deciding to embark upon a PhD journey. The emotional engagements, twists and turns not only contributed to my understanding for being an insider and/or outsider but also informed my diasporic Pakistani ethnic identity. During the post-research phase the emotions that came to the forefront were those of envy and admiration. I wrote the following entry in my journal:

> writing-up my PhD thesis ... looking through the interview transcripts and scraps of paper with casual conversation findings ... yet again ... I am REALLY envious of the second-generations (return) travels to Pakistan ... the glowing look on their faces when they spoke of their visits to their ancestral villages in Pakistan, the meetings with their relatives that were special to them, and how they wanted to make their parents happy by return-ing to the birth place of their mum and dad ... whereas I had nothing to talk about ... I was envious because the second-generation were able to substan-tiate their diasporic Pakistani ethnic identity because they had (re-)visited Pakistan but I could not ... this was missing from my life ... I admired the first-generation Pakistanis for helping their children to establish and main-tain a 'link' with Pakistan ... the second-generation were lucky in a sense that they were exposed to both the 'Pakistani' and 'British' aspects of their identity as British-Pakistanis.
>
> (Personal research journal entry, 21st December 2005)

Conclusions

The emotionalised reflexive accounts presented in this paper emphasise the importance of the process of reflexivity to critically interpret the positioning of both my emotions and myself in the research setting. The emotionalisation of reflexivity is essential to understanding the impact of research informants on the (altering) emotions of the fieldworker while conducting a study. My emotions affected the way I chose to negotiate my insiderness and outsiderness in the research and the extent to which I deliberately felt certain things over others as a means of respecting and appreciating the informant experiences. For example, I did not have to feel empathy, but I did because of the sensitive nature of various matters discussed (e.g. migratory experiences and separation from kin). I con-cluded from my emotional encounters in the field that emotions, whether posit-ive or negative, are central to my professional and personal development. Moreover, I found that the emotional influence of my study was never-ending and a few years after completing my PhD studies the sentiments experienced before, during and after the research process are still present. I found it (and still find it) difficult to emotionally detach myself from my research, and therefore I decided to travel to Pakistan this year (April 2010), 29 years after my first visit. The main reasons prompting my trip, other than attending a family wedding, was to overcome emotions of embarrassment and envy; to reduce feelings of anxiety in future inquiries with the UK Pakistani diaspora; and, to be able to empathise better with future informants.

Future research is needed to further understand the emotionalisation of reflexivity in qualitative tourism research in the context of other investigators studying diasporas which they consider as their 'own'. Responding to the Critical Tourism Studies network's call for creating Academies of Hope, this article seeks to encourage researchers not to hold back in revealing their emotions, to promote creative emotionalised reflexive vistas in the interpretation of tourist behaviours and movements, to engage in critical dialogue with other fields of study to give emotional entanglements a voice, and for tourism studies to act as an innovator of emotionalisation of reflexivity.

Note

1 Kuhn and McPartland (1954) devised the Twenty Statement Test (TST) in which the subject was given twelve minutes to respond to the question 'Who am I?' on a sheet of paper containing 10 numbered blanks for 'I am' and 10 numbered blanks for 'I am not'. Hutnik (1991) modified the TST in her research investigating the ethnic profiles of Asians, Afro-Caribbeans and English people, which I adapted for use in this research study.

References

Abercrombie, N., Hill, S. and Turner B. S. (1994) *The Dictionary of Sociology*, London: Penguin.

Ali, N. (2007) 'Researcher reflexivity: a stranger amongst my "own"?' in C. Harris and M. Van Hal (eds), *The Critical Turn in Tourism Studies: promoting an Academy of Hope? Book of papers*, University of Wales Institute Cardiff: Wales, Wageningen University: The Netherlands, Institute for Tourism: Croatia, pp. 5–16.

Ali, N. (2010) 'Researching diaspora tourism: journeys of the UK Pakistani community to the ancestral homeland', *LSA Newsletter*, 87, November: 10–18.

Blum, S. C. (1997) 'Current concerns: a thematic analysis of recent hospitality issues', *International Journal of Contemporary Hospitality Management*, 9 (7): 350–361.

Bondi, L. (2005) 'The place of emotions in research: from partitioning emotion and reason to the emotional dynamic of research relationships', in J. Davidson, M. Smith and L. Bondi (eds), *Emotional Geographies*, Hampshire: Ashgate, pp. 231–246.

Bourne, J. (1998) 'Researchers experience emotions too', in R. S. Barbour and G. Huby (eds), *Meddling with Mythology: AIDS and the social construction of knowledge*, London: Routledge, pp. 90–130.

Carlisle-Gaye, S. (2007) 'Extensive living and working within tourism research settings: ethics and practice of participant action-research (PAR)', paper presented at *The 2nd*

International Critical Tourism Studies Conference: The Critical Turn in Tourism Studies – Promoting an Academy of Hope?, Split: Croatia, 20–23 June 2007.

Cohen, S. (2010) 'Reflections on reflexivity in leisure and tourism studies', *LSA Newsletter*, 87: 27–29.

Decrop, A. (1999) 'Triangulation in qualitative tourism research', *Tourism Management*, 20 (1): 157–161.

Denzin, N. K. and Lincoln, Y. S. (1994) 'Introduction: entering the field of qualitative research', in N. K. Denzin and Y. S. Lincoln (eds) *Handbook of Qualitative Research*, Thousand Oaks, CA: Sage, pp. 1–17.

Denzin, N. K. and Lincoln, Y. S. (2000) 'Introduction: the discipline and practice of qualitative research', in N. K. Denzin and Y. S. Lincoln (eds), *Handbook of Qualitative Research* (2nd edition), Thousand Oaks, CA: Sage, pp. 1–28.

Down, S., Garrety, K. and Badham, R. J. (2006) 'Fear and loathing in the field: emotional dissonance and identity work in ethnographic research', Faculty of Commence: Faculty of Commence Papers, University of Wollongong, New South Wales, Australia, pp. 1–35. Retrieved from: http://ro.uow.edu.au/cgi/viewcontent.cgi?article=1313&context=commpapers (accessed 5 July 2010).

Dunkley, R. (2007) 'A PhD journey on the road less travelled', paper presented at *The 2nd International Critical Tourism Studies Conference: The Critical Turn in Tourism Studies – Promoting an Academy of Hope?*, Split: Croatia, 20–23 June 2007.

Everett, S. (2007) 'Lessons from the field: reflecting on a tourism research journey around the "Celtic" periphery', paper presented at *The 2nd International Critical Tourism Studies Conference: The Critical Turn in Tourism Studies – Promoting an Academy of Hope?*, Split: Croatia, 20–23 June 2007.

Fielding, N. (1993) 'Ethnography', in N. Gilbert (ed.), *Researching Social Life*, London: Sage, pp. 150–171.

Glesne, C. (2006) *Becoming Qualitative Researchers: an introduction* (3rd edition), Boston, MA: Pearson Education, A & B.

Goleman, D. (1995) *Emotional Intelligence: why it can matter more than IQ*, London: Bloomsbury.

Gray, B. (2008) 'Putting emotion and reflectivity to work in researching migration', *Sociology*, 42 (5): 935–952.

Guba, E. G. and Lincoln, Y. S. (1989) *Fourth Generation Evaluation*, Newbury Park, CA: Sage.

Hedican, E. J. (2006) 'Understanding emotional experience in fieldwork: responding to grief in a northern Aboriginal village', *International Journal of Qualitative Methods*, 5 (1): 17–24.

Hertz, R. (1997) 'Introduction: reflexivity and voice', in: R. Hertz (ed.), *Reflexivity and Voice*, Thousand Oaks, CA: Sage, pp. vii–xviii.

Hochschild, A. R. (1998) 'The sociology of emotion as a way of seeing', in G. Bendelow and S. J. Williams (eds), *Emotions in Social Life: critical themes and contemporary issues*, London and New York: Routledge, pp. 3–15.

Holland, J. (2007) 'Emotions and research', *International Journal of Social Research Methodology*, 10 (3): 195–209.

Holliday, A. (2002) *Doing and Writing Qualitative Research*, London: Sage.

Hollinshead, K. (2004a) 'Tourism and third space populations: the restless motion of diaspora peoples', in T. L. Coles and D. J. Timothy (eds). *Tourism, Diaspora and Space: travels to the promise lands*, Abingdon: Routledge, pp. 33–49.

Hollinshead, K. (2004b) 'A primer in ontological craft: the creative capture of people and places through qualitative research', in J. Phillimore and L. Goodson (eds), *Qualitative Research in Tourism: ontologies, epistemologies and methodologies*, London: Routledge, pp. 63–82.

Hollinshead, K. (2004c) 'Ontological craft in tourism studies', in J. Phillimore and L. Goodson (eds), *Qualitative Research in Tourism: ontologies, epistemologies and methodologies*, London: Routledge, pp. 83–101.

Holmes, M. (2010) 'The emotionalization of reflexivity', *Sociology*, 44(1): 139–154.

Hughes, J. A. (1990) *The Philosophy of Social Research*, London: Longman.

Hughes, J. and Sharrock, W. (1997) *The Philosophy of Social Research* (3rd edition), London: Longman.

Hutnik, N. (1991) *Ethnic Minority Identity: a social psychological perspective*, Oxford: Oxford University Press.

Kleinman, S. and Copp, M. A. (1993) *Emotions and Fieldwork*, Newbury Park, CA: Sage.

Kuhn, M. H. and McPartland, T. S. (1954) 'An empirical investigation of self-attitude', *American Sociological Review*, 19: 1: 68–76.

Lewis, M. (2000) 'Self-conscious emotions: embarrassment, pride, shame and guilt', in M. Lewis and J. M. Haviland-Jones (eds), *Handbook of Emotions* (2nd edition), New York and London: The Guildford Press, pp. 623–636.

Lincoln, Y. S. and Guba, E. G. (1985) *Naturalistic Inquiry*, Newbury Park, CA: Sage.

Lincoln, Y. S. and Guba, E. G. (2000) 'Paradigmatic controversies: contradictions and emerging confluences', in N. K. Denzin and Y. S. Lincoln (eds) *Handbook of Qualitative Research* (2nd edition), Thousand Oaks, CA: Sage, pp. 163–188.

Lupton, D. (1998) *The Emotional Self*, London: Sage.

McLaughlin, C. (2003) 'The feeling of finding out: the role of emotions in research', *Educational Action Research*, 11 (1): 65–78.

Matthews, G., Zeidner, M. and Robers, R. D. (2004) *Emotional Intelligence: science and myth*, Cambridge and Massachusetts: The MIT Press, pp. 3–29.

Mauthner, N. S. and Doucet, A. (2003) 'Reflexive accounts and accounts of reflexivity in qualitative data analysis', *Sociology*, 37 (3): 413–431.

May, T. (1998) 'Reflexivity in the age of reconstructive social science', *International Journal of Social Research Methodology: Theory and Practice*, 1 (1): 7–24.

Mayer, J. and Salovey, P. (1997) *Ability Model of Emotional Intelligence.* Retrieved from: http://emotionaliq.com/ (accessed 14 June 2009).

Luton Borough Council (2003) *Sticking Together: embracing diversity in Luton*, Luton: Community Cohesion Scrutiny Panel.

National Statistics Online (2001) *Census 2001*, London: National Statistics. Retrieved from www.statistics.gov.uk (accessed 5 March 2004).

Nightingale, D. J. and Cromby, J. (eds) (1999) *Social Constructionist Psychology: a critical analysis of theory and practice*, Buckingham: Open University Press.

Phillimore, J. and Goodson, L. (2004) 'Progress in qualitative research in tourism: epistemology, ontology and methodology', in J. Phillimore and L. Goodson (eds), *Qualitative Research in Tourism: ontologies, epistemologies and methodologies*, London: Routledge, pp. 1–29.

Riley, R. W. and Love, L. L. (2000) 'The state of qualitative tourism', *Annals of Tourism Research*, 27 (8): 164–187.

Rosenberg, M. (1990) 'Reflexivity and emotions', *Psychology Quarterly*, 53 (1): 3–12.

Sartre, J. P. (1957) *Existentialism and Human Emotions*, New York: Citadel Press.

Scherer, K. R. (2005) 'What are emotions? And how can they be measured?', *Trends and Developments: research in emotions,* 44:4, pp. 695–729,

Schutz, A. (1967) *The Phenomenology of the Social World*, London: Heinemann Educational Books Ltd.

Schwandt, T. A. (1994) 'Constructivist, interpretivist approaches to human inquiry', in N. K. Denzin and Y. S. Lincoln (eds) *Handbook of Qualitative Research*, Thousand Oaks, CA: Sage, pp. 118–137.

Schwandt, T. A. (2000) 'Three epistemological stances for qualitative inquiry: interpretivism, hermeneutics and social constructivism', in N. K. Denzin and Y. S. Lincoln (eds) *Handbook of Qualitative Research* (2nd edition), Thousand Oaks, CA: Sage, pp. 189–213.

Tribe, J. (2001) 'Research paradigms and the tourism curriculum', *Journal of Travel Research*, 39: 442–448.

Tucker, H. (2009) 'Recognising emotion and its postcolonial potentialities: discomfort and shame in a tourism encounter in Turkey', *Tourism Geographies*, 11 (4): 444–461.

Turner, J. H. and Stets, J. E. (2005) *The Sociology of Emotions*, Cambridge and New York: Cambridge University Press.

Williams, S. J. and Bendelow, G. (1998) 'Introduction: emotion in social life – mapping the sociological terrain', in G. Bendelow and S. J. Williams (eds), *Emotions in Social Life: critical themes and contemporary issues*, London and New York: Routledge, pp. xv–xxx.

Willig, C. (2001) *Introducing Qualitative Research in Psychology: adventures in theory and method*, Buckingham: Open University Press.

2 The political ends of tourism

Voices and narratives of Silwan/the
City of David in East Jerusalem[1]

Chaim Noy

Introduction: the performative power of tourism

Imagine that you wake up one morning and realize that your house and your
neighborhood are now part of a tourist site located inside a National Park. Worse
yet, you are now residing inside a highly ideological heritage site, the narrative
of which has *you* playing the role of a rival, of an enemy. Reminiscent of a
Kafkaesque tale, things – even if not yourself – have transformed irrevocably. In
this chapter I examine how tourism discourses and practices are effectively put
into use for political objectives. I hold that commonly both tourism scholarship
and tourists overlook the pervasive political aspects associated with tourist sites,
attractions, and discourses, which are the way that the industry serves in promoting and perpetuating hegemony. Empirically, the study explores a Jewish heritage site located in Occupied East Jerusalem. It exposes the mechanisms by
which the site serves political aims, and how these aims are effectively de-
politicized for the benefit of the sovereign authority and ideology. The chapter
also documents the initial phases of my own move into political activism in the
context of the Israeli Occupation of East Jerusalem, and my appreciation of how
the tourism industry, with its awesome powers of worldmaking, plays a role in
this affair of which significance cannot be undermined.

In both academic orientation and research methods I am inspired in attitude
by critical approaches in tourism studies, which (in tourism and beyond) always
relate to various disciplinary and theoretical backgrounds that share emancipatory aims (Aitchison 2001, Chambers 2007, Hall and Tucker 2004). With
regards to critical studies in the context of tourism in Israel, the most burning
issues seem to be related to *national ideology*, namely contemporary forms of
Zionism. These issues touch primarily on the Israeli–Palestinian Conflict, but
also on such matters as militarism in Israeli society, issues of feminism, ethnicity
and more. Hence stating that the burning issues that beseech critical investigation concern the relationship between Zionist ideology and tourism, actually supplies a rather wide agenda for critical studies.

Indeed, studies assuming various critical perspectives within the Israeli–
Palestinian Conflict have explored discourses, practices and representations that
concern how both sides construct social reality according to national ideologies

and goals (Brin 2006, Brin and Noy in press, Feldman 2008, Isaac 2010, Paine 1995, Stein 2008). Schematically, these studies, which discuss political and/or alternative tourism, agree that tourism serves hegemonic aims and ideologies, and that the industry does so in seamless and uncanny ways. I will refrain now from elaborating theoretically on the relations between political tourism on the one hand, and critical studies in tourism, on the other. Suffice to note that these domains are mutually informing, and that at the risk of stating a tautology it can be said that studying tourism critically is a political act, and vice versa – that attending to the political interfaces of tourism requires critical sensitivities.

I employ the concept of performance (or performative power) in tourism in line with previous research and theorizing (Noy 2004, 2008), which in the present context serves within a larger post/colonial theoretical framework (Veijola and Jokinen 1998). I revert to related concepts of voice and narrative, which I draw from the influential work of Mikhail Bakhtin (1968). Together, these terms supply the conceptual framework with which we can appreciate the worldmaking powers of tourism, and the struggle over the ability to shape symbolic *and* material realities that the industry has. I understand the notion of voices as relating to the *social agents* that are effective in a given social scene and have annunciation capacities in that scene; the notion of narratives I see as referring to the 'content', or to what is being argued and what are the implied meanings. Voices and narratives are readily critical concepts, primarily due to the notion of *plurality* which they convey. The very plurality of these terms suggests, again in line with Bakhtinian concepts (such as polyphony and authoritative discourse), that even when there is seemingly only one (dominant) voice, if one listens carefully, other voices – often subversive and silenced – can be discerned, and other, often resistive narratives, can be heard.

Silwan or the 'City of David National Park and archeological site'

The City of David is the name of an archeological site and National Park located to the southeast and very close to the Old City of Jerusalem. The site was declared a National Park by Israeli authorities in 1974 after the occupation and then annexation of East Jerusalem following the 1967 War. The City of David National Park is located inside the large and densely populated Palestinian neighborhood of Silwan, with a population of approximately 40,000 residents, and specifically inside the neighborhood of Wadi Hilwah (with approximately 5,000 residents).

As a Jewish heritage site that is run by Israelis and that is located inside a densely populated urban Palestinian area, the way that the site operates, how it is framed and how it shapes its neighborhood in terms of symbolizing and representing Jewish nationhood, suggests a fervent site of political contestation; a site where the Israeli Occupation of East Jerusalem is promoted as a tourist attraction. This, I will show, is accomplished by claims concerning tourism preservation and development, which mobilize the powerful colonial discourse and visual imagery of tourism. Visitors to the site consist mainly of organized groups of local Israelis and international Jewish tourists. Many of the visitors consist of groups of schoolchildren from the secular, orthodox and ultra-orthodox educational systems in Israel, groups of armed forces and security institutions, and many international Jewish groups and organizations that visit Israel through organized Zionist tours (such as the Birth Right Tour).

The site of the City of David National Park is a major Jerusalemite attraction, and one of the most frequently visited National Parks in Israel, reaching approximately 400,000 visitors annually (in 2009).[2] In terms of visits to local archeological National Parks, it is second only to the Masada National Park. From a critical perspective it is noteworthy that while the ideological narrative unfolded in Masada (where archeological findings and narrative are also mobilized in the aims of Zionist national ideology) has been discussed in academic literature quite extensively (Zerubavel 1995), to the best of my knowledge the site of the 'City of David' has never been researched prior to the present study. It can only be speculated that the main reason for this disparity – over and above the statistics concerning number of visitors (Masada has nearly twice as many visitors) – is that it is somewhat more convenient to discuss a site located in a remote and unpopulated area in the southern Judean Desert, which is under no national contestations (such as Masada), than to get one's hands into the heated and messy politics of the densely populated and highly contested urban neighborhoods of East Jerusalem and its Occupation by Israel.

Critical methodologies/activist research

For the aims of this research I have documented discourses, images and practices presented and pursued publically by the main actors in Silwan/the City of David, with the aim of socially constructing the site's meanings. Collecting these types of data is accomplished primarily via ethnographies of the various actors' different tours in the site (elaborated below), documenting various texts (brochures, websites, signs, etc.), and conducing observations of and informal (in situ) interviews with visitors, operators, neighborhood residents and political activists there. Analysis follows interdisciplinary critical sensibilities and sensitivities, inspired by the fields of critical discourse analysis (Fairclough 1995, Jaworski and Pritchard 2005), semiotic analysis (Jewitt 2009, Kress and Van Leeuwen 2006), and as indicated earlier, by my lasting interest in performance approaches to tourism. I first seek to identify the actors – those agentic organizations and institutions, and the narratives and the power structures that shape the symbolic meanings of the site, and how these meanings serve to oppress and/or exclude various populations – in the present case Palestinian residents. At the same time, I am also highly interested, even intrigued, by how these actions are naturalized, or how they assume a de-politicized appearance.

Thus far I have attended six tours – three were official tours of the City of David, and three were guided by the activist organization of Emek Shaveh (described later). I visit Silwan neighborhood and the site frequently because I am increasingly involved with the activities of Emek Shaveh there. Hence my visits are recurrent and the clear distinctions and boundaries between formal, 'neutral' academically oriented activities, and political activism blur. Indeed, my initial interest in the site as a field of research arose as a result of my affiliation with an activist organization of Israeli archaeologists, which seeks to expose and transform the political aims to which archaeology is put to use in the site. Throughout my visits to Silwan with activist Yonathan Mizrachi, my scholarly appetite grew, and I began contemplating the veiled politics of the site via critical academic lenses. In this regard, the research story corresponds with other researchers' narratives, where the personal, political and academic mutually inform and shape each other (Ateljevic *et al.* 2005; Chatterton *et al.* 2010).

Narratives and counter narratives: in Silwan/the City of David

ElAd's hegemonic voice

Undoubtedly, the dominant ideological agent acting in and running the site of Silwan/the City of David is the Orthodox Jewish settler organization of ElAd (Hebrew acronym of 'to the City of David'). Established in 1986, the organization's expressive aims are, 'continuing King David's legacy and strengthening Israel's current and historic connection to Jerusalem through four key initiatives: archaeological excavation, tourism development, residential revitalization and educational programming.'[3] While the site's logo is identical to the logo of ElAd, it is important to observe that the organization's name and its ideological orientation are hidden from sight (at the site and elsewhere), and are unknown to most visitors or to the general population. In addition, crucial information about ElAd is hard to reach because the organization was granted a special permission from the Israeli authorities, which allows it to avoid revealing the names of its donors (a crucial bit of information with regards to non-governmental organizations).

I use the term hegemonic in the subsection's heading with regards to the ElAd organization, in order to indicate that at present, the ideological narrative told by ElAd is most influential and uncontested, to an extent that most of the visitors to the site are not aware of alternative or contesting narrative possibilities. The term hegemony, adopted from Antonio Gramsci's (1971) work, suggests not only that this narrative is prevalent, but crucially that it is *the account that is sustained by the state's official authorities*. In other words, adopting the Gramscian notion of hegemony sheds light not simply on the number of rivaling narratives that compete over the hearts and minds of tourists; rather, it hints that at stake is an ideological narrative that is being promoted by national authorities (Israeli ministries and the municipality of Jerusalem), even if the institution that voices this narrative is a *private organization*.[4]

Indeed, in 2005 the ElAd organization became the *sole agent* legally authorized to operate the National Park of the City of David, as well as the sponsor of the extensive excavations taking place there. This is a rare if not singular case where, of some 115 national parks run by The Israeli Nature and Parks Authority, the operation of a national park was wholly assigned to the hands of a private organization. Ever since, ElAd's personnel are in charge of all activities at the site, from selling tickets and guiding tours, to securing the premises, funding the archeological excavations there, and advancing various projects taking place in and around the site.

As a settler organization that is active in East Jerusalem (Ir Amim 2009: 11), ElAd's broader political aims lie beyond those that concern the site of the City of David, and include promoting a demographic shift in the entire area of the Holy Basin. This aim is pursued by purchasing land and buildings and populating them with Jewish settlers. In addition, ElAd and other Jewish settler organizations seek the eviction of Palestinians by various means. During the last decade, ElAd has gained ownership of a number of Palestinian buildings inside the premises of the City of David, and has populated them with Jewish settlers (many of whom work at the site), together with dozens of armed Israeli guards who patrol the neighborhood. Again, here is a rare case where, of all Israeli National Parks, in the City of David ElAd members actually reside permanently and have achieved ownership of spaces and buildings in the site. Conceptually, then, this site is a hybrid, combining an archeological national park, a tourist heritage attraction, and a Jewish settlement. Further plans have recently been approved by the municipal planning committees. These plans include the demolition of dozens of local (Palestinian) houses and the eviction of their residents from the neighborhood, with the aim of expanding the site's recreational areas (hotels, restaurants, parks and parking lots).[5]

It is hopefully clear by now why the tourist site of the City of David is highly instrumental for settler colonial activities, such as the Judaization of the site and the surrounding neighborhoods. In addition, insofar as the site functions as a Jewish (national) heritage site, it plays a role in fastening the emotional ties between foreign Jews and Israelis, on the one hand, and the 'unified' city of Jerusalem, on the other. Here, too, political goals are at stake, which become clear when acknowledging that any serious reconciliation between Israelis and Palestinians would require a withdrawal of Israel from the areas of East Jerusalem.

Hegemonic discourse and practice: the symbolic erasure of Palestinians

In line with ElAd's attempts at Judaization of the site and at binding the emotional connection to Jerusalem, the narrative that the organization elaborates at the site establishes an organic connection – a link that seems obvious and powerful – between contemporary Orthodox Jewish settlers in the site and Jewish communities in the past. Also, and in a complementary way, the hegemonic narrative seeks to symbolically erase Palestinian presence. In the scope of this chapter, three representations and practices that serve these aims are described and briefly discussed.

First there is the question of the *name of the site* – how the tourist site is commonly indexed. There are two points here. First, there is the Hebraization of Arab names of townships, neighborhoods, streets, as well as of natural landscapes, which is part of a much larger and pervasive Zionist practice (Cohen and Kliot 1992). At stake is a change of the entire linguistic landscape of the site and of its surrounding urban area (Shohamy and Gorter 2009). This change is accomplished with the support of Jerusalem's municipality, which attempts to change the names of Palestinian streets and neighborhoods. Figure 2.1a presents an official sign that was posted recently near the entrance to the City of David (on one of the main roads of Wadi Hilwah), designating the name of the neighborhood as the City of David (note that on the photo's upper left side an improvised post is depicted, which was hung by local residents and which indicates the location of the alternative Information Center down the road. I will return to this later).

There is a more nuanced point here, which concerns a shift in the site's name between *different Hebrew terms*. Throughout the centuries, and for some time after the annexation of East Jerusalem in 1967, other Hebrew terms were employed to refer to the site, including the Shilo'ah Spring (in Hebrew, *Ma'ayan Ha-Shilo'ah*, which is actually the site's biblical name). Hence the term that is presently used (i.e. City of David) is recent. It became widespread after the Israeli annexation and specifically after the term was gainfully picked up by ElAd during the late 1980s. This Hebrew term represents a planned linguistic ideology promoted by the Israeli authorities and settlers. The differences between the Hebrew names are striking, especially in light of the fact that the name *Ma'ayan/Niqbat Ha-Shilo'ah* is biblical, and carries ancient and holy echoes for Jewish ears. Yet the term City of David brands the site, and unlike the other term it connects back to a notion of Jewish Kings and Kingdoms, and is construed in the context of contemporary politics and the Israeli–Palestinian Conflict as a manifestation of Jewish ethno-nationalism.

The second issue concerns representational devices in the shape of maps and visual illustrations. The political roles that maps play in the Israeli-Palestinians Conflict, as part of the discursive means of advancing each side's political claims, is not unique in the case at hand (Collins-Kreiner 2008). At stake here are tourist maps, and not geographical or cartographical maps, which, with the

Figure 2.1 A Jewish heritage site or a Palestinian residential neighborhood?

help of tourism imagery, *erase the present of Palestinian populations at and near the tourist attraction.* Figures 2.2a and b include images of the City of David and its surroundings, which are offered in the brochures that are handed out at the site, and in its award-winning website.[6] The figure on the left (2.2a), is a schematic map depicting the entire area of East Jerusalem and the Old City, with the City of David site at its center (marked as 1); the figure on the right (2.2b) supplies a visual illustration of 'Ancient Jerusalem.'

With regards to the schematic map on Figure 2.2a, which visually resembles typical schematic maps supplied to tourists, what is noticeable is the fact that all the Arab names (places, streets, neighborhoods, sites of worship, etc.) have been omitted. This is striking because the map covers the area of East Jerusalem, which is a distinctly Palestinian area with approximately 150,000 residents and dozens of large neighborhoods. For instance, inside the Old City, the Jewish Quarter is indicated, but not the Muslim Quarter, thereby omitting the commercial center of East Jerusalem, the large neighborhoods of Ras al-Amud, Sheik Jarrah, Wadi Al-Joz, and more. This deletion corresponds with the title of the map, which allegedly concerns 'Ancient Jerusalem' (and not the present city).

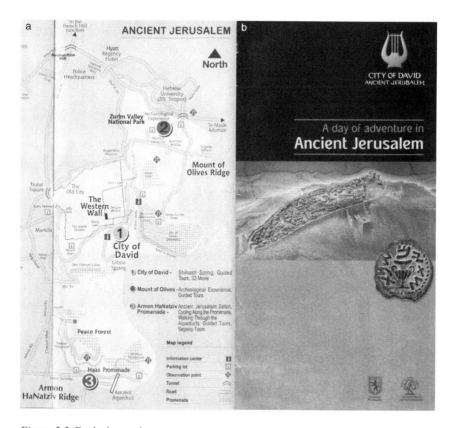

Figure 2.2 Exclusionary imagery.

Yet this title is metaphorical, as many of the buildings and points of interest indicated in the map are in fact contemporary structures and were built rather recently.

The illustrative image in Figure 2.2b depicts the walled city of Ancient Jerusalem, secluded inside a deserted desert territory. The yellowish-greyish (moonlike) grounds that surround the city are completely barren of human settlement. The image communicates the notions that (a) in the past, Ancient Jerusalem was completely sealed, and (b) that the area around it was completely void of people. What is in effect conveyed by this image is not an archeologically informed figure of an ancient city, but a *purist fantasy of a homogenized ethno-national (Jewish) life*. Very much in line with the oft cited Zionist dictum: 'A land without a people for a people without a land,' Figure 2.2b is a cleansed image that tells not so much of a mythic past, but of a projected mythic future and of the fantasies of an eradication of the Other, i.e. the Palestinians. Indeed, in all the official tours in which I participated, and in various media operating in the site (such as a three-dimensional movie that presents the history of the site), no references are made to the presence of Palestinians living in the grounds of the site and in the urban areas around it whatsoever.[7] Ignoring the Palestinian urban environment becomes particularly salient when explanations concerning the site's location and perimeter are supplied by the guides during the tours. In a number of instances, guides made references such as, 'Can you see those houses there?' or 'That neighborhood that's located on that mountain slope' without making any mention of the obvious fact that the entire urban surround is inhabited by Palestinian populations.

The complementary side of the ideological discourse of cleansing the symbolic presence of the Arab population, is the over-presencing of the Jewish population, and importantly, drawing a religious connection that seems natural and inevitable between the Jewish settlers who live in the site today and those that lived there during the periods of the First and Second Temples (tenth to sixth centuries BCE, and fifth century BCE to first century CE, respectively). Discursive illustrations aimed at constructing a shared Jewish national character of these periods are prevalent. For instance, when describing the archeological excavations and findings, tour guides generally ignore the many cultures that have thrived in the site, moving on the timeline between First and Second Temple, on the one hand, and present day Orthodox Jewish settlers, on the other. The leaps between these two time periods are accomplished discursively through the use of first person plural. Guides use the term 'we' repeatedly, easily alternating between groups that are indexed by this powerful term (for the use of identity markers in tourism discourse see Noy 2009). In the tours 'we' sometimes designated the present-day Jewish settlers, and sometimes the Jews of the eras of King David and King Solomon; sometimes the term referred to Zionist Pioneers, and sometimes – in the same tour – the term designated the members of the group of visitors (which usually consist mostly of Jews). All the official tours that I took ended after three hours of walking through the excavated ancient tunnels and paths, in a dramatic, highly moral tone (note that all the guides were Orthodox

Jews who lived in settlements in the Occupied Territories). The guides always had a moral concerning the cohesion of the 'People of Israel' with their past, and the present connection to the Jerusalem.

> You want to know what the people of Israel are worth? Go look at their ancestors [...] the people [of Israel] believed that this city could not be *destroyed*, and they had a point but they just got it wrong: it's not the stones that you cannot destroy – it's the people. And *we* [hand gesture referring to the group] are the best proof of that: walking these paths, again, after two thousand years [...] and so I see *us* as kind of pilgrims of Jerusalem being thirdly built.

In this text, 'we' and 'us' are the Jewish groups of (heritage) tourists, who supply a continuation and a connection between the Jewish People and the City of Jerusalem. The reference to 'Jerusalem being thirdly built,' concerns the construction of the Third Temple, due in the time of the arrival of the Messiah. In yet other cases, the guides concluded the tours by performing a Jewish prayer, to which the visitors replied with an 'Amen,' which reinforced the ethno-religious ties between Jews and City of David, validating Jewish political right over Jerusalem.

The settlers' control over the City of David National Park, manifested in the shape of ElAd's ability to effectively tell a narrative of ethno-national heritage about the site and in its ability to evacuate Palestinian residents and take over their houses, has gone unchallenged until recently. During the last few years, grassroots activist organizations have been challenging this hegemonic narrative, offering alternative and subversive narratives.

'The story behind the tourist site': subversive narratives and the politicization of tourism

Two other organizations that play an important role as social agents, and which have a voice and offer a counter narrative concerning the site of Silwan/the City of David, are the Palestinian *Wadi Hilwah* Information Center (WHIC) and the Israeli *Emek Shaveh*. The activities of these organizations focus on the area of the site and the neighborhood in which it is located, and they both promote a humanist anti-colonial agenda that resists the Judaization of the Holy Basin and of East Jerusalem. Like ElAd, WHIC and *Emek Shaveh* have tourism discourses, images and practices as their vehicles in the struggle over visitors' consciousness and over the larger public opinion in Israel and aboard. In other words, these organizations make use of the performative power of tourism in order to promote an emancipatory social change. Although they are considerably smaller than ElAd, and were established recently (during the last three years), they are nonetheless agents that are active in voicing subversive narratives, and have been receiving growing media attention and public recognition locally and internationally.

I will address these organizations jointly, because their activities and goals are coordinated. Indeed, the cooperation between these organizations – which includes the fact that tours conducted by *Emek Shaveh* conclude at the WHIC, where the tourists meet and talk with residents, and that both organizations' websites and promotional material cross-reference each other – is not incidental. Rather, it is *in itself a political statement*, signifying that Palestinians and Israelis can – and perhaps should – cooperate in their struggles. These organizations' shared aims concern first and foremost the uncovering of the political aims that lie behind the ElAd-owned Jewish heritage site, and preventing these aims (i.e. the demolition of Palestinian houses, restrictions and hindrances on Palestinian mobility, etc.) from being fulfilled.

As stated by these organizations, the first step towards remedying the present condition is acknowledging the fact that the 'City of David' is in effect a highly political endeavor, and that this fact, its mechanisms and implications should be exposed. In other words, at stake is the (re)politicizing of the tourist site. In what follows I shall briefly describe each organization and its discourse and a few of the activities that it undertakes. It should be noted that just as a critical perspective was needed in order to uncover the ideological organization that stands behind the title 'the City of David' (i.e. ElAd), recognizing the presence and work of these organizations is by no means trivial and could have been missed. In other words, outlining the social agents that are active in the scene of Silwan/the City of David is not trivial, and is in itself an important and ethical research process.

Emek Shaveh ('common grounds' in Hebrew) was established in 2008 as 'a non-profit organization of archaeologists, local residents and human rights activists working to change the role archaeology plays in the Israeli–Palestinian conflict'.[8] Since the City of David site revolves primarily around archeological findings, and as its discursive power is conveyed through mobilizing the scientific findings of archeology, Emek Shaveh archeologists challenge its colonial-scientific approach. They propose an alternative perspective with regards to the meanings of archeological practices (excavations, interpretations, representations, etc.) and findings. One of the main vehicles that serves Emek Shaveh in reaching and changing public opinion are tours that they conduct at the site. Each tour lasts about three hours, and takes place right at the site – more or less along the route of the formal tour. In these tours a different narrative unfolds, one which is humanist and universalist, and which explicitly undermines the official and hegemonic narrative. Of course, the site's management are displeased with subversive tours conducted on the(ir) premises, but since these activities are legal, there is little that can be done besides interfering with and harassing the Emek Shaveh tour (which ElAd's personnel do).

Emek Shaveh's use of the performative power of tourism in its tours, via the discourses of archeology and authenticity, is accomplished by considerably broadening the scope of knowledge that is deemed relevant and that is, consequently, shared with the visitors. The two points that I found most impressive in this regard are, first, the way that these tours refer to the *cultural heterogeneity* that existed at the site. In the tours, different past cultures are discussed in light of the archeological findings in situ, and this has the effect of de-centering the binary structural that excludes all but Jewish culture(s) in past and in the present. In these tours a new and different cultural narrative is revealed, promoting the value of cultural diversity and heterogeneity rather than cultural exclusion and (Jewish) exclusivity. Table 2.1 reproduces part of a handout that is provided to visitors in the Emek Shaveh tours, where different historical periods and corresponding cultures are indicated. The document, which tells of the many cultures that flourished at the site, does not exclude any of these cultures, but rather portrays a diverse and rich image of the site.

The timeline in Table 2.1 carries an additional effect: it indicates (and advocates) cultural continuity by leading from cultures of the past to present day populations and cultures. Contrary to what might be expected of archeological discourse, here the past leads in a continuous way to the present, and the qualities of Otherness and mysteriousness associated with archeological findings – emphasized and mystified in the official tour – are mitigated. Hence events of the twentieth century too have their role in the history of the site, including the Israeli Occupation and annexation of the neighborhood in 1967.

Finally, the notions of cultural diversity and intercultural interaction are effectively conveyed in Emek Shaveh's tour by meetings with Palestinian residents and local activists. These meetings take place regularly at the tour's conclusion, and they *embody* the idea of cultural diversity and cooperation. In

Table 2.1 Cultural diversity: Emek Shaveh's archeological timeline

Date	Period	Event
37 BCE	Roman Period	The King Herod
Around AD 20–33	Roman Period	Jesus of Jerusalem
AD 70	Roman Period	Roman Period
		The destruction of the Second Temple
AD 324	Byzantine Period	Christian rule in Jerusalem
Fifth century	Byzantine Period	Empress Eudocia
AD 638	Islamic Period	
AD 661	Islamic Period	The Umayyad Caliphate
AD 750	Islamic Period	The Abbasid Caliphate
AD 969	Islamic Period	The Fatimid Caliphate
AD 1033	Earthquake	
	Silwan area abandoned	
AD 1099	Crusader Period	
AD 1187	Islamic Period	Ayyubid Dynasty
		Salah Ad-din
AD 1250	Mamluk Period	
Sixteenth century	Silwan resettled	
AD 1517	Ottoman Period	
1917	British Mandate	
1948	Part of Jordan	
1967	Israeli Occupation	
	Silwan annexed to Jersualem	

the political context of Silwan/City of David (and more broadly of the Israeli-Palestinian Conflict), these acts are rare and are usually perceived as radical statements. These meetings allow tourists to interact directly with residents, and to hear in an authentic and unmediated way their perspectives on their everyday experiences under the Jewish heritage site and so on.

The second organization that is active is the Wadi Hilwah Information Center (WHIC, see silwanic.net), which was established in 2009 as a non-profit voluntary organization of local residents. The organization's goals are giving voice to residents, monitoring and reporting activities that are promoted by the combined policies of ElAd and the Municipality of Jerusalem, as well as various social and welfare activities in the neighborhood. As the WHIC's website indicates:

> We, the residents of Wadi Hilwah, did not delegate anyone to convey the information on our behalf, and we do not allow any person to obscure our deep rooted identity which lies in the houses, stones, trees, gardens, springs, and sky of our village [...] We [...] have decided to open an Information Center for those who wish to hear the voice of the indigenous people, to tell the stories of our forefathers and keep the light in the way of youth, and to keep the hope on the thresholds of doors.[9]

Observably, the performative power of the discourse produced by WHIC stems from the fact it is conveyed in the words of the local/native residents. While not making any specific mention of the Jewish heritage site, the narrative in this text is subversive because it has as its point of departure the misinformation supplied to tourists *above the heads* of the indigenous Palestinian population. At stake here are issues of voice, authenticity and authority. The text, where the deictic 'we' is again evinced, represents the residents' attempt to regain the grounds of their neighborhood and of their everyday spaces of livelihood. The text discloses its authors' understanding of the performative narrative power of tourism: such terms as 'voice' and 'stories' are used with an emancipatory aim. The WHIC offers not only alternative information, but also awareness that tourism is an ideological battleground where identities and places are being narrated into existence or otherwise silenced and erased.

Part of the organization's attempts to symbolically regain the space of the neighborhood of Wadi Hilwah concerns re-marking its area as one which belongs to the Palestinian residents and not to the Jewish settlers. As indicated in Figures 2.1b and 2.1c, spontaneous and planned resistive activities are carried out in this capacity. For instance: (a) hanging improvised street signs (Figure 2.1b), which indicate the Arabic name of the streets (Wadi Hilwah St.) and not its tourist Hebraized name, and (b) drawing graffiti (Figure 2.1c), which also serves to indicate the identity of the place as perceived by the residents in opposition to the colonial expansion of the Jewish tourist site (Here is Silwan; and in Arabic: Silwan is Arab).

In one of its recent publications, WHIC relates to a number of issues under such headings as: 'Archaeology in ElAd's Era,' 'A Visit to a National Park or a

Settlement?' and 'National Park: Private Property!', which expose the ideo-logical aims and means of the ElAd run Jewish heritage site, and the grave con-sequences that they carry for local residents. Under a picture that shows children playing in the neglected and crowded neighborhood of Silwan, the text says:

> Behind the scenes of the tourist site live people. They should be seen, heard and helped to oppose the injustices they face. The residents of Wadi Hilwah ask the people of Israel and the world to support their struggle for the right to live in their village as part of a multi-cultural Jerusalem based on princi-ples of equality and peace. [10]

The WHIC text politicizes tourist stages by indicating that the choice of what to show on these stages concerns also the choice of what is hidden and expunged. The voice of local residents, as expressed in and through this WHIC text, tries to access tourists directly; attempting to bypass the institutional and hegemonic voice (which admittedly presently comprises of 'the scenes'). As with Emek Shaveh, here too, the address is peaceful and multicultural: the goals that are presented include creating a multicultural (and perhaps also multinational) co-existence in Jerusalem.

Conclusions

This chapter commenced with an allusion to Kafka, suggesting that tourism sometimes plays a mean role in transforming populations and in instilling them with a sense of helplessness. Yet at times transformations are not imposed, and can be assumed willingly: as academics, we have room to decide if we want to shift our research perspectives and goals. This chapter documented my shift to an activist academic framework, offering a case study that illustrates the gains achieved when a critical perspective in tourism research is adopted. As indicated, no research has been conducted on Silwan/the City of David heritage site thus far – a fact that can be viewed as a silence that 'says' something; if I had not accessed the field from the perspective of someone associated with an activist organization, I might not have considered the site for research or, alternatively, my research would have been very different (namely, siding unknowingly with the hegemonic narrative).

For myself, and perhaps for others in the community of tourism scholars, sub-versive voices, which are by definition weaker and flickering, are oftentimes not heard and are not recorded in research/as research data. Social activism of sorts offers ways of accessing interesting and otherwise easily unobserved sites of research and fascinating empirical material. At the same time, activism can also supply theoretical perspective and conceptual sensitivities, and in this way a much needed and fruitful bridge is sustained between academic work and grass-roots activism, and between the different knowledge(s) that are fostered in these spheres.

Notes

1 This chapter was conceived at the 3rd Critical Tourism Studies Conference (June, 2009, Zadar, Croatia), specifically after hearing a lecture titled 'Living stones and dead children: Palestine and the politics of tourism', by Freya Higgins-Desbiolles. Moving lectures can have this effect, as conferences can be places of (academic) activism. An earlier version of this chapter was presented at the Annual Meeting of the Israeli Association of Tourism Research, 17 February 2010, Hebrew University of Jerusalem, Israel. I am indebted to comments made to this chapter by Jonathan Mizrachi and Dana Hercberg.
2 Israeli Nature and Parks Authority. Retrieved from: www.parks.org.il/BuildaGate5/ general2/company_search_tree.php?mc=378~All (accessed 5 June 2010).
3 Retrieved from: www.cityofdavid.org.il/IrDavidFoundation_Eng.asp (accessed 24 January 2010).
4 Many of the activities of the ElAd organization, such as changing ownership of houses and land from Palestinian hands to Jewish hands, were successful and prompted by much support of state authorities and municipality agencies. In fact, the Jerusalem municipality accounted for the total handover of the City of David National Park to the High Court of Justice by arguing that ElAd is 'an arm of the municipality'. This point is of particular importance because it indicates that in terms of agency, the ElAd organization is supported by Israeli State authorities (Ir Amim 2009: 20).
5 Retrieved from: www.nytimes.com/2010/06/22/world/middleeast/22mideast. html?scp=3&sq=east%20jerusalem&st=cse (accessed 29 June 2010).
6 Retrieved from: www.cityofdavid.org.il/map.asp (accessed 18 January 2010).
7 The only exception to non-Jewish presence in the past is the earlier Canaanite culture, which is mentioned in the tours. This bygone culture serves as a cultural 'Other', which (having perished long ago) does not pose any threat to ethno-national Jewish ideologies.
8 Retrieved from: www.alt-arch.org/index.php (accessed 22 January 2010). A disclosure note: the author acts as a board member of this organization.
9 Retrieved from: http://silwanic.net/?page_id=684 (accessed 26 January 2010).
10 *The Story Behind the Tourist Site*, unknown year and place of publication. Retrieved from: http://silwanic.net/?page_id=57 (accessed 28 May 2010).

References

Aitchison, C. (2001) 'Theorizing other discourses of tourism, gender and culture: can the subaltern speak (in tourism)?' *Tourist Studies*, 1 (2): 133–147.

Ateljevic, I., Harris, C., Wilson, E. and Collins, F. L. (2005) 'Getting "entangled": reflexivity and the "Critical Turn"', *Tourism Recreation Research*, 30 (2): 9–21.

Bakhtin, M. M. (1968) *Rabelais and His World* (trans. H. Iswolsky), Cambridge, MA: M.I.T. Press.

Brin, E. (2006) 'Politically-oriented tourism in Jerusalem', *Tourist Studies*, 6 (3): 215–243.

Brin, E. and Noy, C. (In press) 'The said and the unsaid: performative guiding in a Jerusalem neighborhood,' *Tourist Studies*.

Chambers, D. (2007) 'Interrogating the "critical" in critical approaches to tourism research', in I. Ateljevic, N. Morgan and A. Pritchard (eds), *The Critical Turn in Tourism Studies: innovative research methodologies*, Amsterdam: Elsevier Publications, pp. 105–119.

Chatterton, P., Hodkinson, S., and Pickerill, J. (2010) 'Beyond scholar activism: making strategic interventions inside and outside the neoliberal university', *ACME: An International E-Journal for Critical Geographies*, 9 (2): 245–275.

Cohen, S. B., and Kliot, N. (1992) 'Place-names in Israel's ideological struggle over the Administered Territories', *Annals of the Association of American Geographers* 82 (4): 653–680.

Collins-Kreiner, N. (2008) 'Maps as a tool for understanding territorial conflicts: the case of Israel', *Map and Reality*, 1: 10–32.

Fairclough, N. (1995) *Critical Discourse Analysis: the critical study of language*, London: Longman.

Feldman, J. (2008) 'Constructing a shared Bible Land: Jewish Israeli guiding performances for Protestant pilgrims', *American Ethnologist*, 34 (2): 351–374.

Gramsci, A. (1971) *Selections from the Prison Notebooks of Antonio Gramsci* (trans. Q. Hoare and G. N. Smith), London: Lawrence & Wishart.

Hall, C. M. and Tucker, H. (eds) (2004) *Tourism and Postcolonialism: contested discourses, identities, and representations*, London: Routledge.

Ir Amim (2009) *Shady Dealings in Silwan*, report. Retrieved from: www.ir-amim.org.il/eng/?CategoryID=254 (accessed 24 January 2010).

Jaworski, A. and Pritchard, A. (eds) (2005) *Discourse, Communication, and Tourism*, Clevedon, UK: Channel View Publications.

Jewitt, C. (2009) *The Routledge Handbook of Multimodal Analysis*, Abingdon: Routledge.

Isaac, K. R. (2010) 'Alternative tourism: new forms of tourism in Bethlehem for the Palestinian tourism industry', *Current Issues in Tourism*, 13 (1): 21–36.

Kress, G. R. and Van Leeuwen, T. (2006) *Reading Images: the grammar of visual design* (2nd edition), New York: Routledge.

Noy, C. (2004) '"The trip really changed me": backpackers' narratives of self-change', *Annals of Tourism Research*, 31 (1): 78–102.

Noy, C. (2008) 'Pages as stages: a performance approach to visitor books', *Annals of Tourism Research*, 35 (2): 509–528.

Noy, C. (2009) '"I WAS HERE!": addressivity structures and inscribing practices as indexical resources', *Discourse Studies*, 11 (4): 389–408.

Paine, R. (1995) 'Behind the Hebron massacre', *Anthropology Today*, 11 (1): 8–15.

Shohamy, E. G. and Gorter, D. (eds) (2009) *Linguistic Landscape: expanding the scenery*, New York: Routledge.

Stein, R. L. (2008) *Itineraries in Conflict: Israelis, Palestinians, and the political lives of tourism*, Durham: Duke University Press.

Veijola, S. and Jokinen, E. (1998) 'The death of the tourist: seven improvisations,' *European Journal of Cultural Studies*, 1 (3): 327–351.

Zerubavel, Y. (1995) *Recovered Roots: collective memory and the making of Israeli national tradition*, Chicago: University of Chicago Press.

3 The challenge of critical approaches to rural tourism studies and practice

Heather Mair

Introduction

With this chapter, I present a reflexive look at some practical implications of becoming a critical tourism researcher. Linked to recent (and essential) discussions about reflexivity and ethics, not to mention the challenges of critical tourism research, I consider the opportunities and obligations inherent in intervening to foster change. Trained in critical social research approaches, feminist theories, human geography, and political economy, I've sought to embrace a critical approach to tourism studies for nearly a decade of research, writing, teaching, and mentoring. In 2008, as I approached two coveted milestones of academia (tenure/promotion and sabbatical leave), I began to reflect on these rites of passage, considering, as hooks (1994) does, the ramifications of 'success' in this chosen career. I use this chapter not only to expose and consider my experiences with these 'entanglements' (Ateljevic *et al.* 2005), but also to contribute to a growing discussion in our field about the contexts and constituencies of (critical) tourism research.

The chapter has three parts. First, I argue as others have argued recently (see especially Tribe 2008; Ateljevic *et al.* 2007) that critical tourism scholars are developing tools to situate tourism within the broader social, cultural, political, economic, and ecological context, and yet their work must also include an effort to change the discourse of tourism and to challenge mainstream approaches. Engaging in our work critically and reflexively helps build an atmosphere where we can set out our assumptions, consider power relations both on the ground and in academia, sharpen our skills, and strive to make our work as effective and transparent as it can be. Next, I follow Botterill (2003), Ateljevic *et al.* (2005), Hall (2004), and others who have legitimated these kinds of presentations to reflect on nearly a decade of working with small communities in Canada. Primarily interested in tourism policy and issues of process in development, I foreground some of the challenges, tensions, and opportunities shaping my experiences – first as a student and now a newly tenured professor. While I'm heartened by opportunities to discuss tourism (research) critically, experience on the ground and in communities suggests that we need to go much further to challenge mainstream discourse and to re-frame everyday assumptions and expectations.

Last, I ask: What's next for maturing critical tourism research(ers)? If, as Franklin wrote (2007), tourism can best be thought of as a fundamental, yet ever-changing ordering of social life, what if any role do I/we have in this process? Given the potential of critical paradigms, can we transcend the false dichotomies of objectivity/subjectivity and describing/prescribing? Jamal *et al.* considered the potential of a new paradigm for (eco)tourism research and action, 'not driven by the instrumental reason of managerial and scientific interests, but rather … envisioned on the basis of participatory democracy and human and ecological well-being' (2006: 147). Add to this questions with which I've been struggling: How can researchers counter the conventional wisdom that tourism is an adequate way to keep small communities alive? Given the broader context of the current global economic slump, are traditional tourism researchers, business leaders and policy makers finally ready to say that Tourism-the-Emperor has no clothes? How can I/we make sure that tourism development and research comes closer to its emancipatory potential?

A role for reflexivity: facing the challenge of critical tourism research

Some time ago, Tribe (1997) set out the distinction between academics and industrialists in tourism – a not completely comfortable division between knowing and doing. He also indicated that power seemed to rest increasingly in the realm of the latter. Later, Tribe also engaged Lyotard's post-modernism, a critically oriented approach that seems to have vanished from more recent post-modern orientations:

> One consequence of Lyotard's analysis is that the business of tourism part of the field of tourism exerts a strong pull on knowledge production and that much tourism knowledge is generated for profitability. Epistemology is led by functionalism, and the aim of knowledge production becomes not an impartial uncovering of truth but a search for truths which are useful in terms of marketability and efficiency.
>
> (Tribe 2004: 55)

Jamal and Everett (2007) used Habermasian language to consider how tourism research has met the needs and interests of scientific and economic rationalisation shored up by a focus on technical and practical knowledge, which occludes opportunities for meaningful participation and emancipation. Unfortunately, and despite the growth in critical approaches to knowing tourism that have an activist edge, the so-called business of tourism still dominates development policy as well as university and college curricula. Rowe (2005) reflected critically on his experience conducting applied tourism research and consultancy. gainst the backdrop of decreased public funding for research and the tightening relationship between universities and the private sector, Rowe exposed the broader socio-political economic context of tourism consultancy and applied research:

tourism researchers, consultants, and advisors, both in and outside government, are therefore often charged with the task of demonstrating to communities that tourism is inherently a 'good thing' and, once persuaded of this argument, how 'to do tourism' (Rowe 2005: 129).

For small communities in particular this has created a rather limited, constrained and homogenised approach as many are merely encouraged to replicate ideas from other places including 'building museums, halls of fame, and spectacular "big things" that diminish the very differences they are seeking to promote' (Rowe 2005: 134; see also Mair 2006). Tribe (2004: 55) summarises Hollinshead's (1999) contention that tourism researchers are among the power-brokers whose research and publishing choices mask opportunities for change.

The power of surveillance is shown by Hollinshead as an authoritative mix of normalising discourse and universalising praxis which routinely privileges particular understandings of heritage, society, and the world in and through tourism. Hollinshead argues tourists and those who work in tourism can be seen as *Homo docilis*, participating in the regulation of the world and in the mastery of its social cultural, natural and geographical environments, but also in regulating and constraining themselves.

Environmental concerns in particular have elicited deep thinking about the role of research(ers) in tourism management. Wearing *et al.* (2005) called for a de-commodifying approach to tourism. They highlighted research paradigms that would foster a process, led by NGOs, wherein tourism management confronts the dominance of market-oriented perspectives. Jamal *et al.* (2006), after Gramsci (1971), call on tourism researchers to be 'organic intellectuals' and entreat us to become directly involved in participatory research and praxis (see also Jamal and Everett 2007). More critical, however, and central to the discussion here, is the on-going reluctance to question the existence or encouragement of tourism. Indeed, the goals and processes underscoring most tourism research rarely include encouraging non-tourism options. Why?

Humberstone (2004: 122) argued that tourism research 'needs to engage with issues around the nature of knowledge and its production'. This means we must contend with the political, economic and social contexts within which knowledge is constructed and especially how it is used in communities and by whom. Reflexivity is an increasingly useful tool both for individual researchers to come to terms with their work but also for encouraging others to do the same and to build a larger, reflexive conversation that can only strengthen our field. For those involved in social research, the critiques of their own motivations, assumptions and impact can be uncomfortable, humbling and unsettling. Nonetheless, critical reflexivity is central to identifying these tensions and thereby for improving practice and research. Organised chronologically within an inter-related framework of contexts and constituencies (i.e. mutually reinforcing experiences, places and people), the next section presents a reflexive assessment of my efforts to instill practice and research with a critical edge.

Resisting and reifying conventional wisdom

Contexts and constituencies I: building a value-full researcher

I grew up in a small village on the Atlantic Coast of Canada. Like my siblings, I could barely wait to leave for university in a bigger, more central Canadian city. An undergraduate degree in political science with a focus on international development studies fostered a keen if skeptical interest in rural development. A graduate degree in political economy, and research on the collapse of the Atlantic Canadian groundfishery in the early 1990s, fostered a romantic desire to protect and conserve the small communities blighted by human-made environmental, economic and social disaster. Tourism didn't enter my mind until it became clear that a significant formal policy response to the ruin of many communities in Atlantic Canada included tourism development projects. My feminist, critical, political economy trained mind (and heart) knew it could never be that simple. In an unpublished final paper, I wrote that researchers needed to:

> interrogate this effort to sell the region on account of its beauty and simplicity in terms of the impact these changes might have on the way in which women and men relate to these spaces and each other. An interesting study would attempt to determine whether this has led to an increase in home-centered tourism (for example, bed and breakfasts) wherein women open their homes to travelers, redefining their relation to the homespace to accommodate the whims of global capital and make some extra money.
>
> (Mair 1995: 65)

Contexts and constituencies II: becoming a critical tourism researcher

When I was 27, I returned to the community where I grew up and was taken aback by the indelible imprint of tourism on many communities in the area. I worked first at the local paper mill and then with a quasi-governmental environmental group and became increasingly aware of the complexity of development in an economically depressed region. At 29, I moved again to a mid-sized city in central Canada to attend university. Over the course of the doctoral degree, I worked on small projects assessing rural tourism development and planning in a number of communities. I knew that my own doctoral work would inevitably have to come to terms with what I saw as a short-sighted and wrong-headed answer to the conundrum of rural development. And yet, despite what I thought was a finely honed, critical lens, I can now see significant differences in how I used this lens to shape my thesis research and paid research work. In short, I was asking 'why tourism' (i.e. policy) in one world but questioning 'how tourism' (i.e. process and planning) in the other. As I put these two questions together, I can see how I was trying to help communities resist tourism and yet was reinforcing tourism in many ways.

Shortly after starting the doctoral programme, I was in the throes of my first tourism-related research consultancy project. My supervisor was invited to a meeting in a community torn into factions as a result of disagreements about the nature of tourism development. This tiny village had created two tourism brochures and had opened two tourism information booths, each selling a different image of the community. That this was an untenable situation was not lost on many members of the community, and my supervisor, well known in the area as an 'expert' in rural development, was invited to a meeting by the president of the Business Improvement Association. My job (as a new doctoral student) was to present our 'community-based approach' to rural development and to talk about our participatory philosophy. I talked enthusiastically about inclusive planning processes and the impacts of tourism development without community consent and/or collaboration. In addition to the broad literature on tourism impacts, I had been reading Freire (1970), Friedmann (1987), and Forester (1989); the gurus of inclusivity, conscientisation, participatory processes and social change. The dozen or so people in attendance (although this was a meeting advertised widely in the community and open to all) seemed to have neither patience nor interest. I could feel them getting bored. It became clear those in attendance were from one side of the debate and I remember how during the course of the discussion that followed, they kept turning to my supervisor (a very tall, middle-aged, white man) hoping he might tell them how to win. He kept saying, 'I can't give you the answers but I have some ideas about ways you can come together to talk about this collectively and sort this out as a community.' We reinforced our message and offered to facilitate any future meetings the community might host should they wish to undertake a more inclusive, participatory approach. While this experience provided fodder for a few in-depth qualitative interviews about the split in the community, and, following from that, conference presentations and publications, we were never invited back. We were left to describe the tensions we saw but not to engage in addressing them.

This experience left a deep awareness of both the lack of power inherent in my student (perhaps young female) status but also in regards to the importance of the wider social, economic and political context within which (tourism) planning is always situated. Economic restructuring, particularly the downturn of some natural resources-based economies (and now manufacturing in North America) sets the stage for a ready acceptance of a services-based approach to economic growth. At least from a policy standpoint, tourism fits this service-led growth agenda well. Add to this the atmosphere of uncertainty and insecurity permeating most small communities and it doesn't bode well for a commitment to process-oriented planning approaches and long-term views. Ultimately, I was disappointed that my 'truth' hadn't been embraced. I thought that the 'proper' planning process would help the community understand that tourism was at best only part of the solution.

In 2000, partly as a result of the experience described above, my supervisor and I decided to develop what we considered to be a community-based tourism planning process. Soon, we had crafted a hands-on, plainly written tourism planning manual that members of rural communities could use on their own. We based the manual on the model of a community search conference (Emery and Purser 1996) and set out to 'test' it in as many communities as possible. After a few presentations at rural development conferences, leaders of three communities approached us and volunteered to help. It should be noted that these communities were undergoing forced amalgamation – a controversial process whereby their governments and services were merged as part of a broad trend of making local government 'more efficient' that was sweeping through the province of Ontario upon the election of deeply conservative leadership.

I had also started teaching my first course on tourism and recreation planning and was determined to encourage students to think about relations of power in communities and about the benefits of a collaborative approach. I was reading Reed (1999), Ritchie (1999) and others who were committed to undertaking an approach to tourism planning that was at least sensitive to power relationships. When time came to work with the communities, I was determined to encourage participants to engage equally in a dialogue about community health and development *before* talking about tourism. Together with another doctoral student, I developed and held a series of collaborative planning events. Participants were keen to take the lead in the process we facilitated. While attendance was low, the outcomes (strategies) developed were centered on meeting community needs that went beyond tourism-led responses to economic concerns. However, when my supervisor and I made a presentation to the local government (our funders) on the results of this project, councilors were much more interested in hearing our thoughts on the tourism potential of the area and possible economic development opportunities. One of our key recommendations was that communities undertake this process again, on their own with more participants and as a newly amalgamated group, and to do it at regular intervals such as every five years. This recommendation elicited next to no discussion, and to my knowledge it has not been taken up.

As with the previously mentioned project, the details of these events have been presented and published elsewhere as we sought to describe the process and to encourage other researchers to undertake similar activities. However, despite irregular contact with a key player in one of the communities, engagement with these communities and their tourism planning endeavours has ceased.

These experiences stand out among the few opportunities to encourage a tourism planning process built on assumptions about community power and where tourism is deemed a secondary focal point. And yet, as with Rowe's experience, the discussion of process and encouragement of critical reflection about the nature of development itself was neither actively supported nor maintained, especially at leadership levels. Rowe noted that 'a deeper, reflexive research process may take the participants far from conventional boosterist platitudes, imitative strategies, and "safe" recommendations, and provide critical perspectives of local culture and its future directions that may not be entirely welcome' (2005: 135).

Indeed, the broader context of fear and insecurity that permeates much thinking about development in small communities often overrides even the best intentions of praxis. While I cherish these important experiences, they reaffirm the challenge inherent in decoupling tourism from the overriding discourse of economic growth. I'd softened my sense of having a kind of truth to instill; nevertheless, I was still firmly committed to process. And yet, at the time I felt quite powerless to find ways to excite and engage other small communities in these kinds of planning endeavours. Doctoral research allowed me to return to the ivory tower as I satisfied myself with undertaking a critical analysis of the trajectory of tourism and rural development policy in two provinces over 25 years. Two case studies of small communities (one was close to where I grew up and the other was one of the communities mentioned above) assessed the impact of those development policies at the local level. Upon completion of the degree, I felt I'd contributed to the field but had not moved any closer to the goal of social change. As Tribe (2007) outlines, critical approaches not only embrace the paradigmatic shift from 'is' to 'ought' but attempt to help move the process along.

Contexts and constituencies III: finding community or 'the Dubrovnik effect'

Perhaps one of the reasons why I've struggled with the challenge of putting praxis at the forefront of work with members of rural communities considering tourism development is because there are few others around me who think this way. Certainly, 'community-based tourism' is a major theme in tourism research, but, as authors such as Blackstock argue, the use of this term often signifies an inherent disconnect from 'the bottom-up, anti-oppressive, empowering ethos of community development' (2005: 46). Not only do many researchers and planners ignore the local context as well as the complexity of community (rife with power struggles and competing values), as Blackstock argues, the community may be co-opted and tourism privileged over other development options, opening the door for the advancement of a neo-liberal agenda. Certainly in the North American context, tourism conferences seem dominated by market-oriented approaches and lack critical insight, quite unreflective of major paradigmatic shifts in our field.

I realised that intellectual isolation was taking its toll when I attended the first Critical Tourism Studies conference in Dubrovnik, Croatia in 2005. I was overcome by a feeling of being in a community for the first time since I'd returned to university. The conference became, as I would describe later to colleagues, a 'support group' for critical tourism researchers. From 1999 until 2005, I had satisfied myself with presentations on tourism planning processes at conferences – turning my critical sights towards 'how tourism' and away from 'why tourism' – and feeling a growing frustration. Needless to say, when I got to Dubrovnik, not only had I found a group I could relate to, I realised how far the field had come. While I had thought deeply and written a bit about the potential of critical and interpretive approaches to tourism research, papers by John Tribe, David Botterill, Irena Ateljevic, Nigel Morgan, and Annette Pritchard indicated others were pushing the field in exciting new directions. I returned home refreshed and rejuvenated and committed to unapologetically injecting a critical spirit into every aspect of my work. And yet...

Contexts and constituencies IV: being critical in an increasingly constrained (and uncritical) world

I had started my first academic appointment in 2004 and, as noted above, was determined to continue to foster this critical and praxis-oriented approach to rural tourism research. The paradigmatic revolution so well articulated by Goodson and Phillimore (2004) and Ateljevic *et al.* (2007) have shaken the foundations of tourism research and scholarship. The on-the-ground context of university research, not to mention neo-liberalism, however, has made things increasingly difficult. Other research projects, limited time, teaching and supervisory commitments, as well as funding challenges, have meant that I've had to be satisfied with teaching about the challenge of community-based processes and doing critically oriented research in communities where this process *ought* to have been undertaken. In 2006, I traveled to a community in western Canada and was immediately caught by its endeavour to craft a tourism theme connected to an enduring popular culture icon. It became immediately clear that not everyone in the community supported this development but that economic downturn in the early 1990s had led a small group to push the idea through as an attempt to keep the community afloat economically. I had been teaching a graduate course in tourism dynamics and included a section on theming and branding. I was reading Hollinshead (2004), Paradis (2002), and Mordue (2001) and was thinking about ontological developments and how places are performed in and through tourism and what this means for those who live there. As indicated by this entry in my research journal during the second visit to the community, however, I found myself once again struggling with my own ideological viewpoints and those of community members who seemed desperate to make tourism work:

> So, it's clear that these are emotional issues – I'm trying really hard to be positive and not critical while keeping the critical lens at the front ... but I feel for this community and its attempts to stay afloat. The little history description [name of interview participant] gave me begins with, 'In the 1980s, [our community] was in trouble, stores were closing and being boarded up' so we can see what people think the options are – my concern is how it comes to pass that these are the options when the stakes are so high for members of this community. [Name of interview participant] seems to see it as a question of making sure people agree with the image and can somehow see themselves in it ... I wonder if the two can co-exist when we are talking about tourism.
>
> (Research journal entry – 5 December 2006)

Interestingly, this paragraph was included in the paper I prepared for the second Critical Tourism Studies conference in Split, Croatia, yet I ultimately removed it when preparing the final version for publication. I was concerned about word count and reflexivity didn't seem to fit the overall tone of the paper. In this sense, then, I feel I've moved even further from my initial motivations for academic work. My research in this community did little more than reinforce the argument that tourism should be encouraged (albeit in more inclusive ways). In short, I did not challenge the conventional wisdom of tourism-led rural development. In the presentation and journal article, I put the critical analysis at the forefront but also, as Thomas (2005) would argue, in the shadows, as only other academics might see it.

Three weeks after undertaking research in the community described above, I received a phone call from an economic development officer from a town nearby. She had read a story in the local paper about my research (an impromptu interview with the editor of the paper led to a description of me as an expert in rural tourism development). She asked for my help in creating a big attraction or theme. Specifically, she wanted my help in convincing members of her community that building the world's largest motorcycle would be a good use of limited resources (instead of a swimming pool for which most members of the community appeared to be asking). I explained to the officer that I was reluctant to offer support for such tourism projects in small communities, especially when they appeared to be developed in the face of community resistance. I offered to send her a copy of the tourism planning manual I'd developed as a graduate student and she said she'd 'take a look'. I also offered to come to her community to facilitate a community-based tourism planning process that might help elicit some other, more supported ideas about development. She seemed mildly interested in this offer. I put the manual in the mail the next day and never heard from her again. A recent check on the Internet indicates that the community does not appear to have built said motorcycle.

As I reflect on these experiences, it's clear members of many communities are generally not prepared to think beyond the tourism agenda. This is the greatest challenge to my work. What might I have done differently in these cases? How could I have encouraged community members and their leaders to more actively engage a collaborative process that fosters critical thinking about the potential of tourism? Why was I reticent about sharing my values (sceptical of tourism as I am) more directly with community members? While I remain emotionally and intellectually committed to the ethos of a critical praxis-oriented approach, I have yet to attain that goal, let alone 'conscientisation' or 'emancipation'. In a recent publication written with my doctoral supervisor, we re-visited transformative and collaborative planning traditions (cf. Forester 1989; Healey 1997) and tried to come to terms with the practicalities of tourism policy and planning as we had experienced it. Alas, our paper concluded with an imagining:

> It is possible to consider the role that tourism development can play not just in expressing community uniqueness and values, but also in countering the growing infiltration of the economic development imperative into considerations of community development more widely. Allowing for tourism to

form one component of community development engenders its de-centering and re-prioritization. Moreover, this approach may even provide opportunities to build skills that can help oppose or re-design unwanted tourism developments and/or off-set some of the homogenizing tendencies of global cultural change and economic restructuring more generally.

(Mair and Reid 2007: 420)

As tourism research(ers) enter(s) what Macbeth (2005) called a sixth platform of developing self-awareness – considering and becoming clear about ethical positions and reflecting upon their implications – perhaps it is time to consider the potential for a more mature, critical tourism research(er).

Finding the heart of my/our work

Thinking about the course of my admittedly short tenure and reflecting on discussions with students and colleagues, I'm led to the conclusion that I/we need to work even harder to build an environment (academic and practical) that fosters a critical discourse and where counter-hegemonic language is not marginalised. Through the creation of what Hollinshead and Jamal call 'critical texts', researchers can build communicative spaces, where 'we might be able to struggle dialectically and gainfully to reconceptualize and reshape some of the existing myths and the dominant social constructions of and about nature and environment' (2007: 113).

Botterill highlights a critical realist tourism research agenda, which has researchers looking beneath the surface of tourism and 'thinking about the underlying mechanisms and powers that act to create or constrain tourism' (2003: 105). This is a central issue and not just for researchers. Indeed, how do we create more opportunities for people in communities to discuss (and resist) these mechanisms and powers? The answer may rest in process and ethics. Macbeth (2005) called for ethically reflexive, prescriptive, and value-full scholarship in our field. While I loathe to prescribe a particular ethical orientation, he encourages all policy makers, planners, developers, critics and commentators to come to terms with their own ethical standpoints. Then, he makes the following plea:

> one needs to be prepared to argue for no tourism! More precisely, treat this industry like any other development option and assess its viability to contribute to the wider sustainable development of the region, the state, the country and the 'living earth', but without ignoring the political economic of the North–South divide in the early 21st century.
>
> (Macbeth 2005: 980)

Jamal *et al.*, have invited researchers to embrace an ethic of care and well-being when 'using, managing, and living within the physical, social and spiritual systems that sustain our existence' (2006: 161). Surely part of this ethic of care involves questioning not just the *practice* of tourism research and development but the very *presence* of tourism.

By offering this chapter, I hope to create a dialogic, reflexive, critical text about an unfinished process. The question must always be: now what? The task remains for me, then, to spread the 'Dubrovnik effect' in the places where I research, learn and teach and to keep at the forefront considerations of social change. For Hrezo, social change:

> comes through the daily efforts of human beings who are able to use their bodies and their minds to organize and complete the tasks required to accomplish mutually agreed upon goals. Thus the freest and least evil society is the one in which the most people are obliged to think while acting, exercise as much control as possible over social life, and have the largest amount of independence to choose the ends of their actions. Such people cannot overcome necessity, but they can learn to use love and reason to persuade necessity, thereby eliminating social oppression and affliction to the extent possible.
>
> (2000: 102)

At the end of our second-to-last gathering in Croatia, we were asked: 'What lies at the *heart* of your work?' The heart of my work must be fostering and facilitating empowerment in small communities so that they may be increasingly involved in defining their own future. Other aspects of my work lead me to help craft places and spaces where community members can gather and build relationships and, subsequently, be able to create the networks and skills that will help them resist unwanted developments. Encouraging a wider discussion where saying 'no' to the tourism-led agenda is a viable and supported option must become part of the heart of our collective work. In this time of economic downturn where the façade of tourism-led growth is exposed like never before, the time is right for this agenda to gain legitimacy.

References

Ateljevic, I., Harris, C., Wilson, E. and Leo Collins, F. (2005) 'Getting "entangled": Reflexivity and the "critical turn" in tourism studies', *Tourism Recreation Research*, 30 (2): 9–21.

Ateljevic, I., Prichard, A. and Morgan, N. (eds) (2007) *The Critical Turn in Tourism Studies*, Oxford: Elsevier.

Blackstock, K. (2005) 'A critical look at community based tourism', *Community Development Journal*, 40 (1): 39–49.

Botterill, D. (2003) 'An autoethnographic narrative on tourism research epistemologies', *Leisure and Society/Loisir et Société*, 26 (1): 97–110.

Emery, M. and Purser, R. E. (1996) *The Search Conference*, San Francisco, California: Jossey-Bass.

Forester, J. (1989) *Planning in the Face of Power*, Berkeley: University of California Press.

Franklin, A. (2007) 'The problem with tourism theory', in I. Ateljevic, A. Pritchard and N. Morgan (eds), *The Critical Turn in Tourism Studies*, Oxford: Elsevier, pp. 131–148.

Freire, P. (1970) *Pedagogy of the Oppressed*, New York: Herder and Herder.

Friedmann, J. (1987). *Planning in the Public Domain*, Princeton, New Jersey: Princeton University Press.

Goodson, L. and Phillimore, J. (2004) 'The inquiry paradigm in qualitative tourism research', in J. Phillimore and L. Goodson (eds), *Qualitative Research in Tourism: ontologies, epistemologies and methodologies*, London: Routledge, pp. 30–45.

Gramsci, A. (1971) *Selections from the Prison Notebooks* (trans. Q. Hoare and G. Smith), New York: International Publishers.

Hall, M. (2004) 'Reflexivity and tourism research: situating myself and/with others', in J. Phillimore and L. Goodson (eds), *Qualitative Research in Tourism: ontologies, epistemologies and methodologies*, London: Routledge, pp. 137–155.

Healey, P. (1997) *Collaborative Planning: shaping places in fragmented societies*, Vancouver, British Columbia: University of British Columbia Press.

Hollinshead, K. (1999) 'Surveillance of the worlds of tourism: Foucault and the eye of power', *Tourism Management*, 20 (1): 7–23.

Hollinshead, K. (2004) 'A primer in ontological craft: the creative capture of people and places through qualitative research', in J. Phillimore and L. Goodson (eds), *Qualitative Research in Tourism: ontologies, epistemologies and methodologies*, London: Routledge, pp. 63–82.

Hollinshead, K. and Jamal, T. (2007) 'Tourism and "the third ear": further prospects for qualitative inquiry', *Tourism Analysis*, 12: 85–129.

hooks, b. (1994) *Teaching to Transgress*, New York: Routledge.

Hrezo, M. (2000) 'Composition on a multiple plane: Simone Weil's answer to the rule of necessity', in R. L. Teske and M. A. Tétreault (eds), *Conscious Acts and the Politics of Social Change*, Columbia: South Carolina University Press. pp. 91–106.

Humberstone, B. (2004) 'Standpoint research', in J. Phillimore and L. Goodson (eds), *Qualitative Research in Tourism: ontologies, epistemologies and methodologies*, London: Routledge, pp. 119–136.

Jamal, T. B. and Everett, J. (2007) 'Resisting rationalisation in the natural and academic life-world: critical tourism research or hermeneutic charity?', in I. Ateljevic, A. Pritchard and N. Morgan (eds), *The Critical Turn in Tourism Studies*, Oxford: Elsevier, pp. 57–76.

Jamal, T., Borges, M. and Stronza, A. (2006) 'The institutionalization of ecotourism: certification, cultural equity and praxis', *Journal of Ecotourism*, 5 (3): 145–175.

Macbeth, J. (2005) 'Towards an ethics platform for tourism', *Annals of Tourism Research*, 32 (4): 962–984.

Mair, H. (1995) 'New spaces in Atlantic Canada: towards the future of the Atlantic groundfishery', unpublished thesis, Carleton University, Canada.

Mair, H. (2006) 'Global restructuring and local responses: investigating rural tourism policy in two Canadian communities', *Current Issues in Tourism*, 9 (1): 1–45.

Mair, H., and Reid, D. G. (2007) 'Tourism and community development vs. tourism for community development: conceptualising planning as power, knowledge and control', *Leisure/Loisir*, 31 (2): 403–426.

Mordue, T. (2001) 'Performing and directing resident/tourist cultures in *Heartbeat* country', *Tourist Studies*, 1 (3): 233–252.

Paradis, T. W. (2002) 'The political economy of theme development in small urban places: the case of Roswell, New Mexico', *Tourism Geographies*, 4 (1): 22–43.

Reed, M. (1999) 'Collaborative tourism planning as adaptive experiments in emergent tourism settings', *Journal of Sustainable Tourism*, 7 (3–4): 334–378.

Ritchie, J. R. B. (1999) 'Interest based formulation of tourism policy for environmentally sensitive destinations', *Journal of Sustainable Tourism*, 7 (3–4): 206–239.

Rowe, D. (2005) 'Some critical reflections on research and consultancy in cultural tourism planning', *Tourism Culture & Communication*, 5: 127–137.

Thomas, H. (2005) 'Pressures, purpose and collegiality in UK planning education', *Planning Theory & Practice*, 6 (2): 238–247.

Tribe, J. (1997) 'The indiscipline of tourism', *Annals of Tourism Research*, 24 (2): 638–657.

Tribe, J. (2004) 'Knowing about tourism', in J. Phillimore and L. Goodson (eds), *Qualitative Research in Tourism: ontologies, epistemologies and methodologies*, London: Routledge, pp. 46–62.

Tribe, J. (2008) 'Tourism: a critical business', *Journal of Travel Research*, 46 (3): 245–255.

Wearing, S., McDonald, M. and Ponting, J. (2005) 'Building a decommodified research paradigm in tourism: the contribution of NGOs', *Journal of Sustainable Tourism*, 13 (5): 424–439.

4 The under-conceptualisations of tourism studies

The case for postdisciplinary knowing

Keith Hollinshead

Introduction: the call for contextual/dialogic/open understandings

This chapter inspects the need for critical researchers to recognise the canonicities of disciplinary outlooks. Extending the recent demand of Coles *et al.* (2006) for the more commonplace application of postdisciplinary thoughtlines on studies of tourism and related arenas of human experience and representational activity, it thereby questions whether those who work in international tourism and in Tourism Studies are too frequently held captive by such canonicities, and are thus not decently tuned into to the contemporary dialectics of emancipation and enunciation which compose the changing contours of 'local being' and 'cultural becoming' around the world today.

It develops the view that a global and axial field like Tourism Studies should have a high proportion of researchers defamiliarising themselves with the hard domain boundaries and the closed disciplinary systems of analysis. It argues that within a panoramic domain like Tourism Studies – which has to admit manifold competing social/cultural/institutional notions of 'place-construction' and 'space-construction' in every corner of the world – neither domain purity nor disciplinary/interdisciplinary/multidisciplinary purity will axiomatically 'get things done' to reliably secure interpretations and communicate findings to the myriad of interested/involved audiences which are now (in each city/region/ nation) turning to 'tourism' to be not only seen but also heard by distant populations. Hence, this presented case (for more commonplace *postdisciplinary research* in Tourism Studies) seeks to describe more flexible, cogenerative, and permeable ways of designing research studies which – rather than unquestioningly uphold universal laws and generalised cultural values here, there, and everwhere – endeavour to respond differentially to the new sorts of inculcations of being and becoming that are arising in every nation and across every continent.

In the effort to secure research approaches which imaginatively and relevantly trespass beyond the strictures of disciplinary (and interdisciplinary/multidisciplinary) knowledge, this chapter critically assesses the agency and authority of tourism/Tourism Studies on these shifting grounds of knowledge and aspiration upon which newly emancipated peoples think and hope as they declare or project 'their' culture, heritage, and nature to others.

In explicating such emergent (and pungently postcolonial/coproductive) kinds of *postdisciplinary knowledge*, this chapter suggests that much work in Tourism Studies research will increasingly take place in complex 'contested realms' where heavily disciplinary approaches are so often insufficiently responsive to the multiple truth settings and the open-to-the-future interpretations which are required today – especially in scenarios where the representational projections of tourism have deep political symbolism or otherwise have complex local, indigenous, or newly hybridised cosmological/spiritual/psychic significations.

To these critical purposes, the chapter ends by drawing attention to a number of recent trends in the theory and craft of qualitative/interpretive inquiry (after Denzin and Lincoln 2005a), which warrant creative (but rich and rewarding?) deployment under postdisciplinary lines of inquiry in international Tourism Studies.

Background: tourism and unaccounted knowledge

The existence of 'multiple worlds'

Over the last two or three decades immense shifts have occurred in the social sciences as the old tenets of *universalism* and *generalisability* have been assaulted and (in many spheres of understanding – but not all) replaced by new postulations about the need to pay lead respect to *particularism* and *local contextuality* (Imayatullah and Blaney 2004). 'Global change' specialists like Agathangelou and Ling (2009) have called for *worldist* cognitions, which envision world politics (or world social studies/world humanities) not perpetually as a single and unvariant place, but as a site of multiple lived worlds. The unfolding concept of 'worldism' principally acknowledges not only the many differences that come from these plural points of lived perspective, but also how those multiple worlds necessarily and inevitably are entwined amongst themselves.

Much of these new high-in-particularism/high-in-local-contextuality contemporary social science reinterpretations of human, cultural, psychic, and political life today recognise that 'selves' and 'others', in fact, resonate richly, and yield all sorts of new/fresh/distinctive multi- and trans-subjectivities (Bauman 2000). These new multiple reverberations of being and becoming tend to be built upon (or further generate) all kinds of inheritance contestations and cultural/intercultural conflicts (Bhabha 1994), and all kinds of struggle for 'reconstruction … reconciliation and resistance' (Agathangelou and Ling 2009: 86). These new/fresh syncretic arrangements gainsay (or variously conceal, disguise, distort, gloss-over) many inter-societal contretemps as specific groups/communities/subnational populations (and even transnational peoples) rise and fall in the effort to protect their felt legacies and thereby announce, declare or re-project themselves (Appadurai 1996). Such is the aftermath of the violent erasures of imperialism and colonialism that constitutes our contemporary moment (Loomba 1998).

The endeavour to identify 'multiple worlds' in social science: the call for postcolonial geographies

In each social science field, a pool of radical thinkers has tended to emerge in recent decades to challenge the very complicity *of their own field* in the continuing imperialist and colonialist dominion over the world, and hence over the places and spaces of these gradually recognised (and in some senses reluctantly recognised) multiple worlds. Since room is at a premium under the word-ceiling available for this chapter, an illustration will now be given of just one such within-discipline entreaty, that of geography. Sixteen years ago, Crush (1994: 336–7) condemned the discipline of geography for being one riddled with the representations of colonial discourse, and one totalised via metropolitan sorts of theory that simply failed to account for people and places of different cultures/ different traditions/different contexts in their own light. Carrying on the critique, Blunt and Wills (2000) called for a reappraisal of 'the geographical imagination' and a decolonisation of the field. To them, a new sort (or rather, new sorts) of *dissident geography* was required which challenged the ruling ethnocentrisms of the field and took informed and sensitive steps to produce a healthier and more responsive academy. To them, new forms of dissident geography were required which (correctively and reflectively) honoured the interests and aspirations of non-metropolitan populations who had been (if often inadvertently and unsuspectingly) heavily marginalised by the imperialist/colonialist (and pungently gendered) received geography of the last two (and more) centuries.

The endeavour to identify 'multiple worlds' in tourism studies: the call for postdisciplinary outlooks

While Tourism Studies has – over the last several decades – regularly been condemned for being conceptually rickety (Crick 1989; Hall 1992; Franklin and Crang 2001; Echtner and Jamal 1997; Tribe 2001; Goeldner 2005), the field has actually had its thinkers who have called for more flexible modes of knowledge production which are able to meaningfully describe and analyse the multiple worlds of the turn-of-the-century moment. One specific team of authors (that of Coles *et al.* 2006) warrants singular elaboration. In their critique of the institutionalisations of Tourism Studies, Coles *et al.* have produced a rigorous examination of the field's territoriality and its seeming parochialism. While they acknowledge the presence of a litany of skilled researches in the field who have worked with adaptable styles of synthetic and synergistic research (experimenting on interdisciplinary, multidisciplinary and transdisciplinary fronts), they note that the ultra-strong grip of business school mentalities and the quest for a solid and secure academic discipline of 'Tourism Studies/Tourism Management' in its own right have been paramount amongst the manifold factors that have tended to restrict what is seen in and through the evolved/bureaucratised field. While Blunt and Wills – for geography – had called for more innovation and creativity of a *dissident* nature which correctively privileges *postcolonial* forms of knowing,

Coles *et al.* – for Tourism Studies – call for more innovation and creativity of a *dialogic* nature which creatively advances *postdisciplinary* outlook on the world and bridges the gaps between the held mindsets of received fields. In citing what Beier and Arnold (2005) have termed the search for a 'supradisciplinary' approach to knowledge production, Coles *et al.* bemoan the contrived ends of disciplinary approaches per se – and (by implication) the contrived ends of inter-disciplinary and multidisciplinary ones, too. Their call for much more experi-mentation with hybrid forms of postdisciplinary knowledge production stands as an effort to help the field escape from the production of rather 'siloed' units of information acquisition and processing in favour of the generation of multiple approaches to knowing which can more flexibly help navigate the webs of inter-action through which labour, capital, and information flow (they cite Urry 2002 here), and which can more flexibly negotiate the 'multiple truth' scenarios (they cite Tribe 2006 here) that were outlined – via the 'worldism' of Agathangelou and Ling – at the start of this chapter. Clearly, Coles *et al.* do not call for the wholesale rejection of disciplinary (or interdisciplinary/multidisciplinary/other 'discipline-based') perspectives. What they cogently offer, instead, is the recog-nition that 'the shackles of disciplinary policy' must be removed when tourism/travel projects are complex, multi-scalar, or otherwise cover questions of context where messy kinds of poorly monitored, less-predictable, hybrid, or evolving mobilisations occur. But – as they recognise themselves – that is no small arena: the above messinesses are ubiquitous and oh-so-frequently deep-seated. To them, the potential for postdisciplinary contributions is thereby 'enormous' (Coles *et al.* 2006: 313).

Aim of the chapter: mapping the conceptual territory 'beyond disciplines'

The Coles *et al.* commentary is a landmark assessment in the call for postdisci-plinary enquiry and it is a long-overdue exposition of the need in Tourism Studies for a primer on the benefits (and the costs) of integrated cum extra-disciplinary (after Tribe 2004) understanding. But the Coles *et al.* manuscript is just one journal article on those deep matters of ontology and epistemology and it cannot be expected to raise the alarm, point out the deficiencies in and of current practice, *and* then map out the methodological, operational, and curriculum-bored road ahead ... or, rather, roads ahead. Following the efforts of Coles *et al.* on some of these cardinal weaknesses in the institutionalisation of research in Tourism Studies/Tourism Management, it is now the purpose of this short chapter 'to carry the conceptual baton' on a little further by explaining for researchers who are active or interested in Critical Tourism Studies (and related fields) just what they may need to turn their attention to, if they have not already done so. The aim is not to comprehensively map out the terrain of *postdiscipli-narity* (for it is really a realm of postdisciplinairities – i.e. a spectrum of many different moods, conditions and imperatives), it is rather to be illustrative of some of the key kinds of postdisciplinary insights and outsights which have not been used in Tourism Studies with frequency or conviction, yet. The purpose of this limited-in-size 6,000 word chapter is therefore to be suggestive: to show just where and how certain the potential of postdisciplinary perspectives can help researchers (particularly of international tourism) become more comfortable with the cultural constructions, the social constructions, the psychic constructions, and the political constructions which may be foreign to their own experience and schooling, or which otherwise are remote and unfamiliar to the playmaking institutions and interest groups that they investigate or have contact with.

Focus: postdiscipinarity distilled

Contribution of Coles et al.

Before some of the noted promontories of the terrain of postdisciplinarity are signposted and illustrated, perhaps a more substantial account ought to be given as to what Coles *et al.* have covered. Their *Current Issues in Tourism* manuscript is one which:

- in terms of its objectives

seeks to point out how those who work in Tourism Studies (like those who work in any discipline or field) tend to become fast institutionalised into ways of seeing some aspects of the world and not seeing others. Coles *et al.* (2006: 296, 300) quite rightly imply that there is almost an ordinary ubiquity and an ordinary inevitability to these matters of normalisation (and their purblind consequences) across each and every singular field.

- in terms of its general critique of postdisciplinarity

seeks to point out that while all disciplines and fields have their known and undersuspected imperialisms (and their known and undersuspected blind alleys), postdisciplinarity is no perfect panacea, and can itself readily become yet another overprized god of reason and over-praised god of justification. Coles *et al.* (2006: 295, 305) make it clear that while under disciplinary (and to a lesser extent interdisciplinary and multidisciplinary) approaches boundaries between disciplines readily become fetishised, specific postdisciplinary approaches may have own forms of 'discipline' which might (for instance) leave the imbued researcher with a strong commitment towards transgressive knowledge (almost as a goal in and of itself) but with no commitment towards aggregative/dialogical understanding across cultures.

- in terms if its specific critique of 'Tourism Studies'

seeks to point out that the field of Tourism Studies/Tourism Management is one (like all others) where particular vested interests have naturalised the field to their own institutional and direct and indirect financial gain. Coles *et al.* (2006: 294) join many other commentators in condemning Tourism Studies for continually privileging the immediate problem-focus of business interest/managerial development activity at the expense of more open outlooks which otherwise might endeavour to weigh up (at a necessarily slower pace!) the complexities of cultural and cosmological fit of a given tourism project or development.

- in terms of the resultant need for an improved and world-responsive social science of Tourism Studies

seek to significantly reduce the degree to which those who work in Tourism Studies (or practitioners in international tourism) work and think in cocooned isolation, championing the institutional and professional warrants of the hallowed field, yet not being alive and responsive to the many other contesting realities held within it. Coles *et al.* (2006: 301) thereby state the case for the cultivation of more flexible and fluid forms of understanding that are suited to longitudinal explanations of the world's cultural, social, psychic and political hybridities through time, and which are more capable at producing dialogic communication between the various found multiple-truth standpoints in the examined contexts.

Such are the key conceptual insights of the *Current Issues in Tourism* manuscript. But before an effort is made to delineate the sort of corrective or complementary postdisciplinarity that the Coles *et al.* article appears to beckon but is not able to substantiate (no doubt owing to its own size limitations!), perhaps a short clarifying observation ought to be made on how postdisciplinary knowledge-production indeed differs from (in particular) interdisciplinary cum multidisciplinary understanding. Coles *et al.* do cover the matter, but they do so in very rushed fashion.

The special singularities of postdisciplinarity

If Tourism Studies researchers are to sincerely and faithfully become aware postdisciplinary thinkers (or rather individuals and teams who are *more openly alert* to the situational and contextual merits of postdisciplinary enquiry!), it is important that the claimed strengths of the approach (or rather of postdisciplinary approaches, plural) are examined a little more roundly. In this respect, the recent work of Repko (2008) can add a little more conceptual pigment where the coloration of Coles *et al.* is thin. Repko – the Director of an Interdisciplinary Studies Programme at the University of Texas (Arlington) – is a longstanding exponent of research projects that straddle disciplines. To him, *multidisciplinarity* is the act of 'placing side by side [the] insights from two or more disciplines' (Repko 2008: 346), but in his view it is generally a more limited exercise than *interdisciplinarity* which necessarily requires the hard work of 'integration'. He thereby defines 'interdisciplinary studies' as being:

a process of answering a question, solving a problem, or addressing a topic that is too broad or complex to be dealt with adequately by a single discipline and draws on disciplinary perspectives and integrates their insights to produce a more comprehensive understanding or cognitive advancement.

(Repko 2008: 344)

Interestingly, Repko does not offer a definition of *crossdisciplinary* forms of inquiry, but he does supply one for *transdisciplinarity*, and he sees it as the application of theories, concepts, or methods across disciplines and sectors of society where the decided effort is made to include stakeholders in both the public and private domains with the overall intent of developing an umbrella synthesis. Thus, to him a transdisciplinary study is:

a focus on a mega and complex problem or theme such as 'the city' or 'sustainability' that requires collaboration among a hybrid mix of actors from different disciplines, professions, and sectors of society.

(Repko 2008: 352)

Some soft scientist and interpretive philosophers may find Repko's explanation of transdisciplinarity to be a little conceptually limited – that is, somewhat illustrative and instrumental rather than being broadly panoramic and situationally fecund. It conceivably suggests that no transdisciplinary study could ever be possible if the government or the corporate sector was not involved: by his judgement, it would also not be nominally possible for different fields within the walls of a single university to come together to mount a bona fide transdisciplinary study!! Many extradisciplinary or supradisciplinary thinkers might thus prefer to follow the 'living systems' approach of Miller's (1978) and of Checkland's (1981), an activity which calls for transdisciplinary studies which are established in terms of emergent (abstract) concepts, ipso facto, whomever is involved, where (under Miller and under Checkland), the researcher/the research team generally searches for new or empowering concepts or models which describe in complex situations and in distant/unmapped scenarios the interactions between elements which have been painstakingly/rigorously found 'there'.

Sadly, there is not the space in this chapter to ruminate further on what Repko would term such matters of 'wide' or 'extended' interdisciplinarity. But there is room to offer a brief explanation of what *postdisciplinarity* – a subject that surprisingly does not make the subject index of Repko's 393 page compendium, let alone his 19 page glossary – might be. Please refer to Exhibit 4.1.

Exhibit 4.1 Delineation of and about postdisciplinary studies

A comparison of the orientations of postdisciplinary work with that of disciplinarity and interdisciplinarity ... an extension of the ideas of Repko on process and theory

1   ◆ **Studies based on an established discipline**
Claim a body of knowledge about certain subjects or objects.
★ *Interdisciplinary studies*
Claim a burgeoning literature of increasing sophistication, depth of analysis, and thus utility. This literature includes subspecialities on interdisciplinary theory, programme administration, curriculum design, research process, and assessment. More importantly, a growing body of explicitly interdisciplinary research on real-world problems is emerging.
▶ *Postdisciplinary studies*
Seek to work with relevant contextual understandings rather than with the bodies of knowledge exclusively contained within a single discipline or within singular disciplines. Aim to help those involved at the setting(s) in question see under and beyond the veils of ignorance that come with each discipline, and with universalist/hegemonic understandings – particularly those freighted with 'the comfortable make believe' of the historical configurations of colonialism.

2   ◆ **Studies based on an established discipline**
Have methods of acquiring knowledge and theories to order that knowledge.
★ *Interdisciplinary studies*
Make use of disciplinary methods, but these are subsumed under a research process of its own that involves drawing on relevant disciplinary insights, concepts, theories and methods to produce new knowledge.
▶ *Postdisciplinary studies*
Tend to be flexible in the use made of methods and theories – and disciplines – thereby being designed to compensate for knowledge produced where an iron cage of privileged understanding has built up around a received or dominant mindset. Tend to be particularly active where a felt need is found to compensate for an ordered or systematic denigration of 'the other' ('an other').

3   ◆ **Studies based on an established discipline**
Seek to generate new knowledge, concepts, and theories within or related to the domain.
★ *Interdisciplinary studies*
Produce new knowledge, more comprehensive understandings, new meanings, and cognitive advancements.
▶ *Postdisciplinary studies*
Seek to cultivate new knowledge normally grounded to or within a specific local/host/emic setting. Importantly recognise that all knowledges are contested and shifting.

4   ◆ **Studies based on an established discipline**
Possess a recognised core of courses.
★ *Interdisciplinary studies*

Are beginning to form a core of courses.

▶ *Postdisciplinary studies*

Are inclined to resist or minimise reliance upon the ubiquitous application of core cognitions and established (normalising) templates. Are inclined – within courses of study – to celebrate so-called 'alternative' ways of seeing and telling, especially those (today) that are 'non-European', genderised, decolonised and decentered.

5 ◆ **Studies based on an established discipline**

Have their own community of experts.

★ *Interdisciplinary studies*

Are forming their own community of experts.

▶ *Postdisciplinary studies*

Are decidedly dubious about the generalisability of 'expertise', tending to recognise (instead) the power and reach of situated know-how which faithfully respects and sincerely reflects the ontologies (i.e. the societal cosmologies/the cultural thoughtlines) and the epistemologies (i.e. the local ways of producing, accepting, and registering 'knowledge').

6 ◆ **Studies based on an established discipline**

Are self-contained and seek to control the said domain as it relates to others.

★ *Interdisciplinary studies*

Are largely dependent upon the disciplines for their source material.

▶ *Postdisciplinary studies*

Tend to resist closure and containment, being open to all sorts of insight whether they be academic or non-academic. Tend to be notably responsive to postcolonial forms of critique that help constitute the new or the recovered fantasies of silenced or suppressed populations.

7 ◆ **Studies based on an established discipline**

Train future experts in the discipline-specific master's and doctoral programmes.

★ *Interdisciplinary studies*

Are training future experts in older fields such as Cultural Studies through its Masters and Doctoral programmes and undergraduate majors. Interdisciplinary Studies 'units' or departments still often hire those individuals who have disciplinary PhDs.

▶ *Postdisciplinary studies*

Gear individuals and (importantly) teams to work on projects where the studies development or issue is examined co-generatively in terms of the broad values and wide aspirations it is reflexive with.

Give researchers/practitioners an axial awareness of how events/places/things are conceivably connected to larger held-truths or cultural/institutional warrants – whether that co-articulation is manifest or latent.

Key: ◆/★ = The received assessments of Repko.
▶ = The emergent assessment of Hollinshead.
Source: Form of exhibit modelled on Repko (2008: 9), drawing on Vickers (1998: 34); augmented (in terms of the insight on postdisciplinarity by observations from Clayton (2008) and Venn (2006).

Exhibit 4.1 is provided as an extension of Repko's work on integrated study. While the first two points in each section of the exhibit are taken from Repko's (2008: 9) own table (where he compared the work of 'Established Disciplines' with that of 'Interdisciplinary Studies'), the third point is added by this author (Hollinshead) to reveal some of the tenets (or rather, the nuances) of postdisciplinary thinking. Thus, a starting definition for *postdisciplinary studies* – to match what Repko has yielded for other terms – might now stand as:

> Forms of systematic or exhaustive longitudinal (through time) and latitudinal (through place) critique which utilise scholarly and non-scholarly reasoning to map the multiple truths which exist in a found context or setting, and which pay distinct attention to emic/local/grounded understandings which have significant communal, public, and/or political support there, whether that be based upon felt or claimed longstanding inheritances or otherwise upon emergent and dynamic projections of being and becoming. Such forms of critique tend to serve as dialectical open-to-the-future inspections which uncover or account for the plurality of important (i.e. well-supported) outlooks which have been overlooked, ignored, or suppressed either historically (or which are being subjugated in the present) by dominant authorities/dominant cognitions.

These explanatory matters of what postdisciplinarity is (and can be for Tourism Studies) have also been recently inspected elsewhere – see Hollinshead (in press).

The current re-conceptualisation in soft science: the tillage of a broader postdisciplinary imaginary

In many nooks and crannies of the soft sciences, the last two decades have witnessed an increased sensitivity towards multiple-world understandings (Holmes and Marcus 2005). Critical and interpretive researchers in the social sciences and the humanities have become much more self-aware of the idolatries of control that course ordinarily through the exercise of their phenomenological approaches to knowing, and as the number of concerned doubting-Thomases has escalated, the arena of the soft sciences has become not only a site of philosophical and methodological revolt, but a milieu for the rise of many new breeds of counter-enlightenment (Ellingson 2009). The soft sciences themselves – and gradually the extended field of the social sciences and the humanities – have become much more 'provisional' and much less 'authoritative' (Kukla 2000).

The current period of re-conceptualisation in the soft sciences has perhaps best been monitored in the top-selling publication *The Sage Handbook of Qualitative Research*, the magnum opus of editors Denzin and Lincoln which has expanded from its monster (volume one) size of 1994, via its extra-monster (volume two) size of 2000, to its super-monster (volume three) 1,210 pages in 2005 (Denzin and Lincoln 2005a). This top-selling compendium is not merely an aid for the deployment of qualitative techniques (as its name might at first imply), it is an expansive overview of the whole panoply of ontological and epistemological issues which undergird the many movements in the social sciences and humanities that have championed the shift from 'culture-finding' essentialist approaches to 'culture-situated' processual approaches. Thus, the three Denzin and Lincoln handbooks – where most of the early chapters are updated in the succeeding volumes – are a vital read for soft science/critical/interpretive researchers who wish to contextualise their work within broader streams of cultural significance. *The Sage Handbook of Qualitative Research* (notably volume three [2005a]) is thus an important at-hand text for those researchers who have slowly or suddenly turned towards the mediated intimacies (after Marcus 2001) of postdisciplinary thinking. It is a work in which many of its 46 chapters offer prime coverage of the sorts of imperatives and obligations that critical and interpretive researchers (namely, notably those who have perhaps become disillusioned with *the continued disciplinarities* of 'interdisciplinary research' and with *the insufficient malleabilities* of 'multidisciplinary research') face today in the search for more accommodating collaborative and dialectical approaches to knowing. It is a compendium which frequently positions the researcher not inherently and axiomatically as the grand lord or lady of the research exercise but as a mere partner in the given knowledge-quest who must work in association with (or in alliance with) the local/host/contextual 'community'. Thus, Denzin and Lincoln (2005a) is a work which articulates not just new versions of old styles of ethnography, it is a work which shines the light on *whole new discernments of para-ethnography* (Holmes and Marcus 2004) – that is of approaches to the world that decidedly hold back from universal outlooks and which seek collaboratively to trace the received cosmologies and the lived realities of such local/host/contextual 'community' groups and individuals.

The sought trajectory of the thinking behind the panorama of approaches in *The Sage Handbook of Qualitative Research* is clearly stated in the second paragraph of the work, where the editors (Denzin and Lincoln 2005b: 1) maintain that many existing forms of qualitative research and related styles of ethnography act as a metaphor for colonial edifices of knowledge, power and truth. The subsequent 45 chapters are principally offered in recognition of the view that longstanding positivist and neo-positivist 'hegemonic ways of seeing and interpreting the world' are still rife in the received soft sciences, often based upon a single/dominant aesthetic mode (Atkinson and Delamont 2005: 823). In implicit postdisciplinary hue, the Denzin and Lincoln contributors thereby generally call for the development of a wider imaginary across the soft/critical/interpretive sciences, that is one that harnesses complictous forms of collaboration to examine the collateral counterpart knowledge of the contextual zones and layers that are pertinent to the given study (Holmes and Marcus 2005: 1100). Such is the work's cumulative call for *postgraduate curricula* (i.e. for *graduate curricula* in North America) which constitute a new tradition of activist and intellectually open sorts of enquiry which are relatively free of the disciplinary straitjackets of yesteryear (Finley 2005: 683).

Exhibit 4.2 now attempts to cover much of the range of these hailed kinds of activist and supposedly more intellectually open approaches to understanding which are highlighted in the strategies of enquiry and the interpretive practices of the Denzin and Lincoln (2005a) handbook. In presenting the information, the aim here is not to peddle a new orthodoxy of 'techniques' per se, but to encourage soft sciences/critical/interpretive researchers in Tourism Studies (and related fields) to look over the methodological fence and reflect upon what other researchers are struggling with or freshly contemplating in their own qualitative/ phenomenological bailiwicks (see Hollinshead 2006 here).

Exhibit 4.2 Trends in the theory and craft of qualitative inquiry: social justice practices with a bearing on postdisciplinarity

The key issues according to the contributors to Denzin and Lincoln (2005a)

A synthesis of some of the recent trends in critical and interpretive practice that are consonant with the call for postdisciplinary approaches.

1   **A sensitivity towards understanding about_multiple worlds/multiple truths**
    Recent corrective and/or freshly energised critical and interpretive practices generally hover around a sensitivity to the muiltiplicity of worlds that exist, many of which are non-mutual with dominant 'Western'/'Eurocentric'/'North Atlantic' worldviews. Soft science researchers have to beware of thinking and appearing monologically as they learn to think differently about the different registers of being and the varied layers of meaning which exist not only across the continents (in perhaps distant/removed spaces) but also in urban-industrial places (which might perhaps be 'closer to home'). Soft scientists have to frequently learn to look beyond the limited scope of interdisciplinary and multi-disciplinary approaches to tap the more flexible understandings of counterdisciplinary, postdisciplinary, and adisciplinary thoughtlines.

2   **A questionning of researcher expertise**
    Recent corrective and/or freshly energised critical and interpretive practices generally necessitate that the researcher guards against axiomatic reliance upon the 'Western'/'patriarchal' canon, and thereby learns to avoid the flaunting of received orthodoxies which trample over local/indigenous/other forms of knowing. Soft science researchers have to come to terms with – when called in as specialists on particular matters – the dilemmas of expertise. They might indeed have conventional forms of understanding that have some ubiquity to them, but they must guard against undue reliance upon prefabricated sorts of knowledge, and against trite and insincere forms of evaluatory research/participative planning which might be based on facile or hollow styles of constructivism (social constructivism/social constructionism).

3   **A strong interest in collaborative forms of research**
    Recent corrective and/or freshly energised critical and interpretive practices tend to look beyond the gain of lukewarm or short-term forms of rapport with

local/indigenous/other populations, and respect the more demanding need to cultivate longer-term forms of complicity in the research effort. Soft science researchers have commonly to learn to operate within cogenerative styles of inquiry rather than relying automatically upon top-down processes. The rise in engagement in these 'public' or 'communal' styles of ethnography will frequently demand that the researcher (from outside the group/population in question) has to take time and effort to understand how it may have been seething (in under the surface ways and not just in immediately articulated ones); he/she may also have to build in time and effort to not just uncover lost/hidden voices, but to be agentic in helping those voices be heard and understood in authoritative fashion.

4   **A recognition of the need for ethnoesthetic insight**
Recent corrective and/or freshly energised critical and interpretive practices often give rise to the researcher indulging in 'border crossing' activities where he/she has to be competent at operating both within the developing social science conceptual academy and within local/emic contextual settings and ways-of-valuing-things. Soft science researchers have thereby to develop competency at blurring the genres, by mixing intelligence that may have come academically from what have formerly been distinct corners of the humanities (such as, perhaps, 'feminism', 'continental philosophy', 'anthropological inquiry', 'whatever') with cosmological insights from the sacred or the secular inheritances of the space/place in question. In so doing, the researcher must learn how to listen acutely when the poesis (the ethnopoesis) is different from what he/she is used to, or from that of neighbouring peoples in that locality or that milieu. Such are the ethnoaesthetic demands of moral entrepreneurship, where (on occasions) the researcher may inevitably be drawn into (and ought to respect) the call for revolutionary pedagogy.

5   **A suspension of conclusive judgments in the interpretation of culture**
Recent corrective and/or freshly energised critical and interpretive practices generally require the researcher to learn to think otherwise (as points 1 to 4 above, have stressed): this is not an easy craft to learn, and commonly occasions the need for long periods of in situ engagement. Soft science researchers have to learn to resist jumping to early judgements about who is doing what to whom and when and why in cultural or cosmological settings which are foreign to them, and they have to particularly guard against prematurely celebrating a singular, new, 'postcolonial truth' which is (suddenly) advocated by or for an emergent 'postcolonial' population. In the generation of decently substantiated or decently demonstrable new 'local knowledge', the goal is often not the development of a single (all-purpose) truth, but the contextual mapping of 'varieties of truth'. Such contextual monitoring may regularly involve the heavy use of internarrative skills and competencies.

6   **A strong support of and for counter-enlightenment thinking**
Recent creative and/or freshly energised critical and interpretive practice will often involve the researcher promoting counter-enlightenment forms of knowing which run unequivocally in counter-direction to dominant or normalised ways of viewing the world. Soft science researchers must take care (in projecting such counter-philosophies or counter-practices) to avoid working within kneejerk, binary, or preconceived views about who or what that 'other'/'counter-enlightenment' population is. They may need to work with

conviction and force to help smash the walls-of-presumption that have denied or neutralized the counter-truth in the past, and they may need to convince many mainstream observers (including themselves!) to place less reliance upon 'sight', and more upon steadily corroborated or decently confirmed understandings. At all times, the soft science researcher will need to self-regulate against the commonplace and slippery ventriloquisms involved in 'speaking for others'. On occasions, in the projection of counter-truths, the researcher may need to engage in particular acts of cultural objectification/cultural reification by indulging in forms of strategic essentialism – which itself may seemingly run counter to his/her 'orthodox' or 'received' social science teaching.

7   **A strong support of and for indigenous meaning and voice**
Recent corrective and/or freshly energised critical and interpretive practices are inclined to warn of the danger of preconceiving people or things in binary ('they are different than us') fashion concerning the other population being encountered. Soft science researchers – in particularly dealing with indigenous populations in distant/removed locations – often have to work via difficult-to-grasp forms of spiral discourse in order to understand indigenous forms of the sacred and/or the secular, and they must recognise that many such peoples will inevitably seek to mask or hide their precious knowledge and traditions. Again, in dealing with indigenous populations, it has to be stressed that the making visible of revered things and beliefs is demanding of considerable ethnopoetic and ethnopolitical craft on the part of the usually etic researcher. Many such 'outsider' investigators have to learn to drop their received or established predilection for 'theme-work' inquiry, and replace it with 'voice-generative' approaches which are designed to empower the right sort of elder/authority figure/spokesperson from that indigenous/host/culture-carrying people to speak in the right sort of settings for that poulation.

8   **A recognition of the frequent need for aggressive 'new-sense' sense-making**
Recent corrective and/or freshly energised critical and interpretive practices tend to heed the lessons of 'resistance postmodernism' of the 1980s and 1990s and accept the need (on occasions) for external researchers to help internal community or group members (in the populations they are dealing with) engage in distinct forms of defiance, impediment, or prevention towards some felt cultural invasion or cosmological intrusion. Soft science researchers often have to learn not just the how, when, and where of sense-making, but the geographies and temporalities of bona fide aggressive sense-making. Often working via triage-calculative forms of para-ethnography in close harmony with lead members of the local 'concerned population' (in lieu of working via at-distance styles of conventional ethnography), the embedded researcher may need to help communicate potent statements (testimonies) which have been freshly generated/systematically generated on the issue in question – or they may need to conduct their engaged research in and with that population via decidedly more attritional sorts of counter-hegemonic action.

9   **A regular appreciation of the need to situate things and events within broader cultural meanings**
Recent corrective and/or freshly engaged critical and interpretive practices are inclined to stress the need for 'closeness' and 'engagement' at the expense of

the old tenets of 'objectivity' and 'neutrality'; such embedded and iterative styles of understanding commonly require the researchers to work not so much with found 'gatekeepers' or happenstance 'informants', but with a stronger pool or team of knowledge-cogenerators who are appointed by and within that community, and with whom a more durable relationship has to be established. Soft science researchers have to reflexively cultivate the skill to work via a strong commitment to ethical relationships in/amongst/with their co-researchers in this perduring fashion, 'working at the hyphens' of established and emergent understanding to generate broad (broader?) understanding of the cultural and contextual meaning of things. Thus, experienced soft scientists today learn the competencies of searching for (and co-deciphering) the preludial (i.e. the beyond-the-immediate-awareness) reach of things. Such matters of cultural architectonics commonly bond that people to the environment in particular ways, but they may have other not immediately apparent cosmological connectivities which the researcher may need time and painstaking effort to recognise and identify.

10 **An awareness of the general need for a more open cultural/social/psychic/ political imaginary (able to accommodate the cosmologies of different populations)**
Recent corrective and/or freshly energised critical and interpretive practices (as raised in points 1 to 9 above) cumulatively demand the fertilisation of a wider imaginary to receive and describe 'other populations'. Today, soft science researchers generally have to learn to work with more open-to-the-future cognitions of and about the world, which are polycultural (rather than multicultural) in their significances. At times these more responsive (yet always reflexive) efforts to uncover the imaginary worlds of others will necessarily involve the close reading of what may have been 'hidden', 'unrealised', radical or 'under-realised' human possibilities, or it may necessitate the co-production of a radical politics of possibility. In particular cases where a felt oppression or deep subjectification of an inspected population has been felt or identified, the engaged soft scientist ought nowadays also expect himself/ herself to become involved in the hard praxis of militant utopian cultural criticism in order to faithfully carry out the co-productive research act.

In encouraging Tourism Studies researchers towards more open-to-the-future styles of inquiry which can accommodate what Holmes and Marcus (2005: 1100) call *collateral counterpart knowledge*, the intent (in presenting the information in Exhibit 4.2) is to encourage soft science (and hard science!) researchers in Tourism Studies to reflect upon how the mindsets they currently operate with (and within!) might be heavily collusive with existing hegemonic (?)/still-imperialising (?)/still-colonising structures of understanding (Smith 2005: 91). Hopefully, such reflexive critique might help even stalwarts in Critical Tourism Studies recognise that they themselves still conceivably serve as hegemonic/imperialist/colonialist servants of penetrative forms of undue metropolitan or urban-industrial surveillance, wherever their studies take them to across the continents (after Smith 2005: 87). A self-critique based on the open-to-the-future thinking which is frequently explicitly (and often implicitly) espoused in and amongst the mentalities of the contributors – and (hopefully and faithfully) captured here in Exhibit 4.2 – can be manifest in helping the given soft science researcher in Tourism Studies not only reimagine the rights of 'other', 'indigenous', and 'distant' peoples, but can help the said investigator more collaboratively and deeply appreciate just where, when, and why dominant centrifugal cognitions are resisted by (perhaps) an other, an indigenous, a distant population in the particular elsewhere. If that appreciation is recognised, then that activist and hopefully open-to-different-futures – and, conceivably, that postdisciplinary – researcher can actively learn where, when, and why he/she (herself) must act to disrupt the ruling governances of (perhaps) neo-positivist thought and sight, or (perhaps) of lingering imperialising/colonising though and sight.

Endnote: the prospects for the adoption of postdisciplinary architectures of knowing

Since space is at a premium in the short chapter for this book, no expansion can be offered here to clarify or qualify the ten key issues given in Exhibit 4.2. All that may be immediately stated is that soft science researchers who are (in bona fide fashion) heavily embedded in or engaged upon a good number of the ten critical and interpretive practices (as highlighted in the exhibit) are already active or 'proto postdisciplinarians'. Only personal preference and the passage of time will tell whether they want to become (or declare themselves to be!) card-carrying-members of this movement (?)/this church (?)/this fellowship (?) of like critical methodologists. But many will resist such labelling: it is the mere winning of other multiple, contesting, and open knowledges and the development of broader imaginations that will tend to count for them.

Hopefully the proposed International Conference on *Postdisciplinarity In and For Global Tourism Studies* (currently mooted for November 2011 at NHTV University in The Netherlands) can indeed help the field of Tourism Studies move to embrace more open and responsive forms of knowing which are rather more dialectically fluid and anti-canonical. Hopefully this long overdue conference (being nurtured by a team chaired in Breda by Professor Vincent Platenkamp) can help encourage the international field of Tourism Studies towards what Thomas (an Australian ethnographer on the reach and agency of the historicist normalisations of tourism and travel [see Thomas 1994]) called the imperative need for *exhilarative trespass* across and beyond our received forms of knowing.

References

Agathangelou, A. M. and Ling, L. H. M. (2009) *Transforming World Politics: from empire to multiple worlds*, London: Routledge.

Appadurai, A. (1996) *Modernity at Large: cultural dimensions of globalisation*, Minneapolis: University of Minnesota Press.

Atkinson, P. and Delamont, S. (2005) 'Analytic perspectives', in N. K. Denzin and Y. S. Lincoln (eds), *The Sage Handbook of Qualitative Research*, Thousand Oaks, CA: Sage, pp. 821–840.

Bauman, Z. (2000) *Liquid Modernity*, Cambridge: Polity.

Beier, J. M. and Arnold, S. L. (2005) 'Becoming undisciplined: towards the supradisciplinary study of security', *International Studies Review*, 7 (1): 41–62.

Bhabha, H. (1994) *The Location of Culture*, London: Routledge.

Blunt, A. and Wills, J. (2000) *Dissident Geographies: an intrduction to radical issues and practice*, Harlow, UK: Pearson-Education.

Checkland, P. (1981) *Systems Thinking, Systems Practice*, New York: Wiley.

Clayton, D. (2008) 'Imperial geographies', in J. S. Duncan, N. C. Johnson, and R. C. Schein (eds), *A Companion to Cultural Geography*, Malden, MA: Blackwell, pp. 446–468.

Coles, T., Hall, C. M. and Duval, D. T. (2006) 'Tourism and post-disciplinary enquiry', *Current Issues in Tourism*, 9 (4, 5): 293–319.

Crick, M. (1989) 'Representations of international tourism in the social sciences: sun, sex, sights, savings, and servility', *Annual Review of Anthropology*, 18: 307–344.

Crush, J. (1994) 'Postcolonialism, decolonization, and geography', in A. Godlewska and N. Smith (eds), *Geography and Empire*, Oxford: Blackwell.

Denzin, N. K. and Lincoln, Y. S. (eds) (2005a) *The Sage Handbook of Qualitative Research*, Thousand Oaks, CA: Sage.

Denzin, N. K. and Lincoln, Y. S. (2005b) 'Introduction: the discipline and practice of qualitative research', in N. K. Denzin and Y. S. Lincoln (eds), *The Sage Handbook of Qualitative Research*, Thousand Oaks, CA: Sage, pp. 1–32.

Echtner, C. and Jamal, T. B. (1997) 'The disciplinary dilemma of tourism studies', *Annals of Tourism Research*, 24 (4), pp. 868–883.

Ellingson, L. L. (2009) *Engaging Crystallization in Qualitative Research: an introduction*, Los Angeles: Sage.

Finley, S. (2005) 'Arts-based inquiry: performing revolutionary pedagogy', in N. K. Denzin and Y. S. Lincoln (eds), *The Sage Handbook of Qualitative Research*, Thousand Oaks, CA: Sage, pp. 681–694.

Franklin, A. and Crang, M. (2001) 'The trouble with tourism and travel theory', *Tourist Studies*, 1: 5–22.

Gilroy, P. (1997) *The Black Atlantic: modernity and double consciousness*, London: Verso.

Goeldner, C. R. (2005) 'Reflections on the historic role of journals in shaping tourism knowledge', *The Journal of Tourism Studies*, 16 (2): 44–51.

Goeldner, M. J. (2001) *Cultural Metaphors: readings, research translations, and commentary*, Thousand Oaks, CA: Sage.

Hall, C. M. (1992) *Tourism and Politics: policy, power, and place*, Chichester: John Wiley.

Hollinshead, K. (2006) 'The shift to constructivism in social inquiry: some pointers for tourism studies', *Tourism Recreation Research*, 31 (2): 43–58.

Hollinshead, K. (in press) 'Tourism studies and confined understanding: the call for a "new sense" postdisciplinary imagination', *Tourism Analysis*. [For publication in 2011.]

Holmes, D. R. and Marcus, G. E. (2004) 'Cultures of expertise and the management of globalization: toward the refunction of ethnography', in A. Ong and S. J. Collier (eds), *Global Assemblages: technology, politics, and ethics as anthropological problems*, London: Blackwell, pp. 232–252.

Holmes, D. R. and Marcus, G. E. (2005) 'Refunctioning ethnography: the challenge of anthropology and the contemporary', in N. K. Denzin and Y. S. Lincoln (eds), *The Sage Handbook of Qualitative Research*, Thousand Oaks, CA: Sage, pp. 1099–1114.

Imayatullah, N. and Blaney, D. L. (2004) *International Relations and the Problem of Difference*, New York: Routledge.

Kincheloe, J. L. (2001) 'Describing the bricolage: conceptualizing a new rigor in qualitative research', *Qualitative Inquiry*, 7 (6): 679–672.

Kincheloe, J. L. (2005) 'On the next level: continuing the conceptualisation of the bricolage', *Qualitative Inquiry*, 11–3: 323–350.

Kukla, A. (2000) *Social Constructivism and the Philosophy of Science*, London: Routledge.

Loomba, A. (1998) *Colonialism/Postcolonialism*, London: Routledge.

Marcus, G. (2001) 'From rapport under erasure to the theater of complicit reflexivities', *Qualitative Inquiry*, 7: 519–528.

Miller, J. G. (1978) *Living Systems*, New York: McGraw-Hill.

Repko, A. F. (2008) *Interdisciplinary Research: process and theory*, Los Angeles: Sage.

Smith, L. T. (2005) 'On tricky ground: researching the native in the age of uncertainty', in N. K. Denzin and Y. S. Lincoln (eds), *The Sage Handbook of Qualitative Research*, Thousand Oaks, CA: Sage, pp. 85–108.

Thomas, N. (1994) *Colonialism's Culture: anthropology, travel, and government*, Princeton: Princeton University Press.

Tribe, J. (1997) 'The indiscipline of tourism', *Annals of Tourism Research*, 24 (3): 638–657.

Tribe, J. (2001) 'Research paradigms and the tourism curriculum', *Journal of Travel Research*, 39 (4): 442–448.

Tribe, J. (2004) 'Knowing about tourism: epistemological issues', in J. Phillimore and L. Goodson (eds), *Qualitative Research in Tourism: ontologies, epistemological methodologies*, London: Routledge, pp. 46–62.

Tribe, J. (2006) 'The truth about tourism', *Annals of Tourism Research*, 33 (2): 360–381.

Urry, J. (2002) 'Social networks, travel, and talk', *British Journal of Sociology*, 54 (2): 155–175.

Venn, C. (2006) *The Postcolonial Challenge: towards alternative worlds*, London: Sage.

Vickers, J. 1998. '"[U]framed in open unmapped fields": Teaching the practice of interdisciplinarity', *Arachne: An Interdisciplinary Journal of the Humanities*, 4 (2): 11–42.

Part II

Critical tourism education

Nigel Morgan

There has been a dramatic growth in global tourism education provision but in the midst of this expansion, more voices are arguing that undergraduate and postgraduate programmes need to better prepare students for the pressing challenges which confront the tourism industry and the wider world. Driving these calls is a recognition that universities need to move beyond a present-minded, narrowly focused industry-serving curriculum to one which looks long-term to the attainment of a more sustainable human and planetary future. The following five chapters demonstrate that such a transformation requires a restructuring of the education system (Sheldon, Fesenmaier and Tribe), the transformation of universities from 'ivory towers' to 'watch towers' (Lidburd and Hjalager), the willingness of the academy to build strong coalitions for change (Schwarzin), and tourism scholars to have the courage and foresight to embrace new intellectual engagements (Liburd and Hjalager, Leopold, Caton and Schwarzin).

This part of the book is opened by Pauline Sheldon, Daniel Fesenmaier and John Tribe, who contend that there is a pressing need to radically overhaul the tourism education system – not merely in terms of its content but also in terms of its delivery. They outline a framework for the future development of tourism education, one that is values-based, proactive and action-oriented as proposed by the Tourism Education Futures Initiative (TEFI). Crucially, this initiative foregrounds ethics, stewardship, knowledge, professionalism and mutuality and advocates that universities prepare tourism graduates to be responsible leaders and destination stewards. This chapter is followed by Janne Lidburd and Anne-Mette Hjalager's essay on the emerging new order of copyleft intellectual creativity, prompted by the novel learning environments facilitated by Web 2.0 platforms such as INNOTOUR. Lidburd and Hjalager illustrate fresh ways of knowledge building, learning and collaborating in tourism education. They argue that such new knowledge pathways require everyone with a stake in education – researchers, educators, students and business users – to adopt different behavioural ethics, pedagogies, and modes of collaboration and critical reflexivity.

This is a serious challenge since, as Peter McLaren and Nathalia Jaramillio underlined in their foreword essay, today's universities are dominated by neoliberal managerial structures and market values. Of course, such philosophies are not uncontested and as Theresa Leopold comments in Chapter 7, there is a growing sense that tourism curricula should develop more critical thinkers. She firmly moves the discussion into the classroom to consider critical thinking, its role in subject and pedagogic knowledge content and how it can be encouraged. Leopold contends that, through critical thinking, we can truly develop the university classroom as a place where educators and students engage in co-transformative dialogue and creative conversations to build environments of learning, knowledge and scholarship.

In the next chapter, Kellee Caton reminds us that we enter all our tourism encounters (whether in the classroom or the wider world) with our heads full of broader cultural imaginaries, mythologies and memories, which challenge us to consider tourism's worldmaking power (see Hollinshead, this volume). Our ability to recognise and reflect on this power is, however, stifled by the dominant hyper-real and infantilising discourses and technologies, which have real consequences for our contemporary tourism educational encounters and tourism experiences. Caton argues that the strength of our determination to think creatively and critically as researchers and educators will decide the extent to which we can transform our interactions inside and outside the classroom. This line of thought is then developed by Lisa Schwarzin, who reflects on her own experiences as a tourism postgraduate student to consider education as an inspirational and empowering force. She argues that too many student experiences are ones of passivity and domination as universities increasingly serve as mere gatekeepers to the professional world. Fittingly closing part two, Schwarzin concludes with an empassioned call to action, contending that transforming the educational process into a genuine partnership between students and educators offers change possibilities rather than 'certain' predictabilities and creates real opportunities for pedagogies of hope.

5 The Tourism Education Futures Initiative (TEFI)

Activating change in tourism education[1]

Pauline J. Sheldon, Daniel R. Fesenmaier and John Tribe

Introduction

Tourism is a hallmark activity of the postmodern world. As such, it is a significant factor in world-making and people-making. The same can be said for universities – they are major enterprises and, historically, have been important sources of innovative thinking and change. The intersection of tourism and universities is, therefore, a powerful nexus of potential influence. From an industry perspective, tourism employment in the coming decades must have a very different profile than it does today. In 2020, students will be applying for jobs that do not even exist today, and much of what we teach our students is obsolete by the time they graduate. Students entering the uncertain world of the future and, in particular, the vulnerable tourism sector needs different skills, aptitudes and knowledge to succeed. To meet the challenges of the next few decades, tourism educational systems, however, are in need of radical change. Indeed, Wallis and Steptoe (2006) and many others argue that a fundamental re-tool and re-design is necessary; not incremental change, but change in the nature of what is taught and how it is taught. Further, skills and knowledge sets must be redefined, structures and assumptions need to be questioned; thus, the 'old ways of doing things' must be transcended.

The challenges facing the tourism industry and tourism educators call out for a new paradigm of tourism education. In an attempt to address these challenges, the Tourism Education Futures Initiative (TEFI) was born by a few concerned tourism educators (Sheldon *et al.* 2008). The purpose of this chapter is to outline a framework developed by TEFI for the future development of tourism education. Its content is based on the input of about 80 experienced educators and industry leaders who met four times between 2007 and 2010 to discuss and debate the need for change and to provide recommendations for a framework for a new tourism curriculum for 2015–2030. Specifically TEFI has the following mission: *TEFI seeks to provide vision, knowledge and a framework for tourism education programs to promote global citizenship and optimism for a better world.* The vision of TEFI is to not only work to reshape tourism education worldwide, but to help the leaders of the tourism industry follow practices that are rooted in basic values.

The TEFI was born in 2007 when a few tourism educators and industry met in Vienna, Austria to discuss the status of tourism education. During this meeting, a process emerged that provides a framework for the development of TEFI. Subsequent meetings in Hawaii, USA, Lugano, Switzerland, and San Sebastian, Spain built on the work in Vienna. TEFI is organized around a process which is both *proactive* and *action oriented*, focusing on translating the core values articulated by the participants into implementation to bring about fundamental change in tourism education.

An important initial outcome of the TEFI process is a set of five values-based principles that tourism students should embody upon graduation to become responsible leaders and stewards for the destinations (including hospitality and other tourism related businesses and organizations) where they work or live. The five value sets are: Ethics, Stewardship, Knowledge, Professionalism, and Mutuality, and are discussed in more detail later in this paper. They are portrayed as interlocking values because of their interconnectedness and their permeability. This paper provides more detail on these value sets, how they can be incorporated into the learning experience for tourism students, and examples of courses incorporating these values.

Another dimension of the TEFI process is the Working Groups that develop a range of tools for educating tourism students. These Working Groups are now involved in a number of activities including: a faculty and student Code of Ethics; an outreach pilot program to universities worldwide; and a 'values inventory' to be used as part of program assessment. Working Groups are currently finalizing their tools and outcomes. The next TEFI meeting will be the *TEFI World Congress: Activating Change in Tourism Education* at Temple University Philadelphia, USA, May 18–21, 2011. Educators and industry leaders from around the world are invited to attend.

Background and rationale

The intersection of the tourism industry and universities is a powerful nexus for tourism education in that both universities and tourism are products of the world —hence, a paradox exists in that they are both shaped by the world and have the potential to shape it. This paradox presents a challenge for tourism educators. Being part of the world, and not distant or removed from it, is of course important so that academics do not retreat to ineffectual ivory towers. That is to say, they should offer participation as well as critique and therefore universities should not just become places of critique. They should contribute to a productive world by developing a highly skilled workforce. But being shaped by the world also means that tourism education faces a number of challenges.

The first of these challenges is avoidance of unthinking reproduction (Apple 1990). Here, the existing world model and machine, buttressed with solid structures and deeply impregnated by ideology (Althusser 1984) has an innate tendency to reproduce itself in its current form. If caught in this simple, yet possibly blind cycle of reproduction, students learn to fit in passively to the world that exists (Minogue 1973) rather than to create challenging vistas.

Related to this is a second tendency to concentrate on means rather than ends. That is to say, our present configuration of the tourism world tends to create a number of immediate problems that need solving (for example in marketing, operations, service quality, and logistics). Universities are called upon to produce human resources that can solve these problems. The urgency of the day to day inevitably competes for space with the equally urgent, but never quite so pressing issues of the future. Here, we can allow the vocational to supplant the philosophical (Tribe 2002), giving insufficient attention to questions of desirable ends and the kind of tourism world we wish to create.

The late 1980s saw the crisis of communism marked by the symbolic fall of the Berlin Wall. The year 2008 saw the crystallization of a third significant challenge—the crisis of capitalism marked by the symbolic fall of major banks including Lehman Brothers. This has surfaced the challenge of appropriate corporate and broader societal values. Here, university business schools have been fiercely criticized for a failure to give adequate attention or leadership to this part of the curriculum for future business leaders.

The fourth challenge relates to sustainability and is neatly captured by Giddens' Paradox (Giddens 2009). This is the paradox of climate change where Giddens notes that since we are not currently unduly affected by the outcomes of climate change we fail to act. But when we are finally pressed into action by its consequences, it will be too late to do anything about them.

The fifth challenge is that tourism might be read as another product of some form of Washington Consensus (Williamson 1997). For example, its terms of trade (between supplier and consumer), its rules of engagement, its allowed and disallowed moves, its tolerance of inequality, indeed its general configuration performs to generate a predictable structure of winners and losers legitimized by a script of neoliberalist values.

A sixth and final challenge is that of extent and pace of change. Patterns of consumption, technological change and supply innovation in tourism as elsewhere are in a constant state of transformation. This mean that graduates may find that their degrees only offer a few years of currency rather than a lifetime of expertise (Cooper *et al.* 2007). This clearly stresses the need to understand and promote lifelong learning to underpin professional expertise.

These challenges set the context for TEFI. A central task is to educate tourism graduates (e.g. undergraduate and graduate students) to satisfy the demands of the market place as productive employees for a fast-changing world. The tourism industry expects its workforce to be well trained, and society might expect a contribution from universities in terms of enhanced economic performance. But any deep consideration of the term 'society' generates other inescapable questions about what kind of tourism is to be developed. Here, it is argued that we need to re-think and re-engineer our tourism courses and our students' experiences. Further, it is argued that we ourselves and our graduates need to lead the debate about a set of values that should govern the development of the tourism world. If we achieve this, we would be at the forefront of people-making and world-making through tourism.

The TEFI process

As highlighted previously, the seeds of TEFI are based upon the general recognition that higher education and, more particularly, tourism education must change in order to meet the challenges that face tourism and society. Additionally, it was recognized that many people (e.g. academicians, teachers, industry professionals, and government leaders) throughout the world have expressed their concerns regarding the future. Led by these voices, a number of innovators concerned about the future of tourism education met in Vienna, Austria to discuss the status of tourism education and to assess the degree to which there was an agreement concerning the need to develop alternative models for tourism education. During this meeting, a process emerged that provides a framework for the growth and development of TEFI. That is, TEFI is largely organized around a process that is both *proactive* and *action oriented*, focusing on translating the core values it has articulated into action and implementation to create a fundamental change in tourism education. The TEFI process includes two important action settings: 1. An Annual Summit, which brings together innovators from around the world to consider issues related to tourism education; and, 2. Working Groups, which throughout the year seek to develop tools that can be used to affect tourism education.

The Annual Summit has been comprised of 30–40 leading scholars and industry professionals and has included a series of lectures and breakout discussion groups. The lectures are conducted to stimulate thinking and to challenge the status quo. For example in the first Summit, Dr. Jim Dator, a leading futurist from the University of Hawaii, challenged the TEFI members to develop scenarios of future worlds, and then to propose possible solutions/responses to these scenarios. In the second Summit, Dr. John Tribe (University of Surrey) articulated a vision of hope for the future of society and tourism education, in particular. But he also challenged the group to take personal responsibility in shaping this future world. Dr. Gianna Moscardo (James Cook University) focused on the learning styles of the next generation, arguing that how we teach is just as important as what we teach. And, Scott Meis, former director of research for the Tourism Industry Association of Canada, demonstrated quite conclusively that the industry need for qualified employees will become even more critical over the next decade. The third Summit focused on barriers to change within universities (as discussed by Dr. Thomas Bieger of the University of St. Gallen) and strategies for programmatic change (as exemplified in lectures by Drs. Irena Ateljevic, Simon Wong, Loredana Padurean, and Betsy Barber). These presentations clearly demonstrated barriers and potential strategies for changing educational processes within the university; they also highlighted a number of conflicts within higher education in realizing the changes. The fourth Summit in San Sebastian, Spain focused on the status of the Working

Groups and the various tasks they have considered over the year, and on preparation for the TEFI World Congress to be held at Temple University, Philadelphia, USA, May 18–21, 2011.

While the "lectures" provide the starting point of discussion, the main work of TEFI is in the breakout groups that provide the setting for ideation, creativity, dialog and problem resolution. Throughout the TEFI Summits, the group members are tasked to develop position statements regarding the various issues related to the theme of the annual meeting. Then, the results of these efforts were presented to the entire TEFI body for clarification and ultimate approval.

The second pillar of the TEFI process is the Working Group. These Groups are tasked to move the TEFI agenda forward between Summits by providing essential energy and direction resulting in concrete action-oriented tools that can be used by TEFI. For example, prior to the first TEFI Summit, a Working Group identified a core set of readings that established a foundation—a common language and set of ideas and ideals—for discussion. In addition, the Working Group conducted a pre-meeting survey of participants regarding key knowledge and skill sets needed for the tourism graduate of the future. Three different Working Groups emerged from the first Summit, focusing on defining a set of values to drive the TEFI agenda forward, identifying case studies in values-based education, and evaluating outcome-based education as a tool to assess programmatic changes. Each of the Working Groups developed working papers and presentations that are then presented and discussed at the next TEFI Summit.

And finally, as the result of the third Summit, a series of Working Groups were identified to create concrete "tools" for supporting TEFI-based initiatives. These Working Groups included proposing a Faculty Code of Ethics, developing an outreach pilot program to universities worldwide, and developing a 'values inventory,' which may be used as part of program assessment.

TEFI values

The first TEFI Summit explored various futuristic scenarios of society that tourism education programs would need to adapt to. It was decided that attempting to modify tourism education programs to fit a multitude of possible world scenarios, or even a single preferred scenario was a task fraught with too much specificity and too much uncertainty. Instead, a consensus among TEFI participants concluded that whatever the world scenario in the future, certain values would provide the students with the foundation to meet the multitude of uncertainties of the future. Given this consensus, the work of TEFI moved to define these value sets.

The five values-based principles that TEFI identified to be embodied in tourism education programs so that students become responsible leaders and stewards for the destinations where they work or live are shown in Figure 5.1. Specifically the five values are: ethics, stewardship, knowledge, professionalism, and mutuality. They are conceptually portrayed as interlocking value principles demonstrating their interconnectedness and permeability. It is envisioned by TEFI members that educators can use subsets of the five value principles to integrate into their courses

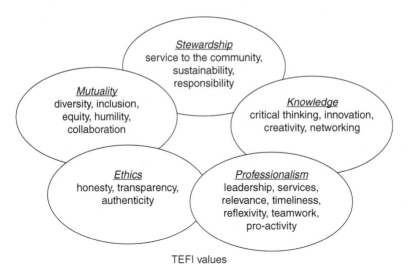

Figure 5.1 The TEFI values of tourism education.

as appropriate. Each values-based principle is discussed below with an emphasis on how that concept can be incorporated into the tourism student learning process. For each principle we describe its definition, the content that should be included in the learning experience, and specific learning objectives.

Ethics

Definition

Ethics is concerned with distinguishing between behavior that is right and behavior that is wrong. It is the basis for good action and provides a framework for judging actions that are questionable. Ethical behavior means striving for actions that are deemed "good" based on principles and values. It also involves making such principles and values explicit and rendering the processes that lead to decisions transparent. Recognizing that good actions do not occur in a vacuum but are derived from specific value systems further requires understanding and respect for actions based on different systems.

Content

Teaching ethics involves:

1   Introducing students to ethics as a field of study with practical importance:

   a   defining ethics;

    b   encouraging reflexivity and decolonization of the self;

    c   recognizing diversity;

    d   outlining the practical importance of ethical behavior;

    e   discussing the specific issues and challenges in the context of tourism;

    f   exemplifying the implications of unethical behavior;

    g   identifying the stakeholders in certain ethical dilemmas.

2   Exposing students to different ethical traditions and principles:

    a   helping students understand what traditions and principles exist (e.g. Utilitarianism, Kantian ethic of respect for others, Aristotelian virtue ethics, religion, principles of benevolence, honesty, autonomy, justice, etc.);

    b   explaining the evolution of these traditions;

    c   illustrating how these traditions and principles influence actions;

    d   highlighting differences and potential areas of conflict.

3   Equipping students with the means to achieve reconciliation:

    a   explaining how ethics inform judgment;

    b   engaging students in principles of negotiation;

    c   illustrating ways in which conflicts can be resolved and compromises reached.

4   Drawing connections to issues of power and politics:

    a   identifying sources of power;

    b   discussing the importance and principles of the legitimization of power;

    c   emphasizing the role of existing power structures in determining ethical outcomes.

5   Evoking actions:

    a   exposing students to sources which can guide their actions;

    b   encouraging students to develop their own codes of conduct;

    c   having students identify and implement good actions.

Specific student learning objectives in the tourism context

Students who study ethics in the tourism context should be able to:

- recognize its importance in general and specifically for tourism;
- judge their own and others' actions;
- value transparency;
- respect different ethical traditions/approaches;
- identify potential and actual conflicts and set actions in place to mitigate them;
- know which resources are available when dealing with ethical concerns;
- provide ethical leadership and initiate changes for the better.

Knowledge

Definition

Knowledge can be described as: 1. expertise and skills acquired by a person through experience or education; 2. the theoretical or practical understanding of a subject, 3. facts and information about a field, or 4. awareness or familiarity gained by experience of a fact or situation. This implies that knowledge is more than data (summary descriptions of parts of the world around us) and more than information (data put into a context). Knowledge comes in both explicit and tacit formats. In most instances, it is not possible to have an exhaustive understanding of an information domain so knowledge is ceaselessly incomplete. Knowledge is created through processes of selecting, connecting, and reflecting. Knowledge is always already predicated by existing knowledge, which means that knowledge involves interpretation and contextualization and existing knowledge should be challenged.

Content

The knowledge creation process should address *creativity*, *critical thinking*, and *networking* for change and innovation through complex cognitive processes of perception, reasoning, learning, communication, association, and application.

Creativity

Creativity has been identified as a key factor to adequately address the seismic changes facing contemporary society and as a driving force towards knowledge creation and socio-economic advancements (European University Association 2007). It is often useful to explicitly distinguish between creativity and innovation. Creativity is typically used to refer to the act of producing new ideas, approaches or actions that are appropriate to the problem at hand, while innovation often begins with creative ideas and involves a process of both generating *and applying* such creative ideas in a specific context for a human, cultural, or economic purposes. The ethical dimension of creativity and creative knowledge should be addressed. Dealing with future insecurity and uncertainty requires "thinking outside the box," looking at existing domains and problems from a new angle. Promoting such a culture of creativity that acknowledges and seeks to learn from failure encourages students to move from hypothesis and conventional knowledge towards possibilities and originality. Creativity and knowledge formation takes place in an organizational set-up, for example but not exclusively, in the format of educational institutions or business organizations. It is essential to envisage outcomes consisting of both factual and procedural knowledge, and that finding a balance between the two are essential for the comprehension and application of knowledge.

Critical thinking

Critical thinking calls for an unrelenting examination of any form of knowledge and the knowledge creation process to recognize the existence (or non-existence) of the use and power that supports it and the further conclusions to which it tends. It is important that knowledge is contextualized in order to recognize unstated assumptions and values. Critical thinking is not only about criticizing but being critical of the constitution of knowledge and underlying dogmas. Students should therefore be encouraged to make the implicit explicit and identify ethnocentric bias and prejudice whenever deciding upon or solving a problem. Embodying an ethical dimension in mainstream disciplines in social sciences can enrich the thinking and add relevant dimensions of critical thinking, not only for the critique as an academic exercise, but critique as part of a constructive pursuit. Responsible citizenship evolves through knowledge enhancing critical thinking.

Networking

The dissemination and development of knowledge take place in social environments. Social networks can create or assist in refining the use of knowledge. Bridging social networks can link different repositories of knowledge with the potential innovation effects. Networks and knowledge repositories are become more open as a consequence of the development of technical and institutional remedies connected to the social media. Hereby, problem solving and identification increasingly take place through sharing and cooperation in open knowledge systems, where providers and users of knowledge meet and exchange information. Students and higher institutions of education must understand and address the issues of open knowledge sources and open innovation, which are in contrast to issues of knowledge hoarding, protection and monopolizing in closed learning environments. New ways of thinking about the professions are essential. Higher educational institutions must prepare students to become practitioners, researchers, philosophical scholars, and knowledge brokers throughout their studies and in their subsequent careers.

Specific student learning objectives in the tourism context

As a phenomenon, industry, career and lifestyle tourism constitutes exceptional learning opportunities. The specific student learning objectives in the tourism context are:

- understanding the value and power of knowledge rather than data or information;
- the art and skill of sharing knowledge, including new codes of conduct;
- harvesting from new knowledge intermediaries;
- developing equitable ways of communication with industry and community—across national borders and disciplines;

- humility and courage in the fields of data creation and management, information management and knowledge creation and management;
- the art of questioning the answer—challenge what is taken for granted;
- letting go—risking the adventure of creative journeys, using creativity tools and new ways of collaboration;
- strengthening students' critical thinking skills through interactive teaching processes;
- shifting from solely valuing and rewarding individual achievement toward collective action, participation and contribution.

Stewardship

Definition

Stewardship implies the responsibility to care for something, or someone, and the accountability to exercise responsibility. The value of stewardship is deeply reflected in sustainable development (Lidburd 2010). It implies that the earth is a divine gift, which we are permitted to use and take care of for the benefit of future generations. This definition also suggests that tourism faculty and students should learn to take leadership in three distinct aspects of stewardship:

- sustainability;
- responsibility;
- service to the community.

All stakeholders have responsibility for the environment and society, and power and/or influence are necessary to exercise responsibility. Responsibility also implies the existence of rights. If all stakeholders are to take responsibility for the future of the planet in tourism, empowerment of those who are currently in a position of powerlessness is called for, just as the restraint of power of others may be necessary. Whereas local communities may help facilitate liaison building based on a shared sense of contextual responsibility, it is important to recognize that communities are not homogenous units that easily reach consensus. Service to the community is one way that stakeholders can demonstrate their commitment to taking responsibility.

Content

A frequent claim made in the literature is that sustainable tourism development can be achieved. Arguing that sustainability is achievable over a period of time fails to understand that change and ever-evolving processes are the norm rather than the exception. Choice in lifestyle, cultural preferences, and patterns of consumption and communication are not the same between generations and these are rather unpredictable. Similarly, it is not feasible to assume that tourism that stays the same 'will go on forever' (Hall and Butler 1995: 102). These arguments indicate that the very idea of striking a balance in which the environment, economy and social and cultural elements are in equilibrium can be seen as an oxymoron. Appreciating the complexities of socio-cultural values, quality of life aspirations, and the biophysical and economic systems in which tourism takes place over time, an integrated approach to stewardship is of importance. Consequently also discarding the notion of sustainable development as a goal that can be achieved is called for.

Stewardship implies that individuals and organizations acknowledge their responsibilities and act accordingly. All stakeholders have responsibility for the environment and the society, requiring the use of influence or power. Responsibility and stewardship also imply the existence of rights. If all stakeholders take responsibility for the future of the planet in tourism, empowerment of those who are currently powerless is necessary, as is the restraint of power of other groups. The stakeholders with responsibilities include destination governments, generating country governments, tourism industry firms and organizations, employees, tourists, host communities, media, and investors.

Finally, stewardship includes service to the destination community, allowing stakeholders to take responsibility. In the context of tourism education, in addition to the destination host community other communities worthy of consideration are students, graduates, and the global tourism academic community. Volunteer-tourism is an example of implementing service to the destination community.

In order to implement knowledge of stewardship in the tourism curriculum we propose that students are exposed to debates that will challenge conventional ideas and taken-for-granted discourses. Educators must also consider whether they have the right or the responsibility to inculcate particular values in students. Including stewardship in the tourism curriculum will require this self-reflection by the educators.

The specific learning objectives are:

1 understand social and ecological systems;
2 be able to explain environmental governance and policies;
3 be able to apply adaptive management and adaptive co-management concepts;
4 understand tourists' ecological footprint;
5 understand the precautionary principle;
6 know environmental management systems;
7 understand the relationship between climate change and tourism;
8 understand different kinds of sustainable business practices and operations;
9 know how destinations can be managed to become more sustainable;
10 critically evaluate the impact of their own vacations;
11 undertake tourism-related projects that serve a community;
12 understand the various motivators of stakeholders in the tourism system, and the various power structures between these stakeholders.

Professionalism

Definition

'Professionalism' is a rather nebulous term as it implies not only a profession and the skills, competencies or standards associated with it, but also an attitude and behavior that reflect these. It has also been defined as the ability to align personal and organizational conduct with ethical and professional standards that include a responsibility to the customer or guest and community, a service orientation, and a commitment to lifelong learning and improvement.

Professionalism is defined as incorporating leadership, a practical approach (practicality), attention to services, concern for the relevance and timeliness of evidence, reflexivity, teamwork and partnership building skills, and pro-activity. Pro-activity involves taking the initiative to address problems in one's service domain and a commitment to excellence in one's domain of expertise. According to Bateman and Crant (1993: 105), "[p]roactive people scan for opportunities, show initiative, take action, and persevere until they reach closure by bringing about change. They are pathfinders who change their organization's mission or find and solve problems". This is in keeping with leadership, which is the ability to inspire individual and organizational excellence, to create and attain a shared vision, and to successfully manage change to attain the organization's strategic ends and successful performance.

Content

The core values of professionalism are a requirement for all tourism and hospitality academic programs. It is educators' responsibility to expose students to high quality and appropriate professionalism. The term "new professionalism" is used by Sachs (2003) to distinguish between "old" forms of professionalism which debate characteristics of professions and the extent to which occupational groups might be acknowledged as professions, and "new" forms which, claims Sachs, assume a "changed analytical perspective" and are seen to be more "positive, principled and postmodern" (p. 182). The distinction between old and new forms of professionalism is useful, although the notion that new forms of professionalism are necessarily "positive" and "principled" should be considered with caution, as there is also evidence of a less "principled" discourse in action.

While there is no overall agreement as to what constitutes a profession, certain key aspects are commonly cited that seek claim to professional status. These generally include reference to specialist knowledge, autonomy and responsibility (Hoyle and John 1995). Professionalism, therefore, implies that such characteristics are evident in an individual's work. It is also linked to ethics or ethical behavior. Some refer to it as an emotion, or a feeling of being professional. TEFI appears to include some of both, where professionalism is a series of behaviors and beliefs. To achieve success in the behavior of professionalism requires an attitude (ethical belief) of what makes a true professional. It also seems that leadership is key; because the professional that exhibits the most positive leadership often displays the other components in a positive manner as well.

Specific student learning objectives in the tourism context

The desired learning outcome can be synthesized as having students aspire to the highest levels of professionalism and committed to continuous improvement of that professionalism. The two sections below identify the content to be transferred in the learning process. The way in which this can be done is discussed in general at the end of the two sections.

1 Relevance, timeliness, reflexivity

The rapid evolution of the demand and supply characteristics in the tourism industry require the professional to constantly think in terms of innovation and improvement to their own professionalism and also to the product, the processes and the services delivered. The learning environment must encourage students to understand the importance of timeliness in a variety of professional situations. It must also ensure that students understand that their work must be relevant to the ever-changing environments in the travel industry. It must also introduce the students to the importance of reflecting on their work and contributions.

The learning process must help students understand which information is relevant to address the issue at hand, the importance of timeliness in the decision-making process, and the need to reflect on the outcome once decisions have been made. It is critical that students understand the options available and can assess the appropriateness of each of the areas that might require attention and/or investment in the quest for professionalism. These three qualities of relevance, timeliness, and reflexivity are important in their contribution to the tourism product, process, and service innovation and improvement also. Innovation is often high risk, and involves *substantial investment in people*, time and money. All dimensions of professionalism can be introduced in a sector by adopting accreditation and certification schemes.

2 Practicality, partnership, leadership

Tourism is an inherently conservative industry; slowly reacting to market trends and demands rather than predicting and preparing for them. Within reason and practicality, the ability of operators to discard their risk aversion is one of the first steps to take in becoming more innovative and, ultimately, more successful. Professionalism is critical when we look at the roles played inside the organisation, at all levels. It is the tertiary sector where the organizational competencies such as leadership, practicality, relevance, timeliness, reflexivity, teamwork, and partnership are critical needs.

Innovation pivots on intrinsically motivated individuals, within a supportive culture, informed by a broad sense of the future. Intrinsic innovation in the workplace evolves from an environment in which new ideas and creative thinking are genuinely encouraged. It requires an environment and leadership that allows ideas to be aired, tested, and allowed to flourish. Students must gain a full appreciation of the types of innovation that exist, the costs and benefits associated with each, the partnerships or team approaches required to bring them to fruition, and the leadership role that, in time, they will be called upon to exhibit within their organization. Various types of innovation are business model innovation, marketing innovation, supply chain innovation, and organizational innovation which involves the creation or alteration of business structures, practices, and models.

Learning objectives for the professionalism value would be knowledge and comprehension of the concepts underpinning professionalism (students should be able to list, define, describe, identify, show, label, collect, examine, summarize, describe, interpret, contrast, differentiate, and discuss). Then the skills involving application and analysis must be introduced (apply, demonstrate, calculate, illustrate, show, solve, examine, classify, experiment, discover, analyze, separate, order, explain, connect, compare, and select). Finally, synthesis and evaluation must be introduced (combine, integrate, modify, plan, create, design, invent, compose, prepare, generalize, rewrite, assess, decide, grade, test, measure, recommend, convince, judge, explain, discriminate, support, conclude, and summarize) (Bloom 1956). Students could be exposed either to a case study or to an actual experiential learning environment (e.g. internship) where the assessment criteria would be incorporated into the learning objectives and the assignments given.

Mutual respect

Definition

Within the TEFI framework mutual respect has been initially defined as *diversity, inclusion, equity, humility, collaboration*. However, during the TEFI III summit the meaning of this value was refined and extended by the participants. *Mutual respect is seen as a value grounded in human relationships that requires attitudinal developments that are evolving, dynamic, and involve acceptance, self-awareness of structural inequalities, open-mindedness, empowerment, and ability to revisit one's cultural understanding of the world.*

Content

Several important elements of the mutuality value are highlighted:

1   Mutuality is a *process* that is evolving and dynamic, emphasising that achieving mutual respect is a long-term and even life-long learning process that can be developed at different levels, starting from the individual to the society and global levels. It also can apply to human–animal relationships,

particularly in the context of how animals are used in tourism. This development from survival values of one's own isolated existence to relational/ global consciousness of mutuality has been researched for the last 25 years by eminent sociologist Ronald Inglehart (1990; 1997). In his longitudinal World Values Survey covering two-thirds of world population he has been capturing global evolution of the personal, social, public, and cultural values which he conceptualizes under a theory of a 'Spiral of Values' (see also Webster 2001).

2 Mutuality starts with *self-awareness* and understanding of own identity, values, cultural drivers, and behavioural patterns. Understanding self-identity is a prerequisite to understanding values and believes of other people, and developing positive attitudes to diverse identities. It is important to recognize that structural inequalities exist, including race, sex, gender, religion, etc, and acknowledge these inequalities to eliminate the bias. Self-awareness also helps to question "I versus Them" attitude and move from comparing and contrasting to accepting and sharing. Self-awareness also helps to perceive self as a positive change agent.

3 Mutual respect is about *behaviours and attitudes.* Respect of self and others is an attitude that involves recognition and acknowledgement of other people's views. It goes beyond formal structures and legal frameworks for social inclusion and diversity, and it is grounded into early age education.

4 Mutuality is grounded in *human relationships.* Respect of self and others is developed through open interactions, through constructive communication and discussions, conflict avoidance and management, empathy and acceptance. Mutuality is about developing respectful relationships between self and people through sharing and understanding values and attitudes. Mutuality starts with changing our own mindset and the way of constructing and perceiving reality. It involves open discussions and appreciation of diverse opinions.

Tourism education is a medium through which mutual respect can be promoted. However, we believe that mutuality is a process that starts from self and therefore cannot be taught directly as a subject but rather facilitated through the whole variety of general self-awareness and conflict resolution courses which would need to be a compulsory part of the whole tourism program (undergraduate and postgraduate). Another way of incorporating mutual respect into the tourism curricula is to ensure that students are exposed to diverse social and cultural values and behaviors, and to encourage positive attitude towards diversity.

Specific learning objectives are:

- the promotion of respect and the feeling of recognition;
- innovative thinking and learning methods;
- closer cooperation with "real life" through joint development projects with the industry;

- students as active participants and decision makers, creating an atmosphere of mutual respect and support;
- the role of teachers should change from "fact tellers" to facilitators of a student's own development;
- a learning environment that is inclusive, safe and dynamic, where students are not afraid to take the initiative should be created;
- self-awareness as a prerequisite to mutual respect should involve faculty, because teachers should understand their role as a positive change agents to promote mutuality;
- continuous training for all staff members to build an understanding of diverse cultural backgrounds and value systems;
- teachers should be able to recognize their own values and be open to question and revisit these values;
- mutual respect should be promoted between staff members as well as between teachers and students.

Mutual respect is a process of self-development and thus is unique for every individual. Therefore, mutuality cannot be measured and assessed as a learning outcome in the curriculum. However, it is vital to incorporate mutuality elements and principles into study modules. Tourism curricula should be based on a variety of approaches, experiences, and knowledge. It should incorporate courses related to professional and personal development, sociology, theology and cultural studies to facilitate students' understanding of drivers for change. Critical thinking skills should be emphasised in the curricula, and student's ability to initiate open dialogue, manage conflicts and reach mutually beneficial agreements should be rewarded. Programs promoting cooperation, inclusion, and diversity should be included in tourism studies.

Summary of value-based principles

The ideas presented above are meant to be used creatively by educators in their course materials. The specifics of how to incorporate them are left to the educator. Ways in which the TEFI Values can be incorporated into student learning and industry operations are discussed below.

The way forward

With the goal to fundamentally transform tourism education, TEFI is poised to progress in a number of ways. First, as we move forward it is critical that we engage all stakeholders. In particular, TEFI will work with leading university educators and industry professionals to define a new model of education for the tourism industry. In addition, we will invite students into the process to add their understanding to the redesign of education. Finally, we will also invite those in the upper levels of administration of university programs including deans, rectors, chancellors, provosts, etc. to gain their unique perspective and implementation possibilities.

TEFI fellows are already creating linkages with other organizations with similar visions, distributing a White Paper broadly to educators, industry, students, and associations of educators worldwide. TEFI fellows are beginning to develop pilot programs in the university context to test the values framework and are planning two future TEFI Summits to bring their initiatives to its fruition. Each of these initiatives is discussed below.

Networking with other organizations

- To influence accreditation and certification agencies such as United Nations World Tourism Organization (UNWTO) through the TedQual certification, Accreditation Commision for Programs in Hospitality Administration (ACPHA), and others
- To share outcomes with other agencies/groups working to change education such as Principles for Responsible Management Education (www.unprme. org), Academy of Hope
- To present the TEFI Guidelines at international, national and regional conferences such as International Society of Travel and Tourism Educators (ISTTE), Business Enterprises for Sustainable Tourism Education Network (BESTEN), Council of Australian Universities in Tourism and Hospitality Education (CAUTHE)—particularly those focusing on education and future leadership of the industry.
- To partner with industry associations such as World Travel and Tourism Council (WTTC).
- To partner with the International Academy for the Study of Tourism.
- The creation of online TEFI courses where faculty and students at multiple campuses engage in professional course delivery and assignments based on the TEFI values.

Grants

Numerous funding agencies have been identified for possible funding of the TEFI initiative. In particular, proposals will be written to obtain funds to support the development and evaluation of alternative educational strategies/programs/methods for integrating TEFI values into tourism curricula.

Future TEFI summits

TEFI will hold a World Congress open to all tourism educators and industry leaders. It will be titled: *TEFI World Congress: Activating Change in Tourism Education*, and will be held at Temple University, Philadelphia, USA May 18–21, 2011. This World Congress will be an opportunity for all involved in the tourism education process from around the world (educators, administrators at all levels, industry, students and governments) to come together to learn about the initiative, to design strategy for its implementation on a global scale, and to identify new challenges and opportunities that tourism education is likely to face between now and 2030.

Pilot projects

A few universities are beginning to structurally infuse their programs with TEFI values. For example, Modul University Vienna is using the values to create an oath that all students agree to upon graduation. Temple University in the USA is already using the values-based framework in its course design ensuring that each value set and its sub-values get coverage. James Cook University in Australia and University of Hawaii are both in the initial stages of implementing the values-based framework. Many individual members of TEFI are changing their individual courses to reflect the TEFI initiative.

Additionally, a TEFI Scholarship of Hope has been created at Modul University Vienna to encourage excellent students to continue their tourism studies. This scholarship is given to the winner of an essay competition in which the students must show how the values relate to stewardship and leadership in their lives.

TEFI faculty code of ethics/conduct and student oath

The need for faculty to 'walk the talk' in addition to 'talking the talk' has been discussed numerous times at the various TEFI Summits. The role of faculty as mentors, role models and a source inspiration and knowledge for students is paramount in this initiative. The creation of a Code of Ethics will be developed to help guide faculty in playing this larger role in students' lives. In line with this code, examples of student codes that imbibe the TEFI values will be created.

TEFI values assessment inventory

Tools to assess how students' values are being advanced within the TEFI framework are being developed and will be an important guideline to measure the success of the program. A TEFI Values Assessment Inventory currently under development will measure the values of students prior to being exposed to TEFI courses and also upon completion of the courses.

In summary, the TEFI initiative is dynamic with many institutions and players involved. It is our hope that this collaborative effort will succeed in shifting the focus of tourism education worldwide to provide more responsible graduates and better stewardship for destinations and their environmental and socio-cultural resources. We invite as many people as possible to walk this path with us and help to redefine tourism education and provide leadership for this vital field into the future.

TEFI has benefitted from the incredible participation of educators and industry members from around the world. This paper reflects their insight, creativity and concern for the future of tourism education. Working Groups have been led by various individuals who have played a key role in bringing the initiative to this point. Four meetings have been held to date that have been financially sponsored by universities from around the world with strong tourism programs: Temple University, University of Hawaii, and Virginia Polytechnic University, USA, University of Queensland, La Trobe University and University of Victoria, Australia, Bocconi University, Italy, Modul University Vienna, University of Lugano, Switzerland, and CICtourGUNE, University of Duesto, San Sebastian, Spain. They have also been sponsored by the *International Academy for the Study of Tourism*, and the *BEST Education Network*. The Steering Committee that has guided TEFI includes Drs. Leo Jago, Janne Lidburd, John Tribe, Karl Wöber, Pauline Sheldon, and Daniel Fesenmaier. We would also like to thank numerous TEFI participants who have contributed significantly to this paper: they include but are not limited to: Drs. Marion Joppe, Irena Ateljevic, Betsy Barber, John Swarbrooke, Ulli Gretzel, Darko Prebezac, Julia Nevemrzhitskaya, Rico Maggi, Gianna Moscardo, Anne-Mette Hjalager, Christina Mottirini, Loredana Padurean, and Tiger Wu. We also owe a special thank you to David Fennell for his thoughtful review of this paper and the suggestions he made.

Note

1 This paper was originally published in the *Journal of Teaching in Travel and Tourism* and has been re-printed with permission by Taylor and Francis.

References

Althusser, L. (1984). *Essays on Ideology*. London: Verso.

Apple, M. (1990). *Ideology and the Curriculum*. London: Routledge and Kegan Paul.

Bateman, T. S., & Crant, J. M. (1993). The proactive component of organizational behaviour. *Journal of Organizational Behaviour*, 14, 103–118.

Bloom, B. S. (ed.) (1956). *Taxonomy of Educational Objectives: The Classification of Educational Goals*. New York: Susan Fauer Company, Inc. pp. 201–207.

Brotherton, B. (1999). Towards a definitive view of the nature of hospitality and hospitality management. *International Journal of Contemporary Hospitality Management*, 11(4), 165–173.

Bynum, T. (2008). Computer and information ethics, in Zalta, E. N. (ed.), *The Stanford Encyclopedia of Philosophy*. Online at: http://plato.stanford.edu/entries/ethics-computer/.

Bynum, T. W., & Rogerson, S. (Eds.) (2004). *Computer Ethics and Professional Responsibility*. Oxford: Blackwell.

Cooper, T., Hofheinz, R., & Purdy, M. (2007). *Skills for the Future*. London: Accenture.

Enghagen, L. K. (1990). Teaching ethics in hospitality and tourism education. *Hospitality Research Journal*, 14(2), 467–474.

Enghagen, L. K., & Hott, D. D. (1992). Students' perceptions of ethical issues in the hospitality and tourism industry. *Hospitality Research Journal*, 15(2), 41–50.

European Universities Assocation (2007). *Creativity in Higher Education: Report on the EUA Creativity Project 2006–2007*, Brussels: EUA Publishers.

Fennell, D. A. (2000). Tourism and applied ethics. *Tourism Recreation Research*, 25 (1), 59–69.

Floridi, L. (2008). Information ethics, its nature and scope, invited chapter for moral, in van den Hoven, J. and Weckert, J. (eds), *Philosophy and Information Technology*. Cambridge: Cambridge University Press, pp. 40–65.

Giddens, A. (2009). *The Politics of Climate Change*. London: Polity Press.

Haga, W. J. (1976). Managerial Professionalism and the Use of Organization Resources, *American Journal of Economics and Sociology*, 35, 337–47.

Hall, S. S. (ed.) (1992). *Ethics in Hospitality Management: A Book of Readings*. East Lansingham, MI: Educational Initiative of American Hotel & Motel Association.

Hall, C. M., & Butler, R.W. (1995) In search of common ground: reflections on sustainability, complexity and process in the tourism system – a discussion between C. Michael Hall and Richard W. Butler. *Journal of Sustainable Tourism*, 3 (2), 99–105.

Hoyle, E., & John, D. (1995). *Professional Knowledge and Professional Practice*. London: Cassell.

Hudson, S., & Miller, G. (2005) Ethical Orientation and Awareness of Tourism Students. *Journal of Business Ethics*, 62, 383–396.

Hudson, S., & Miller, G. (2006). Knowing the difference between right and wrong: the response of tourism students to ethical dilemmas. *Journal of Teaching in Travel and Tourism*, 6 (2), 41–59.

Inglehart, R. (1990) *Culture Shift in Advanced Industrial Society*. Princeton, NJ: Princeton University Press.

Inglehart, R. (1997) Modernisation and postmodernisation. Princeton, NJ: Princeton University Press.

Jamal, T., & Menzel, C. (2008). Good Actions in Tourism. In J. Tribe (ed.), *Philosophical Issues in Tourism*, pp. 227–243. Bristol, UK: Channel View Publications.

Jaszay, C. (2001). *An Integrated Research Review of Ethics Articles in Hospitality Journals 1990 to 2000*. Report. Isbell Endowment for Hospitality Ethics, Northern Arizona University. Retrieved May 15, 2009 from: http://www2.nau.edu/~clj5/Ethics/jaszay1.pdf.

Jaszay, C. (2002). Teaching ethics in hospitality programs. *Journal of Hospitality & Tourism Education,* 14(3), 58–63.

Jaszay, C. (2006). *Hospitality Ethics Curriculum*. New Jersey: Prentice-Hall.

Kim, N. Y., & Miller, G. (2008) Perceptions of the ethical climate in the Korean tourism industry. *Journal of Business Ethics*, 82(4), 941–954.

Kwansa, F. A., & Farrar, A. L. (1992). A conceptual framework for developing a hospitality educators' code of ethics. *Journal of Hospitality & Tourism Research*, 15(3), 27–39.

Laudon, K. C. (1995). Ethical concepts and information technology. Communications of the ACM, 38(12), 33–39.

Lidburd, J. J. (2010) Sustainable Tourism Development. In: Lidburd, J.J., & Edwards, D. (eds.), *Understanding the Sustainable Development of Tourism*. Oxford: Goodfellow Publishers, pp. 1–18.

Lieberman-Nissen, K. (2005). *Ethics in the Hospitality and Tourism Industry*. East Lansing, MI: Educational Institute of American Hotel and Lodging Association.

Minnaert, L., Maitland, R., & Miller, G. (2007) Defining social tourism: linking the concept to its ethical foundations. *Tourism Culture*, 7(1), 7–17.

Minogue, K. (1973) *The Concept of a University*. London: Weidenfeld and Nicolson.

Oddo, A. R. (1997). A framework for teaching business ethics. *Journal of Business Ethics*, 16(3), 293–297.

Reisinger, Y. (2009). International tourism: cultures and behavior. *Cultural Influences on Ethics*, pp. 243–261. Oxford: Elsevier-Butterworth-Heinemann.

Resnik, D. B. (2007). *What is Ethics in Research and Why is it Important?* Retrieved from: www.niehs.nih.gov/research/resources/bioethics/whatis.cfm.

Rikowski, R. (2006). Teaching ethical issues in information technology: how and when. *Information for Social Change*, 23, 128–153. Retrieved from: http://libr.org/isc/issues/ISC23/B9a Ruth Rikowski.pdf.

Sachs, J. (2003). Teacher professional standards: controlling or developing teaching. *Teachers and Teaching: Theory and Practice*, 9 (2), 175–186.

Satris, S. (2002). The South Carolina State House and the Confederate flag – ethics case study (heritage tourism). *Teaching Business Ethics*, 2(2), 71–76. (See also and the comments online at: www.rit.edu/cla/ethics/seac/Vol. 2.2.html)

Shamoo, A., & Resnik, D. (2003). *Responsible Conduct of Research*. Oxford: Oxford University Press.

Shannon, J. R., & Berl, R. L. (1997). Are we teaching ethics in marketing? A survey of students' attitudes and perception. *Journal of Business Ethics*, 16(10), 1059–1075.

Sheldon, P., Fesenmaier, D. Wöber, K., Cooper, C., & Antonioli, M. (2008). Tourism education futures 2010–2030: building the capacity to lead. *Journal of Teaching in Tourism and Travel*, 7(3), 61–68.

Smith, M., & Duffy, R. (2003). *The Ethics of Tourism Development*. Abingdon: Routledge.

Stevens, B. (2001). Hospitality ethics: responses from human resource directors and students to seven ethical scenarios. *Journal of Business Ethics*, 30(3), 233–242.

Tribe, J. (2002). The philosophic practitioner. *Annals of Tourism Research*, 29, 338–357.

Vallen, G., & Casado, M. (2000). Ethical principles for the hospitality curriculum. *Cornell Hotel and Restaurant Administrative Quarterly*, 41(2), 44–51.

Velasquez, M. G. (1998). *Business Ethics, Concepts and Cases*. New Jersey: Prentice-Hall.

Vessuri, H. (2002). Ethical challenges for the social sciences on the threshold of the 21st century. *Current Sociology*, 50(1), 135–150.

Wallis, C., & Steptoe, S. (2006). How to bring our schools out of the 20th century. *Time*, December 10.

Webster, A. (2001) *Spiral of Values: the flow from survival values to global consciousness in New Zealand*. Hawera, NZ: Alpha Publications.

Weckert, J. (ed.) (2007). *Computer Ethics*. Farnham, UK: Ashgate.

Williamson, J. (1997). The Washington consensus revisited. In: Luis Emmerij (ed.), *Economic and Social Development into the XXI Century*. Bounder, CO: Inter-American Develpment Bank, Lynne Reinner Publishers, pp. 48–61.

Yaman, H. R. (2003). Skinner's naturalism as a paradigm for teaching business ethics: a discussion from tourism. *Teaching Business Ethics*, 7(2), 107–122.

Yeung, S. (2004). Hospitality ethics curriculum: an industry perspective. *International Journal of Contemporary Hospitality Management*, 16(4), 253–262.

Yeung, S., & Pine, R. (2003). Designing a hospitality ethics course content from the students' perspective. *Journal of Teaching in Travel & Tourism*, 3(2), 19–33.

6 From copyright to *copyleft*

Towards tourism education 2.0

Janne J. Lidburd and Anne-Mette Hjalager

Introduction

Widely accepted for protecting the rights of the original creator, copyright laws provide control of distribution, reproduction, adaptation, and translation of digital and broadcast rights. Copyright regulation is regarded as an essential infrastructure in society as forms of licensing and control that are maintained through more-or-less concealed codes and surveillance. Licenses act as a mechanism of social ordering to help constrain and stabilize the interactions of the involved developers. As owners of intellectual property, tourism academics are familiar with assigning these rights to a publisher in full, or by way of granting these in return for some 'benefit'. Intellectual property rights directly affect the lives of all those who work, study and research in tourism education. Over the years, powerful enforcement of intellectual property rights demonstrates the risks connected to copying and citing without recognition and payment, an issue that university students are reminded of unendingly as part of their academic socialization process (Ryan 2005; Tribe 2007). *Copyleft* is a play on the word copyright to describe the licensing practice of removing or modifying copyright restrictions when distributing copies and modified versions of the work of others while requiring that the same freedoms be preserved in future versions. Emerging from the phenomenon of free or open source software, copyleft practices are spreading rapidly into other areas of intellectual production such as text, pictures, video-films, designs and manifestation of art.

This chapter outlines the contours of an emerging new order of intellectual creativity and property and analyzes the implications of innovativeness in tourism education. It contrasts the copyright paradigm against the *copyleft* paradigm, which more openly invites knowledge reuse by copying, remixing and transformation with no or limited acknowledgement of the original author(s). The aim is to critically discuss the challenges and dilemmas for university education, and in particular for tourism education by uncovering the implications of the changing knowledge monopoly and new learning environments facilitated by Web 2.0. In contrast to the first generation of the internet, Web 1.0, where users were limited to the passive viewing of information and downloading in frozen formats, Web 2.0 allows users to interact with others to alter and generate online content. Increasingly, the dissemination and development of knowledge takes place in social environments that are characterized by information sharing and social interaction across traditional boundaries. Outlining the conceptual divide between copyright and *copyleft* we argue that there is a compelling need for open and innovative content generation and knowledge dissemination – not only within but also beyond the traditional classroom setting (Lidburd and Hjalager 2010). The Web 2.0 platform, INNOTOUR, which distinctly lends many of its ideas from the *copyleft* concept, is used to illustrate new ways of learning and collaborating in tourism education. Balancing between copyright and *copyleft* requires entirely new behavioral ethics, pedagogies and calls upon new modes of collaboration and critical reflexivity by tourism students, researchers and business users as they become co-producers of knowledge. Drawing on Heidegger's (2000) notion of *Poeisis* – meaning to bring forth, to lead – tourism education 2.0 implies not only taking a critical stance but more fundamentally, embarking onto a creative journey through the democratizing paths constituted by equitable conversation and production, which are in dire contrast to never-ending patterns of consumption.

The conceptual divide

Adopting the Biblical image from the *Song of Solomon* of the ivory tower as a symbol of noble purity, in contemporary usage the ivory tower is applied to intellectuals willfully engaged in pursuits that are disconnected from practical concerns of everyday life. Kant, in his 1798 work *The Conflict of the Faculties*, wrote that universities should 'handle the entire content of learning by mass production, so to speak, by a division of labor, so that for every branch of the sciences there would be a public teacher or professor appointed as its trustee.' This mass-production university model has led to separation where there ought to be collaboration and to ever-increasing specialization (Taylor 2009). The following will expand on the idea by former president of the University of California, Berkeley, Clark Kerr (1963), who argued that a large, modern university had to operate as part of society, no longer as an ivory tower apart from it. More recently addressed by partners in the European University Association (2007), universities were encouraged to transcend the conventional position and balance active engagement in society with a certain distance from the world, thus transforming the ivory tower into a "watch tower". The crowds have been given voice (Surowiecki 2004), and the entry barriers to contribute to knowledge have been altered.

Following the immense success of the GNU/Linux software that gave up traditional methods of copyright protection and code secrecy in favour of a common ownership model, the concepts of open source and *copyleft* have received considerable scholarly interest (Berry 2008; Bettig 1996; Gordon 2003; Thurow 2006). Still, the implications for further education in general and tourism education in particular have only been marginally explored (Alger 2002; Brown and Adler 2008; Iiyoshi and Kumar 2008). To address this gap we first question what can be the subject of property, and here specifically the property of academic knowledge. Next, we systematize the key issues of *copyleft* against copyright, which is then critically discussed in the context of tourism education.

To understand what can be subjected to property and thereby copyright in tourism education, the genealogy of property rights offered by Roman law is informative. Roman law transgresses modern binary oppositions of either public or private ownership domains and, as skillfully demonstrated by Berry (2008); it is particularly useful to highlight the expansion of property right in the realm of intellectual and immaterial things. Drawing on Foucault's genealogy of the common (1989, 1990), Figure 6.1 is intended to help expose the contingent and contested nature of copyright, which opens for critique of what we commonly take for granted.

The concept of the commons in Roman law on the classification of things (*res*) was used to represent different forms of property ownership. *Res Nullis* are un-owned things, unclaimed objects, which is also the state to which copyrighted works return when falling outside of copyright protection. Privately owned things, such as a house, books and clothes are specific to individuals (or other legal entities, such as corporations), and publicly owned things, e.g., roads, state buildings and ports are usually understood as controlled or owned by the state. *Res Communes* are things held in common, capable of non-exclusive ownership, or incapable of ownership, like the oceans, the air, outer space and finite natural

Figure 6.1 Redefining the commons (adapted from Berry 2008: 79–97).

resources. Tourism academics will recognize Hardin's (1968) notion of the *Tragedy of the Commons* in this type of ownership. *Res Universitatis*, from which also the term 'university' derives, was granted by the state to own large group assets described by Hyde (2006: 83) as property on the outside and commons on the inside. *Res Imperium* are things owned in the international domain, such as treaties agreed by the United Nations World Intellectual Property Organization, deep sea probes and satellites. Finally, *Res Divini Juris* were originally within the control of the gods (e.g., religious, sacred, holy things) and thus beyond the control of the state or any single individual or corporation. Following Berry's (2008) proposition in the context of open source and intellectual property, we argue that *Res Divini Juris* represent a common ownership model that could not only innovate tourism education by making educational assets accessible, but furthermore, it signifies the possibility of global, collective ownership by academic communities of practice (for instance in tourism education) espoused by *copyleft.*

Teasing out some of the key characteristics of copyright versus *copyleft*, Table 6.1 is based on general theories and concepts of the economy of knowledge and information (mainly on Boisot 1999; McInerney 2002; Spender and Scherer 2007).

Overall, the *copyleft* column suggests that knowledge is to be considered as an ever-changing entity (McAfee 2006), and a matter of continuous reflectivity of the producers, acquirers and users (Wenger *et al.* 2003; Ren *et al.* 2010). Access to social and educational networks can create or assist in refining the use of knowledge. Knowledge flows in unpredictable streams of abundance, which leaves attempts of hoarding and monopolizing obsolete. Elements of participation and reciprocity are prevalent, suggesting that the notion of a success depends on the ability to become a contributing member of a community. While the original author is still recognized, some, but not all rights that are specified under copyright law are surrendered to end users in *copyleft* licensing, such as *creative commons*. Such *copyleft* licenses permit the use of normally copyright restricted/protected source codes and/or content. The *copyleft* principle thus indicates an inherent generosity and equitable communication between voluntary contributors who understand the art and skill of sharing knowledge. Emerging business models suggest that *copyleft* is as efficient as copyright in terms of generating economic value, albeit in other formats (Anderson 2007; Chesbrough 2006; Davenport 2008).

Copyright, as described in the right-hand column, is not to be perceived as an archaic model of knowledge handling. Worldwide, powerful institutions are involved in reproducing the copyright system, for example, through *Res Privatae* laws and regulations of intellectual property and *Res Communes* organizations that make a living out of intermediating knowledge and information. Copyright is a legal term that gives statutory expression to the moral and economic rights of creators to their literary and artistic works, and describes the rights of the public to access those creations (World Intellectual Property Organization 2010). Many elements of information possess an exclusive and extreme

Table 6.1 Copyright versus *Copyleft* – conceptual characteristics

Themes in the knowledge chain	Copyleft	Copyright
Knowledge provision	*Abundant* Knowledge is in abundance, and organizing and selecting it are primary challenges	*Scarce* Knowledge is scarce; finding it is a primary challenge
The repository of knowledge	*Transmural* Knowledge is shared across institutional boundaries due to flows of human beings and interlinkages of information systems	*Intramural* Knowledge is contained in institutions: with university staff, in libraries, R&D departments, and other closed communities of knowledge
Circulation	*Never-ending process* Half-finished, comment inviting products are launched, asking for continuous improvements	*Completed works* Fully quality ascertained versions are published, the knowledge has a status of "truth"
Price	*Free* No or low costs, but moral obligation to credit. The price is detached from the production costs	*For sale* The price reflects the market value of knowledge. Scarce knowledge is produced at high cost
Trade	*Withholding* Giving away and still keeping the knowledge	*Renouncing* The knowledge is transferred and valuated by others
Organization	*Democratic* Anyone can enter the knowledge zone to utilize or to contribute	*Hierarchical* Access depends on status, privileges, funds, etc.
Success criteria	*Contributing* Activity and interaction, increasing the quality of work	*Honoring* Paying credit to the original version
Business models	*Long tail* Free services, supplied with a variety of supporting service and licenses derived from the main knowledge	*Off-shelf* The core information products sold as licenses, patents, in books, etc.

value for the individual or corporate owner, such as groundbreaking results in scientific research, resulting in reluctance to share and disseminate knowledge without ensuring direct remuneration to the owners. The hierarchical structures in the academic world and the associated privileges also tend to contribute to the entrenchedness of copyright procedures (Alger 2002). Forms of recognition and incentives are closely intermingled with the economic mechanisms perpetuated by publishers, libraries, academic meriting, neoliberal quality assurance and accreditation systems (Ayikoru *et al.* 2009). In most cases the duration of copyright lasts for the life of the creator plus 50 years, after which his or her work enters what is known as the 'public domain', *Res Nullis*.

Focusing next on the implications for tourism education, three concerns emerge. First, whereas the professional world and the exchange of knowledge is becoming increasingly global (OECD 2008; Soete 2010), with Internet technology as a principal driver, it is questionable whether educational practice in today's higher education institutions, including those of tourism, are preparing graduates for the world of tomorrow. Are we as academics turning a blind eye to the crumbling walls (Carson 2009), more concerned about reproducing traditions (ourselves?) and standing guard around the ivory tower? Second, authoritative knowledge – notably knowledge derived from university research and teaching – is still relatively immune to creative and collaborative contributions from broader user environments, for example business actors, NGOs, administrators and community groups. And third, how are the well-established forms of hording knowledge challenged by *copyleft*, open source and web 2.0?

Tourism education, open source and *copyleft*

As a global social and economic phenomenon, tourism represents exceptional learning and career opportunities. Increasingly, tourism students insist that their studies need to offer relevance and perspectives for their future, based on a comprehendible and logical integration of theory and practice. Concerned with the future of tourism education, Sheldon *et al.* (2008) argue that tourism employment in the coming decades will have a very different profile. Yet, in less than a decade, tourism students will be applying for jobs that do not even exist today, and much of what and how we teach offers only a few years of currency (Cooper *et al.* 2007), hardly enough to adequately prepare tourism students for a working life in a rapidly changing and complex industry. This raises the need to understand and promote lifelong and self-directed learning to underpin professional expertise.

Whereas most tourism educators have been using the Internet and other digital technologies to develop and disseminate knowledge for years, the majority of learning materials remain locked up behind passwords, copyrights and other proprietary systems unreachable for outsiders. Over the past decade, many innovative tourism educators have adopted e-learning environments, and contributed to open source initiatives by sharing resources and educational materials on tens of thousands of course websites that are now freely available (Richardson

2006; Sigala 2007; Iiyoshi and Kumar 2008). At the same time, numerous tourism programs have joined collaborative exchanges of students and faculty, and taken part in international consortia, networks and alliances to develop and share educational expertise, resources and repositories of knowledge. To mention but a few examples, the European Commission's Erasmus Mundus program promotes structured cooperation between higher education institutions to enhance quality in joint master and doctorate programs, including tourism. Furthermore, UNESCO sponsors the Virtual University, and the OECD's Centre for Educational Research and Innovation actively explores issues of e-learning in higher education (see reference list for URLs).

Tourism educators need to be mindful that open source innovation is not just a form of technical activity taking place online but it implies a wider range of democratic aims. Whereas the interest in open education, and joint and online collaboration is burgeoning, many innovative educational efforts remain isolated and in closed domains (Iiyoshi and Kumar 2008) as *Res Communes, Res Universitatis* and *Res Privatae.* They are not shared beyond the classroom, as disciplines and institutions involved in tourism programs operate against diseconomies of scale in many cases. Suggesting that the tourism academe still tends to stand guard around the ivory tower by intrinsically reproducing itself in its current form, an overarching tendency in tourism education is to concentrate on means of problem solving and meeting immediate industry needs (for example marketing, facility management, service quality and logistics) as opposed to focusing on ends and desirable futures. Airey (2008) and Shaw and Williams (2009) further argue that there is obvious needs to search for new possibilities to assist the tourism industry to not only overcome barriers towards innovation but to facilitate much wider capacity building and knowledge transfer through education.

Education is currently traded and treated as a commodity, which students purchase and consume based on prescribed, tacit rules of engagement, including those of copyright. Rather than teaching students to fit in passively to the world that exists (Minogue 1973), a holistic approach to tourism education similar to Tribe's (2002) 'philosophical practitioner' is needed to explicitly address the broader objectives of society and the industry in tourism curriculum. Critical reflection on the value of education in society is also called for. It is arguably a human right for all people in the world as opposed to a commodity produced and consumed by few. If education is 'aimed at the democratic, social, cultural and economic development of society and the preparation of every citizen for active and responsible participation in society' (Education International 2010) tourism educators must address the issues of sustainability and stewardship, including the kind of tourism to be developed and what the final objectives behind these activities should be (Lidburd 2010). Whether for improving learning in a single classroom or creating broader stewardship competences, the transformative and innovative opportunities posed by open source innovation, *copyleft* and Web 2.0 appear to escape current educational practice in tourism.

New arenas of learning constitute themselves as a result of Web 2.0. It is still a very open question whether Web 2.0 paves the road for fostering cognitive attributes in students that equip them with or enable them to approach what solemnly can be called wisdom, in the sense outlined by McKenna (2005): "wise action, although reasoned, requires us to act and think outside the bounds of rationality and accepted, codified knowledge; that is grounded in worldly day-to-day activity; assumes that life is contingent; and is virtuous and humane" (p. 40). Wisdom is not solely a commodity of individuals, *Res Privatae*, but always already predicated by existing knowledge *Res Divini Juris.*

INNOTOUR and Web 2.0 education in tourism

Through genuine cross-disciplinary research underpinning tourism education, in 2009 the University of Southern Denmark launched an innovative platform for education, research and business development entitled INNOTOUR (www. INNOTOUR.com). INNOTOUR is an experimental wiki platform for collaborative knowledge creation and dissemination. INNOTOUR contains case studies in tourism innovation, interactive innovation tools and tests, a range of academic resources, remedies for communication and collaboration for students, academics, and business actors, etc. INNOTOUR is international from the very outset, underpinning cross-border and cross-institutional collaboration. Using the case of INNOTOUR, an applied understanding about Web 2.0, *copyleft*, and open innovation processes in tourism education will be explained.

Moving beyond content delivery and transmission of knowledge, often in the form of shooting bullet points at students in power point format, Web 2.0 affords active, student-centered participation and multi-way communication. Students are required to take an active role with the educator assuming the role of facilitator in applying and enhancing knowledge (McLoughlin and Luca 2002; Sigala 2007). Web 2.0 refers to certain forms of activities characterized by collaborative content generation. While taking place on the World Wide Web, or to a large extent utilizing web-mediated resources, Web 2.0 is not concerned with the use of specific technologies. Web 2.0 activities lend themselves to continuous production, reproduction and transformation of individual and collaborative knowledge and material in use and reuse across contexts. Inherent in such Web 2.0-activities is a view of communication as interaction, of knowledge as transitory and in flux, of competence as situated doing, and of learning as participation, theoretically launched in Lave and Wenger's (1991) classical contribution. It implies a shift from solely valuing and rewarding individual achievement and *Res Privatae* toward collective action, participation, critical thinking and contribution as *Res Divini Juris*. INNOTOUR is an inviting structure open to students, educators, researchers and business users worldwide. The Web 2.0 platform aims at building bridges between research, education and business practices by including different, although extensively shared, repositories of knowledge and activities in which the learner participates. Students and educators are encouraged to question established ideas, to go beyond conventional knowledge and strive towards originality. Promoting such a culture of creativity that acknowledges and seeks to learn from failures encourages students to move from hypothesis and conventional knowledge towards possibilities and originality.

The ethical dimension of creativity and creative knowledge should be addressed; there is ample historical evidence of innovations that have led to ethically disastrous consequences. Ethics must be embedded in tourism education to enrich and add relevant dimensions of critical thinking in Web 2.0 collaborative learning. Striving for learning and co-creation through activities that are deemed "good" involves making moral principles and values explicit as a transparent measure of ethical behavior. This calls for self-monitoring in problem solving and mutual respect between users, potentially as a long-term and even life-long learning process that can be developed at different levels; starting from the individual to the societal and global levels. Mindful of the global digital divide, INNOTOUR encourages respect of self and others through open interactions, equitable access and communication between users. Building on Heidegger's (2000) idea of *poeisis* in the sense of creating, bringing forth and producing as opposed to simply consuming and exploiting, INNOTOUR is committed to forming 'a common gathering' (Berry 2008: 200) through distributed authorship, ownership and/or renunciation of copyright.

E-learning has a relatively long history, but until recently electronic learning resources and devices have mostly been considered auxiliary attributes to the "real" classroom teaching (Salmon 2002; Vest 2006; Sigala 2007; Dohn 2009). Advanced learning through knowledge sharing is still novel and notable resistance can be observed at the personal (students and staff) and institutional (management) levels (Haven and Botteril 2003; Morris 2008). For students, Web 2.0 is commonly not regarded as a tool for learning and educational purposes but predominately as part of social software used in the leisure sphere, such as Facebook, YouTube, and weblogs (Lidburd *et al.* 2010). Students are challenged by implicit demands in a Web 2.0 setting (Parker and Chao 2007; Thomson 2007; Asraf 2008).

Whereas a number of positive motivational factors are readily acknowledged, including student motivation, and personalized and collaborative knowledge formation (Sigala 2002), the inherent epistemology of Web 2.0 practices and the formal educational system pose conceptual tensions. The conception of knowledge in Web 2.0 as on one hand *process* and *activity* and a community of practice is contrasted with knowledge as a *state* possessed by the individual, and learning as an *acquisition* of this state within the formal educational system (Dohn 2009). Furthermore, active student engagement for personalized learning may enhance relevance and authenticity for the learners through user generated content.

Yet, the established regimes of teacher expertise and power are not easily transformed. Educators typically find that changing and providing new learning opportunities are time consuming, and so is the interaction with tourism enterprises and other stakeholders. Dale and Povey (2009) argue that both tourism/experience enterprises and universities can, in a far more integrated effort raise competitiveness and innovativeness by ensuring new ways of accessing knowledge and environments where knowledge is created, transformed and disseminated. This further challenges conventional management regimes; as such activities are generally neither rewarded nor encouraged in current neo-liberal notions of research excellence (Lidburd and Hjalager 2010). In a wider perspective, the INNOTOUR platform and associated research are thus considered of importance for continuous innovation in higher education, amendment of competition policies for the tourism sector, as well as to facilitate international interaction and open knowledge dissemination.

Critical challenges – creativity and collaboration

INNOTOUR facilitates a new way of teaching, learning and collaborating in academia and with the industry. It stipulates fairly radical changes in the conceptualization of (tourism) education, and thus opposition and doubt can be anticipated. The initiative hits the nerve of more general challenges in contemporary higher education, as does the mere thought of breaking into a new era in teaching with rebalanced understandings of copyright and *copyleft*. According to Kotter (2008), the changes are smoothed by a sense of urgency. Universities are facing several coinciding pressures, not in the least through economic requirements to deliver still more educational content and quality at still lower costs. Each individual educator cannot plausibly invent his/her own personalized and unique teaching package every semester, and therefore efficient and flexible ways of transferring content and activities between practices emerge. The urgency for sharing teaching materials in accountable ways, to find methods for the students to co-create and to share among themselves must be interpreted as an apparent necessity. Urgency is, however, not sufficient, as tradition-bound systems like universities tend to continue until every slack resource is engulfed, until standards have been leveled down, or until more privileged faculty have found means to escape teaching. Again following from Kotter (2008), strong coalitions have to be built to carry change. By understanding change and unpredictability as part of a complex adaptive system, which can cause multifaceted and non-linear outcomes that are hard to foresee (Malanson 1999; Gunderson *et al.* 2005; Miller and Twining-Ward 2005), coalitions, or communities of practice, can reinvent themselves by continuously learning and adapting in line with contextual changes (Andrus 2005).

Coalitions are not yet visibly adjusting to the new practices of *copyleft*. In spite of its principled openness, the INNOTOUR platform also has to pay attention to *Res Privatae* by urging users to verify the liability of any text, picture, film, abstract, etc that they are about to upload. The joint ventures in the fields of immaterial property rights are profoundly manifested and guarded by rigid regulation, enforced as a consequence of significant economic interests. Only gradually are new ways of handling these delicate issues emerging, for example in the institutionalization of "Creative Commons". The reader is referred to MIT's OpenCourseWare for more inspiration (http://ocw.mit.edu/index.htm).

The formation of coalitions also has another beneficial dimension in this context, as it embraces the collaboration between universities and academia in borderless structures. After decades of neoliberal orientation with encouragements to sharpen and increase competiveness, the plea for collaboration – or generous competition intertwined with mutual respect and assistance – is not effortless. Trust has to be re-established together with ethical standards for the handling of someone else's content. In due course it is of pivotal importance that tourism students and academia understand the opportunities and intrinsic ethics of *copyleft*. Living out a vision in communicable manners, empowering the collaborators, and giving progress momentum are steps in successful change processes. As noticed by Huber and Hutchings (2008), open learning has an advantage in terms of space for experimentation, although only marginally exploited. They advocate modest steps toward a larger ambition, recognizing the risks inherent to all change processes and the need to ensure a culture shaping consolidation. Harnessing the collective wisdom of tourism educators, which is not confined to the tourism academe as a type of community of practice, may open space for collaborative content generation, innovativeness and creativity.

The soundness of the *copyleft* movement and the need to embed new principles in a broader political vision for the future is underlined by the fact that organizations like the OECD (2007) and the Swedish Research Council (2009) address the need for making publicly funded research results accessible and "giving knowledge for free", as it is phrased by OECD. These organizations are searching for new economic models, pragmatically realizing that good intentions and ethical standards will not suffice, and neither will small fractions of educators, no matter how enthusiastic. In the field of higher tourism education, national governmental bodies are to be alerted. At the time of writing, there are hardly any convincing examples of initiatives that set new regulatory and institutional frameworks. Equally, the powers of international structures and accreditation agencies as drivers or inhibitors of change, including the UN World Tourism Organization, should not be underestimated. Up until now, the plea for a *copyleft* practices in tourism and higher education worldwide still has the character of an idealistic movement, which seeks a legitimate platform to sustain its transformative potentials.

References

Airey, D. W. (2008) *Tourism Education: life begins at 40.* Paper. School of Management, University of Surrey. Retrieved from: http://epubs.surrey.ac.uk/cgi/viewcontent.cgi?art icle=1039&context=tourism (accessed May 1, 2009).

Alger, J. R. (2002) "Legal issues in on-line education", *Educause*, April. Retrieved from: http://net.educause.edu/ir/library/pdf/NTW0204.pdf (accessed October 2, 2009).

Anderson, C. (2007) *The Long Tail: how endless choice is creating unlimited demand*, London: Random House Business.

Andrus, D. C. (2005) "The wiki and the blog: toward a complex adaptive intelligence community", *Studies in Intelligence* 49 (3). Retrieved from: http://ssrn.com/abstract=755904. (accessed May 1, 2010).

Asraf, B. (2008) "Teaching the Google-eyed YouTube generation", *Education + Training*, 51 (5/6): 343–352.

Ayikuru, M., Tribe, J. and Airey, D. (2009) "Reading tourism education: neoliberalism unveiled", *Annals of Tourism Research* 36 (2): 191–221.

Berry, D. M. (2008) *Copy, Rip, Burn: the political of copyleft and open source*, London: Pluto Press.

Bettig, R. V. (1996) *Copyrighting Culture: the political economy of intellectual property*, Boulder, CO: Westview Press.

Brown, J. S. and Adler, R. P. (2008) "Minds on fire: open education, the long tail, and learning 2.0", *Educause Review*, 43 (1): 16–32. Retrieved from: www.educause.edu/ EDUCAUSE+Review/EDUCAUSEReviewMagazineVolume43/MindsonFireOpenEd-ucationtheLon/162420 (accessed May 16, 2010).

Boisot, M. (1999) *Knowledge Assets: securing competitive advantage in the information economy*, Oxford: Oxford University Press.

Carson, A. (2009) "The unwallet garden: growth of the OpenCourseware Consotium, 2001–2008", *Open Learning*, 24 (1): 23–29.

Chesbrough, H. (2006) *Open Business Models: how to thrive in the new innovation land-scape*, Boston: Harvard Business School Press.

Cooper, T., Hofheinz, P., and Purdy, M. (2007) *Skills for the Future*, London: Accenture.

Dale, C. and Povey, G. (2009) "An evaluation of learner-generated content and podcast-ing", *Journal of Hospitality, Leisure, Sport & Tourism Education*, 8 (1): 117–123.

Davenport, T. (2008) "Enterprise 2.0: the new, new knowledge management?" *Harvard Business Online*. Retrieved from: http://discussionleader.hbsp.com/davenport/2008/02/ enterprise_20_the_new_new_know_1.html (accessed April 8, 2010).

Dohn, N. B. (2009) "Web 2.0: Inherent tensions and evident challenges for education", *International Journal* of *Computer-Supported Collaborative Learning* 4(3) Retrieved from: http://www.citeulike.org/journal/springerlink-120055 (accessed May 2, 2009).

Education International (2010) "Principal aims". Retrieved from: www.ei-ie.org/en/ aboutus/aim.htm (accessed May 17, 2010).

European Commission (2010) "Erasmus mundus". Retrieved from: http://ec.europa.eu/ education/external-relation-programmes/doc72_en.htm (accessed May 27, 2010).

European University Association (2007) *Creativity in Higher Education: report on the EUA Creativity Project 2006–2007*, Brussels: EUA Publications.

Foucault, M. (1989) Discipline and Punish, Harmondsworth: Penguin.

Foucault, M. (1990) History of Sexuality, Harmondsworth: Penguin.

Gordon, W. (2003) "Introduction", in W. Gordon and R. Watt (eds), *The Economics of Copyright*, Northampton, MA: Edward Elgar, pp. xiv–xxii.

Gunderson, L. H., Holling, C. S., Pritchard, L. and Peterson, G. D. (2005) "Resilience of large-scale resource systems", in L. H. Gunderson and L. Pritchard, Jr. (eds), *Resilience and the Behaviour of Large-Scale Systems*, Washington DC: Scope 60, Island Press, pp. 3–18.

Hardin, G. (1968) "Tragedy of the commons", *Science*, 162: 1243–1248.

Haven, C. and Botteril, D. (2003) "Virtual learning environments in hospitality, leisure, tourism and sport: a review", *Journal of Hospitality, Leisure, Sport & Tourism Educa-tion*, 2 (1): 76–93.

Heidegger, M. (2000) "The question concerning technology", in D. F. Krell (ed.), *Martin Heidegger: basic writings*, London: Routledge.

Huber, M.T. and Hutchings. P. (2008) "What is next for open knowledge?" in T. Iiyoshi and M. S. V. Kumar (eds), *Opening up Education: the collective advancement of edu-cation through open technology, open content, open knowledge*, Cambridge, MA: MIT Press, pp. 417–428. Retrieved from: http://mitpress.mit.edu/opening_up_education/ (accessed October 2, 2009).

Hyde, L. (2006) *The Gift: how the creative spirit transforms the world*, London: Canongate.

Iiyoshi, T. and Kumar, M. S. V. (ed.) (2008) *Opening up Education: the collective advancement of education through open technology, open content, open knowledge*, Cambridge, MA: MIT Press. Retrieved from: http://mitpress.mit.edu/opening_up_education/ (accessed October 2, 2009).

Kerr, C. (1963) *The Uses of the University*, Cambridge, MA: Harvard University Press.

Kotter, J. P. (2008) *A Sense of Urgency*, Boston: Harvard School of Business Publishing.

Lave, J. and Wenger, E. (1991) *Situated Learning*, Cambridge: Cambridge University Press.

Lidburd, J. J. (2010) "Sustainable tourism development", in J. J. Lidburd and D. Edwards (eds), *Understanding the Sustainable Development of Tourism*, Oxford: Goodfellow Publishers, pp. 1–18.

Lidburd, J. J. and Hjalager, A.-M. (2010) "Changing approaches to education, innovation and research: student experiences", *Tourism Journal of Hospitality and Tourism Management*, 17: 12–20.

Lidburd, J. J., Hjalager, A.-M. and Christensen, I.-M. F. (2010) "Valuing tourism education 2.0", *Journal of Teaching for Travel Tourism* (forthcoming).

Malanson, J. P. (1999) "Considering complexity", *Annals of the Association of American Geographers*, 89: 746–753.

McAfee, A.P. (2006) "Enterprise 2.0: the dawn of emergent collaboration", *Sloan Management Review*, 47 (3): 21–28.

McInerney, C. (2002) "Knowledge management and the dynamic nature of knowledge", *Journal of the American Society for Information Science and Technology*, 53 (12): 1009–1018.

McKenna, B. (2005) "Wisdom, ethics and the postmodern organization", in D. J. Rooney, G. N. Hearn and A. Ninan (eds), *Handbook on the Knowledge Economy*, Cheltenham, UK and Northampton, MA: Edward Elgar, pp. 37–53.

McLoughlin, C. and Luca, J. (2002) "Experiential learning online: the role of asynchronous communication tools", in P. Parker and S. Rebelsky (eds), *Proceedings of the World Conference on Educational Multime*, Chesapeake, VA: AACE, pp. 1273–1278. Retrieved from: http://www.editlib.org/p/9980 (accessed May 1, 2009).

Massachusetts Institute of Technology (2010) *OpenCourseWare*. Retrieved from: http://ocw.mit.edu/index.htm (accessed May 15, 2010).

Miller, G. and Twining-Ward, L. (2005) *Monitoring for a Sustainable Tourism Transition: the challenge of developing and using indicators*, Wallingford: CABI Publishing.

Minogue, K. R. (1973) *The Concept of a University*, Los Angeles: University of California Press.

Morris, D. (2008) "Economies of scale and scope in e-learning", *Studies in Higher Education*, 33 (3): 331–343.

OECD (2007) *Giving Knowledge for Free: the emergence of open educational resources*, Paris: OECD.

OECD (2008) *Open Innovation in Global Networks*, Paris: OECD.

OECD (2010) "Centre for Educational Research and Innovation".Retrieved from: www.oecd.org/department/0,3355,en_2649_35845581_1_1_1_1_1,00.html (accessed May 27, 2010).

Ren, C., Pritchard, A. and Morgan, N. (2010) "Constructing tourism research: a critical inquiry", *Annals of Tourism Research*, doi:10.1016/j.annals.2009.11.006.

Richardson, W. (2006) *Blogs, Wikis, Podcasts and Other Powerful Web Tools for Class-room*, Thousand Oaks: Corwin Press.

Ryan, C. (2005) "Ethics in tourism research", in Brent W. Ritchie, Peter M. Burns and Catherine A. Palmer (eds), *Tourism Research Methods*, Wellingsford: CABI, pp. 9–20.

Parker, K. R. and Chao, J. T. (2007) "Wiki as a teaching tool", *Interdisciplinary Journal of Knowledge and Learning Objects*, 3. Retrieved from: http://ijklo.org/Volume3/IJK-LOv3p057–072Parker284.pdf (accessed May 27, 2010).

Salmon, G. (2002) *E-tivities: the key to active online learning*, Abingdon: Routledge Falmer.

Shaw, G. and Williams, A. (2009) "Knowledge transfer and management in tourism organisations: an emerging research agenda", *Tourism Management*, 30 (3): 325–335.

Sheldon, P., Fesenmaier, D., Woeber, C., Cooper, C. and Antonioli, M. (2008) "Tourism education futures 2010–2030: building the capacity to lead", *Journal of Travel and Tourism Teaching*, 7 (3): 61–68.

Sigala, M. (2002) "The evolution of Internet pedagogy: benefits for tourism and hospitality education", *Journal of Hospitality, Leisure, Sport & Tourism Education*, 1 (2): 27–42.

Sigala, M. (2007) "Integrating Web 2.0 in e-learning environments: a socio-technical approach", *International Journal of Knowledge and Learning*, 6 (3): 628–648.

Soete, L. (2010) *The Role of Community Research Policy in the Knowledge-based Economy*, Luxembourg: Publications Office of the European Union.

Spender, J.-C. and Scherer, A. G. (2007) "The philosophical foundations of knowledge management: editors' introduction", *Organization*, 14 (1): 5–28.

Surowiecki, J. (2004) *The Wisdom of Crowds*, New York, NY: Doubleday.

Swedish Research Council (2009) *Remit*. Retrieved from: www.vr.se/inenglish/aboutus/remit.4.44482f6612355bb5ee780001601.html (accessed May 29, 2010).

Thomson, J. (2007) "Is education 1.0 ready for Web 2.0 students?" *Journal of Online Education*, 3 (4). Retrieved from: www.innovateonline.info/pdf/vol. 3_issue4/Is_Education_1.0_Ready_for_Web_2.0_Students_.pdf. (accessed May 31, 2010).

Thurow, L. L. (2006) "Needed: a new system of intellectual property rights", in D. Vaver (ed.), *Intellectual Property Rights: critical concepts in law*, New York: Routledge.

Tribe, J. (2002) "The philosophic practitioner", *Annals of Tourism Research*, 29 (2): 338–357.

Tribe, J. (2007) "Critical tourism: rules and resistance", in I. Ateljevic, A. Pritchard and N. Morgan (eds), *Critical Turn in Tourism Studies: innovative research methodologies*, Oxford: Elsevier, pp. 29–38.

Tylor, M. C. (2009) "The end of the university as we know it", *New York Times*, April 26. Retrieved from: www.nytimes.com/2009/04/27/opinion/27taylor.html?_r=1 (accessed May 1, 2009).

UNESCO (2010) "Virtual University". Retrieved from: www.unesco.org/iiep/virtualuniversity/forums.php (accessed May 27, 2010).

Vest, C. (2006) "Open content and the emerging global meta-university", *EDUCAUSE Review*, 41 (3): 18–30. Retrieved from: http://connect.educause.edu/Library/EDUCAUSE+Review/OpenContentandtheEmerging/40626 (accessed May 1, 2009).

Wenger, E. R., McDermott, R. and Snyder, W. M. (2002) *Cultivating Communities of Practice*, Boston: Harvard Business School Press.

World International Property Organization (2010) "Copyright and related rights'. Retrieved from: www.wipo.int/about-ip/en/copyright.html (accessed May 16, 2010).

7 Critical thinking in the tourism curriculum

Teresa Leopold

Introduction

It is tempting to dive straight into discussing the complexity of critical thinking, however this would be to ignore the argument, which initiated my journey to critical thinking – the ongoing search for finding a balanced tourism curriculum, which is informed by tourism management theory but also social science approaches to tourism. This is not as easy as it might seem, as curriculum development is dynamic and complex and is underlined not only by pedagogic but also political reasoning. Curricula develop in the, often, neoliberalist managerial structures that many universities have come to adopt. The neoliberal drive and search for increased social and economic productivity and stability, the notion of competition, as well as economical and political developments impact upon tourism programmes in higher education institutions through changing funding systems and increasing the need for industrial collaboration (Ayikoru *et al.* 2009). These developments place universities within a competitive business environment using corporate language, which changes the values of universities:

> Where once college presidents meant what they said when they spoke of excellence or providing opportunity, today such sentiments come across as advertising slogans, carefully crafted with the latest market research findings in mind. Rosenzweig (2001) had it exactly right when he said, 'The values of the market are not the values of the university' (p. 210), and the issue facing the academy is that the values of the market are steadily encroaching on and transforming the values of the university.
>
> (Steck 2003: 68)

What tourism academics need to consider in light of these developments is their effect on curriculum design, subject content knowledge and pedagogical content knowledge as education is indeed 'faced with the complex requirements of the world and employment today' (O'Brien 2002: 4).

In addition to this development, the tourism curriculum has to cater for the diverse stakeholder expectations and requirements that come with such a fragmented industry. It has to acknowledge the request for training, which dominated higher education tourism curricula in the 1980s and early 1990s and has, to some extent, re-emerged with the focus on graduate employability skills (Churchward and Riley 2002; Ayikoru *et al.* 2009). Meanwhile there is the call to 'move away from narrow but important issues on curriculum, teaching and learning to broader issues related to power, ideology and discourse' (Ayikoru *et al.* 2009: 214). However, rather than moving away from these issues, this chapter suggests to acknowledge and put a spotlight on critical thinking within teaching, learning and curriculum of tourism higher education programmes to provide students with the tools to deal with today's complex issues and global changes. Thus, tourism curricula would follow Barnett and Coate's (2005: 39) framework by not only reflecting the social context in which they are located and the 'power of the knowledge field' but also become 'pervasive and powerful' by focusing on understanding and thinking processes. Tribe (2002: 340) provides a key contribution in the study of tourism curriculum with his exploration of graduates as 'philosophical practitioners'. This would allow the 'balance between satisfying the demands of business and those of the wider tourism society and world' (Tribe 2002: 340). While Tribe (2002) acknowledges the need for critical thinking by philosophical practitioners, this chapter furthers the discussion by focusing on critical thinking as the crucial skill within tourism curricula.

It seems that in our quickly advancing global world of technology and globalisation, developing critical thinking is more important than ever (Halpern 2003, Pithers and Soden 2000); see, for example, Cho and Schmelzer's (2000) discussion on the need for critical thinking for hospitality managers of the future. It is an invaluable asset for students as it prepares them to deal with issues and challenges not only in their careers but also in their daily lives (Tsui 2002). Global developments have influenced the way many people work, with job changes throughout careers being a normality, and rapidly changing work environments through globalisation, technological development and internationalisation. Thus, workers and, in particular, university graduates are expected to be lifelong learners rather than pure subject knowledge specialists. The argument is thus made that developing critical thinking in students would give them the key to be able to deal with such developments and expectations and thus enable them to become 'well-rounded' and responsible citizens.

In this chapter I put forward the call to acknowledge, become aware of and embed critical thinking within all tourism curricula as a tool to move tourism curricula into the future. By doing so, students will be equipped, not only with imperative subject knowledge necessary to work in their area of interest, but also with a critical thinking ability which will allow them to become lifelong learners. What should be considered here is that it is difficult to develop a serious counterargument to claim that the tourism curricula should not develop critical thinkers. There seems to be a consensus that curricula should be designed to encourage thinking (Pithers and Soden 2000). Yet, to encourage critical thinking to become a fixed and acknowledged aim in tourism curricula, we need to establish what critical thinking entails, its role in subject and pedagogic content knowledge and ultimately how critical thinking could be taught.

I start therefore with some scenarios in which critical thinking skills are employed in tourism curricula:

> Angela is asked in a tutorial to take on the role of a tour operator in a debate on the potential introduction of a speed limit on a lake in a National Park.

> Students are asked to write their views on the film 'Cannibal Tours' while watching it during class.

> Joanne is a tourism student who needs to establish the feasibility for a potential tourism attraction for a destination.

> Phillip has to write an essay. The title is 'Critically evaluate and reflect on your visit to the tourist attraction using managerial concepts'.

> Mary is a tourism postgraduate student and has found a journal article that relates to her topic area. She now needs to assess the relevance and validity of the article.

The scenarios clearly illustrate that critical thinking can take place across a huge variety of different learning environments and levels as well as situations and subject areas. However, even though thinking skills are taught and assessed, these are often not recognised enough due to a focus on repeated subject content rather than reasoning processes (Van Courland Moon 1986).

What is critical thinking?

Over the last two decades, critical thinking has become a buzz word in educational studies (Fisher 2001), embedded within institutional objectives and development of curricula (Potts 1994), and is seen as a product of liberal undergraduate education (Greenlaw and DeLoach 2003). The popularity of the term and its recognition as important key graduate attribute or key graduate skill (such as at University of Essex, University of Sydney, Canterbury Christ Church University, Bristol University) highlight the importance of the concept of critical thinking. This leads to the assumption that everyone knows what critical thinking is (Moon 2008): 'The idea of critical thinking has been around for a long time and I suspect that most academics would accept it as a fundamental concept that truly defines what a "higher" education might be' (Harland 2008: 5). While the significance of critical thinking for higher education has been recognised by many researchers (such as Dewey 1938; Kuhn 1999; Pithers and Soden 2000), the practicalities and awareness of teaching critical thinking are often complex and absent in tourism curricula.

Numerous definitions exist which frame critical thinking (such as Ennis 1985: 45; Brookfield 1987: 13–14; Halpern 2003: 6; Paul 1995, cited in Walker 2003: 264; Cottrell 2005: 2), most of which are build on similar elements (objective reasoning with indefinite solutions), though it can be explored using different approaches, such as logic, development approaches, skills components, pedagogy, etc. (Garside 1996; Moon 2008). Willingham (n.d. cited in hooks 2010: 8) defines critical thinking as being capable of 'seeing both sides of an issue, being open to new evidence that disconfirms young ideas, reasoning dispassionately, demanding that claims be backed by evidence, deducing and inferring conclusions from available facts, solving problems, and so forth.' While there are clearly more than two sides to an issue, the key message is that critical thinking involves questioning personal and others' assumptions, knowledge and beliefs and determining 'what matters most' (hooks 2010: 9). Thus, critical thinking can be seen as a learning process but rather than just learning, the thinker develops a way to question knowledge (Moon 2004, 2008). Subject content, for instance whether a student analyses the management operation of a tourist attraction or the tourist behaviour at the tourist attraction, will of course lead to the consultation of different sources, however the critical thinking processes will be much alike (such as understanding, analysing, etc.). In other words, critical thinking informs the analysis and questioning of existing knowledge to develop new knowledge (Moon 2008).

The question was once put to me – 'Why *critical* thinking? Why not just thinking?' The answer is that critical thinking is more than just the pure process of thinking as it acknowledges and entails the 'tools of manipulation of knowledge' (Moon 2008: 14). Within this context, the importance of the skill set underlying critical thinking becomes crucial as it enables us to manipulate knowledge.

Focusing on actual skill components allows us to gain an understanding of the specific competences involved in critical thinking, rather than seeing it as a logical development process, where one skill leads to the other (this is discussed in the next section). Numerous critical thinking skills exist and have been discussed in academic literature (such as Cottrell's 2005 book *Critical Thinking Skills*; Beyer 1985), identifying the following critical thinking skills: to identify and detect unjustified assumptions, biases and flaws in arguments; to find, evaluate and be able to distinguish relevant from irrelevant sources of evidence; to recognise logical inconsistencies or fallacies in an author's line of reasoning and thus assess the quality of the argument; to distinguish between warranted and unwarranted claims and thus recognise assumptions and implicit arguments; to find and evaluate sources of evidence and determine their reliability; and, to identify argument and non-argument. In addition, Cottrell (2005) acknowledges the ability to process critical reading and note taking, while other researchers highlight the ability to *evaluate* (e.g. Sadler 1989; Bell 1995) and *reflect (*e.g. Fisher 2001; Moon 2008) as key skills for critical thinking. Students who become critical thinkers start to question concepts and beliefs, which they have constructed based on their past knowledge and experience. This is closely linked to the learning theory of cognitive constructivism in that learners question and construct concepts based on their past and new knowledge (Stewart 2004).

Critical thinking can also be seen as a development process, as new knowledge needs to be gained and questioned, new thinking skills need to be learned and employed, and new knowledge needs to be constructed (Moon 2008). Thinking has been conceptualised as a development process by many authors (such as Bell 1995; Fisher 2001; Cottrell 1999; Halpern 1998). Bloom's taxonomy (1956) becomes important within this context, as it is one of the most common frameworks for thinking. In the taxonomy, thinking is described in a nearly linear way from pure knowledge gain to comprehension, application, analysis, synthesis and evaluation, with the latter representing the most complex thinking level. The question arises, though, whether conceptualising thinking as a strict hierarchical approach allows for recognition of the complexity of critical thinking and students' diverse foundational knowledge. Halpern (1998) suggests a four part process to become a critical thinker, which involves learning the skills needed for critical thinking (1), developing and using these skills through mindful practising (2), being aware of the need for critical thinking in situations which are beyond one's subject knowledge (3) and being able to monitor and judge one's critical thinking (4).

Employing a specific and systematic thinking skills development process (such as suggested by Halpern 1998) as a scaffolding process for students to understand their thinking process seems sensible. This would encourage a student-centred orientation, which builds on 'facilitating understandings, promoting conceptual change and intellectual development' (Pithers and Soden 2000: 247). Reflecting on thinking skills, which should underline tourism curricula, it becomes obvious that most thinking skills and processes will be applicable to situations outside the specific subject content. Thus, regardless of whether subject content of curricula is focused on tourism management or tourism studies, if graduates are able to think critically they should be able to use this skill across their career and daily life.

Pedagogy, epistemology and critical thinking

bell hooks (2010), a renowned African American cultural critic and educator, describes in her reflection on her schooling in the 1950s how education was upheld as the surest route to freedom. However, her romanticised image of universities as 'paradise of learning' was shattered by 'teachers who appeared to derive their primary pleasure in the classroom by exercising their authoritarian power over my fellow students, crushing our spirits, and dehumanizing our minds and bodies' (hooks 2010: 2).

To me, critical thinking is represented in different aspects within bell hooks' narrative/memory: first, the need of universities to provide positive environments for critical thinking and learning; second, the influence of teachers' epistemological beliefs upon the learning environment they are creating; and, third, the belief that power of knowledge can bring about changes or, in other words, allow and foster critical action. I will now explore the first two aspects by considering the role of teachers' epistemological beliefs in providing a learning environment, which allows for critical thinking at universities.

Day-to-day political, economic and social developments affect how subject content knowledge and pedagogical content knowledge are embedded in design of curricula, but often result in a dominant focus on subject content (Pithers and Soden 2000). Teachers are already faced with a dilemma of having to teach complex social dilemmas within the backdrop of blurring disciplinary boundaries (O'Brien 2002). Thus, integrating a stronger focus on critical thinking skills and, potentially, assessing them requires a very balanced subject and pedagogical content. Inui *et al.* (2006: 34) describe the two key elements of tourism education as 'preparing students to be employable' and 'facilitate critical thinking and moral decision making'.

However, each year, teachers encounter students who seem to show little interest in thinking, clearly evident in their actions and expressions. It seems that what they expect is pure subject knowledge, ideally spoon fed to them, rather than actual thinking (hooks 2010). Fortunately, there are some teachers who, whether aware or unaware of it, embrace effective pedagogy to provide students with a renewed interest and joy in thinking critically. Engagement plays a fundamental role in this development (Bryson and Hand 2007). It is largely built on trust relations between student and teacher, as well as the provision of an active learning environment, which allows for critical thinking to develop (Howard *et al.* 2000).

Little is known of the interrelations between teachers' subject content knowledge and pedagogical content knowledge (Evan 1993). Pedagogical content knowledge can be defined as 'the ways of representing and formulating the subject matter that make it comprehensible to others as well as understanding what makes the learning of specific topics easy or difficult' (Evan 1993: 94). Thus, pedagogical content knowledge presents a crucial element of the teacher–learner interaction. However, often teaching is primarily seen as imparting subject knowledge, treating it as a kind of commodity that can be conveyed to the students (Fox 1983). Moon (2008: 134) argues, 'staff knowledge and development have a crucial role in fostering critical thinking'. In particular, teachers' epistemological beliefs have a direct influence on teaching strategies (Hashweh 1996), what focus they put on learning, decision making in the classroom etc. (Chan and Elliott 2000). Given that critical thinking requires individuals to question knowledge, the importance of recognition for teachers' but also students' epistemological understanding of today's society becomes crucial; particularly in light of today's students' diverse backgrounds and ethnicities within one classroom. Exploring and recognising teachers' and students' epistemological beliefs would provide an understanding of 'how individuals come to know, the theories and beliefs they hold about knowing, and the manner in which such epistemological premises are a part of and an influence on the cognitive processes of thinking and reasoning' (Hofer and Pintrich 1997: 88). Thus, what needs to be recognised is that the link between students' epistemology and the ability to think critically is influenced not only by a teacher's ability to teach and his/her understanding of teaching and learning, but also issues of teachers' and students' gender, ethnicity, culture, motivation, beliefs, interest in the subject content, age and education. This was already recognised by Freire (1970) when arguing that students construct their knowledge based on their life experience and later by Pinnars and Bowers (1992: 186): 'Fundamental problems plague the contemporary effort to study the politics of curriculum. These are problems associated with gender, race, and culture; they are embedded in the modes of cognition as well as the themes and slogans of critical scholarship'. It seems that there has been little advancement in these issues since then, even though today's classrooms are becoming more diverse and international than ever. The need for teachers to be aware of students' individual foundation of assumptions, knowledge and beliefs, and explore links to new knowledge has become of even greater importance.

The question then remains whether critical thinking should be taught specifically or whether it should be embedded within subject content. Pedagogic researchers (such as Dewey 1938; Halpern 1998) have long called for the recognition of thinking as a central purpose of education and emphasised the need to move beyond teaching subject knowledge to teach students to learn how to think. Still we have to recognise that 'the nature of thinking of an individual is under the control of that individual and one person cannot make another think critically' (Moon 2008: 131; original emphasis removed). Nevertheless, there are a number of ways to encourage critical thinking among learners, such as challenging students to think beyond their comfort zone (Moon 2008; King and Kitchener 1994), providing a positive and encouraging classroom environment and using assessments as a way to not only encourage learning but also critical thinking (Moon 2008; Leopold and Vickerman 2010). MacPherson (1999) reports her success in developing critical thinking among management students by providing an explicit lecture and seminar on critical thinking, followed by peer reviewed student presentations throughout the remainder of the year. Her research demonstrates the positive results that might derive from an awareness of critical thinking strategies and skills by teachers and students. In her discussion on how to foster critical thinking, Tsui (2002) reviews positive teacher-influenced classroom interactions, which encouraged students' critical thinking. These are encouragement, praise and usage of student ideas, students' level of classroom participation and involvement as well as the amount of student interaction encouraged during a course.

In the discussion on pedagogy and critical thinking, we also have to consider the changing nature of the delivery of tourism programmes. Developments ranging from universities' funding structures, today's neoliberal environment to global mobility have impacted on today's higher education offer. Thus, an increasing number of distance learning programmes as well as higher education off-campus centres in countries around the globe are being opened, resulting in the need for technological advances that move beyond classroom settings. With the emergence and growing importance of technological tools and social media, also for student/teacher and institution/student interaction, ways to incorporate critical thinking through technology have advanced: Al-Fadhli and Khalfan (2008) explore e-learning as tool to 'construct' knowledge and thus develop critical thinking, Greenlaw and DeLoach (2003) focus on electronic discussion to foster critical thinking and van Gelder (2001) reflects on the University of Melbourne's *Reason!Able* software, which has proved successful in enhancing students' critical thinking skills through technology. These studies clearly promote e-learning environments and technologies as suitable tools and advances to encourage critical thinking among students in higher education (Al-Fadhli and Khalfan 2008).

Concerns have been voiced with regard to the difficulty of assessing critical thinking within subject content and the question of how we can assess thinking (Pithers and Soden 2000), particularly as it 'involve(s) qualitative changes in thinking and complex interactions between thinking and value formation' (Thoma 1993: 133). Greenlaw and DeLoach's (2003) suggestions regarding how to assess critical thinking align with the concept of different thinking levels, ranging from the provision of pure unilateral descriptions (level 1), simplistic alternatives (level 2), basic analysis and reasoning (level 3) to theoretical inference (level 4), empirical inference (level 5) to, finally, the merging of values with analysis (level 6). Other studies (such as Tsui 1999 and Astin 1993 cited in Tsui 2002) highlight a range of assessment techniques that encourage critical thinking such as group project work, class presentations, essay exams etc. What is prevalent in studies is the recognition of writing, reading and in-class discussion, often key elements of formative and summative assessments, to facilitate the development of critical thinking (Tsui 2002; Tieney *et al.* 1989). Reflective enquiry is another key skill of critical thinking (Fisher 2001; Moon 2008) as it is a meaning-making process and requires active engagement of the individual (Rodgers 2001; Rodgers 2002). This is reflected in Tribe's (2002) discussion and suggestion to focus on vocational and liberal reflection as two key domains that should inform curricula for tourism higher education. Encouraging students to reflect on their own epistemology through reflective diaries, learning journals and reflective essays would thus encourage students to develop their thinking (Pithers and Soden 2000; Duron *et al.* 2006; Moon 2006; Leopold and Vickerman 2010).

Final thoughts on critical thinking

The chapter has aimed to locate critical thinking within the tourism curriculum to provide students with more than just the necessary subject content, but also with lifelong learning skills. To encourage critical thinking among students is to step beyond teaching pure subject content knowledge to wanting to share the intellectual journey of students. It builds on recognising students as individuals and developing a trust relationship and thus a positive learning environment in which students feel safe to take the initiative to explore their own thinking. To achieve this, there is the need to be aware of teachers' and students' epistemology and employ pedagogy to provide the confidence and awareness to start questioning the construct of knowledge.

It follows that we need to recognise the crucial role of academic staff members in fostering critical thinking but, more importantly, we have to ensure an awareness of this responsibility among staff. Acknowledging academia as a continuing conversation that is based on a culture of scholarship, learning and knowledge (Steck 2003) highlights the need for interaction and critical thought among and between staff and students. Engagement and trust, as discussed above, play key roles in allowing 'conversations' to take place in classroom situations and foster critical thinking. Thus recognising critical thinking as a key element of tourism curricula would provide a common stand between management focused or social science focused approaches to tourism curricula.

References

Al-Fadhli, S. and Khalfan, A. (2009) 'Developing critical thinking in e-learning environment: Kuwait University as a case study', *Assessment & Evaluation in Higher Education*, 34 (5): 529–536.

Astin, A. (1993) *What Matters in College?* San Francisco: Jossey-Bass.

Ayikoru, M., Tribe, J. and Airey, D. (2009) 'Reading tourism education: neoliberalism unveiled', *Annals of Tourism Research*, 36 (2): 191–221.

Barnett, R. (2000) 'Supercomplexity and the curriculum', *Studies in Higher Education*, 25 (3): 255–265.

Barnett, R. and Coate, K. (2005) *Engaging the Curriculum in Higher Education*, Berkshire: Open University Press.

Barnett, R. and Hallam, S. (1999) 'Teaching for supercomplexity: a pedagogy for higher education', in P. Mortimore (ed.), *Understanding Pedagogy and its Impact on Learning*, London: Paul Chapman.

Bell, J. (1995) *Evaluating Psychological Information*, Boston: Allyn and Bacon.

Beyer, B. (1985) 'Critical thinking: what is it?' *Social Education*, 39: 270–276.

Bloom, B. (1956) *A Taxonomy of Educational Objectives, Handbook 1: cognitive domain*, New York: McKay.

Brockbank, A. and McGill, I. (2007) *Facilitating Reflective Learning in Higher Education* (2nd edition), Milton Keynes: Society for Research in Higher Education and Open University Press.

Brookfield, S. (1987) *Developing Critical Thinking*, Milton Keynes: Society for Research in Higher Education and Open University Press.

Bryson, C. and Hand, L. (2007) 'The role of engagement in inspiring teaching and learning', *Innovations in Education and Teaching International*, 44 (4): 349–362.

Chan, K.-W. and Elliott, R. G. (2000) 'Exploratory study of epistemological beliefs of Hong Kong teacher education students: resolving conceptual and empirical issues', *Asia-Pacific Journal of Teacher Education*, 28 (3): 225–234.

Cho, W. and Schmelzer, C. D. (2000) 'Just-in-time education: tools for hospitality managers of the future', *International Journal of Contemporary Hospitality Management*, 12 (1): 31–36.

Churchward, J. and Riley, M. (2002) 'Tourism occupations and education: an exploration study', *International Journal of Tourism Research*, 4: 77–86.

Cottrell, S. (1999) *The Study Skills Handbook*, Basingstoke: Macmillan.

Cottrell, S. (2005) *Critical Thinking Skills*, Basingstoke: Palgrave MacMillan.

Dewey, J. (1938) *Experience and Education*, New York: Collier Macmillan.

Duron, R., Limbach, B. and Waugh, W. (2006) 'Critical thinking framework for any discipline', *International Journal of Teaching and Learning in Higher Education*, 17 (2): 160–166.

Ennis, R. H. (1985) 'A logical basis for measuring critical thinking skills', *Educational Leadership*, 43: 44–48.

Evan, R. (1993) 'Subject-matter knowledge and pedagogical content knowledge:

prospective secondary teachers and the function concept', *Journal for Research in Mathematics Education*, 24 (2): 94–116.

Fisher, A. (2001) *Critical Thinking: An Introduction*, Cambridge: Cambridge University Press.

Fox, D. (1983) 'Personal theories of teaching', *Studies in Higher Education*, 8 (2): 151–163.

Freire, P. (1970) *Pedagogy of the Oppressed* (trans. M. Bergman), London: Penguin Books Ltd.

Garside, C. (1996) 'Look who's talking: a comparison of lecture and group discussion teaching strategies in developing critical thinking skills', *Communication Education*, 45 (3): 212–227.

Greenlaw, S. A. and DeLoach, S. B. (2003) 'Teaching critical thinking with electronic discussion', *Journal of Economic Education*, 34 (1): 36–52.

Halpern, D. E. (1998) 'Teaching critical thinking for transfer across domains: dispositions, skills, structure training, and metacognitive monitoring', *American Psychologist*, 53: 449–455.

Halpern, D. F. (2003) *Thought & Knowledge: an introduction to critical thinking* (4th edition), New York: Taylor & Francis Group.

Harland, T. (2008) 'What could Barnett mean by critical action?' *Akoranga*, 3: 5–6, Dunedin: University of Otago.

Hashweh, M. Z. (1996) 'Effects of science teachers' epistemological beliefs in teaching', *Journal of Research in Science Teaching*, 33: 47–63.

Hofer, B. K. and Pintrich, R. (1997) 'The development of epistemological theories: beliefs about knowledge and knowing and their relation to learning', *Review of Education Research*, 67 (1): 88–140.

hooks, b. (2010) *Teaching Critical Thinking: practical wisdom*, New York: Routledge.

Howard, B., McGee, S., Schwartz, N. and Purcell, S. (2000) 'The experience of constructivism: transforming teacher epistemology', *Journal of Research on Computing in Education*, 32 (4): 455–465.

Inui, Y., Wheeler, D. and Lankford, S. (2006) 'Rethinking tourism education: what should schools teach?', *Journal of Hospitality, Leisure, Sport and Tourism Education*, 5 (2): 25–35.

King, P. and Kitchener, K. (1994) *Developing Reflective Judgment*, San Francisco: Jossey-Bass.

Kuhn, D. (1999) 'A development model of critical thinking', *Educational Researcher*, 28 (2): 16–26, 46.

Leopold, T. and Vickerman, P. (2010) *Learning and Teaching Guide on Critical Thinking*, Subject Guide, Higher Education Academy Network for Hospitality, Leisure, Sport and Tourism. Retrieved from: http://www.heacademy.ac.uk/hlst/resources/subjectspecificguides.

MacPherson, K. (1999) 'The development of critical thinking skills in undergraduate supervisory management units: efficacy of student peer assessment', *Assessment & Evaluation in Higher Education*, 24 (3): 273–284.

Moon, J. (2004) *A Handbook of Reflective and Experiential Learning*, London: Routledge.

Moon, J. (2006) *Learning Journals: a handbook for reflective practice and professional development* (2nd edition), London: Routledge Farmer.

Moon, J. (2008) *Critical Thinking: An exploration of theory and practice*, London: Routledge.

O'Brien, M. (2002) *New Pedagogies in the Knowledge Society: why this challenge is an epistemological one*, refereed paper presented at Australian Association for Research in Education AARE International Conference 2–6 December 2002, Brisbane.

Pinars, W. F. and Bowers, C. A. (1992) 'Politics of curriculum: origins, controversies, and significance of critical perspectives', *Review of Research and Education*, 18: 163–190.

Pithers, R. T. and Soden, R. (2000) 'Critical thinking in education: a review', *Educational Research*, 42 (3): 237–249.

Potts, B. (1994) 'Strategies for teaching critical thinking', *Practical Assessment, Research & Evaluation*, 4 (3).

Raths, L. E., Wasserman, S., Jonas, A. and Rothstein, A. (1966) *Teaching for Critical Thinking: theory and application*, Hillsdale, NJ: Erlbaum.

Rodgers, R. (2001) 'Reflection in higher education: a concept analysis', *Innovative Higher Education*, 26 (1): 37–57.

Rodgers, C. (2002) 'Defining reflection: another look at John Dewey and reflective thinking', *Teachers College Record*, 104 (4): 842–866.

Sadler, D. R. (1989) 'Formative assessment and the design of instructional systems', *Instructional Science*, 18: 119–144.

Steck, H. (2003) 'Corporatization of the university: seeking conceptual clarity', *Annals of the American Academy of Political and Social Science*, 585: 66–83.

Stewart, M. (2004) 'Learning through research: an introduction to the main theories of learning', *JMU Learning & Teaching Press*, 4 (1): 6–14.

Thoma, G. A. (1993) 'The Perry framework and tactics for teaching critical thinking in economics', *Journal of Economic Education*, 24: 128–136.

Tierney, R. J., Soter, A., O'Flahavan, J. F. and McGinley, W. (1989) 'The Effects of Reading and Writing upon Thinking Critically', *Reading Research Quarterly*, 24 (2): 134–173.

Tribe, J. (2002) 'The philosophic practitioner', *Annals of Tourism Research*, 29 (2): 338–357.

Tsui, L. (1999) 'Courses and instruction affecting critical thinking', *Research in Higher Education*, 40: 185–200.

Tsui, L. (2002) 'Fostering critical thinking through effective pedagogy: evidence from four institutional case studies', *The Journal of Higher Education*, 73 (6): 740–763.

Van Courtland Moon, J. (1986) 'Teaching critical thinking to management students', in J. Golub (ed.) *Activities to Promote Critical Thinking*, Urbana, USA: National Council of Teachers of English.

van Gelder, T. (2001) 'How to improve critical thinking using educational technology', in G. Kennedy, M. Keppell, C. McNaught and T. Petrovic (eds), *Meeting at the Crossroads: proceedings of the 18th annual conference of the Australasian Society for Computers in Learning in Tertiary Education*, Melbourne: Biomedical Multimedia Unit, The University of Melbourne, pp. 539–548.

Walker, S. (2003) 'Active learning strategies to promote critical thinking', *Journal of Athletic Training*, 38 (2): 263–267.

8 Thinking inside the box

Understanding discursive production and consumption in tourism

Kellee Caton

Introduction

Travel's potential to unite people across the lines of culture and nationality has long captivated the popular and scholarly imagination, and recent events such as the IIPT European Conference on Peace through Tourism demonstrate that this age-old concern has lost none of its fervor. Early work on tourism as a catalyst for cross-cultural understanding (e.g. Milman *et al.* 1990) focused largely on the actual tourism encounter—a not-too-surprising approach, given the anthropological and social-psychological disciplinary paradigms that then dominated much of tourism studies. But as later cultural studies work would clarify, focusing on the encounter alone is insufficient because human understandings are not completely born from the realm of direct experience. Instead, we enter tourism encounters with a head full of preconceived expectations based both on our own memories and on broader cultural imaginaries that quietly saturate our consciousness. We therefore need work that explores the production and consumption of tourism representations as part of the "worldmaking" labor of tourism—Hollinshead's (2007) collective term for the "creative and collaborative [processes of] essentializing/naturalizing/normalizing" that occur through all types of social interactions including tourism, the fruits of which, in the case of tourism, are collectively or disjointedly produced mythologies of spaces and cultures (p. 166). Such work can contribute greatly to furthering our understanding of the role of travel in promoting or inhibiting the development of cross-cultural understanding, respect, and compassion because it calls attention to the broader discursive environment in which tourism experiences are enmeshed.

Although popular culture has tended to valorize travel as a path to intercultural harmony, much scholarship has concluded otherwise, arguing that tourism often promotes essentialized views of people and cultures (e.g. Bruner 1991). This outcome occurs through multiple and mutually reinforcing practices, as tourism brokers first employ established representations of destinations for promotion, and then produce sites in accordance, to avoid tourist disappointment (Buck 1977; Bruner 2005). Tourists' experiences at such sites thus often serve to reinforce extant stereotypes, and when they return home, they share stories and photographs that augment the supply of narratives rearticulating dominant discursive themes. This cycle of stereotyping is particularly problematic in situations when vast inequalities exist between tourist-sending and tourist-receiving societies (Echtner and Prasad 2003). A growing mountain of empirical studies, discussed below, continue to convincingly demonstrate that western tourism contributes to the social construction of nonwestern people and cultures as exotic, primitive, sensual, servile, morally inferior, and dependent on the West. This "western imaginary" serves to polarize the western Self and the nonwestern Other and promote a superiority ideology that legitimates inequality.

Despite its many important contributions, work in this vein has been somewhat limited, in that it has tended to focus primarily on calling attention to the presence and power of particular patterns of depiction but has stopped short of exploring why those patterns occur, why they continue to have resonance despite changing global political and economic conditions, and why they seem so hard to do anything about. Tourism representations have tended to be abstracted from their specific conditions of production, such that the connections between messages and the circumstances of their creation go underexplored and underarticulated, but it is precisely this kind of analysis that is needed if we are to truly understand their power and to begin to imagine ways to change them.

In this chapter, I thus attempt to highlight discourse as a key feature of the tourism phenomenon that must be addressed both on a more theoretical level and in a manner that is more dialectical with actual sociocultural conditions if tourism is indeed to serve as a force for cross-cultural understanding, empathy, and peace. I begin by sketching a backdrop for considering tourism as a space where imagination is richly at work, and then proceed to build a theoretical framework that I hope will help to elucidate the process of discursive production and consumption as constrained activities that operate through external conditions to produce particular outcomes. Thus, I seek to go beyond articulating the messages produced through tourism media products, site framing, and tourist encounters to broadly explore *how* those messages come to be produced and consumed through these practices, given contemporary sociocultural conditions.

Tourism as a space of imagining

Although much work in tourism studies derives from a business studies perspective, it has long been recognized by anthropologists, geographers, sociologists, cultural studies scholars, and many others that tourism is much more than an experiential product to be sold. Instead, it is a site at which individuals and groups encounter one another (sometimes directly, sometimes in the virtual space of media products like magazines and Internet sites), lugging with them the cultural baggage of their heritages, ideologies, and past experiences, and then attempt to make sense of one another. Through these sense-making encounters, understandings are produced that have consequences, ideological, but also material. Thus, tourism helps to produce the world in a particular shape, both in terms of the way it is imagined and in terms of the material outcomes that flow from the choices people make about how to treat each other based on their perceptions of one another. Thus, we have Hollinshead's (2007) notion of tourism as a "worldmaker": a space of cross-cultural understanding or misunderstanding, a catalyst for social justice and peace or a Neverland where toxic dreams of the Other as an object of pleasure, realized through tourism productions, invite escape from social responsibility and rationalization of excessive privilege in a grossly unequal world.

This darker side of tourism as a realm of imagining has been brought to life through the careful empirical work of discourse analysts who have deconstructed tourism imagery and written text across a variety of travel-related mass-media formats, including travel brochures (Echtner and Prasad 2003; Morgan and Pritchard 1998; Caton and Santos 2009), guidebooks (Chang and Holt 1991), postcards (Albers and James 1983, 1988), promotional websites (Caton and Santos 2009), magazines (Lutz and Collins 1993), travel stories (Santos 2006), and television programs (Fürsich 2002). Their work has generally proceeded through a framework of postcolonial theory, which argues that, even in the absence of formal political colonialism, imperialism is still alive and well in the ideological legacies colonialism has left behind (Said 1978, 1993). As the studies above illustrate, tourism is one site of such ideological production, as western tourism media products tend to sort the world into "us" and "them," articulating the West and the Rest through binaries such as modern–traditional, subject–object, powerful–dependent, dynamic–unchanging, master–servant, moral–devious, and industrious–lazy. Although work on discursive consumption in tourism has been less prolific, Bruner's analysis of cultural tours in Kenya and Indonesia and Caton and Santos's (2008) exploration of student-produced imagery in a study abroad yearbook begin to suggest what happens on the receiving end, as tourists reproduce in their own interpretations the fantasies they are nurtured on. These deconstructive studies help us to understand the *outcomes* of the imaginative labor that is occurring through contemporary tourism. The *process*, however, still bears exploring.

Boxed in: discursive production and consumption as situated processes

Despite recognition that tourism has an important role to play in ideological production, there has been little theoretical work on this front. A conceptual framework can thus provide some grounding for this analysis. Discourses do not appear from nowhere; they circulate and produce their "effects of truth" (or "truthiness," as modern comedian-commentator Jon Stewart of the *Daily Show* would put it) by working through larger systems to which they are tied (Foucault 1980: 131). Ways of understanding the world are not fixed and inevitable, but socially and relationally produced (Hall 1997). The worldmaking agency of tourism thus exists not as a force unto itself; it works *through* a variety of external conditions that both constrain and enable particular outcomes. If we want to question hegemonic discourses, and ultimately to change them, then we have to understand their logic—where they come from and why they "make sense." In other words, we have to learn how to think *inside* the box: the overarching nexus of conditions that governs ideological production in tourism in the contemporary moment.

In Figure 8.1, I attempt to tackle this entanglement by proposing a representation of the discursive process as a situated phenomenon. The blue circle surrounding it denotes what I shall call the regulatory framework of discursive production and consumption. This framework consists of elements that mediate the discursive process, elements which can be grouped, in an ideal-typical sense, into three broad categories: material conditions, historical understandings, and human experience.

Material conditions include aspects of the physical world that bear on human understanding; they include tangible elements, such as economic resources and physical characteristics of spaces, as well as more abstract entities such as formal legal codes. The inclusion of material conditions here captures the Marxian notion that human understanding exists very heavily in reference to one's place in the social hierarchy, as determined by his or her access to resources, as well as the Foucauldian notion that ways of making sense of a phenomenon at any given time are partially a product of the reigning institutions and available resources of the day.

Historical understandings refer to the body of thought and speech already existing about a particular phenomenon up to the present moment. This idea captures Gramscian notions of the power of ideological, in addition to material, aspects of culture to shape human beliefs (Hall 1986). Religious, ethnic, national, and other cultural traditions all influence the way elements of the life-world are understood, and new understandings are always situated, in some way, in relation to old ones.

In contrast to the previous two notions, which emphasize the way our understandings are at least partially determined for us by forces larger than ourselves, human experience refers to the way that lived, embodied encounters mediate

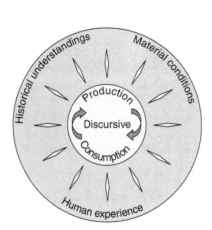

Figure 8.1 Discursive production and consumption as situated processes.

human understandings. Human beings are not mindless drones, infinitely programmable by larger ideological and material forces; we are creative, cognitive, and moral creatures constantly in the process of interpreting that which we encounter. Although, as many thinkers such as Goffman (1974) have noted, we always interpret the world in light of what we have already come to know, we are also capable of modifying what we know based on new data we encounter. Thus, human experience is a powerful player in regulating the production and expression of understandings, and its inclusion in this scheme captures the contribution of philosophical hermeneutics scholars such as Gadamer, who emphasize existence as an ongoing dialogic encounter between human beings and that which lies outside us (Baronov 2004).

The regulatory framework thus constitutes the web of conditions through which imaginative labor occurs. It is enabling as well as constraining—an inescapable forcefield which favors some outcomes and inhibits others. At the same time, however, discursive processes also exert outward pressure on the framework itself. Material conditions can be altered as a result of changing discursive patterns, new discourses eventually become part of historical understandings, and extant discourses bear on humans' interpretations of their experiences. As we shall see, this framework, which highlights the entanglement of discourse with forces and conditions external to itself, can help us to better understand the unique contours of ideological production in the context of contemporary tourism.

Below, I attempt to flesh out this framework by exemplifying but a few of the myriad ways that material conditions, historical understandings, and human experiences can come together to drive problematic ideological outcomes through tourism. As I illustrate below, the unique features of the regulatory context of contemporary tourism tend to lead to a situation in which notions of the Other as an exotic object of difference are more easily buttressed than resisted.

Constrained encoding

Much work in discourse analysis has focused on reading and deconstructing marketing messages, but less thought tends to be given to the conditions that produce the messages. Marketing choices obviously relate to an organization's specific goals, and tourism organizations are no different. It has become fashionable in leftist circles to emphasize the pursuit of profit in the commercial sector as the sole driver of organizational decision-making, and this is clearly an important factor. Commercial tourism brokers exist to sell a product, and in the case of cultural tourism, that product is people, their spaces, and their behaviors and practices. Extant tourism research indicates that images are key in tourists' decision-making processes (Sirakaya and Sonmez 2000), and "destination decisions may be based on the symbolic elements of the destination (as conveyed in visual imagery) rather than the actual features" (MacKay and Fesenmaier 2000: 417). As such, tourism brokers must to some degree engage standardized images or "hooks" to attract tourists to the destinations they feature (MacKay and Fesenmaier 2000). Thus, commercial tourism brokers are logically heavily invested in imagery that is evocative of destinations, as filtered through potential customers' preconceived notions of those places—imagery that tends to speak the language of fantasy of an exotic world lying beyond the frontiers of the western tourist's daily existence. In turn, there is a tendency to manage tourist attractions in ways that reproduce this framing, such that the trip will live up to tourists' expectations and disappointment will be avoided (Bruner 1991; Dann 1994).

It is overly simplistic, however, to assume that problematic images in tourism promotion and site management are solely the result of a system in which callous commercial travel brokers, trawling the gutters of global culture for easy imagery, exploit potential tourists' desires for exoticism by offering them a buffet of rehashed colonialist stereotypes in order to sell them the world. This is so for several reasons.

First, although it may play a comparatively larger role in their decision-making processes, commercial brokers are not the only ones with a bottom line. Public and private-nonprofit agencies in the tourism industry, including study abroad programs, museums, cultural centers, and many other types of organizations, are not without their own financial pressures. Such agencies must find a way to keep the doors open and the lights on, to pay the salaries of their employees, and to invest in the content of the programs they offer, and in the pursuit of attracting participants or visitors, they must inevitably, if involuntarily, compete with a variety of other organizations, including those in the commercial sector, for potential participants' limited resources of money and time. Although this pressure may have at one time been offset by subsidies of public money and private charitable contributions, the increasing milieu of privatization has led to a situation in which educational and cultural organizations are being forced to rely more and more on nonstate funding sources, which in turn taxes a limited resource base for charitable giving. This turn toward privatization reflects changing ideologies about the importance of investing in shared public goods, once a hallmark of liberal democratic prioritization but now the increasing casualty of a public that is at once both suspicious of the motives and competence of its own elected officials in managing tax revenues and powerfully manipulated by a sophisticated system of global capitalism that stands to benefit from the perpetuation of misinformation regarding the importance of investing in anything beyond satisfying one's own immediate wants and pleasures (Barber 2007). Thus, even public and private-nonprofit agencies in the tourism industry can not fully escape the binds of a capitalist economy, with its hallmarks of competition, attention-mongering, and individual gratification, because the ideology of privatization undermines such organizations' resource base and because inevitable limits in tourist time, energy, and money force organizations into competition with each other and with agencies in the commercial sector.

The hardline distinction turns out to be artificial also because agents in the commercial sector, too, may be driven by goals other than profit. Although they typically do not emphasize humanitarian, educational, or other collective social goals to the degree that public and private-nonprofit organizations do, they may be concerned, at least to some degree, with corporate social responsibility. Certainly, there has been a growing discourse of social responsibility in tourism marketing, affecting commercial and noncommercial organizations alike, in terms of the way both tourists and destinations are depicted (e.g. Macbeth 2005; Buzinde *et al.* 2006; Yaman and Gurel 2006). Its existence illustrates the way that concerns external to simply "doing business" are beginning to find their way onto the agendas of tourism managers, a process that is sorely needed if tourism is going to truly benefit the world over the long term (Belhassen and Caton, forthcoming). Apparently, however, given the findings of work on postcolonial theory and tourism representations, this discourse has not penetrated deeply enough to induce critical reflexivity regarding the way nonwesterners are represented in travel media products.

One reason for this seems to lie in the complicated nexus between late capitalism, cultural fantasies, and the quest for identity. When travel brokers deal in exotic imagery, it seems unlikely that they typically are purposely attempting to exploit or stereotype the people living in toured places. More likely, they believe that the images they use are celebrating the beauty and uniqueness of the destinations they feature (and, of course, beauty sells). Aesthetics, however, are not a natural but a cultural phenomenon; beauty may be only skin deep, but the notion of beauty is incredibly complex. At the dawn of the twenty-first century, the combination of globalization and the spread of the post-Fordist economy, in which individuals have increasingly come to rely on market products to define and communicate (an arguably even to understand) their own identities, has resulted in the foregrounding of racial and ethnic diversity in modern consumer-culture aesthetics, both because of corporations' increasing need to manufacture and market niche products and because of their need to find new markets for the ever more highly differentiated raw materials of identity in which they deal (Giroux 1993). Race and ethnicity have become an increasingly frequently tapped well for fueling this production of niche products, as the popularity of everything from world music to "third world cinema" to ethnically inspired fashion readily attests. In the words of Davidson (1992: 199), "capital has fallen in love with difference." Such a situation has made it possible for traditional imagery of the Other, of the type featured in glossy *National Geographic* spreads—once the fodder of armchair anthropologists and geographers—to find a new home in the pages of fashion magazines and other venues of hip, youthful popular culture.

Thus, when travel brokers seek to advertise the people and cultures of the world as their products, they are acting not only under the influence of a contemporary travel culture which prizes the nineteenth century notion of the exotic and untouched authentic Other that functioned as the handmaiden of empire, but also under broader twenty-first century pop cultural constructions of nonwestern cultures as infinitely unique and intriguing—interpretations which have quite a grip, backed as they are by the interests of corporations whose lifestyle products they help to move. Western consumers, seeking self-definition in the post-ascriptive identity playground left in the wake of the retreat of the traditional regulatory forces of church and tribe, suture themselves anew to "lifestyle identities," derived in part through the appropriation of the tokens of Others' forms of cultural expression (see Maira's [2000] discussion of the *bindi*'s reincarnation as a western fashion statement for an excellent example of this phenomenon). Remnant colonialist fantasies and contemporary, market-driven aesthetic imaginaries therefore work hand in hand. Regardless of whether they key into modernist fantasies of the search for a primitive Other, who represents an earlier stage of human development when life was more authentic, or postmodernist western hipster dreams of uniqueness, fragmentation, and identity differentiation, travel brokers find themselves working with the same aesthetic palette—and it is hard to escape this language of difference.

It is thus clear that promotion and management patterns are the result of a complicated set of material and ideological factors, of which this discussion has attempted only to scratch the surface. It is overly simplistic to assume that the presence of the corporate profit motive can easily and singlehandedly explain contemporary tourism's exotifying tendencies, although it certainly plays its part, and concerns about global capitalism being at odds with forms of cultural production that further human dignity are not misplaced. Instead, it is necessary to look deeper, to the place where economic pursuits meet notions such as self, community, history, identity, truth, and beauty. These cultural understandings, forged and distorted through the often perverse mechanisms of a market economy that pulls even public and private-nonprofit endeavors into its own gravity, help to produce the world largely in the shape of difference, dividing people and cultures into binaries and helping these social constructions to become common sense.

Constrained decoding

On its monthly list of what's "in" and what's "out," a recent issue of *People Style Watch* magazine (May 2010: 108) declares vacations spent "holing up at the hotel" to be so last season. People—or at least the young, wealthy urbanites we are told we should want to emulate—the feature claims, now "want to experience cultural immersion." They are searching for travel experiences that involve "authentic" engagement with destinations. Borat is apparently not the only one interested in acquiring "cultural learnings" these days.

Indeed, it has been recognized in the literature that educational travel is a growing phenomenon in the realm of tourism more broadly. Richie (2003) provides a helpful orientation, in which he characterizes educational tourism as a spectrum that ranges from participation in formal programs like student exchanges to informal behaviors of tourists who seek individually to include learning experiences into travels they may take largely for other purposes, such as relaxation. The move toward tourism experiences that are more overtly educationally based is not an isolated occurrence, but part of a larger sociocultural trend marked by the collapsing of the notions of information, education, and entertainment into each other in ways that re-contour the human experience of interfacing with the world around us. The awareness of this change has spawned a fount of popular neologistic portmanteaux—*infotainment, infomercial, edutainment, mockumentary*—as scholars and journalists seek to articulate the cultural dimensions of the information age. That knowledge has become fashionable is evident in everything from the popularity of broadcast media like the History Channel, Discovery Channel, and Animal Planet to the success of quasi-academic entertainment ventures like Oprah's Book Club, and it should not surprise us to see this trend in tourism as well.

At cross-tendencies with the public's increased enjoyment of the educational (or perhaps simply reflected in it, considering the idea of "edutainment"), however, is another cultural trend that has been commented on by many, but by none more eloquently than Benjamin Barber: the rise of "infantilization." In a sweeping analysis of postmodern consumer culture, Barber (2007) argues that a new ethos is on the rise, which is characterized by the encouragement and legitimation of lifelong childishness. Behaving in infantilized ways is, of course, not the result of rational choice, but rather is a pattern that arises from a reinforcing nexus of our own worst tendencies (laziness, selfishness, greed) at play with manipulative market forces that speak to the Peter Pan in all of us by exploiting impulsive and irrational decision-making to peddle immediate gratification and convince us that "consumer empowerment" is a substitute for civic freedom, along with political ideologies of privatization that rationalize immediate personal gain (for example, through aversion to taxation) at the expense of investing in the public sphere for the greater good over the long haul. In hyper-privileged societies, where citizens have few real needs, the market must generate wants in order to continue to move products and turn profits, and childish faddishness and impulsiveness are more useful characteristics to cultivate than adult deliberateness and restraint in the push to encourage compulsive shopping activities to which mature and careful judgment would be an impediment.

The infantilized desire for easy over hard, fast over slow, dogmatic over deeply considered clearly has implications for the modern experience of education, as would-be learners come to expect information to be "delivered to them" (itself a problematic notion) in the form of easily digestible sound bites, the grown-up equivalent of feeding babies using the "here comes the airplane" method. Thus, learning is becoming hip at the same time that other forces are operating simultaneously to produce a citizenry that is becoming less willing and able to engage substantively with that which it encounters.

Tourism is perhaps a natural site for the expression of this tendency because of its temporality and its association with leisure. Although travel can be a lengthy pursuit, as exemplified by "gap year" youth tourists and retirees on extended excursions, for most, it is a short affair. The binds of work and family that characterize life's long midsection between adolescence and retirement generally mean that travel for leisure will be squeezed into, at most, a few weeks a year. Thus, although certainly there are individuals who choose to return to favorite travel haunts time and again, most tourists will never spend more than a few days pursuing experiential learning in any given destination. Despite the best of intentions, there are inevitable limits to what can be learned in such a format, and tourists, acclimated to a culture of edutainment in which entertaining, informative snippets generally stand in for deep learning, are not led to demand more. Also, despite the desire of increasing numbers of tourists to have cultural experiences that are educational, vacationing—pleasure travel, if you will—is still fundamentally about just that: pleasure. If it isn't fun, then it isn't fulfilling its role of providing tourists with either a means of escape to recharge batteries for returning to an occupational or civic life that is psychologically and spiritually under-rewarding (i.e. the push hypothesis), nor is it succeeding in producing a sense of "personal enrichment" in travelers (i.e. the pull hypothesis), defining, as they may, the concept of enrichment within a consumer-culture framework that tends to shy away from that which is truly intellectually challenging in favor of experiences that result in simpler, more immediately accessible forms of mental stimulation.

Anthropologist Ed Bruner's (2005) illuminating, if discouraging, anecdotes from his work as a tour guide in Bali lend life and color to these ideas. Hired to convey educational legitimacy to cultural tours in an area where he had spent many decades doing fieldwork, Bruner found himself thwarted at every turn as he attempted to move the tours beyond simple cultural voyeurism to more critical cross-cultural engagement. When he attempted to demystify Balinese dance performances by inviting the dancers to speak with the audience in their street clothes after the show and to provide an informational narrative that interpreted Balinese culture as dynamic and continuously invented instead of frozen in time, he was accused by the tour operator of "ruining her tour." When he attempted to persuade the group to delay in order to witness a religious event the tour happened upon that would offer a rare window into Balinese traditions, the tired, hot, hungry tourists drowned out his pleas with a preference to instead head back to the bus for the next event on the itinerary, claiming with reference to a staged performance they had attended earlier in the tour that they had "already seen it." Bruner's stories illustrate the way that living in a milieu of consumerism and instant gratification can dupe us into believing that we can achieve the same depth of engagement with life, including in our relationships with others and in our attempts to learn about the world, with less investment of time, money, and energy. This something-for-nothing attitude, of which we are generally not even reflexively aware, leads us to choose the easy over the challenging without thinking critically about the differences in what we are reaping by making this choice. Thus, in tourism, cultural understanding becomes something that can be easily bought and consumed as entertainment.

All this talk of "edutainment" and "infantilization" tends to give the feeling of placing a lot of blame on the tourist. Sweeping cultural sensibilities clearly can not be said to be the fault of particular individuals, but there is nevertheless a moralizing undertone of personal criticism to such cultural critiques, as though individual tourists should simply grow up, snap out of it, and demand more sophisticated and challenging travel experiences that help them to transcend superficiality and truly connect with foreign people and cultures. Such a position deeply underestimates the psychic dimensions of life in an era of advanced communications and transportation technologies. Several postmodern philosophers, including Baudrillard (1988), Boorstin (1964), and Eco (1986), have written extensively about the notion of hyperreality, a condition in which consciousness becomes unable to distinguish reality from fantasy. This condition is usually characterized as being the product of a media-saturated world, in which real phenomena are repeatedly represented in diverse, fragmentary forms, and simulations which look like reality, but whose only value is symbolic, abound. Objects are taken as truth, when in fact they are only simulacra—representations based on other representations. The oft-cited example par excellence is the image of Jesus, which is, of course, simply the outcome of other images of Jesus, as no period depictions of this individual actually exist. Working in consort, however, these overlapping images combine to create a shared public understanding of what Jesus looked like (again, a "truthiness" of Jesus's appearance, if you will) that is rarely questioned unless one thinks deeply about where this depiction came from.

In this hypermediated existence, the line between real phenomena, simulations, representations of reality, and representations of simulations begins to blur; reality gets lost in the sea of possibilities. Advanced communications technologies are usually held to blame. A potent example of such critique in a pop culture performance art context can be seen in the rock band U2's demonstration of this condition of postmodern consciousness through a performance vignette featured in its 1992–1993 "Zoo TV" tour, in which frontman Bono wields a giant remote control, flipping through a series of channels, the content of which is displayed Andy Warhol–style in a repeating grid on the faces of individual television monitors that compose a wall of visual media. Using his remote control, Bono cycles through footage of military combat, sports matches, news reports, and soap opera dramas, illustrating the way that real events and seductive fantasies have come to live side by side, each receiving equal weight and being expressed in the same visual language in the undifferentiating virtual space of television.

Contemporary communication technologies, however, are not the only developments that can help to throw individuals into a state of hyperreality: transportation technologies can do this as well. Modern transportation capabilities, combined with unprecedented levels of disposable income in some areas of the world, mean that actual places can be experienced viscerally in rapid succession to a degree not heretofore possible. Contemporary tourism allows for an intense juxtaposition of the real, *and* this uniquely modern experience occurs in the context of an already hypermediated world populated by substantive phenomena and simulacra alike. It thus becomes easy to imagine why travel experiences can leave people's heads spinning. Being able to transition from the familiarity of home to the foreignness of anywhere else on the scale of hours via modern aviation capabilities provides contemporary humans, with each trip, the psychic experience of stepping through a surreal gateway into an unfamiliar world already in progress, from which they can then retreat equally seamlessly at the end of the excursion, as though simply switching channels on a virtual-reality TV. And thus is superficiality woven into the very mechanics of postmodern life. Is it any wonder, then, that discursive patterns which cast the Other as object tend to persist despite a growing, half-articulated sensibility among tourists themselves that travel should somehow be about reaching beyond cultural boundaries to learn something real, and that much of cultural tourism therefore remains as akin to pornography (or, perhaps, to social cannibalism, as cultures and heritages are treated as products to be consumed) as it does to deep education and open global fellowship?

Closing the circle

Discursive production and consumption do not stop when tourists return home from a trip. For the rest of their lives, returned travelers share stories and photographs that contribute to the supply of images and understandings circulating in their home societies, rearticulating old discursive themes or creating new ones through this process. These "travel tales" serve many purposes, including seeking affinity with others or entertaining them, attempting to acquire status through a demonstration of cultural capital, and attempting to make sense of one's own life by narrating profound events and feelings that give the human journey texture and meaning (Bruner 2005). Thus, a storyteller may engage particular discourses for a variety of reasons: to delight a listener, to enlighten her, to impress her, to avoid confrontation by telling the listener what she wants to hear, to place the teller in a position where he can be viewed in his own best light (by the listener, himself, or both), or to work through his own past lived experiences in order to arrive at new understandings. It is easy to imagine that some of these purposes may be more amenable to the reproduction of stereotypes, whereas others may provide a basis for statements of personal resistance to dominant belief patterns. Thus, the decoders become the encoders, and discourses echo across space and time, often reconsolidating themselves but occasionally stretching in new directions as statements are made that challenge the integrity of the logic of the whole.

Conclusion

The features of the current regulatory framework of discursive production and consumption in tourism overdetermine the outcomes, making it challenging to foster discourses of resistance. Change will have to come from many angles at once: some direct, such as movements for socially responsible marketing in tourism, some more oblique, such as work to nurture a culture of visual literacy through liberal education or to re-link the notions of work and reward in the public mind. Such are cultural struggles, in Gramsci's (1971) terminology, "wars of position" rather than "wars of maneuver." In the battle for social equality and human solidarity, tourism is but one field site, currently occupied by ideological forces that champion materialism, consumption, and the simple sorts of pleasure that can be had by casting Others as objects in our own narratives of desire. As humanity has long sensed, however, it holds the promise of becoming something more, and freedom starts with understanding the cage.

References

Albers, P., & James, W. (1983). Tourism and the changing photographic image of the Great Lakes Indians. *Annals of Tourism Research*, 10, 123–148.

Albers, P., & James, W. (1988). Travel photography: A methodological approach. *Annals of Tourism Research*, 15, 134–158.

Barber, B. (2007). *Consumed: How markets corrupt children, infantilize adults, and swallow citizens whole*. New York: W.W. Norton and Company.

Baronov, D. (2004). *Conceptual Foundations of Social Research Methods*. Boulder, CO: Paradigm.

Baudrillard, J. (1988). Simulacra and simulations. In: M. Poster (Ed.), *Selected Writings* (pp. 168–184). Stanford, CA: Stanford University Press.

Belhassen, Y., & Caton, K. (Forthcoming). On the need for critical pedagogy in business education. *Tourism Management*.

Boorstin, D. (1964). *The Image: A guide to pseudo-events in America*. New York: Atheneum.

Bruner, E. (1991). Transformation of self in tourism. *Annals of Tourism Research*, 8, 222–245.

Bruner, E. (2005). *Culture on Tour: Ethnographies of travel*. Chicago: University of Chicago Press.

Buck, R. (1977) The ubiquitous tourist brochure: Explorations in its intended and unintended use. *Annals of Tourism Research* 4, 195–207.

Buzinde, C., Santos, C. A., & Smith, S. (2006). Ethnic representations: Destination imagery. *Annals of Tourism Research*, 33, 707–728.

Caton, K., & Santos, C. A. (2008). Closing the hermeneutic circle? Photographic encounters with the other. *Annals of Tourism Research*, 35, 7–26.

Caton, K., & Santos, C. A. (2009). Images of the Other: Selling study abroad in a postcolonial world. *Journal of Travel Research*, 48, 191–204.

Chang, H-C., & Holt, G. R. (1991). Tourism as consciousness of struggle: Cultural representations of Taiwan. *Critical Studies in Mass Communication*, 8, 102–118.

Dann, G. M. S. (1994). Tourism: The nostalgia industry of the future. In: W. F. Theobald (Ed.), *Global Tourism: The Next Decade* (pp. 55–67). Oxford: Butterworth-Heinemann Ltd.

Davidson, M. (1992). *The Consumerist Manifesto*. New York: Routledge.

Echtner, C., & Prasad, P. (2003). The context of Third World tourism marketing. *Annals of Tourism Research*, 30(3), 660–682.

Eco, U. (1986). *Travels in Hyperreality*. New York: Harcourt Brace Jovanovich.

Foucault, M. (1980). *Power/Knowledge*. New York: Pantheon Books.

Fürsich, E. (2002). Packaging culture: The potential and limitations of travel programs on global television. *Communication Quarterly*, 50(2), 204–227.

Giroux, H. A. (1993). Consuming social change: The "United Colors of Benetton." *Cultural Critique*, 26, 5–32.

Goffman, E. (1974). *Frame Analysis: An essay on the organization of experience*. New York: Harper & Row.

Gramsci, A. (1971). *Selections from the Prison Notebooks*. New York: International Publishers.

Hall, S. (1986). Gramsci's relevance for the study of race and ethnicity. *Journal of Communication Inquiry* 10(5), 5–27.

Hall, S. (1997). The work of representation. In: S. Hall (Ed.), *Representation: Cultural representations and signifying practices* (pp. 13–74). London: Sage.

Hollinshead, K. (2007). "Worldmaking" and the transformation of place and culture: the enlargement of Meethan's analysis of tourism and global change. In: I. Ateljevic, A. Pritchard, and N. Morgan (Eds.), *The Critical Turn in Tourism Studies: Innovative research methodologies* (pp. 165–196). Amsterdam: Elsevier.

Lutz, C., & Collins, J. (1993) *Reading National Geographic*. Chicago: University of Chicago Press.

Macbeth, J. (2005). Towards an ethics platform for tourism. *Annals of Tourism Research*, 32, 962–984.

MacKay, K. J., & Fesenmaier, D. R. (2000). An exploration of cross-cultural destination image management. *Journal of Travel Research*, 38, 417–423.

Maira, S. (2000). Henna and hip hop: The politics of cultural production and the work of cultural studies. *Journal of Asian American Studies*, 3(3), 329–369.

Milman, A., Reichel, A., & Pizam, A. (1990). The impact of tourism on ethnic attitudes: The Israeli–Egyptian case. *Journal of Travel Research*, 29, 45–49.

Morgan, N., & Pritchard, A. (1998). *Tourism Promotion and Power: Creating images, creating identities*. Chinchester: Wiley.

People Style Watch. (2010). What's in what's out. May, 108.

Richie, B. (2003). *Managing Educational Tourism*. Clevedon, UK: Channel View.

Said, E. (1978). *Orientalism*. New York: Random House.

Said, E. (1993). *Culture and Imperialism*. New York: Random House.

Santos, C.A. (2006). Cultural politics in contemporary travel writing. *Annals of Tourism Research*, 33(3), 624–644.

Sirakaya, E., & Sonmez, S. (2000). Gender images in state tourism brochures: An overlooked area in socially responsible tourism marketing. *Journal of Travel Research*, 38, 353–362.

Yaman, H.L., & Gurel, E. (2006). Ethical ideologies of tourism marketers. *Annals of Tourism Research*, 33, 470–489.

9 To act as though the future mattered

A framework for hopeful tourism education

Lisa Schwarzin

Fear and hope: the state of the world – a sad story?

What might historians tell future generations of earthlings about this period at the beginning of the twenty-first century? It's likely to be a sad story – 'Humans in the era of unsustainability kept dipping their greedy hands deeper into the earth's crust, extracting its stores of resources. A lot of what they dug up, they burned, filling the atmosphere with greenhouse gases that set in motion a vicious cycle of climate change. Sea levels rose, rivers dried up, deserts spread.'

Today, humanity is facing significant challenges to ensure the sustainability of its own habitat. Despite contrary propaganda in media and politics, most climatologists agree that the environmental crises are indeed anthropogenic (IPCC 2007; Steffen 2010; Weart 2010). We don't show much more respect for each other either, clinging to our 'tribes', in-groups, fractions, which by definition exclude 'the Other'. In itself, this isn't all bad; our communities are, to varying degrees, spaces of care, love and respect. However, we seem to be inept at extending empathy to people who are unlike us, who dress, speak, look, pray, eat, think, act differently. Our contempt leads us exploit, compete with, and wage war against those in the out-group, and we do it on all scales of society; bullying, racism, neo-liberal capitalism, neo-colonialism, fundamentalism and militarism are but a few of the symptoms of our lack of empathy. Last but not least, we abuse ourselves, blindly accepting our place in the machine, unable to escape the rat-race, as the post-modern consumer society that now engulfs (admittedly to varying degrees) almost every corner of the earth turns us into docile servants of greed.

What a pessimistic story, but it's only one side of the coin. As people all over the world are becoming more aware of our pressing contemporary issues, activist organizations are pushing for a more just, equitable world, consumers seem to become more conscious, and the term sustainability has become an exhortation in the worlds of policy making, civil society, research, business, education, and increasingly in the minds of 'you and me'. As Jeremy Rifkin shows in his latest work, humans are, despite their flaws, fundamentally empathic beings, and our growing interconnectedness provides stimuli for societies to increasingly reflect this capacity for empathy (Rifkin 2009). From the optimists' corner, we can then hope that the practices that are 'regarded as common sense or natural today may well be thought of as inhuman and barbaric in the future' (Venn 2006: 147).

Another ray of light amidst the doom and gloom is the nascent academic discourse around transmodernity, which concerns itself with describing an emerging societal paradigm shift that holds potential for overcoming exploitative world-systems by re-invigorating common values and ethical principles of mutuality and interconnectedness, along with encouraging the celebration of diversity and mindful and respectful (inter)action in all spheres of life, with one another and the environment (cf. Ateljevic 2009; Dussel 2004; 2009; Magda 2004; Venn 2002; 2006). In spite of the powerful hold that Eurocentric neo-liberal hegemony exerts today, some place hope in the variety of local and global movements that in various ways counter oppressive forces, finding space to pursue emancipatory goals (Ateljevic 2009; Venn 2006). Through such resistance, a potentiality emerges for genuine dialogue among cultural innovators of the South and the North (Dussel 2004; 2009), among cultural creatives (Ray and Anderson 2000), activists, academics, and social entrepreneurs who embody and nurture the transmodern paradigm shift, without even having a unified language or terminology to describe it (Ateljevic 2009).

While for many of us, inertia prevails in the face of uncertainty and fear, a beacon of hope is the evermore present discourse and practices of sustainable development, which has transpired into many levels of policy making, including the arena of education. This chapter considers the role of (tourism) education as a catalyst for a societal shift in mindset and practice towards a future more hopeful, sustainable and just than the one currently in prospect. It is written from the (in educational debates often overlooked) perspective of an MSc student, only just on her way to become an academic activist. After contextualizing the role of education in raising planetary citizens with regard to tourism studies, I will attempt to provide a glimpse of what (tourism) education might look like if it was to foster learning for change; education for a transmodern world. I will then share some insights that emerged from student-led initiatives, one of which explored 'learning for life' in higher education, and another that promoted inspirational teaching amongst tourism educators. Drawing on the work of a third initiative that is co-creating transformative sustainability curriculum, I will move on to provide a framework for 'hopeful tourism education' that integrates four essential dimensions of transformative learning. Finally, this chapter concludes with a call to action for students and educators to see themselves as co-facilitators of learning and to walk the talk of the Academy of Hope.

Education and empowerment – raising planetary citizens

The call for education as learning for change

Who is responsible for change? What needs to be done? Who takes the first step? While we wait for these questions to be answered, we tend to hang in limbo; business as usual. Sure, there are no quick fix solutions, and we can't possibly know with certainty what measures to take. But the way the odds are stacked, it appears we (all) need to do *something*.

I am a student. I am a small cog in the wheel, with very little power to speak and act. Yet, I have an (expanding) sphere of influence. I can make choices – choices of what and where (not) to buy; choices of what to read and who to listen to; choices of who to work for and what to work on; choices of where and how and why to travel.... Yet, I did not always think this way. For large parts of my teens and twenties I felt powerless, disgusted by the machine, yet unable to step out of 'the systems of thought that establish the rationality and authority of the current post- and neo-hegemonic orders' (Venn 2006: 125). That was until I learnt about the interplay of structure and agency (cf. Bourdieu 1990; Giddens 1984), about the power of the individual to resist the forces placed upon us, and to do what is within our capacity to shape new ways of thinking, being, relating, and acting that eventually make the current exploitative social forms obsolete. *And* my empowerment occurred in the context of education. As an MSc student enrolled in one of the rare tourism studies programs that actually place emphasis on critical thinking, I was inspired by passionate and caring teachers who showed me that we do have a choice between (creating) a future that is dehumanizing, and perhaps even uninhabitable, and a world in which 'one lives well with and for others in just institutions' (Ricoeur 1992: 330). It is difficult to describe how intensely affirmed and heartened I felt in my up until then thwarted desire to make a meaningful contribution to what I was beginning to comprehend is a society in constant making, and therefore always *potentially* moving towards brighter prospects.

While I consider myself extremely fortunate to have experienced (parts of my) university education as empowering, I also believe certain things to be severely wrong with the way students are 'instructed' and 'schooled' – many fellow students don't find education very inspiring at all. Nevertheless, it is important to recognize the great potential of education to raise what Haigh terms planetary citizens (2008), a call that is echoed also by academic fields like critical pedagogy, eco-pedagogy, transformative learning, citizenship education, and environmental education, as well as in policy initiatives like the UNESCO Decade for Education for Sustainable Development, which encourages value-based curriculum for critical thinking and changes in 'unsustainable' attitudes and habits (UNESCO-DESD 2009).

The realization that teaching can and should be a catalyst for positive societal change is also transpiring in the relatively young field of tourism. In the introduction to the first edition of *The Critical Turn in Tourism Studies*, Irena Ateljevic, Nigel Morgan and Annette Pritchard (2007b) put forward the call for an *Academy of Hope*, a notion that now provides the frame for this second edition. This call aims to raise critical tourism scholarship beyond a way of knowing to a *way of being*, 'a commitment to tourism enquiry which is pro-social justice and equality and anti-oppression' (Ateljevic *et al.* 2007a: 3). Critical education is, along with critical research and critical action, one central element of this academy of hope, and the push for tourism education that raises philosophic practitioners (Tribe 2002) is reflected in a variety of initiatives, such as the *Critical Tourism Studies Network*, which supports and promotes tourism scholars who (dare to) transcend the managerial and economic discourse that dominates tourism research and curriculum[1]; the *Tourism Education Futures Initiative*[2], which promotes value based learning for raising a next generation of ethical tourism practitioners (Sheldon *et al.* 2007; Sheldon *et al.* 2009); the INNOT-OUR Web 2.0 platform 'for education, research and business development in tourism' that aims to introduce 'a culture of creativity [that encourages] students and researchers to question established ideas, to go beyond conventional knowledge, and strive towards originality'[3] (see also Lidburd and Hjalager 2011, this book); and the BEST Education Network, which is committed to sustainable tourism, education, and training.[4]

From dreary classrooms to engaged learning

These initiatives show that educators are increasingly asking what education is actually for. The Latin word *educare* means to 'lead into life', and the Greek concept of *paideia* (to which the term pedagogy is related) implies that 'the goal of education is not mastery of subject matter, but of one's person' (Orr 1991: 55). Once upon a time, education may well have lived up to this ideal; however, with the advent of the 'modern age' and industrialism, education was progressively hijacked to serve the needs of the labor market. Some historical 'events' shaped the modern mind and were instrumental in this plight; Francis Bacon's proposed union between knowledge and power, Galileo's separation of the intellect, and Descartes' radical separation of self and object (Orr 1991). These and other related developments led to a state where, as Venn argues by drawing on Foucault and Bhaba, the authorizing narrative of instrumental rationality, ultimately concerned with constituting appropriate subjectivities for a well-oiled apparatus of production, is maintained by co-articulated 'technologies of the social that connect the barracks with the schoolroom with the factory with the family with the law courts to establish the machinery of normalization working to form and regulate subjects and citizens' (2006: 147). At present then, (most) educational programs prepare (tourism) students for work, i.e. for carrying out a range of tasks in a well-defined professional (or academic) environment. They breed compliance, encouraging potential critics of society to fit into the system, unquestioningly – to me; this carries uncomfortable connotations of totalitarianism.

In a spectacular waste of potential, the very institutions of education can turn inquisitive, curious, creative children into result-driven, unimaginative, extrinsically motivated young adults (Cranton 2008; Robinson 2006) who see higher education as nothing but a gatekeeper to the 'professional' world. The news is: the kinds of work environments where mere *utilization* of skills and knowledge is required are fast disappearing as we transition into a post-mechanical knowledge society (Jaros and Deakin-Crick 2007). A knowledge economy requires not 'workers' but active contributors who are able to think creatively, use knowledge flexibly, and drive innovation (Durišić-Bojanović 2007; Jaros and Deakin-Crick 2007). At the same time, a range of inconvenient truths discover the profundity of the mess we are in, calling for people who can deal with pressing issues in which both stakes and uncertainty are high (Funtowicz and Ravetz 2003). What is highly desirable is to shift the focus of education from acquisition of particular knowledge, skills, and understanding (Jaros and Deakin-Crick 2007) to a primary emphasis on triggering a transformation in which learners integrate new information, perspectives and practices into their own world view, and thereby cause shifts in deeply rooted frames of reference (King 2004).

It transpires that today's educational institutions and programs are quite inappropriate for raising citizens who can take part in critically and creatively shaping a world of which we have no idea what it will look like in 50 years time (Robinson 2006). Sir Ken Robinson, Emeritus Professor of Education at the University of Warwick and prominent leader in the development of creativity, innovation, and human resources, calls for a radical revolution towards personalized education that gives wings to people's dreams and talents rather than stifling creativity (2010) and 'smothering the soul' through institutional policies and procedures, and mandated curriculum in classrooms that reinforce passivity, domination and artificiality (Cranton 2008; Orr 1991). What I believe we desperately need is an emancipatory approach to education that encourages democratic participation and a heartfelt commitment to act as though the future mattered (Devall 1988). As Tony Ward[5] puts it, we 'have to educate differently, using different goals, beliefs and pedagogies, [...] simply because we are faced with nothing less than a transformation of the social, political, economic and environmental awareness of our entire society' (2008: 20).

How then can we transform educational institutions to better respond to the call for hopeful education? As David Orr aptly states, educators and management need to pave the way: 'What is desperately needed are faculty and administrators who provide role models of integrity, care, thoughtfulness, and institutions that are capable of embodying ideals wholly and completely in all of their operations' (Orr 1991: 5).

Insights from student-led initiatives

What I would add to this based on my own experience, is that students themselves also carry a measure of responsibility towards innovating the educational landscape, ideally through co-creative efforts with educators. My own involvement in such efforts was triggered by a teacher who encouraged me to form a student taskforce[6] for educational innovation, which went on to design and implement two projects on innovative tourism education.

The first was a small study entitled *The Future of Tourism Education: Learning for Life at University* and involved a full day workshop for students enrolled in the MSc program Leisure Tourism and Environment at Wageningen University. This workshop, conducted in March 2009, aimed to investigate what students 'learn for life' in higher education and uncover the role of education in shaping the 14 participants' values.[7] The day was spent in an informal environment and students were guided through creative and reflective activities designed to bring to awareness deeper insights and learning (Cranton 2008; Leonard and Willis 2008; Wright 2008). For instance, participants reflected on important moments of their past, big lessons of the present, and steps for achieving their aspirations, and noted their thoughts on pieces of cardboard shaped like footsteps, which they stuck on the floor and walls for others to read.

When inspecting the material collected during the day, several topics could be identified that seemed relevant to critical tourism education. Some of these themes were *critical thinking*, which included remarks about the importance of 'broadening the mind', and *empowerment*, which was about acquiring 'knowledge and skills for social change' and 'carrying critical action into the world'. Other themes we identified were *multicultural learning*, which referred to the benefits of drawing on multiple perspectives through interactive teaching methods, and *engaged learning*, which was concerned with the need for applied education that breaks down barriers between the university and the tourism world by working with and learning from communities.

In the context of this chapter, these themes point to the need for teaching methods that utilize diversity by designing social learning processes (cf. Wals 2006; Wals *et al.* 2009), and to the significance of encouraging tourism students to question existing frames of reference as well as their own potential for contributing to change processes. Furthermore, they indicate that tourism education should foster engagement of students in the world, so that learners can begin making positive impacts in society while being supported by caring and critical educators.

The second project aimed to raise these insights with tourism educators in a workshop on 'Ways of Teaching that Inspire Critical Consciousness and Creative Action', which was held at the 3rd Critical Tourism Studies Conference in June 2009 with a group of about 24 tourism academics. Essentially, we wanted to convey that, from the student perspective, empowerment is extremely important in education, hoping to stimulate tourism educators to reflect on the way they (could) teach. After welcoming the participants and emphasizing that we wanted to encourage open and engaging conversation, we asked participants to sit in small circles of chairs, dared to blindfold their eyes, and bade them hold hands while sharing stories of inspiration. What sounds like an outrageous activity for an academic conference,[8] accomplished, I believe, our intention to foster deep appreciation for the transformative potential of meaningful moments in life.

Subsequently, participants rejoined the large group and engaged in a dialogue on the need for education to inspire students (and teachers!). Here, the aim was to share and mutually enhance ideas that might be useful for raising critical consciousness and promoting critical action in tourism students. One of the main outcomes of this dialogue was that while engagement as a critical educator is certainly very challenging within the existing framework of higher education and with class sizes of several hundred students, it is not impossible if one is committed and willing to experiment, and it can be an extremely rewarding endeavor. As bell hooks so aptly says: 'Learning is a place where paradise can be created. The classroom, with all its limitations, remains a location of possibility' (hooks 1994: 207).

A framework for hopeful tourism education

Around the time I started working on these two projects, I also became involved with a working group of teachers, students, and academics of Wageningen University, who, based on a shared interest in innovative pedagogy, have been co-creating a framework for transformative sustainability education.[9] This framework, developed collaboratively through a process of brainstorming, dialogue and social learning, differentiates between four dimensions of education that we argue need to be in balance in order to promote transformative learning for change (Schwarzin *et al.* 2011); an objective 'IT' dimension; a subjective 'I' dimension; an inter-subjective 'WE' dimension; and an integrative cross-boundary dimension. In what follows, I will discuss each of these dimensions in the context of tourism education, outlining a framework for hopeful tourism education that integrates Tribe's model for encouraging tourism students to become 'philosophic practitioners' who work effectively and efficiently, yet act as stewards for the ethical development of the tourism world (2002).

The 'IT' of hopeful tourism education – critical content and creative context

Contrry to what is taught in many 'traditional' tourism programs, critical tourism educators would agree that tourism students need to learn to apply a diverse range of theories, paradigms, research methods and professional skills that relate to the complexity of the tourism industry. The 'IT' dimension in the framework for hopeful tourism education emphasizes a critical and transdisciplinary approach to the *content* of tourism programs. It holds that graduates who intend to promote a shift towards sustainability and justice within the tourism industry need to be encouraged to develop reflexive awareness of multiple scientific and lay perspectives on highly complex issues (cf. van Asselt 2000) in tourism, and should develop awareness of the complementarities and contradictions between these perspectives (Baumgärtner *et al.* 2008). In this way, students can develop a helicopter perspective of actors and processes of transitions, which enables a more holistic approach to analyzing and contributing to sustainable development of the tourism industry. Hence, the 'IT' dimension combines Tribe's (2002) curriculum elements of *vocational action* (preparation for effectiveness at work through acquisition of a range of tourism related skills), and parts of *liberal reflection* that emphasize multidisciplinary learning and philosophical and skeptical engagement with tourism truths.

Furthermore, the 'IT' dimension recognizes that people learn from their total educational environment (Haigh 2008), which should be designed for collaboration and creativity to emerge. Indeed, in the 'learning for life' student project, the benefit of informal settings for learning for facilitating relaxed and genuine interaction was mentioned. Hence, we need to re-thinking the very nature of the 'classroom' and 'teaching'. It is clear that 'front stage' methods designed to 'deliver' knowledge by bombarding students with bullet points are quite inappropriate when it comes to engaging students and encouraging innovative thought. While the scope of this chapter does not allow for a detailed review of suitable teaching methods, it is worth noting that lateral thinking tools can be used to break uni-directional patterns of thought and encourage cross-pattern thinking (cf. De Bono 1967), and techniques which make use of creativity and dramatic expression are especially suitable to trigger a process of reflexive learning (cf. Florence 2006; King 2007; Wright 2008).

The 'I' of hopeful tourism education – personal development and empowerment

As emphasized before, the lack of critical elements in contemporary education programs breed compliance to the status quo. We need to recognize that in order to stimulate innovative action, tourism students need first to be inspired to challenge 'business as usual', and the curriculum needs to be connected to empowerment and personal development. This is the focus of the 'I' dimension of hopeful tourism education – it seeks to provide guidance for reflexively developing personal and professional passion, nurturing individual talents and fostering change-agency skills. As such, it echoes Tribe's call for *vocational reflection* (critical evaluation of one's learning needs and modification of practical skills and knowledge) and the part of *liberal reflection* concerned with 'becoming', seeking the 'good life' and developing reflexivity (2002).

At the same time, it is important to remember that learners pass through stages of cognitive development in which thinking and acting mature (Murray 2009). For instance, the values and principles identified by the *Tourism Education Futures Initiative* as key to responsible leadership in the tourism industry (stewardship, critical and innovative knowledge creation, professionalism, ethical conduct, and mutual respect) (Sheldon *et al.* 2009) cannot simply be 'lectured'; they need to grow out of reflexive awareness and practice, to which learners first need to open themselves. Furthermore, introspective teaching requires openness from the educator's side, who needs to be skilled in creating learning environments that are conducive to introspection and honest assessment of personal capacities, wishes, and dreams. A deeply empowering learning experience can be created when educators dare to open up an 'otherworld' of imagination and autopoiesis (Wright 2008), encouraging learners to reflexively express and 'create' themselves.

The 'WE' of hopeful tourism education – relationships and social learning

The call for reflexivity implies that tourism educators need to foster trusting and open engagement with students, as the quality and substance of learning relationships is central to ability and motivation for learning (Jaros and Deakin-

Crick 2007). A central tenet of the 'WE' dimension of hopeful tourism education, which Tribe's (2002) framework does not seem to consider, is that 'teachers' and 'students' can learn *from each other* if educational hierarchies and roles are broken down. Educators who act as co-facilitators may promote dialogue that draws on and integrates the insights, ideas and intuition of both students and teachers, shifting from a teacher focused model of instruction to a student focused model of collaboration. Such dialogue requires a range of skills, such as group-reflexivity on objectives, strategies, and outcomes of interaction (Godemann 2008). Furthermore the educator-as-facilitator needs to be wary of dialogue turning into debate; here, awareness of conversational dynamics (cf. Scharmer 2009) and deliberate practice of communication techniques such as dialogic leadership (cf. Isaacs 1999) can be useful.

Students should also learn to apply interaction principles and collaborative learning tools in the field. Tourism is a complex phenomenon involving a great variety of actors; hence, working in tourism most often implies a social context, the challenges and opportunities of which need to be negotiated. The 'WE' dimension highlights the change potential of this diversity and encourages educators to create engaging yet safe opportunities for reflective social learning in heterogeneous groups. Social learning is an educational approach that emphasizes collective meaning making and assumes that 'we can learn more from each other if we do not all think alike or act alike' (Wals *et al.* 2009: 11).

This approach to learning is gaining increasing recognition as a way of dealing with the great complexity of sustainability issues, as it promotes the competence of *Gestaltswitching*, i.e. moving back and forth between different mind-sets (Wals and Blewitt 2010). In well-facilitated processes of social learning, students can come to understand how a variety of perspectives on a particular tourism concern interact, and discuss and develop hands-on ways of dealing with such variety. While the challenges associated with multi-perspectival work might result in confrontation between perspectives and worldviews, discipline-based outlooks and (academic) cultures (Godemann 2008), it is important for educators to keep in mind that the aim is not to impose values or pressure for consensus among learners from different backgrounds (cf. Osberg and Biesta 2008). Indeed, a focus on consensus would disrespect such diversity. Instead, contested perceptions need to be exposed and studied to promote understanding of how differences in views and practices can be utilized for constructive interaction and promising pathways to innovation.

Crossing boundaries in hopeful tourism education – integration in action

An individual examination of these dimensions as presented so far should not invoke the impression that they operate in isolation. In fact, it is only through integration of the elements thus far described that hopeful tourism education can attempt to be transformative. Figure 9.1 illustrates how the dimensions overlap to form a fourth action-focused cross-boundary dimension.

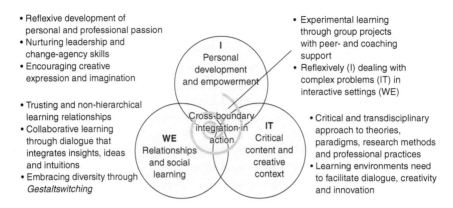

• Reflexive development of personal and professional passion
• Nurturing leadership and change-agency skills
• Encouraging creative expression and imagination

• Trusting and non-hierarchical learning relationships
• Collaborative learning through dialogue that integrates insights, ideas and intuitions
• Embracing diversity through *Gestaltswitching*

I
Personal development and empowerment

Cross-boundary integration-in action

WE
Relationships and social learning

IT
Critical content and creative context

• Experimental learning through group projects with peer- and coaching support
• Reflexively (I) dealing with complex problems (IT) in interactive settings (WE)

• Critical and transdisciplinary approach to theories, paradigms, research methods and professional practices
• Learning environments need to facilitate dialogue, creativity and innovation

Figure 9.1 Hopeful tourism education.

Here, a spiral of experiential learning is created that 'touches all bases' of experiencing, reflecting, thinking, and acting in order to continuously enhance understanding in a way that integrates 'the functioning of the total person – thinking, feeling, perceiving, and behaving' (Kolb and Kolb 2005: 194). This dimension focuses on reflexively (I) dealing with complex problems (IT) in interactive settings (WE). Project-based learning is central here, as it allows for a gradual shift in the students' position from a receptor to that of active agent (Jaros and Deakin-Crick 2007). In problem-posing education,

> people develop their power to perceive critically the way they exist in the world with which and in which they find themselves; they come to see the world not as static reality, but as a reality in process, in transformation
>
> (Freire 2000 [1970]: 83)

The cross-boundary dimension relates to Tribe's (2000) call for *liberal action* in the tourism curriculum, as in the need to foster the translation of critical understanding to emancipatory action. For example, students might be asked to work in small groups to design and implement a local or regional project that is related to sustainable tourism or critical scholarship. Here, it is vital to provide students with continuous peer and coaching support in order to ensure reflection on learning outcomes and the integration of a variety of perspectives in the project. In this way, students can be exposed to challenging tourism cases in a relatively safe environment and develop a sense of power and control (Wals 2006) by realizing that they themselves have a significant sphere of influence to contribute to sustainable tourism development.

Conclusion: a call to action

At the beginning of this chapter, I expressed my belief that if we want to promote a transmodern paradigm shift towards the co-creation of ethical and mindful human societies, then we all need to start walking the talk of environmental stewardship, social justice, cultural dialogue, and institutional transformation. As academics, educators, and/or learners, we can show initiative to promote the kind of critical (and hopeful) tourism education called for by the Academy of Hope. We need to begin making hopeful changes within our own professional (and personal) environment, instead of waiting for change to come to us. We need to ask ourselves where we can make a sustained impact, what our sphere of influence is.

As educators and learners, we should come to see ourselves as co-facilitators of learning. Breaking down the disempowering teacher–student dichotomy, we can co-create learning environments that stimulate for critical action. On the teacher's side, this requires giving up full control of the education process and letting students define parts of the learning process and outcomes themselves. In the same vein, learners need to move out of passive 'student' schemata and become active participants and decision makers. This is by no means easy to accomplish, as such a shift in educational roles requires a lengthy process of q uestioning and re-addressing ingrained patterns of mind and behavior.

However, I believe the transformation towards co-facilitated education to be absolutely crucial to the learning revolution Sir Ken Robinson calls for to prepare future generations for dealing with the pervasive challenges we will continue to face (2010). As co-facilitators of learning, we therefore need to claim the power of our agency. We have a choice to empower others to think critically and reflexively; to raise questions and debate about current hegemonic structures and hopeful vistas for a transmodern future. If we want to re-design education to offer more engaging, interactive, and reflexive tourism curriculum, we should think about rallying support amongst our peers. Acting like a flock of birds in synchronized flight, we can significantly reduce resistance from the institutional ether. If we manage to pull ourselves together to create a critical mass of transmodern thinkers and doers, our future historians may well be able to recount a 'happy end' to the story that seemed so sad at the beginning of the twenty-first century.

Notes

1 See Heather Mair's enlightening reflection in the 'Critical Tourism Research' section of this book.
2 TEFI website: www.quovadis.wu-wien.ac.at/drupal/.
3 INNOTOUR website: www.innotour.com/about-innotour/.
4 BEST Education Network website: www.besteducationnetwork.org/.
5 Tony Ward is a prominent promoter of critical pedagogy whose website (http://tony-wardedu.com/) holds a wealth of information and tools for University educators.
6 At this stage I would like to express my appreciation to the students and educators who attended the two tourism education projects, and my heartfelt gratitude to my colleagues and friends with whom they were co-created; thank you Hermes Arriaga, Saskia Leenders, Arjaan Pellis, and Ana Raguz!
7 See www.vimeo.com/7080439 for a short video of the 'learning for life' workshop.
8 Several participants later expressed how moving this activity was for them, which just

shows how important it is to (trigger others to) step out of one's comfort zone; after all, it is when we are challenged, that we learn.

9 This working group is currently also in the process of applying the framework to the design of a transdisciplinary BSc minor in Sustainable Development, which will also be open to local and international tourism students.

References

Ateljevic I. 2009. Transmodernity – remaking our (tourism) world? In *Philosophical Issues of Tourism: Beauty, Truth and Virtue*, ed. J Tribe. Clevedon: Channel View.

Ateljevic I, Morgan N, & Pritchard A. 2007a. Editor's Introduction: Promoting an Academy of Hope in Tourism Enquiry. In *The Critical Turn in Tourism Studies: Innovative Research Methodologies*, ed. I Ateljevic, A Pritchard, & N Morgan, pp. 1–9. Oxford: Elsevier.

Ateljevic I, Pritchard A, & Morgan N, eds. 2007b. *The Critical Turn in Tourism Studies: Innovative Research Methodologies*. Oxford: Elsevier.

Baumgärtner S, Becker C, Frank K, Muller B, & Quaas M. 2008. Relating the philosophy and practice of ecological economics: The role of concepts, models, and case studies in inter- and transdisciplinary sustainability research. *Ecological Economics* 67: 384–393.

Bourdieu P. 1990. *The Logic of Practice*. Cambridge: Polity Press.

Cranton P. 2008. The resilience of soul. In *Pedagogies of the Imagination: Mythopoetic Curriculum in Educational Practice*, ed. T Leonard, & P Willis, pp. 125–136. New York: Springer.

De Bono E. 1967. *The Use of Lateral Thinking*. London: Jonathan Cape.

Devall B. 1988. *Simple in Means, Rich in Ends*. London: Green Print (Merlin).

Durišić-Bojanović M. 2007. Readiness for changes: New competences for knowledge society. *Zbornik Instituta za Pedagoska Istrazivanja [Serbian Institute for Educational Research]* 39: 211–224.

Dussel E. 2004. *Transmodernity and Interculturality: An Interpretation from the Perspective of Philosophy of Liberation*. Retrieved from: www.enriquedussel.org/txt/Transmodernity%20and%20Interculturality.pdf.

Dussel E. 2009. A new age in the history of philosophy: The world dialogue between philosophical traditions. *Philosophy and Social Criticism* 35: 499–516.

Florence N. 2006. Dialogue to truth in bell hooks and Jane Roland Martin. In *International Handbook of the Religious, Moral and Spiritual Dimensions in Education*, ed. M De Souza, K Engebretson, G Durka, R Jackson, & A McGrady, pp. 107–125. New York: Springer.

Freire P. 2000 [1970]. *Pedagogy of the Oppressed*. New York: Continuum.

Funtowicz S, & Ravetz J. 2003. Post-normal science. *International Society for Ecological Economics: Internet Encyclopaedia of Ecological Economics*.

Giddens A. 1984. *The Constitution of Society*. Cambridge: Polity Press.

Godemann, J. 2008. Knowledge integration: a key challenge for transdisciplinary cooperation. *Environmental Education Research* 14(6): 625–641.

Haigh M. 2008. Internationalisation, planetary citizenship and Higher Education Inc. *Compare* 38: 427–440.

hooks b. 1994. *Teaching to Transgress: Education as the Practice of Freedom*. New York: Routledge.

IPCC. 2007. Summary for Policymakers. In *Climate Change 2007: Mitigation. Contribution of Working Group III to the Fourth Assessment Report of the Intergovernmental Panel on Climate Change*, ed. B Metz, OR Davidson, PR Bosch, R Dave, & LA Meyer. Cambridge, UK and New York: Cambridge University Press.

Isaacs WN. 1999. Dialogic leadership. *The Systems Thinker* 10: 1–5.

Jaros M, & Deakin-Crick R. 2007. Personalized learning for the post-mechanical age. *Journal of Curriculum Studies* 39: 423–440.

King KP. 2004. Both sides now: Examining transformative learning and professional development of educators. *Innovative Higher Education 29*(2): 155–174.

King N. 2007. Developing imagination, creativity, and literacy through collaborative storymaking: a way of knowing. *Harvard Educational Review* 77.

Kolb, AY, & Kolb, DA. 2005. Learning styles and learning spaces: enhancing experiential learning in higher education. *Academy of Management Learning and Education* 4(2): 193–212.

Leonard T, & Willis P. 2008. *Pedagogies of the Imagination: Mythopoetic Curriculum in Educational Practice*. New York: Springer.

Lidburd J, & Hjalager A.-M. 2011. From copyright to copyleft: Towards tourism education 2.0. In *The Critical Turn in Tourism Studies: Creating an Academy of Hope*, ed. I Ateljevic, N Morgan, A Pritchard. London: Routledge.

Magda RMR. 2004. *Transmodernidad*. Barcelona: Anthropos.

Murray, T. 2009. What is the integral in integral education? *Integral Review* 5(1): 96–134.

Orr D. 1991. What is education for? Six myths about the foundations of modern education, and six new principles to replace them. *In Context – A Quarterly of Humane Sustainable Culture: The Learning Revolution* 27.

Osberg, D, & Biesta, G 2008. The emergent curriculum: navigating a complex course between unguided learning and planned enculturation. *Journal of Curriculum Studies* 40(3): 313–328.

Ray HP, & Anderson SR. 2000. *The Cultural Creatives: How 50 Million People are Changing the World*. New York: Harmony Books.

Ricoeur P. 1992. *Oneself as Another*. Chicago: University of Chicago Press.

Rifkin J. 2009. *The Empathic Civilization: The Race to Global Consciousness in a World in Crisis*. Los Angeles: Tarcher.

Robinson K. 2006. Schools kill creativity. In *Technology Engineering Design 2006*. Long Beach, California, USA.

Robinson K. 2010. Bring on the learning revolution! In *Technology Engineering Design 2010: What the World Needs Now*. Long Beach, California, USA.

Scharmer CO. 2009. *Theory U: Leading From the Future as it Emerges: The Social Technology of Presencing*. San Francisco: Berrett Koehler.

Schwarzin L, Wals A, & Ateljevic I. 2011. Collaborative curriculum innovation as a key to sprouting transformative higher education for sustainability. In *GUNI Global University Network for Innovation – Higher Education in the World 4; Higher Education Committed to Sustainability: From Understanding to Action*. Basingstoke, UK: Palgrave-Macmillan.

Sheldon P, Fesenmaier D, Woeber K, Cooper C, & Antonioli M. 2007. Tourism education futures, 2010–2030: Building the capacity to lead. *Journal of Teaching in Travel and Tourism* 7: 61–68.

Sheldon P, Fesenmaier DR, & Tribe J. 2009. The Tourism Education Futures Initiative *e-Review of Tourism Research* 7: 39–44.

Steffen W. 2010. Observed trends in Earth System behaviour. *WIREs Climate Change* 1: 428–449.

Tribe J. 2002. The philosophic practitioner. *Annals of Tourism Research* 29: 338–357.

UNESCO-DESD. 2009. *'Education' – Hompeage of UNESCO Decade of Education for Sustainable Development*. Retrieved from: http://cms01.unesco.org/en/esd/programme/educational-dimensions/.

van Asselt MBA. 2000. *Perspectives on Uncertainty and Risk: The Prima Approach to Decision Support*. Dordrecht, The Netherlands: Kluwer Academic Publishers.

Venn C. 2002. Altered states: Post-enlightenment cosmopolitanism and transmodern socialities. *Theory, Culture & Society* 19: 65–80.

Venn C. 2006. *The postcolonial challenge: towards alternative worlds*. London: Sage.

Wals A. 2006. The end of ESD ... The beginning of transformative learning – Emphasising the E in ESD. In *National High Level Seminar on Education for Sustainable Development*. Helsinki.

Wals A, van der Hoeven N, & Blanken H. 2009. *The Acoustics of Social Learning: Designing learning processes that contribute to a more sustainable world*. Wageningen, The Netherlands: Wageningen Academic Publishers.

Wals AEJ, & Blewitt J. 2010. Third wave sustainability in higher education: Some (inter)national trends and developments. In *Green Infusions: Embedding Sustainability across the Higher Education Curriculum*, ed. P Jones, D Selby, & S Sterling, pp. 55–74. London Earthscan.

Ward T. 2008. *The Ward Method*. Retrieved from: www.tonywardedu.com/images/stories/critical_practice/the%20ward%20method.pdf.

Weart SR. 2010. The idea of anthropogenic global climate change in the 20th century. *WIREs Climate Change* 1.

Wright D. 2008. The mythopoetic body: Learning through creativity. In *Pedagogies of the Imagination: Mythopoetic Curriculum in Educational Practice*, ed. T Leonard, P Willis, pp. 93–106. New York: Springer.

Part III

Critical action in 'the tourism world'

Irena Ateljevic

Since the advent of neoliberal capitalism, academia has embraced market driven research and education ever closer. Faculty are expected to and rewarded for acquiring external funding for research projects, put under pressure to publish at a rate that challenges Fordist targets, and cleverly coerced to offer free labour to publishing companies. Students are efficiently prepared for their working lives, while degree inflation ensures ever increasing income through study fees. The final part of this book calls on tourism scholars to engage in *critical* action, to empower themselves to investigate matters that question the hegemonic rule of neo-liberal capitalism, and to seek out pathways to alternatives.

Freya Higgins-Desbiolles begins part three by investigating how tourism can be linked to the pursuit of justice and human rights. In her exploratory case study of the Hotel Bauen in Argentina, a failed capitalist enterprise that was subject to a workers' takeover or 'recuperation' in 2003 and is now being run as a cooperative, she assesses the potential of tourism to contribute to attaining justice and legal recognition for such recuperated businesses. This is followed by Senija Causevic and Paul Lynch who elaborate on tourism's potential to stimulate social and personal catharsis to overcome issues of injustice and inequality that are the consequence of war and post-war legislation and regulation in Bosnia and Herzegovina. Employing Hegelian dialecticism and reflexivity, the chapter analyses the perspective of tour guides and tourism stakeholders in Bosnia and Herzegovina, identifying tourism as part of a strategy which transforms places, cultures and societies through social reconciliation and urban regeneration following political conflict.

Shifting the focus onto the experience of travellers, Claudia Bell examines how young Antipodeans write about their visit to the Gallipoli war sites in Northern Turkey, where the loss of Australasian soldiers in World War I is commemorated. Analysing blog posts, she investigates the impacts of collective memory and the individual expression of self and nation that are implicit in this ritual form of travel, and asks whether the Antipodean visitors to Gallipoli attain a new level of consciousness and higher moral ground.

Jan Mosedale then moves the debate towards diverse economies and alternative economic practices in tourism, deconstructing the notion of 'the economy' as a singular pervasive abstract entity. Focussing on economic practices in tourism, he analyzes the confluence of structure and agency in respect to economic actions, and examines alternative economic examples in tourism to offer examples of economic practices that follow market, alternative market and non-market exchanges. Shifting the lens from alternative economies to alternative forms of hospitality, Alexander Grit and Paul Lynch conclude this set of chapters by examining the art project Hotel Transvaal to explore the organisation and becoming of hospitality space. Describing how a whole neighbourhood in the city of Den Hague became hotel and all inhabitants became hosts, they use the Deleuzian concepts of 'assemblage' and 'organisational lines' to force us to rethink the notion of 'Hospitality', as a combination of the concepts of 'hotel', 'hospitality', 'neighbourhood' and 'renewal' become entwined.

10 Hotel Bauen

An exploratory case study in justice tourism

Freya Higgins-Desbiolles

Introduction

Recent events including major financial crises are challenging the hegemonic dominance of capitalist globalization and the ideology of neo-liberalism. Within the domain of tourism, alternative tourism can be viewed in the context of an increasingly vigorous challenge to the impacts of corporatized tourism and spreading capitalist globalization (Higgins-Desbiolles 2008). In particular, justice tourism is a new phenomenon that clearly contributes to this agenda. However, to date, justice tourism has received little academic attention; there is a clear need to investigate the aims, strategies, outcomes and limitations of this unusual effort to harness tourism in the effort to secure justice. This chapter offers a case study analysis of the Hotel Bauen of Argentina in an effort to contribute to this research area.

The discussion of justice tourism must be situated in the context of globalizing neo-liberalism. The diminishing of the socialist alternative that occurred when communism was abandoned by the Soviet Union and other nations of the Warsaw Pact has been accompanied by an extraordinary advance in the spread of the ideology of neo-liberalism. According to Stilwell, neo-liberalism's 'core belief is that giving freer reign [*sic*] to market forces will produce more efficient economic outcomes' (2002: 21).

With the rise of the 'Washington consensus', these neo-liberal policies now have global reach. Developing countries are urged to adopt such policies by international financial institutions such as the World Bank, the International Monetary Fund and the development banks. McMichael has claimed that the World Trade Organization offers the promise of development to developing countries as the reward for joining the market so that a 'market rule' is installed whereby the markets and resources of the developing world are accessible (1998: 302–303).

Clive Hamilton has described the central tenets of neo-liberalism as beliefs that 'the central objective of government must be the promotion of economic growth and that markets must prevail' (2003: ix); the former he calls 'growth fetishism'. He states:

In practice, growth fetishism has been responsible for a historic transfer of political authority from the state to the private market. If growth is the path to greater national and personal wellbeing, should not those responsible for growth be encouraged at every opportunity? Growth fetishism therefore cedes enormous political power to business, and corporations are never reluctant to argue that, since they are creators of wealth, it is their interests that should be paramount to government.

(Hamilton 2003: 17–18)

The tourism sector is very important in these processes because the consumption of tourism experiences is a key 'growth' sector in many contemporary economies. In his discussion of volunteer tourism, Wearing (2002) was highly critical of tourism operations within the neo-liberalism context. He stated:

Tourism in a free market economy can exploit natural resources as a means of profit accumulation, and consequently has been described as the commercialization of the human need to travel. The notion of unlimited gain has led to the exploitation of host communities, their cultures and environments. Tourism perpetuates inequality, with the multinational companies of the advanced capitalist countries retaining the economic power and resources to invest in and ultimately control nations of the developing world. In many cases, a developing country's engagement with tourism serves simply to confirm its dependent, subordinate position in relation to the advanced capitalist societies – itself a form of neo-colonialism.'

(Wearing 2002: 238)

The negative environmental and social consequences of tourism development under such an economic system are catalysts of the alternative tourism movement. Lanfant and Graburn have contended that alternative tourism originated in the visions and critiques of tourism NGOs such as the Ecumenical Coalition on Third Wold Tourism (ECTWT) and the Tourism European Network (1992: 89–90) which were strongly influenced by the1960s counterculture movements:

These movements wanted to promote a counterculture by rejecting consumer society. Alternative tourism, in rejecting mass tourism, is a similar radical attempt to transform social relations and is thus part of the larger movement. Is tourism a new kind of development strategy, or more powerfully, a prime force within a new range of international relations?

(Lanfant and Graburn 1992: 90)

Holden of the ECTWT argued for the latter standpoint when he described alternative tourism as 'a process which promotes a just form of travel between members of different communities. It seeks to achieve mutual understanding, solidarity and equality amongst participants' (cited in Pearce 1992: 18). In recognition of such views, Lanfant and Graburn contend that 'for some, "alternative tourism" is not just another kind of tourism, but aspires to become *the* tourism in the promotion of a new order' (1992: 92).

However, as Higgins-Desbiolles (2008) argued, these radical origins of alternative tourism have been weakened by the co-option and usurpation of the corporatized tourism industry.[1] As this alternative tourism movement coincided with the phenomenon of the 'new tourists' (Poon 1993), the industry seized this as a lucrative opportunity to profit from the development of specialized niche tourisms. Justice tourism is perhaps the rare segment where the essence of the original alternative tourism movement remains.

Justice tourism

A useful conceptualization of justice tourism has emerged from the recent theorisation of the ethics of tourism (e.g. Fennell 2006; Hultsman 1995; Smith and Duffy 2003). In Hultsman's attempt to develop an ethical framework for tourism he explored what 'just tourism' might mean (1995). He advocated developing a 'principled' practice and 'ethicality' in tourism and ensuring that this imbues tourism curricula (Hultsman 1995: 559–562). Fennell (2006) and Smith and Duffy (2003) provide invaluable insight into the complexities of applying an ethics of justice to tourism in their brief examinations of Rawls' 'theory of justice' (1971). Using social contract theory, Rawls developed a theory of justice, advocating a 'fair distribution of power, goods, and so on within and between societies' (Smith and Duffy 2003: 92). Fennell (2006: 102) argued that tourism is inherently a justice issue because of its differential impacts on developing and developed communities.

Scheyvens described justice tourism as 'both ethical and equitable' and said it has the following attributes:

- builds solidarity between visitors and those visited;
- promotes mutual understanding and relationships based on equity, sharing and respect;
- supports self-sufficiency and self-determination of local communities;
- maximizes local economic, cultural and social benefits (2002: 104).

Scheyvens outlined five forms of justice tourism, which include the 'hosts' telling their stories of past oppression, tourists learning about poverty issues, tourists undertaking voluntary conservation work, tourists undertaking voluntary development work and revolutionary tourism (2002: 105–119).[2] From this analysis, we can see justice tourism includes diverse phenomena and in effect describes a continuum of practice. Kassis added that at the global level 'justice tourism is a social and cultural response to the policy of cultural domination as reflected in the globalization of tourism' (Kassis, n.d.).

Higgins-Desbiolles (2008) has provided a preliminary survey of the parameters of justice tourism and suggested it may foster an alternative and more just form of globalization. This chapter offers a case study of a particular facet of justice tourism in an effort to contribute to fleshing out the contours, potentials and limitations of justice tourism. The Hotel Bauen, located in central Buenos Aires in Argentina, was a classic capitalistic hotel until the economic collapse of 2001 in Argentina when it became a 'recuperated enterprise'. The changes in the running and management of the hotel that these events sparked provide fruitful insights into a justice tourism initiative that emerged from the needs of the hotel workers for employment in the aftermath of a shocking crisis of capitalism.

Case study of the Hotel Bauen

The Hotel Bauen was an emblematic symbol of neoliberalism in Argentina. (Grupo Alavio 2004). It opened in 1978 as a showcase of tourism development geared to political ends. Argentina was under a right-wing, military dictatorship which was engaging in a violent campaign of suppression of leftist opponents. In an effort to present a palatable image on the world stage, it hosted the FIFA World Cup Soccer tournament. The government gave loans and subsidies to build hotels, including the Hotel Bauen, to host the visitors this mega-event would attract.[3] The hotel became a favourite venue for celebrities and politicians thereafter.

Once one of the most prosperous economies in Latin America and a model of neo-liberalism in the 1990s, the Argentine economy went into meltdown with the debt crisis of 2001. Many factories and businesses shut their doors, leading to widespread unemployment, an increase in poverty and a desperate need to find some way to make a living. Workers at the Hotel Bauen were fired en masse on 28 December 2001, the hotel was abandoned and the owners filed for bankruptcy.[4]

In these dire economic circumstances, some workers turned to a new tactic called 'the take', which involved workers re-occupying their former workplace and re-opening the enterprise on a workers' cooperative organizational model. These businesses are called 'recuperated enterprises' or 'recovered businesses'. Since 2001, some 180 businesses have been 'recuperated' by the workers, providing some 10,000 jobs to unemployed Argentines.

The Hotel Bauen workers received advice from the National Movement of Recuperated Enterprises (MNER) that the hotel was in a perfect situation for a workers' takeover of the premises (Grupo Alavio 2004). On 21 March 2003 some 40 unemployed workers of the Hotel Bauen re-occupied the hotel. The workers were given a limited tenancy permit by the bankruptcy court handling the case (Evans 2007: 47). After months of clean-up and renovations, hotel services were offered. Starting with 40 employees, the hotel now employs 150 people (Trigona 2006a: 2). The hotel workers formed the Hotel Bauen Workers' Cooperative,[5] or the BAUEN, and registered it with the State Cooperative Institute. Arguing that the former owner had forfeited his rights of ownership through his failure to pay back loans given by the government, the workers set about making the enterprise a success and promised to repay the previous owner's debt.

The workers financed the renovations of the hotel; in the first year of operations, they eschewed a pay rise so that profits could be ploughed back into building up the hotel. For instance, they provided $30,000 to develop a new street-front café (Trigona 2006a: 7). A total of nearly $300,000 has been invested to get the hotel operational.

However, after making steady progress on renovating the hotel and expanding its services, the family of the previous owner has re-asserted ownership and has tried to settle the debts owed to the state.[6] They have petitioned the Buenos Aires city government to return the enterprise to them. Despite these challenges, the workers of the Hotel Bauen have created a new workplace environment and kept the hotel going. The discussion will now turn to a more in-depth consideration of the internal context of the hotel and the external context in which it operates.

Internal context

The most interesting contribution that the workers of the Hotel Bauen have made in transforming our understanding of how tourism can be re-directed to more just ends is the internal working environment they have established. In an era in which workers' rights globally have been rolled back under neo-liberalism, it is important to note that the main motivation for 'the take' was to secure employment for dismissed workers from the hotel. As Gladis Alegre stated, 'workers just want to work' (Grupo Alavio 2004).

In establishing a work environment that respects the rights of workers to work, the BAUEN has implemented a democratic decision-making process and horizontal management structure that stands in stark contrast to the previous management approach. The BAUEN has a Board of Directors, but all significant decisions on hiring, re-investment of profits and business strategy are made in a general assembly at which all workers can vote. The general assembly of workers meets every two weeks and votes on all major decisions affecting the enterprise.

Workers' statements indicate a very different working environment than that created under the previous capitalist ownership. For instance, maid Isabel Sequeira claimed that the re-opening of the hotel gave her 'hope for the future' and that the workers now 'work with our conscience, we don't have anyone looking over our shoulders or telling us what to do. We are working so the hotel is clean and beautiful' (Grupo Alavio 2004). This new workers' approach to management has been called 'sin patron' or 'without bosses' and has created a more egalitarian working environment. As Rita Yaquet stated:

> I am now my own boss and I do not have to put up with anyone mistreating me. I look forward to coming to work. I never felt like this before we formed our cooperative. My children benefit because I have an income. I also benefit because I am learning a lot about running a business and am developing strong relationships with the other workers. Although sometimes

there is conflict between the men and the women, we are learning to resolve our differences. We can never go back.

(cited in Pena and Dudley 2005: 156)

Additionally, under the previous ownership, workers were restricted in their movement within the hotel, which meant different categories of workers had little interaction with each other, which inhibited the development of bonds of solidarity. Under the workers' cooperative this has changed dramatically:

We were only compañeros, when we took the elevator to go up to eat, or in the lunchroom. Today the difference is marked ... we are always together and not just in the elevators or only during lunch hour. We are together 24 hours. We have long conversations.

(Anibal cited in Evans 2007: 53)

Workers learn to carry out many work roles and in that way the BAUEN cooperative has ensured that workers' skills and capacities are enhanced. Ordinary service workers have taken on managerial roles such as marketing and accounting and visiting activists are given free accommodation in exchange for teaching English classes to the staff (Raimbeau 2005).

Another characteristic of the Hotel Bauen is the more egalitarian pay scale instituted from the time of the take. Trigona (2006a: 6) stated the cooperative pays each worker the same amount (800 pesos per month). This is, however, disputed by Evans who claims different categories of worker receive different salaries (2007: 55).[7] Freeman (2005) explained this discrepancy: all employees receive an equal base salary, with bonuses given to those with seniority and those who made significant sacrifices during the struggle of the take. Bauen workers certainly now receive more equal and adequate pay than under the previous ownership and their salaries compare well with those of other economic sectors.

However, despite these efforts to create an egalitarian and democratic structure for the new workplace, the Hotel Bauen has its internal tensions. As Evans (2007) demonstrated, the relationships between 'old' workers, or those who participated in the take and experienced the hardships it entailed, and 'new' workers, or those employed in more recent times, is characterized by tensions as exclusions and inequalities creep in. In fact, a key concern for older workers is ensuring that new workers understand the meaning and significance of the hotel and the struggle to keep it. For instance, as the President of the BAUEN cooperative stated, 'We have to bring this worker in and tell him our story. However many days, however much time it takes. We have to find a way to make this worker conscious' (cited in Evans 2007: 49). Evans claimed 'the Bauen's public narrative is used within the hotel to cultivate an awareness and sense of commitment in those workers who had no direct experience of the initial occupation's hardships' (Evans 2007: 49). A key aim of this effort is to foster solidarity internally in the context of a precarious external environment.

External context

Recuperated enterprises such as the Hotel Bauen are at a disadvantage in trying to re-activate derelict enterprises because conventional sources of capital, including low-interest loans and subsidies, have not been made available to them by the state or private sector. They have to compete in a capitalist economy with few of the supports that capitalist enterprises normally receive.

A key tactic is therefore to prioritize developing close ties with other recuperated enterprises and the wider community. One key feature of the new incarnation of the hotel is that it is used as a site for other workers' organizations, community groups and activists to meet (Trigona 2006a: 7). The Hotel Bauen workers have been key activists in organizing and mobilizing the larger workers' struggle in Argentina. The Bauen provides conference rooms and accommodation free of charge or at a 'solidarity price' for members of other workers' cooperatives. As Bauen worker Luisa Casanova stated, 'it is more than just a hotel. Political groups and unions meet here during the week; people from the provinces come here to find job opportunities. Bauen influences other social movements in a positive way' (cited in Loren 2005: 22). Recuperated enterprises are forging bartering arrangements and providing mutual economic support to each other.[8]

One of the most striking achievements of the hotel is the relationships it has developed with its external community. Trigona stated, 'one of the keys to recuperated enterprises' success has been the insertion of the workers' struggle into the community' (2006a: 7). The Hotel Bauen has supported community and cultural events including holding rock concerts and theatre productions attended by hundreds. It has also hosted political meetings at the hotel for workers and activists, supporting the larger struggle.

Horacio Lalli of the Hotel Bauen Cooperative stated, 'There's over 180 recuperated businesses and factories. But there are 5,000 bankrupt businesses in Argentina. Beyond the individual circumstances of each recuperated enterprise, we think there is an alternative for Argentina, we think this is a way to fight against unemployment' (Grupo Alavio 2004).

While some recuperated enterprises have achieved legal status, the Hotel Bauen is not among them. The government approach has been on a case-by-case basis and it frequently only offers a short-term (two to five years) legal mandate for workers to operate the enterprise (Trigona 2006a: 4). In the case of the Hotel Bauen, the problem is with the Buenos Aires city government, which has been sympathetic to the appeal by the sons of the former owner to get the hotel back. On 8 December 2005, despite protests by Bauen workers, the municipal legislature decided to create a commission to manage a negotiation process between the workers and the sons of the former owner with the aim of handing back the business. As a result of the Buenos Aires decision in favour of the former owner, the workers at the Hotel Bauen were given an eviction notice in 2007. The workers have resisted the eviction so far and they have been supported by hundreds of people from other recuperated enterprises, activists and the wider community in rallies to protect their occupation of the hotel (Trigona, personal communication 2009; 'A ray of hope' 2006).

The workers have had to spend considerable energy mobilizing to defend their control of the hotel. In order to address this precarious legal situation, many recuperated enterprises have coalesced and rallied outside a federal court to press for the national government to resolve this situation through a national expropriation law (Trigona 2006b).

The workers of the Hotel Bauen have campaigned also for a specific law of expropriation for their enterprise based on the argument that the state has the right to take the property as payment of the outstanding debt that the former owner failed to repay. This proposed legislation has been approved in the Cooperative, Mutual and NGO Affairs Commission of the National Congress (Trigona, personal communication 2009). Trigona suggests that the National Congress is unlikely to pass the legislation, though, as it will be wary of setting a precedent (personal communication 2009).[9] Nonetheless, the workers of the hotel refuse to give up the struggle. Gladis Alegre says, 'we have to fight for this for it to be a success, save every penny, for us and our family' (Grupo Alavio 2004).[10]

In addition to the extensive network of support the Hotel Bauen workers are tapping within Argentina, there is also now a network of workers' cooperatives in South America which forms the basis of a solidarity network. As Trigona reports:

> Representatives from worker-controlled factories and businesses from Argentina, Uruguay, Venezuela, and Brazil organized the First Latin American Congress on Recuperated Enterprises October 28 and 29, 2005 in Caracas to build coordinated strategies against government attacks and dog-eat-dog markets. Venezuelan President Hugo Chávez inaugurated the event with more than 1,000 self-managed workers present who are putting into practice the slogan: Occupy, Resist, and Produce. The Congress served as an initiative to build an economic and mutual support network among the some 300 businesses and factories currently run by worker self-management in Latin America.
>
> (Trigona 2006a)

At this event, Marcelo Ruarte, President of the BAUEN cooperative, signed an exchange agreement with Venezuela's Ministry of Tourism and the Hotel Kamaratta ('A multinational without a boss' 2005).

The BAUEN has also been effective at tapping wider international support. In 2005 an online appeal was developed petitioning the President of Argentina, Nestor Kirchner, to support the efforts of the workers of the BAUEN by blocking eviction and supporting a national expropriation law; it secured over 7,000 signatures ('International support for the Bauen Hotel', n.d.). Recognized as one site in the global struggle against globalizing capitalism, the hotel is also becoming a destination for revolutionary tourists and anti-globalization activists from around the world who come to see the struggle firsthand.

However, all of these enterprises have had to operate within a capitalist market economy and compete on a very un-level playing field. Additionally, the hostile political forces aligned against them have meant that security has eluded them and precious energies that could have been dedicated to rebuilding the hotel have been spent on struggle.

Discussion

While the workers at the Hotel Bauen and other recuperated enterprises have secured significant achievements, their efforts by no means sound the death knell for capitalism in Argentina. One economics magazine puts it in perspective: 'Two hundred enterprises, representing a fairly random mix of industries, hardly constitute a parallel economy in a country of 40 million' (Kennedy and Tilly 2005). Trigona has noted key challenges facing recuperated enterprises such as the Hotel Bauen:

- workers have had to fight against legal attacks and violent eviction attempts;
- some workers have suffered physical attacks;
- lack of legal certainty results in the perpetual threat of eviction;
- lack of credit and low-interest loans to reinvest in the company have made competition difficult;
- recuperated enterprises struggle with market pressures and lack of infrastructure;
- they need trustworthy professional input;
- they need systematic technical and skills training;
- they need to build an alternative market for their products and services (2006a: 2; 2006b).

Certainly in the five years the workers have run the hotel, it has been clear that national and municipal governments are more aligned with the interests of capital than the rights of the workers, as only a handful of enterprises have been expropriated outright and given to the workers to manage. As Raimbeau notes, these enterprises:

> have never been able to secure either the hoped-for interest-free loans or legislative reforms. Big business has such a hold over the country's political and legal authorities that MPs and judges would rather turn their back on rebel workers than help them – despite the popularity of these salvaged businesses.
>
> (Raimbeau 2005)

However, the example set by the Bauen does indicate the falsehood that capitalist globalization has perpetuated that 'there is no alternative'. Trigona (2006a) describes recuperated enterprises as 'reversing the logic of capitalism'. Table 10.1 contrasts the values and approaches of capitalist enterprises and recuperated

Table 10.1 Contrasting values and approaches of capitalist enterprises and recuperated enterprises

Values and approaches	Capitalist enterprises under neo-liberalism	Recuperated enterprises: the Latin American experiment
Organizational relationships	Employer and workers in a power struggle	Workers share responsibility/democratic decision making
Organizational structure	Hierarchical management structure: owners → managers → supervisors → workers	Horizontal; all workers as co-owners
Organizational logic	Profits, efficiency and growth are the primary focus of organizational attention	Jobs for the employees, worker well-being and community relations with other cooperatives are the primary focus of organizational attention
View of workers	Workers are merely one factor of production	All workers are 'compañeros'; solidarity amongst workers
View of the enterprise	Enterprise is the private property of the venture capitalist; it is an economic enterprise	The workplaces is the workers' and community property; the enterprise has significant social obligations to the community
Conceptualization of rights	Private property rights	Workers' rights
Workplace culture	Competition, insecurity	Solidarity, equality
External context	Neo-liberal power structures support the enterprise in a web of political, social and cultural support	Recuperated enterprises form a network of cooperatives with trade agreements between them
Current situation	Such enterprises proliferated in the 1990s and 2000s but the economic crisis of 2008/09 has undermined the foundations of neo-liberalism as an ideology	A very small minority of businesses, but represents one example of alternatives that may become more visible as the economic crisis provides a possible transformational moment

enterprises in order to show the ways in which the latter can be argued to reverse the logic of capitalism. At the centre of this divergence between capitalist enterprises and worker-run enterprises is the effort to put 'people before profits'.

As Vivanco (2001) has suggested, we need forms of tourism that foster pluralism and self-determination. The Hotel Bauen shows us one example of how a tourism and hospitality business can serve humanistic ends when redirected from the capitalistic blind pursuit of profits to the building of bonds of solidarity between workers, hotel clients and the community.

The first lesson to be drawn from the Hotel Bauen is the centrality of the right to dignified and secure work. Corporatized tourism is known for its low wages, seasonal and insecure working conditions. The Hotel Bauen has shown how workers can take charge of their working environment and create sustained conditions of adequate, reliable and equitable pay. The dignified nature of employment in the new Bauen cannot be underestimated: workers go where they like on the premises and constantly interact with their compañeros. This stands in stark contrast to the servile employee that corporatized tourism is frequently accused of fostering (McLaren 2003). Additionally, this case study reminds us that justice tourism must include a clear articulation of the rights to self-determination and freedom from exploitation not only for host communities but also for workers who serve the tourists in tourism destinations.

For its focus on building ties between workers within the hotel, with other recuperated enterprises in Argentina and with Latin American workers' cooperatives, the Bauen has been called 'Hotel Solidarity' (Loren 2005: 22). This focus suggests that the Bauen workers direct their efforts beyond securing just their own individual needs and as a result they play a part in a larger transformation occurring in society. Such efforts challenge us to rethink the role that such enterprises play in our communities and suggest we could redirect some previously private sector businesses to public ends.

Finally the most significant lesson to be drawn from the case of the Hotel Bauen is the fact that human needs should be put before profits. Capitalism and its affiliated corporatized tourism are under fire for the social, cultural and ecological degradation that accompanies their pathological focus on extracting profits to deliver to a small minority of corporate elites. The BAUEN workers' cooperative, with its egalitarian and democratic management regime, fosters the welfare of workers and, while still operating in the market system, embeds itself in its community and works for equity and justice in the wider Argentine society. It is as much a social justice enterprise as it is an economic enterprise. It suggests a model of how the efforts of enterprise can be freed from the constraints of the narrow, ideological purposes imposed under capitalism. As an alternative model, the hotel is attracting revolutionary tourists and anti-globalization activists much like Chiapas, Mexico before it (see Scheyvens 2002).

Kassis (no date) views justice tourism as a social response to the injustices and exploitation of contemporary tourism under globalizing capitalism. This Hotel Bauen case study demonstrates that corporatized tourism's relentless pursuit of profits can be resisted by *the workers* and the local community who bear the brunt of the impacts of this damaging system. It also offers us an insight into the creative and humanistic possibilities that can appear when people, like the workers of the Hotel Bauen, see through the falsehood that there is no other alternative to capitalistic globalization and corporatized tourism and create their own positive futures.

Conclusion

> Our idea is to not go back to what the Hotel Bauen was. Bauen was an emblematic symbol of the bourgeoisie here in Buenos Aires ... This story is about demanding our rights and finding our dignity. Although it takes time, we've been here for a year and a half. We're taking home a salary. It's not much but we're all taking home 300 pesos. We're doing things.
> (President of the BAUEN cooperative Marcelo Ruarte, Grupo Alavio 2004)

Whether recuperated enterprises are just a short-term reaction to the 2001 economic crisis or a more long-lived assertion of workers' rights remains to be seen. Nonetheless, the Hotel Bauen has presented a rare example of how a formerly capitalistic hotel enterprise can be transformed into a worker-run cooperative that operates according to an entirely new set of values. While this case study analysis has not unequivocally supported Higgins-Desbiolles' (2008) assertion that justice tourism is fostering alternative globalization, it has shown that it makes a contribution to the pluralism and self-determination championed by Vivanco (2001), which is a precursor to an alternative and more just form of globalization. Even if the hotel shuts its doors tomorrow, the workers' precedent of creating a hotel built on the principles of the right to dignified work, workers' empowerment and bonds of solidarity stands undiminished and will continue to reverberate. Their efforts stand as testament to the potential for securing justice through tourism and their struggle challenges us to consider further ways in which tourism can be humanized.

Notes

1 The term 'corporatized tourism' describes the tourism system operating according to the precepts of capitalist globalization. It includes the power demonstrated by transnational corporations (TNCs), which have achieved 'vertical integration' through ownership of diverse sectors of the tourism and travel industry. Under globalizing capitalism, these powerful TNCs and the associated transnational capitalist class are able to manipulate tourism to maximize their profits, often to the detriment of local communities. The logic of corporatized tourism is based on exploitation and commodification of all factors of production including people, cultures and environments. Both alternative and mass tourism can be corporatized as each sector is a lucrative source of profits in a diversifying market.

2 Scheyvens argued that some forms of revolutionary tourism qualify as justice tourism when they are focused on 'building solidarity or a commitment to justice issues' (2002: 117).

3 Trigona cites a report by National Deputy Victoria Donda presented to the National Congress of Argentina, which argued that the former owner of the Hotel, Marcelo

Iurcovich, 'built the hotel with a government loan [of $5 million] from the Banade Bank, to promote the military dictatorship's tourism plan for the nation during the 1978 World Cup' (Trigona, personal communication 2009).

4 Trigona (2007) states, 'Iurcovich [the owner of the hotel] never held the hotel up to safety inspection codes and never paid back state loans. He ran up debts and committed tax evasion while making millions of dollars in profits and acquiring two more hotels. In 1997, Iurcovich sold the hotel to the business group Solari S.A. The Solari group followed in Iurcovich's footsteps, never paying the Banade debt. With little interest in the profitability and maintenance of the hotel, the installations at the Bauen deteriorated until the Solari group filed for bankruptcy in 2001'.

5 In Spanish, the Socios Cooperativa de Trabajo BAUEN; the acronym stands for Buenos Aires Una Empresa National (Buenos Aires, a nationalized business) (Freeman 2005). The cooperative is frequently just called the BAUEN.

6 Iurcovich died in April 2003 in Canada and he left his business interests to his sons (Freeman 2005).

7 Evans argues this narrative of equality and democracy is deployed by members of the cooperative and its external supporters (such as journalist Maria Trigona) in order to mobilize support for the hotel and other recuperated enterprises (2007: 55).

8 The Hotel Bauen, unlike some recuperated enterprises, has benefited from the devaluation of the Argentine peso, which has made Argentina a less expensive destination for tourists.

9 Additionally, if the BAUEN won, it would free up their capacities to even more energetically support other recuperated enterprises in the struggle for recognition (Festival frente al Congreso Nacional, 8 July 2008).

10 Rallies have been held with music and political speeches in favour of the law of expropriation for the Bauen and are available online at: www.revolutionvideo.org/agoratv/programas/empresas_recuperadas/defensa_bauen_13.html, www.revolutionvideo.org/agoratv/programas/empresas_recuperadas/defensa_bauen_14.html, www.revolution-video.org/agoratv/programas/empresas_recuperadas/defensa_bauen_15.html.

References

'A multinational without a boss: Report from the 1st Latin American Conference on Recovered Companies' (2005), *The Take: Occupy, resist, produce website*. Retrieved from: www.thetake.org/index.cfm?page_name=management_without_boss (accessed 19 January 2009).

'A ray of hope for the Bauen Hotel' (2006) *The Take: Occupy, resist, produce website*. Retrieved from: www.thetake.org/index.cfm?page_name=ray_of_hope_bauen_hotel (accessed 3 January 2009).

Evans, W. T. (2007) 'Counter-hegemony at work: Resistance, contradiction and emergent culture inside a worker-occupied hotel', *Berkeley Journal of Sociology*, 51: 33–68.

Fennell, D. A. (2006) *Tourism Ethics*, Clevedon, UK: Channel View.

Festival frente al Congreso Nacional (2008) *Si a la expropiacion del Bauen*. Retrieved from: www.revolutionvideo.org/agoratv/programas/empresas_recuperadas/defensa_bauen_14.html (accessed 3 February 2009).

Freeman, A. (2005) 'Takeover inn Argentina: Argentina's worker-run cooperative movement', *Multinational Monitor*. Retrieved from: www.multinationalmonitor.org/mm2005/092005/freeman.html (accessed 4 March 2009).

Grupo Alavio (2004), *Bauen Hotel: Struggle, culture and work*. Retrieved from: www.revolutionvideo.org/agoratv/secciones/english/bauen01.html (accessed 20 December 2008).

Hamilton, C. (2003) *Growth Fetish*, Crows Nest, NSW: Allen and Unwin.

Higgins-Desbiolles, F. (2008) 'Justice tourism: A pathway to alternative globalisation', *Journal of Sustainable Tourism*, 16: 345–364.

Hultsman, J. (1995) 'Just tourism: An ethical framework', *Annals of Tourism Research*, 2: 553–567.

'International support for the Bauen Hotel' (n.d.) *Petition Online*. Retrieved from: www. petitiononline.com/bauen/petition.html (accessed 3 February 2009).

Kassis, R. (n.d.) *The Palestinians and Justice Tourism*. Retrieved from: www.patg.org/ palestinians_and_justice_tourism.htm (accessed 19 July 2005).

Kennedy, M. and Tilly, C. (2005) 'From resistance to production in Argentina', *Dollars and Sense*, 262: 28–33.

Lanfant, M. F. and Graburn, N. H. H. (1992) 'International tourism reconsidered: The principle of the alternative', in V. L. Smith and W. R. Eadington (eds), *Tourism alternatives*, Chichester, UK: John Wiley and Sons, pp. 88–102.

Loren, S. (2005) 'Hotel solidarity: Worker control opens hotel doors to more than tourism in Buenos Aires', *New Internationalist*, November: 22.

McLaren, D. (2003) *Rethinking Tourism and Ecotravel* (2nd edition), Bloomfield, CT: Kumarian.

McMichael, P. (1998) 'Demystifying globalisation, briefly', in M. Alexander, M. Alexander, S. Harding, P., Harrison, G. Kendall, Z. Skrbis and G. Western (eds), *Refashioning Sociology: Responses to a new world order*, Brisbane: TASA Conference Proceedings, QUT Publications, pp. 299–304.

Pearce, D. G. (1992) 'Alternative tourism: Concepts, classifications and questions', in V. L. Smith and W. R. Eadington (eds), *Tourism Alternatives*, Chichester, UK: John Wiley and Sons, pp. 15–30.

Pena, L. and Dudley, B. (2005) 'Argentina: Lessons from a post-neoliberal economy', *Guild Practitioner*, 62: 153–161.

Poon, A. (1993), 'A global transformation', in A. Poon (ed.), *Tourism, Technology and Competitive Strategies*, Wallingford, UK: CAB International, pp. 85–92.

Raimbeau, C. (2005) *Argentina: The coops' dividend*. Retrieved from: www.care2.com/ c2c/groups/disc.html?gpp=4174&pst+241056 (accessed 3 February 2009).

Rawls, J. (1971) *A Theory of Justice*, Cambridge, MA: Belknap Press.

Scheyvens, R. (2002) *Tourism for Development: Empowering communities*, Harlow, UK: Prentice-Hall.

Smith, M. and Duffy, R. (2003) *The Ethics of Tourism Development*, London: Routledge.

Stilwell, F. (2002) *Political Economy: The contest of economic ideas*, Melbourne: Oxford University Press.

Trigona, M. (2006a) 'Recuperated enterprises in Argentina: Reversing the logic of capitalism', *Citizen Action in the Americas*, 19. Retrieved from: http://americas.irc-online. org/amcit/3158 (accessed 20 December 2008).

Trigona, M. (2006b) 'Workers without bosses at a turning point', *Z Space*, 9 November. Retrieved from: www.zmag.org/zspace/commentaries/2760 (accessed 3 January 2009).

Trigona, M. (2007) 'Hotel Bauen: workers without bosses face eviction', *Z Space*, 9 August. Retrieved from: www.zmag.org/zspace/commentaries/3189 (accessed 2 February 2009).

Vivanco, L. (2001) 'The International Year of Ecotourism in an age of uncertainty', University of Vermont Environmental Symposium, October.

Wearing, S. (2002) 'Re-centering the self in volunteer tourism', in G. S. Dann (ed.), *The Tourist as a Metaphor of the Social World*, Oxon, UK: CABI, pp. 237–262.

11 The dialectics of war, peace and tourism

Senija Causevic and Paul Lynch

Introduction

According to Habermas (1978), there are three types of cognitive interest which guide the creation of three different types of knowledge. The first one is technical interest. It is a determinant of the empirical-analytic approach giving rise to instrumental and exploitable knowledge of control and prediction based on facts and technical denomination. The second interest is determined by the historical-hermeneutic approach leading to discursive knowledge of understanding. The third is emancipatory interest shaped through critically-oriented sciences, for instance the critical theory approach, producing knowledge as the result of the emancipation of historically oppressed voices, thoughts and positions.

This research aims at the creation of emancipatory knowledge through critical theory as a methodological approach. According to Kincheloe and McLaren (1998), critical theory is defined within the context of the empowerment of individuals through an attempt to confront the injustice of a particular sphere within a society. This chapter showcases tourism development in Bosnia and Herzegovina, a country that has been, according to Bec-Neumann (2007), marginalised for centuries, since the fall of the Bosnian Kingdom. In 1463, when the Ottoman Empire occupied the country, Bosnia and Herzegovina remained on the periphery of the Ottoman Empire, its most western border until 1878, when the Empire was defeated and the Berlin Congress reshaped the Balkan Peninsula (Malcolm 1994, Mazower 2000). Subsequently, the Austro-Hungarian Empire occupied Bosnia and Herzegovina, which was treated as a separate entity until 1908 when it was formally annexed by the Austro-Hungarian Empire (Mazower 2000); thereby, Bosnia and Herzegovina became the only colonial territory in Europe. The status of an annexed territory gave to Bosnia and Herzegovina a peripheral and marginal position. After the First World War, a Kingdom of Serbs, Croats and Slovenians, later the Kingdom of Yugoslavia, was formed. Bosnia and Herzegovina was marginalised again, as can be seen from the name of that Kingdom. After the Second World War, Bosnia and Herzegovina was further marginalised in the Yugoslav federation, as their citizens were never treated as equal to the citizens of other former Yugoslav Republics (Malcolm 1994). Nowadays, Bosnia and Herzegovina is on the psychological periphery of the EU. It was this characteristic of marginalisation that demanded the adoption of a critical theory approach for this study.

Although there are many schools of critical theory, all of these streams have one common characteristic, which is liberation of the oppressed through the creation of emancipatory knowledge. This liberation challenges normative theoretical assumptions. Of utmost importance in this endeavour is to position oneself in relation to the research subject. Butler (1997) argues that self is constructed through the conceptulisation of identity construction through the process of otherness. Further, Alcoff (2006) argues that self is defined through the practices and meanings grounded in wider socio-political and economical settings manifesting itself through the multiplicity of relationships and social power dynamics. The research presented in this chapter has used reflexivity/introspection as a tool that has helped in acknowledging Senija's own Bosnian background in the process of creating new knowledge. Reflexivity simply linked and bound the story together, helping to reveal parts of the story that would not be obtainable otherwise. Although many criticise so-called transparent reflexivity for being overly indulgent and narcissistic (Rose 1997, Maton 2003), Ateljevic *et al.* (2005) argue that the purpose of reflexivity is to expose complexities, gaps and negotiations between the researcher and the researched, in this case Bosnia and Herzegovina's settings and Senija. Reflexivity thus resulted in dialectical methodology of thinking and perceiving the world, its presentation of ideas and paths through which normative theoretical assumptions were challenged. Hegelian dialectical discourse, which is actually a predecessor of critical theory, will now be briefly explained.

In *The Philosophy of History*, Hegel argues that dialectical reasoning has shaped history since ancient Greece, where 'customary morality' was a societal base (Singer 1983). Customary morality is identified to be part of a harmonious society where citizens are identified with the community and have no opposition towards it. This stage is called the thesis. In ancient Greece there was an exercise of independent thought conducted through Socratian reasoning in order to question customary morality. This step in creating social theory challenges the thesis, presenting it as inadequate. The questioning resulted in replacing the harmonious community and customary morality with freedom of independent thought, which in a dialectical discourse is called the antithesis. However, the antithesis is not stable. In order to achieve a sustainable social order, antithesis needs to unify with the thesis in order to produce a balance and a 'healthy' base to start moving things forward. Historical and political change occurs through the confluence of many competing forces, none of which actually plan or direct the nature of change.

This chapter gives a brief insight into the relationship between peace, tourism and politics in the tourism literature, not as a comprehensive review but to provide an understanding on how the arguments are presented. A mainstream review, i.e. the thesis, is presented first. The discussion then moves towards an alternative perspective, i.e. the antithesis. Finally, the research gives an overview of the synthesis. Through the thesis, antithesis and synthesis the role of tourism in the process of peace and harmony creation in a post-conflict tourism setting was questioned. The alternative views suggest a strategic use of tourism to provide the transition between war and peace and secure time and space for personal and social catharsis.

Tourism, peace and politics

According to Mihalic (1996), tourism can be a vital force for world peace, and also tourism needs peace for its development and prosperity. However, tourism and peace do not operate in their own bubbles. Politics occupies the space in between. When politics is introduced, tourism tends to be characterised as a very frivolous activity (C. M. Hall 1994). Although tourism and politics are greatly interlinked and tourism needs to take into broad consideration the political context, this is rarely reciprocated. Tourism tends to be positioned extremely low on the political agenda. Sometimes, tourism can be attributed to economic recovery, but if social reconciliation is not embodied in the process, economic recovery can hardly happen (Causevic 2010).

Nevertheless, there are a few instances where governments have utilised tourism activity in order to stabilise international relations. In many cases, governments encourage tourists to visit the country with which they want to establish a good diplomatic and political relationship, for example, solidarity towards former European communist regimes encouraged international tourism between communist states (D. Hall 1991). Furthermore, travel advisories play an important role in mapping the tourist gaze. Richter (1999) and Smith (1999) suggest that a government's will to improve political relations can be observed through the wording of its travel advisories. Moreover, governments use tourism in order to construct a desirable image of their country abroad. Richter (1999) notes General Marcos' attempts to repair his country's deteriorated image through tourism after introducing martial law in the Philippines in 1972. The same applied to Spain during the reign of General Franco (1936–1975) (Holguin 2005). These examples show tourism as a political marionette of autocratic regimes. If tourism is successfully implemented by those autocratic regimes, it may anecdotally suggest that we could also use tourism as a part of the reconstruction and reconciliation process in a post-conflict country.

Although tourism's potential role in political relations is evident, political scientists, planners and researchers have only marginally considered tourism as a part of collaborative research. Mainstream tourism research is very business oriented (Tribe 2004), problem-based, and pursuing technical interest. Such an approach does not encourage checking the societal settings under which tourism takes place. Perhaps the problem is attributable to a tendency in tourism research to seek to generalise results (Jamal and Everett 2004), whereas many issues that cannot be generalised, are consequently marginalised regardless of their actual importance.

Further, in many tourism journals, politically incorrect and insensitive expressions and inaccurate facts are published. For example, Stone (2006) notes genocide in Kosovo (former Yugoslavia), even though genocide happened in Bosnia and Herzegovina according to the War Tribunal Court in den Hague. The author probably confused Kosovo with Bosnia and Herzegovina, although the genesis of conflict in those two areas was completely different. The author took a very much problem-based approach, marginalising the socio-cultural and geo-political settings. Henderson (2000) calls war memorabilia sites 'a tourism attraction' which may be the case for those scholars who understand the war as it is presented in Hollywood movies, where good guys win or save the innocent. Given that much tourism scholarship is characterised by labelling and generali-sations, accordingly the easiest is to marginalise certain socio-cultural character-istics of war memorabilia sites and label these sites tourism 'attractions'. Although the socio-cultural and geopolitical context needs to be acknowledged, in tourism research it is marginalised because it impedes generalisation. This may be a contributing factor to tourism being considered as a frivolous area of study. Tourism is a relatively new field and therefore the responsibility is on tourism researchers to earn trust from their colleagues in other social science departments, otherwise tourism's potential role in the peace process and recon-ciliation is undermined.

Another instance of a direct relationship between politics and tourism is in the interpretation of historical sites. Ashworth (1994) argues that heritage is actually a contemporarily created commodity purposefully created to satisfy current consumption, thus tour guiding is rarely free of politicking. Tour guiding is either perceived as an effective instrument used by government (Reisinger and Steiner 2006) and the parties holding political power (Dahles 2002), or as an instrument which allow tour guides to develop their own agendas based on their own social contexts (Ap and Wong 2001), as demonstrated by Bowman (1992) in the case of visits to the Holy Land, where tour guides shaped tourist experi-ences, based on their own personal agendas.

Although there is a lack of research indicating the circumstances under which tourism can bring reconciliation among nations, there is a widespread assump-tion that it does normalise relations and provides an opportunity for building a culture of peace between nations or groups which were in conflict and remain hostile to one another (Hall 1994, Richter 1999, Kim and Crompton 1990). Many instances show that tourism provides an opportunity for better understand-ing, but does not guarantee a positive outcome. Tourism research usually focuses on actual travel between the subject countries or territories which used to be in conflict. Anastasopoulos (1992) examines the role of tourism in Greek tourists' attitude change towards the Turkish host community. The study shows that travel to Turkey had a negative impact upon Greek travellers regarding the per-ceived quality of life, government institutions and local cultural aspects in Turkey. Similarly, Kim and Prideaux (2003) examine South Koreans visiting Mount Gumgang, situated in North Korea, and argue that tourism helped in sta-bilising intergovernmental relationships. Milman *et al.* (1990) argue that Israeli students, when visiting Egypt, did not improve their opinions of the country. Pizam *et al.* (1991) note similar results with US students' attitude towards the

USSR. As a result, the findings are, at best, only partial, showing that on certain occasions relations become better, and on others they do not. Although all these studies have helped shape scholarship, they were all done through a positivistic approach aimed at measuring impact. However, it is important to ask: what is the purpose of measuring the reactions of individuals towards contested sites? Arguably, research on tourism needs to get a theoretical supplement from other fields of study in order to challenge the harmonious thesis of tourism research, and through that process develop tourism scholarship. This is the beginning of antithesis.

The outcome of contact between countries that were in conflict relies on the conditions under which it takes place, i.e. socio-cultural and geopolitical conditions. As discussed in the previous section, there are many cases where tourism could not address change and become a peace catalyst. The main reason for this failure was that it was not placed in a broader economic, social and political perspective (Amir 1969). Progress towards peace through tourism is not an isolated process and should not be taken for granted. It is a part of larger social change that begins with the recognition that the fundamental social and political order is changing (Kim and Crompton 1990). Amir (1969) argues that the direction of the change of attitudes between members of different ethnic groups depends largely on the conditions under which contact takes place. Favourable conditions, such as equal status between host and guest communities, a favourable social climate, personal instead of superficial contact, etc., tend to reduce prejudices and tensions; unfavourable conditions, such as superficial contact, tend to increase them. Before tourism can start to play an important part in the process of reconciliation, certain preconditions need to be satisfied. The most important is to generate trust (Causevic and Lynch 2009) among communities that used to be engaged in political conflict. Trust is achieved through the interaction in functionally important activities, leading to common goals of higher importance to the group. Cehajic *et al.* (2008) argue for the need to focus on common identities, not differences, through establishing a common goal and intragroup identity. Social psychology studies (for instance, Gaertner and Dovidio 2000, Bec-Neumann 2007, Bar-On 2007) actually dismiss the idea that behavioural developments like these could be happening through tourism, because tourism contacts are not profound, but are superficial, temporary and unable to address societal change. Instead, they argue for promoting high-quality and frequent contacts, which favour beneficial changes (Gaertner and Dovidio 2000). Such contacts can be achieved through cooperation, by working on the same project and having the same aim. Tourism is perceived in a very linear manner in political discourse, i.e. whether it brings peace or not. However, many recent studies have included other dimensions, for instance, history, identity, and societal construction, which will be further examined in the following section, starting with thesis.

Thesis: research settings

Conflict in Bosnia and Herzegovina started in April 1992 and finished in December 1995 with the Dayton Peace Agreement. One of the most important characteristics of Bosnia and Herzegovina is a complete change of socio-cultural setting compared to the one that existed before the conflict, when Bosnia and Herzegovina was a part of former Yugoslavia. The difference between Bosnia and Herzegovina and other Yugoslav republics is that other republics were based on a single nation, i.e. single ethnic grouping, whereas in Bosnia and Herzegovina there are at least three constitutive nations, i.e. Bosniaks, Croats and Serbs (Bringa 1993).

There were hardly any ethnically 'clean' territories in Bosnia and Herzegovina before the conflict. In Bosnian urban areas around 50 per cent of marriages were mixed marriages (Malcolm 1994). After the conflict entire territories were ethnically cleansed. According to Bringa (1993) multiculturalism and living together is a part of Bosnian identity, but it seems that the conflict actually erased that part of Bosnian identity. Bosnians were ghettoised into their ethnic enclaves. Bosnian Serbs now live in an entity called 'Republic Srpska'. Bosnian Croats and Bosniaks live in the entity called 'the Federation of Bosnia and Herzegovina'. The Federation is divided into ten cantons, depending whether Bosniaks or Croats hold the majority. Many people in Bosnia and Herzegovina feel lost and misrepresented under that new order and social setting.

Bosnia and Herzegovina's current ghettoisation is manifested in the Bosnian education system. Bosniaks, Croats and Serbs have been manipulated by their national leaders through different syllabi in schools. Children in schools learn the language of hate, i.e. that their neighbours are their worst enemies (Brkic 2008). There are 'three constitutive nations' in Bosnia and Herzegovina and they all hold power, having a very similar rhetoric, values and philosophy. The Croatian nationalists want prosperity for Bosnian Croats, Serbian nationalists for Bosnian Serbs, and Bosniak nationalists for Bosniaks only. The rhetoric keeps so-called customary morality and 'social balance' alive. People live in their designated territories; they do not live together, but survive next to each other instead. However, there is another, alternative stream led by those who want to bring back multiculturalism and well-being for all citizens of Bosnia and Herzegovina. They have less power than nationality based streams, and they try to disseminate their message from the bottom, through various sources, for example, tourism and tour guiding.

The following section presents part of a larger doctoral fieldwork conducted in Bosnia and Herzegovina in 2006 and 2008. Empirical research, in the form of deep participant observation of guided tours, whereby the field researcher was fully immersed into the situation as a ratified insider, took place in Bosnia and Herzegovina's cities Sarajevo and Mostar. In addition to this, semi-structured and unstructured interviews were carried out with the tour guides, and the representatives of education, consultancy, governmental and private sectors, who all have their own stake in tourism and have the power to make decisions, and in that sense shape the process of tourism development.

Antithesis: findings

> Aristotle wanted to teach that watching tragedy help us to put our own sorrows and worries into perspective. Pity and fear, emotions to be·purified, are most easily aroused, he says, if the tragedy exhibits people as the victims of hatred and murder where they could most expect to be loved and cherished. The characters of tragic heroes are neither supremely good [n]or bad, a character is a person who is basically good, but comes to grief through some great error.
>
> (*Humantia*, in Kenny 1979: 77)

Catharsis emerged from Greek tragedy, discussed in Aristotle's The Poetics and The Rhetorics. Aristotle writes that there are six things necessary for a tragedy: plot; character; direction; thought; spectacle; and melody. In developing post-conflict tourism the interpretation of post-conflict sites plays an important role. However, obscure political situations are also reflected in tourism. In post-conflict societies it is important to have training seminars for tour guides, but there are very few of these in Bosnia and Herzegovina. The problem is to overcome the biggest challenge in the country, which is that it is taught in school that 'the neighbour is the enemy'. That interpretation holds sway in everyday Bosnian life, but does not fit with the philosophy of tourism, which is to promote that it is possible to have a 'language of love' instead of a 'language of hate'. In Bosnia and Herzegovina local enthusiasts organised seminars for tour guides. One of the informants argued this was problematic:

> We organised locally a seminar for the tour guides. We told them, it is up to you what you are going to say. The only thing is that you are not allowed to do is to lie. This is a moral and personal dilemma.
>
> (Local tourism consultant and educator)

It is argued that it is down to one individual, i.e. the tour guide, to construct the interpretation of the site that has witnessed conflicts. This presents a challenge. Tour guides are morally obliged to give the official version of what has happened in Bosnia and Herzegovina during the siege. However, there is no official version; the place is still in the process of social recovery. Victims, perpetrators, and by-standers in Bosnia and Herzegovina have contested versions. It is challenging for tour guides to talk about the recent past, which may have had an impact on their own personal lives. The informants for this study insist that the golden rule of post-conflict tour guiding is that lying is not allowed. Some respondents argued that it would be better to hide this part of history and as a rule not to talk about war; for instance,

> I think that if they are interested in they can read it in every book.
>
> (Tourism Association, retired)

However, visitors to Bosnia and Herzegovina would like to learn about what they have already seen in the media. It is usually not the first motive, but people would like to ask directly, and they do ask directly about what has happened. Therefore, these questions deserve an answer. The danger of an unregulated tourism industry becomes apparent at this point, because in an extreme sense, anyone could become a tour guide and tell their story. The question of social and personal catharsis needs to be addressed first:

> Some people think that talk about last conflict should be avoided because in Bosnia and Herzegovina, the question of moral and social catharsis has not been completely addressed yet. Everyone conceals the war crimes by blaming them on others. Only those who are morally and politically mature can be involved. But how do we know who is morally clear? Therefore it is a bit delicate to develop. If you say to the ordinary Croat that Croats destroyed the bridge they would either refute it or try to justify it by talking about the things which were done to them. Those who did not go through the moral and social catharsis should not be tour guides in Bosnia now.
>
> (Local tourism consultant and educator)

Hiding historical developments and refusing to talk about what has happened may have detrimental consequences. According to Bec-Neumann (2007), silence grants amnesty to the real perpetrators and grants acceptance of collective guilt. Silence is detrimental because if people do not talk about what has happened, they will never know about the detrimental consequences and this all may happen again. Therefore, although it is painful to talk, it is usually more painful to remain silent. Tourism comes as a 'handy tool' to get people talking. To be able to achieve political correctness the most important aspect to be considered is that of social and moral catharsis. Until the whole society goes through the process of a social and personal catharsis, it is difficult to live a normal life. Thus in this sense tourism has a role to play in this social transformation. Tourism accelerates the process, but the most problematic in achieving social catharsis is the education system.

> This city [Mostar] cannot start to live although the war ended 15 years ago. There are very delicate things which need to be addressed. Schools and politics should not teach about the hate, but about the tolerance which enriches society. This is all just talk if not backed up through education.
>
> (Local tourism consultant and educator)

The majority of respondents for this current study argue that the presentation of the sites of conflict in Bosnia and Herzegovina needs to have an almost esoteric character. Political opinion is not important. This can be found in the secondary sources. However, individual feelings are important, especially the anti-war sentiments which are brought to the front during tours. As there are no officially agreed accounts of real events, tour guides are delivering their own subjective version of the truth. This is the version of events undermined through official politics, but this is the only version which has meaning for people currently inhabiting post-conflict Bosnia and Herzegovina.

Thesis – antithesis – synthesis

The Dayton Agreement was arranged according to a British 'departmental view' (Laachir 2007, after Said 1994) which does not impose assimilation and communication between different communities. It does not work well because Bosnia and Herzegovina is one community. The three departments in Bosnia and Herzegovina are artificial and the result of the process of dividing, labelling and classifying (Arendt 1963) people. It may work well in some other societies, but not in Bosnia and Herzegovina (personal reflection) where multiculturalism has been a part of Bosnian identity for centuries (Bringa 1993); it is simply not possible to designate 'departments' and territories in this manner. Negative peace, i.e. the absence of physical conflict (Galtung 1996), is usually the starting point and the first stage in consolidating positive peace. Positive peace (Galtung 1996) includes a creation of social systems that enable the normalisation of social relationships. According to Dahlman and Ó Tuathail (2005), Bosnia and Herzegovina is still in a stage of negative peace. Therefore, ordinary citizens intentionally or non-intentionally want to change that status. They feel claustrophobic and not protected by their governments, who safeguard only those who feel as if they belong to the ghettos, i.e. ethnically homogenic cantons and entities.

One of the methods to change an artificial social balance is to facilitate talk (Bec-Neumann 2007). Tour guides promote the values of peace within society through their narrative. The interpretation given and the stories told during war-themed tours is that the majority of people in Bosnia and Herzegovina were better off before the war than they are now, for instance:

> Look at the statistics; the majority of people in Sarajevo and Bosnia lived better before the war than they live now. These are the facts which are the theme of this tour.
>
> (Tour guide)

Through tour guiding, marginalised ordinary people of Bosnia and Herzegovina are presented as heroes, and through them, an anti-war message is given. Tour guides give the story of ordinary citizens, as it is an easier way to explain events through ordinary people than through high-level politics. Furthermore, it is easier for tourists to understand. Delivering an anti-war message recounted through ordinary people is the most important part of the tour. It gives a moment of rise and rebirth and brings a cathartic experience to both the tourists and tour guides. For instance:

> Bosnia is a fascinating country and people have an interest in visiting simply because they discover themselves here and appreciate their lives a bit more. They go through various cathartic experiences during my tours.
>
> (Tour guide and historian)

Achieving personal catharsis is the antithesis. Silence is interchanged with talk, as one of the tour guides passionately argued in the interview after the tour:

> Everyone is interested in finding out what has happened here.... Sometimes we would not like to talk about it. I think that we should talk about that, but not as if it were exclusively our problem, but to talk about it as a global problem. Nobody should go to war. War is the most stupid thing. People die and trage-dies are everywhere. I think that the tour that I am doing and some of my col-leagues as well, is a kind of educational tour, 100 per cent. It is not that we hate someone and are now trying to put that forward.... This is a kind of a tour that everyone should go on; it should be a part of every school programme. Also another point which we always want to say to our guests, is that we want them to know what happened here, we want them to be able to perceive that this has nothing to do with religion, we do not want people to think that we are some kind of primitives who fought just because of that. We want them to perceive us as normal people who were just a bit unfortunate recently. The main message of my tour is that war is stupid and does not bring anything good to anybody. It is important that those tours exist, but their message should not be directed against anybody, just against the war in general. It is a positive and educational message to the world, some kind of a warning that it should never ever happen again.
>
> (Tour guide)

The main characteristics of the tours in Bosnia and Herzegovina are the anti-war messages, a positive attitude, a focus on facts and ordinary people, and showing respect. The tourists themselves can relate to those ordinary unfortunate people. Thus, it appears that tourism is an important factor in this social transformation. Through the talk, the process of achieving social catharsis is accelerated.

Conclusion

The current 'social balance' and 'harmony' in Bosnia and Herzegovina was achieved through putting Bosnian citizens (Bosniaks, Serbs and Croats) into 'their' ghettoes and may be viewed as embodying a Hegelian thesis. However, the thesis is not sustainable in the long run. The antithesis is to interchange the silence with talk. The locals, i.e. the tour guides, go through a cathartic experi-ence and as a result an alternative social construct is created. This is a synthesis, integrating the voice of the people usually marginalised through powerful nation-alistic rhetoric. The voice belongs to the people who do not want to live in the ghetto in which, according to the thesis, i.e. the 'social balance' agreement, they should belong. The main conclusion for Bosnia and Herzegovina is that the country can go no further unless social catharsis is achieved. However, a problem here is that tourism is seen as an economic enhancer in Bosnia and Herzegovina, not as a reconciliatory tool. Thanks to the frivolity of tourism, guided tours act as a reconciliatory tool and this alternative agenda wins and creates a synthesis that represents life and hope.

Some might argue that the application here of Hegelian philosophy is over-simplified, as many argue that dialectical thinking was actually not that import-ant for Hegel and that it was actually Marx and later on Frankfurt School critical theorists who popularised it. Marx came across dialectical theory at the Univer-sity of Berlin Hegel Club when they discussed a lecture of Professor Chalybäus from the University of Kiel who argued the unity of the trilogy of being nothing and becoming i.e. methodical thesis, antithesis, and synthesis as an example of the schema for all that follows. It is worth noting that neither Professor Chaly-bäus nor his students ever used it afterwards (Müller 1958, in Stewart 1996). The dialectic is a progression from one determinant into another and it appears reduc-tionist to state that the collusion of thesis and antithesis produces a synthesis. Dialecticism is essentially organic and as argued by Hegelian school of thought, the world is made up of multiple interactions of its features and each of them has a part to play. It is a predicament under which the 'thesis-antithesis-synthesis' concept needs to be conveyed. In fact, it is not important whether dialecticism is the simplification of Hegel's philosophy or if it was the essence. Philosophers have been discussing this for some time already. While processing and analysing the data, dialectical thinking put a different perspective on this research and understanding the purpose of custom morality which ghettoised Senija's country Bosnia and Herzegovina and left it in a state in which it cannot move forward.

Custom morality needs to be challenged and tourism might be a trigger. Tourism actually cannot make a difference per se. However, it acts as a tool that can be utilised in order to accelerate the process of post-conflict reconciliation, which is seen as a stepping stone for any possible socio-economic development. This research thus appeared as a 'dialogue' of peace and war, construction and deconstruction, communism and capitalism, and through this 'dialogue', the research theme of tourism in a post-conflict setting was explored through expos-ing complexities, gaps and negotiations between the researcher and the researched.

This current research is actually a microcosm of what is happening in global tourism scholarship. In this respect, the thesis is represented by mainstream tourism voices of tourism scholarship, which appear to be in harmony with themselves. As awareness that tourism needs to be a part of social studies schol-arship has grown (Tribe 2004), critical tourism scholarship has questioned that harmonious order through the emancipation of less frequently heard inputs, pro-viding antithesis to mainstream tourism thought. Synthesis is in the process of becoming, and it may always be in the process of becoming; we may never reach the pure synthesis, and this may not even be our aim. The discourse between thesis and antithesis moves scholarship forward, it is recognised, and according to critical theorists thinking, when society is ready for a change, change needs to happen.

References

Alcoff, L. M. (2006) *Visible Identities: Race, gender and the self*, Oxford: Oxford University Press.

Amir, Y. (1969) 'Contact hypothesis in ethnic relations', *Psychological Bulletin*, 71: 319–342.

Anastasopoulous, P. G. (1992) 'Tourism and attitude change: Greek tourists', *Annals of Tourism Research*, 33 (4): 939–956.

Ap, J. and Wong, K. (2001) 'Case study on tour guiding: Professionalism, issues and problems', *Tourism Management*, 22 (5): 551–563.

Arendt, H. (1963) *Eichmann in Jerusalem: A report on the banality of evil* (revised edition), New York: Viking.

Ashworth, G. J. (1994) 'From history to heritage – from heritage to identity: In search of concepts and models', in G. J. Ashworth and J. Larkham (eds), *Building a New Heritage Tourism: Culture and Identity in the New Europe*, London: Routledge.

Ateljevic, I., Harris, C., Wilson, E. and Collins, L. F. (2005) 'Getting "Entangled": Reflexivity and the "critical turn" in tourism studies', *Tourism Recreation Research*, 30 (2): 9–21.

Bar-On, D. (2007) 'Reconciliation revisited for more conceptual and empirical clarity, in J. Bec-Neumann (ed.), *Darkness at Noon: War crimes, genocide and memories*, Sarajevo: Centre for Interdisciplinary Postgraduate Studies, pp. 63–86.

Bec-Neumann, J. (2007) *Darkness at Noon: War crimes, genocide and memories*, Sarajevo: Centre for Interdisciplinary Postgraduate Studies.

Bowman, G. (1992) 'The politics of tour guiding: Israeli and Palestinian guides in Israel and the Occupied Territories', in D. Harrison (ed.), *Tourism and the Less-Developed Countries*, London: Belheaven Press, pp. 121–134.

Bringa, T. (1993) 'Nationality categories, national identification and identity formation', in *"Multinational" Bosnia, Anthropology of East Europe Review*, 11: 1–2.

Brkic, M. (2008) 'Educational system of Bosnia and Herzegovina as a basic pre-condition of B&H integration into the European Union', *Survey*, Special English Edition, pp. 167–176. Previously published in *Survey (Pregled)*, 1–2, 2006 in Bosnian language.

Butler, J. (1997) *The Psychic Life of Power*, Palo Alto, CA: Stanford University Press.

Causevic, S. (2010) 'Tourism which erases borders: An introspection into Bosnia and Herzegovina', in O. Moufakkir and I. Kelly (eds), *Tourism, Peace and Progress*, London: CABI publishing.

Causevic, S. and Lynch, P. (2009) 'Hospitality as a human phenomenon: Host–guest relationships in a post-conflict Bosnia and Herzegovina', *Tourism and Hospitality: Planning & Development*, 6 (2): 121–132.

Cehajic, S., Brown, R. and Castano, E. (2008) 'Forgive and forget? Antecedents and consequences of intergroup forgiveness in Bosnia and Herzegovina', *Political Psychology*, 29 (3): 351–367.

Charmaz, K. (2002) 'Qualitative interviewing and grounded theory analysis', in Jaber F. Gubrium and James A. Holstein (eds), *Handbook of Interview Research: Context and method*, Thousand Oaks, CA: Sage Publications.

Dahles, H. (2002) 'The politics of tour guiding: Image management in Indonesia', *Annals of Tourism Research*, 29 (3): 783–800.

Dahlman, C. T. and Ó Tuathail, G. (2005). 'The legacy ethnic cleansing: The international community and the returns process in post-dayton Bosnia-Herzegovina', *Political Geography*, 24 (5): 569–599.

Gaertner, S. and Dovidio, J. (2000) *Reducing Intergroup Bias: The common intergroup identity model*, Hove: Psychology Press.

Galtung, J. (1996) *Peace by Peaceful Means: Peace and conflict, development and civilisations*, Oslo: International Peace Research Institute.

Habermas, J. (1978) *Knowledge and Human Interests* (2nd edition), London: Heinemann. Original work, Erkenntniss und Interesse, 1968.

Hall, C. M. (1994) *Tourism and Politics: Policy, power, and place*, Chichester: Willey.

Hall, D. (1991) *Tourism and Economic Development in Eastern Europe and the Soviet Union*, Oxford: John Wiley.

Henderson, J. C. (2000) 'War as a tourist attraction: The case of Vietnam', *The International Journal of Tourism Research*, 2 (4): 269–281.

Holguin, S. (2005) ' "National Spain invites you": Battlefield tourism during the Spanish Civil War', *The American Historical Review*, 110 (5), presented online in association with the History Cooperative. Retrieved from www.historycooperative.org.

Jamal, T. B. and Everett, J. (2004) 'Resisting rationalisation in the natural and academic life-world: Critical tourism research or hermeneutic charity', *Current Issues in Tourism*, 7 (1): 1–19.

Kenny, A. (1979) *Aristotle's Theory of the Will*, New Haven: Yale University Press.

Kim, Y.-K. and Crompton, J. L. (1990) 'Role of tourism in unifying the two Koreas', *Annals of Tourism Research*, 17 (3): 353–366.

Kim, S. S. and Prideaux, B. (2003) 'Tourism, peace, politics and ideology: Impacts of the Mt. Gumgang tour project in the Korean peninsula', *Tourism Management*, 24 (6): 675–685.

Kincheloe, J. L. and McLaren, L. (1998) 'Rethinking critical theory and qualitative research', in N. K. Denzine and Y. S. Lincoln (eds), *The Landscape of Qualitative Research: Theories and Issues*, London: Sage, pp. 260–300.

Laachir, K. (2007) 'Hospitality and the limitations of the national', in J. G. Molz and S. Gibson (eds), *Mobilising Hospitality: The ethics of social relations in a mobile word*, Aldershot: Ashgate, pp. 177–193.

Malcolm, N. (1994) *Bosnia: A short history* (1st edition), New York: New York University Press.

Maton, K. (2003) 'Pierre Bourdieu and the epistemic conditions of social science', *Knowledge, Space and Culture*, 6 (1): 52–65.

Mazower, M. (2000) *The Balkans*, Phoenix: Orion Books.

Mihalic, T. (1996) 'Tourism and warfare: The case of Slovenia', in A. Pizam and Y. Mansfeld (eds), *Tourism, Crime and International Security Issues*, New York: John Willey.

Milman, A., Reichel, A. and Pizam, A. (1990) 'The impact of tourism on ethnic attitudes: The Israeli–Egyptian case', *Journal of Travel Research*, 29 (2): 45–49.

Müller, G. E. (1958) 'The Hegel legend of "thesis-antithesis-synthesis" ', *Journal of the History of Ideas*, 19 (3): 411–414.

Pizam, A., Jafari, J. and Milman, A. (1991) 'Influence of tourism on attitudes: US students visiting USSR', *Tourism Management*, 12 (1): 47–54.

Reisinger, Y. and Steiner, C. (2006) 'Reconceptualising interpretation: The role of 917 tour guides in authentic tourism', *Current Issues in Tourism*, 9(6): 481–498.

Richter, L. K. (1983) 'Tourism politics and political science: A case of not so benign neglect', *Annals of Tourism Research*, 10(3): 313–335.

Richter, L. K. (1999) 'After political turmoil: The lessons of rebuilding tourism in three Asian countries', *Journal of Travel Research*, 38(1): 41–45.

Rose, G. (1997) 'Situating knowledges: Positionality, reflexivities and other tactics', *Progress in Human Geography*, 21(3): 305–320.

Said, E. (1994) *Representations of the Intellectual: The 1993 Reith Lectures*, London: Vintage Books.

Singer, P. (1983) *Hegel: A very short introduction*, Oxford: Oxford University Press.

Smith, G. (1999) 'Toward a United States policy on traveller safety and security: 1980-2000', *Journal of Travel Research*, 38(1): 62–65.

Stewart, J. (1996) *The Hegel Myths and Legends*, Evanston, IL: North-Western University Press.

Stone, R. (2006) 'A dark tourism spectrum: Towards a typology of death and macabre related tourist sites, attractions and exhibitions', *Tourism*, 52(2): 145–160.

Tribe, J. (2004) 'Knowing about tourism: Epistemological issues', in J. Phillimore and L. Goodson (eds), *Qualitative Research in Tourism: Onthologies, epistemologies methodologies*, Abingdon: Routledge

12 Pacifists and partygoers?

Young Antipodeans visiting Gallipoli war sites

Claudia Bell

Introduction

Every year New Zealand tourists, mostly young adults already based in Europe, travel to Gallipoli in northern Turkey to attend a commemoration service. The event marks the loss of New Zealand soldiers at that site in the First World War. This chapter explores the impacts of collective memory, and the individual expression of self and nation, involved in this ritual.

For New Zealanders and for Australians Gallipoli is a powerful marker in nationalist history. My goal in this research was to investigate the responses of young Antipodeans visiting Gallipoli, as posted on their blogs. In their accounts of their visits, how did they communicate their reactions to being at the actual site of national myth and legend? Did rows of crosses marking the deaths of young soldiers, their fellow nationals, provoke reflection on the meaning of war? Did this experience engender a call for peace? I have linked the mobility and cultural logics of leisure and tourism to notions of nationalism for travelers when they are away from home.

This particular tourist migration to the battlefield has become a must-do side trip for youthful New Zealanders on their 'overseas experience' ('OE'). This 'overseas experience' is a tradition in which young adults explore the world for a year or two. Most are based in Britain, where they are eligible for work visas (Wilson *et al.* 2009; Bell 2002).

Tourism to Gallipoli is a local industry, ironically run by Turkish people on the site where perhaps their own ancestors died. That earlier generation suffered the war; their descendants now make a living from it. Similarly for the tourists: their ancestors died here, and now they visit as part of a vacation. Travel capitalism brings together these two historically connected groups. The influx reaches a peak for the ANZAC Day commemoration on April 25th, and there is a steady stream of Antipodean tourists during the rest of the year. It is, after all, relatively cheap for them to travel in Turkey. There is also a network of ANZAC hostels through Turkey, assuring a warm welcome in the English language.

The first section of this chapter is a brief background account of the meaning of ANZAC Day in New Zealand and Australia. Also noted is recent resurgence in its public support. This is followed by reflection on a small sample of tourists' accounts of their visit to Gallipoli, expressed in online blogs. My agenda was to investigate whether these tourists conveyed anything resembling 'a new level of consciousness, to reach a higher moral ground' (Ateljevic *et al.* 2007: 3). Would their moments in the presence of the war-dead engender pacifist sentiments? Or are the distances between the current stories and history, between representation and reality, too vast to make the touristic experience much more than entertainment?

In the next section the travelers are positioned as envoys of family and nation, engaging with the past to maintain the myths and legends in the present. They are on a pilgrimage that folks back home will applaud. However that journey framed as pilgrimage may include socially unacceptable behavior. Until alcohol was banned this year at the Gallipoli site, partying had been a feature of the visit. The conviviality of the assemblage with fellow nationals disturbed some observers.

This is followed by a consideration of the role of tourism in reconfiguring national histories. Tourism is a medium that enables reconstruction and re-interpretation of meaning, short-cutting historic detail in favour of current ideology. The brief conclusion is a reminder about the conservative nature of tourism enacted at such sites.

The ANZAC legend

In the Antipodes ANZAC Day has been an annual commemoration since 1916, honouring the ultimate sacrifice of all soldiers. The term ANZAC stands for Australian and New Zealand Army Corps. April 25th is the annual day of remembrance, with dawn services and other events taking place throughout Australia and New Zealand, and in expat communities globally. In Australia and New Zealand this date is a public holiday.

At those commemorations, and in public collective memory, the 1915 battlefield at Gallipoli in Northern Turkey has particular resonance. As part of the Allied expedition attempting to capture the Gallipoli Peninsula to open the route to the Black Sea, more than ten thousand Antipodeans died through disastrous leadership by the British.[1] They landed at ANZAC Cove, then tried to fight an impossible battle on the steep terrain. New Zealand's loss of 2,700 men at Gallipoli, and a total of 18,000 during World War I, was a significant sacrifice of young men for a tiny, fledgling nation. A further 50,000 were wounded.

In such a small country, barely a community or extended family was personally unaffected. Hence there was unlikely to be 'any challenge to the mythologizing that strengthened with each post war year of public commemoration and memorialisation' (Graham 2008: 431). After the war the survivors and civilians at home created social memories that honored and remembered the dead. War was justified, to make the losses bearable. Physical memorials were erected in every town and district 'lest we forget'. The national narrative has long identified Gallipoli events as New Zealand's 'coming of age'.[2] Wartime experiences were framed within the context of nationhood; social memories supported the development of a unique identity, and distinction from Britain (Winter 2009). In terms of discourse on New Zealand's historic formulation of national identity, Gallipoli provides a specific date for a foundation moment.

Both individual and national identity are constructed through social processes. The national narrative is constantly reiterated. Indeed, any sense of nationhood requires shared stories. Those narratives about citizens of the past and present are fundamental to the identity project of the nation. 'National identity and individual subjectivity of citizens are mutually and simultaneously constitutive, as the stories that construct both phenomena draw on the same discourses' (Harding 2008: 1). The younger generation learns about ANZAC Day at school. It is an annual ritual explained to children, just before that special holiday. They grow up knowing what ANZAC Day is about. This ensures that Gallipoli remains powerful in collective memory and in nationalist history. That carefully constructed social memory which takes place through the agency of the state is greater than, and perhaps different from, the sum of individual subjectivities (Winter 2009). More personal accounts of those events are preserved in households through physical mementoes – war medals, soldiers' diaries and old souvenirs, known to have belonged to a family member – and through family legends.

The ceremonies at the Gallipoli site are presently arranged cooperatively by the governments of New Zealand, Australia and Turkey. In 2008 and 2009 an estimated 18,000 people attended. (Numbers were less in 2010, because of transport disruptions by the Eyjafjallajokull volcanic eruption in Iceland). Most camp overnight at temperatures around minus 3 degrees, waiting for the dawn service. At this event, there are more Australians and Kiwis on that beach than there were in 1915.

> Yet the post-World War II generation barely honoured ANZAC Day. Historian Philips explains that there was resistance to 'anything that elevated the importance of war to the New Zealand identity. We wanted no nukes and to establish our country's identity in pacifist terms ... [but] as people read soldiers' diaries and looked at the human costs of war rather than seeing an interest in war as meaning that you are pro war, attitudes changed. People went to the services [to] honour soldiers who'd gone through awful and horrific experiences ... the worst experiences that Pakeha New Zealanders have ever gone through.... When they came back there was an extraordinary amnesia, a real repression about what the reality of war was like in human terms ... The returning soldiers could not openly discuss powerful emotions'
>
> (Barry 2007: 22)

Since the 1980s New Zealand national identity has been a significant subject of public reflection. The debate was kindled by the Maori Renaissance, immigration, trade and defence policies, globalization, and the maturation of the 'baby-boomers' (Graham 2008; Bell 2002). Simultaneously, the ANZAC story has been the subject of extensive analysis by journalists and academics. Various explanations of its steady re-growth in the popular imagination have been attributed to anti-English sentiment, patriarchal power, re-assertions of masculinity, and to analysis of mateship. Today it is read as affirmation of the pioneering spirit, egalitarianism and racial harmony. Maori are certainly as vigorously honoured for their considerable sacrifices in imperial wars.

The war veteran generation has now gone. But the tucked-away diaries and letters have been found, opened, read, and generally made available as important social documents. That personalized information, alongside the accessibility of travel, may have contributed to the rising interest in Gallipoli. ANZAC Day has not just survived as a grand narrative of nation. Each year its place in the collective memory and consciousness appears to expand rather than contract, even though the original event occurred 95 years ago.

Blogs: so you want the world to read your diary?

There are numerous blogs about visits to Gallipoli, particularly about going there on ANZAC Day. Not only were these people visiting that site, but they were also writing about it.

Blogs have been described as 'an amalgam between a diary, a web site and an online community' (Jones and Alony 2008: 438). Blogs resemble dairies and personal journals, but a significant difference is their addresses to the reader. Readers include people in the bloggers' own known social network, and in the larger blogosphere of unknown readers (Nardi *et al.* 2004: 223). Barlow's research shows that the imagined expansionism of bloggers 'is little more than a new way to talk to the same type of people they would be talking to anyway' (2008: xi). By personalizing content, 'blogs go beyond an informative role and provide a platform for ... the expression of personal identity. With no (internet) access hurdles ... bloggers can present their ideas as they wish' (Bruns and Jacobs 2006: 4–5). Many travellers write their comments to newspaper blog sites, a version of 'letters to the editor' available online.

The rapid uptake of blogging has been an unprecedented personal, active relationship between humans and technology (Barlow 2008). Blogs provide a venue to create and maintain standing and identity, for the surveillance of both familiars and strangers. Nevertheless, any form of diary-writing is a minority habit. Blogs are used as research documents cautiously; the behavior and attitudes of diary and blog writers cannot be proven to be either typical or unusual (Alaszewski 2006).

Every few months, blog numbers double. There are now hundreds of millions of blogs. For qualitative researchers, blogs provide convenient primary data, without need for synchronization between the researcher and the subjects. Purportedly, factual material cannot be relied on; the public nature of this storytelling makes its content selective (true also in face-to-face interviews). However, for the tourism researcher requiring individual unsolicited personal accounts of a journey or holiday, blogs are something of a goldmine.

Over my blog-collecting period (taking in three ANZAC Days, 2008–2010) I checked tourists' chronicles of their trips to Gallipoli. The most effusive described their participation on ANZAC Day, though visitors on other days also wrote of their experience. For some bloggers, the temporary sense of almost-euphoric nationalistic togetherness matches Billig's concept of 'banal nationalism' (Billig 1995):

> The speeches begun and the reefs [sic] were laid, tears flowed as we all came to grips with the events that had laid on these very grounds beneath us, the blood that had been shed and the fear they must have felt.
>
> (www.myway2go.com.au/.../166998,anzac-day--gallipoli-2009.aspx)

> I expected to be very emotional when I first saw Anzac Cove but the feeling was of a great sense of pride. The ANZAC legend of larrikin mateship, distrust of authority and a fair go is firmly implanted in our being and for me this pilgrimage was about renewing these values and paying my respects to those who forged them under great adversity all those years ago.
>
> (www.travelpod.com/travel-blog-entries/pollies/1/.../tpod.html)

These accounts illuminate how such spaces function to reaffirm group identity (Grodach 2002). Before their eyes and beneath their feet at that war site are tangible residues of gruesome events. Those are compelling substantiation of the legends they grew up with.

The bloggers offer a seamless national consensus about what should be remembered from our collective past (Griffin and Hargis 2008). However, for most blog writers anything sacred about Gallipoli is expressed in curious juxtapositions: remembrance and entertainment; profound grief and celebratory fun; commemoration and holiday; sacred ceremony and a party. After the service one blogger reported

> catching up with friends from London on other tours that I bumped into while there, signing the visitors' registry, and generally soaking in the sun in an attempt to lessen my London 'moon tan.' (He also bought a souvenir ANZAC Day T shirt).
>
> (www.masey.com.au/2001/04/anzac-day-gallipoli/)

Others made these observations about participating:

> The trip has become something of a pilgrimage for the Antipodean 20-somethings and by all accounts a bloody good time was had by all.
>
> (www.masey.com.au/tag/travel/)

> (ANZAC Day at Gallipoli) reminds me a bit of Diana-hysteria in 1997. You felt like a major social transgressor if you didn't throw your own ... offerings on the communal heap of rotting flowers. ... It does point, though, to

the need to be part of something big and symbolic, whether it's a nation, a footie team, or 'tradition'.

(inastrangeland.wordpress.com/2008/04/24/anzac-day-atheist/)

Very few of the bloggers reflected on the negative features of war. Those who did chose colourful language:

> Yep, war's a bitch. There's a lot of unthinking adulation and talk of 'heroism' on ANZAC Day. For me, war is too obscene for misty-eyed odes. ANZAC Day does nothing to catch the wild-eyed terror of being attacked, the smell of shit as your mate loses his bowels as he dies, and the dehumanizing rage that makes you bayonet the enemy (himself, a man) again and again and again.
>
> (blogs.
> brisbanetimes.com.au/bluntinstrument/archives/2008/04/the_smell_of_th.
> html)

> Frikken military propaganda … it shits me big time … absolute muddaferkers commemorating the spoils and horrors of war … shame on the lot of ya, it is nothing to celebrate or be proud of.
>
> (blogs.
> brisbanetimes.com.au/bluntinstrument/archives/2008/04/the_smell_of_th.
> htm)

> Days like ANZAC Day serve to remind us how truly horrible war is.
>
> (blogs.
> brisbanetimes.com.au/bluntinstrument/archives/2008/04/the_smell_of_th.
> html)

The most succinct pacifist comment:

> Peace rocks!
>
> (Blogs/nzherald.co.nz/blog/escpaism/2008/6/26/emotional-jounrey-
> gallipoli)

Envoys engaging with the past in the present

For the current mobile generation of Antipodeans, travelling and exploring the world, both family and official collective memory entwine. National identity is not hermetically sealed back in those South Pacific islands, but intrinsic to their cultural baggage.

Present day war tourism at the Gallipoli sites links the present, even prosaic, activities of tourism with the glorified past. As West explains, 'foreign fields often become sanctified in national history as places where ancestor's blood was spilt and, as in the case of the world wars, where many of their remains reside'

(West 2008: 1). Almost a century after those 1915 events, Gallipoli has become a key destination for young New Zealand travellers. Gallipoli is a site for 'international secular pilgrimage' – to a site of national importance, but located outside of the nation itself (Bell 2002). At Gallipoli patriotic emotions are deeply stirred. Few sites external to their own country have such significance to New Zealanders. To visit Gallipoli is to visit a well-established connection with home; indeed, almost a little piece of home, in that 'corner of a foreign field' kind of way.

Exotic as Turkey may seem to young New Zealanders, the very name ANZAC Cove provides a specific connection to home. At Gallipoli they can engage with a means of expressing a symbolic affiliation with nation. As a diaspora of expatriates, living somewhere reasonably accessible to Gallipoli, this event is one in which they can participate. The nostalgia of absence from home may also urge their involvement. As Australian sociologist West explains, working holidaymakers may not be overly patriotic while at home, but away from home banal nationalistic symbols seem to stir greater emotions. This, he suggests, 'points to positive unintended consequences of postmodernity and the resilience of modern forms of identity in a global world' (West 2008: 151–152).

For some travellers it is as if they are seeing this on behalf of previous generations of their own families and fellow nationals, who grew up with the legend, but lacked the opportunity to travel. These are new young family envoys. Their newly acquired narrative does not so much *compete* with versions received at commemoration back home, but complements and enlarges that received account.

At the same time, the travellers are constructing their own life stories. Consumption, including the purchase of travel experiences, forms one's identity. That dual transformation of 'inner state and outer status' (Coleman and Elsner 1995: 6) may be read not just as the outcomes of a journey of spiritual and nationalistic significance, but also as a commercial process within the domain of travel capitalism. Without tourism, such personal enrichment may be far more limited. Humans locate meaning in their lives by recalling and recounting personalized places and events. In this manner they track 'progress' from where they were before (e.g. before going to Gallipoli), to where they see themselves afterwards (enriched by the experience, and far more knowledgeable and sensitive about events of the past).

In New Zealand there are concerns expressed about the mass exodus of the younger generation to perceived greater opportunities elsewhere. Many work, marry and settle overseas. The interest in ANZAC Day and Gallipoli suggests that absence does not necessarily include rejection of the ethos of Kiwi identity. A pilgrimage to that distant site is an affirmation of nationhood. This demonstrates that tourism has a contribution to make in furthering the nationalistic ideologies of the tourists themselves. To them, at this space, national identity is plainly a relevant concept. In the case of the Gallipoli pilgrimage, it can be argued that this takes place through the process of consumption. Travel capitalism depends on travellers as consumers. That same consumption contributes to the continuation of the national legend.

Maffesoli refers to the concept of 'belonging', with the notion of the tribe as a global group united by consumption (1996). This includes the purchase of travel, and touristic experiences. In his analysis members choose the group to belongto through recognition of style, consumer goods, and consumerist behaviours. Constructing self-identity and achieving a sense of belonging become simultaneous processes.

> The tribes are fluid, they ebb and flow across international space; they gather then disperse; then gather again in different configurations and at various venues. The tourists' membership to this tribe is dynamic, changing, ephemeral and uncommitted; an occasional member. Consuming together, they become a community of travelers or a travel subculture.
>
> (Bell 2002: 145)

This is what we see at Gallipoli. As Meuller writes, 'The ANZACs got no further [up the cliff face at Ari Burnu] than they had on the first day, but they dug themselves immovably into the cherished memories of three nations: Australia, New Zealand, and Turkey' (Meuller 1998: 68). Graham suggests that what will be commemorated at the ANZAC centenary in a few years' time 'will reflect the legacy of understanding, interpretation and memory that successive generations of youth have absorbed' (Graham 2008: 444). Touristic access to the actual site has cemented the mythologies.

As exotic as Turkey may seem to New Zealanders, the very name ANZAC Cove provides specific associations. Local ANZAC and Southern Cross hostels, ANZAC bars, and ANZAC grocery shops are further connections. In ANZAC hostel lounges, on the evening before the battle site visit, gathered tourists watch the Australian movie *Gallipoli*.[3] If they have scant knowledge of the actual history, the movie will certainly suffice. As Meuller explains, 'what "Gallipoli" the film does depict accurately is Gallipoli the popular legend' (Meuller 1998: 2). One blogger confused the historic site with a movie location:

> We visited The Nek, where the final scene of the movie Gallipoli is set.
> (realtravel.com/e-205748-gallipoli_entry-anzac_day_the_dawn_
> service – 63k-)

Enacting other traditions

Visiting Gallipoli is an occasion in which to participate with fellow nationals. Holidaymakers may not be overtly patriotic while at home, but when away, nationalistic symbols seem to provoke greater emotion. At Gallipoli the pilgrims move into a space or state of heightened spiritual awareness, uniting those present in a common purpose. This, Scates suggests, 'points to positive unintended consequences of postmodernity and the resilience of modern forms of identity in a global world' (Scates 2006: 14).

A gathering of the expat diaspora is also an opportunity to party.[4] There is no other site where so many young Kiwis and Australians gather annually on a particular date, beyond their home borders.

> It's a party day. There's a lot of beer drinking, to remember the beer drinking of the soldiers, I like to think.
>
> (www.stuartwright.wordpress.com/2007/04/)

> It has, unfortunately, become a drinking trip for many young New Zealanders.
>
> (www/nzherald/co.nz/news/print/cfm?/objected10565299&pnum)

The youthful tourists have no memory of World War I, or of the soldiers who fought. Even if they never attended an ANZAC service, they grew up with the ANZAC Day holiday, people wearing red poppies, and seeing those parades on television. Attending ANZAC Day at Gallipoli is now on the inventory of things to do while on OE – along with the running of the bulls at Pamplona in Spain, or attending the Munich Oktoberfest (Beerfest) in Germany.

> From Anzac day in Gallipolli, through drinking in Belfast, climbing in France, backpacking in Northern and Eastern Europe, travelling and hiking in Peru, skiing and working in Canada.... All the funny, happy, sad, crazy and sometimes downright weird – It's all there to be had and I'm going to try my best to find it.
>
> (www.travelpod.com/travel-blog/tommy/world-adventure/tpod.html)

> Wakelpa's life list [things he's just gotta do!]:
> Visit Gallipoli on Anzac Day
> Do Stand-up Comedy in front of an audience
> Do New Year's Eve in Times Square
> Visit my friend in Kentucky
>
> (www.43things.com/persomn/wakelpa)

Scates explains that

> Gallipoli was another experience, another adventure. The Dawn Service was only a small part of it. Aside from the ceremony on 25th April, package tours offer a visit to Troy, a boat cruise along the coast and plenty of free time in the bars of Cannakale. Tour operators invite the young to join the Anzac experience then wind down back in Istanbul where the fleshpots of Turkish baths and belly dancers eagerly await them.
>
> (Scates 2006: 8)

Partying at Gallipoli has been hotly criticized in the New Zealand and Australian newspapers. Such disrespect is abhorred, not just as shameful behavior by individuals, but as a bad way to represent New Zealand. Numerous bloggers commented on the drinking they observed, or heard about, at Gallipoli.

> What a way to commemorate them, by getting drunk.
> (travel.msn.co.nz/.../lonely-planet-stay-away-from-anzac-service)

> Why should they be encouraged to lie among the gravestones, swilling beer, in party mood?
> (www.smh.com.au/news/Letters/Modern-values-demean-)

> It highlights our country's continuing problem of celebrating the lowest common denominator in our society and anything that is devoid of class or respect and highlights our fixation of embracing laddish and boozing culture and calling it Kiwi culture.
> (www.nzherald.co.nz/news/print/cfm?/objected10565299&pnum)

> Locals would often ask where we were from and when we said NZ they talked about us being drunks and party animals and it saddened me to think that is the reputation we have over there.
> (www.nzherald.co.nz/news/print/cfm?/objected10565299&pnum)

It could be pointed out that in New Zealand and in Australia drinking copious quantities of alcohol has long been an everyday form of celebration or commemoration, another time-tested institution.[5] Not all rituals and traditions practised by some sectors of the population are customs that everyone identifies with, or is proud of.

Tourism reconfigures history

Tourism is a medium that enables reconfiguration of meaning. That people can actually go to Gallipoli, and take in the interpretations available at that site, almost a century later, is to access regurgitation or elucidation of the original historic sequence of events. The new narrative must inevitably compress, create, dilute and distil from residues of the myriad of stories of that site. Those tourists attending commemorations at Gallipoli are participants in and witnesses of both the revisiting of the old, and the propagation of the new collective memories. These are concerned with one dominant meta-narrative, ANZAC Day. In this way, they contribute to keeping the notion of ANZAC Day alive in the present.

To be at the real site, having that genuine physical corporeal experience, walking on that very ground, is to experience the authenticity of the actual arena. This authenticity heightens both the sense of history, and the individual's connection with their nation. Here, young men died. They can be recognized here as named individuals, not just anonymous 'soldiers'. It is shocking to see so many graves of people, fellow nationals, most of them younger than the visitors themselves. It is as if those soldiers are trapped in time, in nationality, in their own youthfulness, in this foreign land, too far away to be visited until now, when travel has become accessible. Patriotic tears are shed.

> When they read all the names of the men, the soldiers who had died here, I got a tear.
>
> (www.stuff.co.nz/national/anzac-day.../Poignant-visit-to-Gallipoli-for-Kiwis)

> Tears were almost obligatory...
>
> (Blogs/nzherald.co.nz/blog/escapism/2008/6/26/emotional-jounrey-gallipoli)

Travelling to Gallipoli is to privilege the bodily and spatial experiences over secondary ways to access information that cannot involve one's physical senses. Here is the context for events. The soil on which they now stand ineradicably enfolds the events of 1915, even if that terrain has been altered from when those soldiers were ordered ashore (modified largely to accommodate visitors – steps, tracks, etc). Gallipoli is both a metaphoric and an actual place. At home in New Zealand, the various cenotaphs and other physical memorials can only *symbolize* or *represent* or *stand for* those events at that distant, authentic space that could not easily be visited. At Gallipoli the dead soldiers each have a grave and a marker, visually restating the awfulness of the sheer numbers who died.

The tourists' role in the maintenance of this segment of the national story is empowered. For most, this will be a cherished 'once in a lifetime' experience. One blogger states:

> I have to stress that ANZAC DAY in Gallipoli has without a doubt become a landmark day in my life.
>
> (www.masey.com.au/2001/04/anzac-day-gallipoli/)

Through participating at that site, they are expressing citizenship and loyalty to their nation, as those young soldiers did. This is an expression of belonging to New Zealand, while far away from home. For the travellers this is one of the few places in the world where an overt sense of connection is prescribed.

And so in distant Turkey where the language and customs are strange, nationalism is reiterated. The tourists can enjoy both their own self-ascribed *cosmopolitanism* as smart, sophisticated travellers, alongside opportunities to express and share their own fervent and sentimental nationalism (Bell 2001). The New Zealand government demonstrates an ongoing commitment to remembering the lives of soldiers lost at that site. This endorsed ritual encourages participation and subscription. Those who attend do so in a communal spirit of honour and support. ANZAC Day appears to be in no danger of being lost.

Yet the initial agendas of young tourists to Gallipoli are not necessarily driven by a vigorous patriotism. We can see their use of group memory as a resource they can adapt to achieve their personal and social purposes (Ross *et al.* 2008).

This particular national memory prescribes another travel adventure, another journey to an exotic place, another story to add to their blog. But once at the site, we can see an affirmation of nationality, while accruing experiences for their own future nostalgia. As Featherstone explains, nationhood is one of the most significant cultural definitions of social identity (Featherstone 2009: 7). Gallipoli is a site for the performance and iteration of national identity. Touristic events at Gallipoli illustrate how individuals and collectives are both constituted by the past, and mobilized in the present (Winter 2009). One Australian who attended the service in 1998 observed,

> I still don't know what any of us are doing here now. Sometimes, as I wander over the overgrown trenches and across the immaculate graveyards, I think that the veneration of Gallipoli is a good thing, that the demonstrated sense of history and the concurrent lack of any kind of nationalistic bitterness is admirable. Then I notice that the Australians represented here are not the Australians I recognize: there is barely a trace, among the pilgrims, of Asian, or Mediterranean, or Baltic, or Middle Eastern ancestry. And I wonder if there isn't somewhere at the depth of the Gallipoli myth, which inspires more and more people to come here each year – something unhealthy, reactionary and frightened
>
> (Meuller 1998: 5)

That writer implies that commemorations may also affirm traditional white dominant ideology (Meuller 1998). The celebration of ANZAC at Gallipoli may be read as a retreat into a conservative pre-multicultural version of New Zealand and Australia, as, during the pilgrimage, the young tourists adapt to the values of their own parents and grandparents.

West suggests that the 'recovery of an enchanted national past is rather predicated on its being commemorated in rituals that facilitate its alignment with contemporary consciousness' (West 2008: 267). It may be that we *need* ANZAC Day as an occasion for unselfconscious expression of sentiments less readily stated at any other time. One blogger reflected on the ritual itself:

> There does seem to be something in people that requires ritual, doesn't there? Something in our would that makes us create and cling to ceremony? Could this very simple human need explain ANZAC Day's resurgence of the past ten years?
>
> (inastrangeland.wordpress.com/2008/04/24/anzac-day-atheist)

Conclusion

Social change since World War I has been extremely extensive. Only through a diversity of re-interpretations can past events be made meaningful to the next generations. Events, experiences and information at tourist sites play a large role in those explanations. But is ANZAC Day tourism at Gallipoli akin to a theme park experience? Actual historic occurrences are safely sanitized by time and distance. One can explore trenches, climb ridges, look at named battle sites: it's like visiting a commercial entertainment venue. That familiar mythology is transposed to activity, the passivity of merely *looking* ameliorated. As Lennon and Foley point out, the past has become the province of tourism as much as history (Lennon and Foley 2000: 162).

In my own published work on the New Zealand OE as a secular pilgrimage (Bell 2002) I noted the following, lining up my analysis with that of Coleman and Elsner's (1995) on religious pilgrimages:

- The secular pilgrimage as a rite of passage (been there, done that!).
- It includes the confrontation of travellers with rituals and/or sacred spaces (the ritual of commemoration at the actual site, long familiar from legend).
- It has metaphorical resonances. (These young travellers, in going to Gallipoli, are on something of an adventure, or at very least a journey to an unfamiliar site. They are recapitulating an expedition made long ago by other young New Zealanders.)
- Their luggage will include tokens of place: their evidence. (Maybe a few stones from Anzac Cove, photographs, or souvenir T-shirts purchased on site.)
- They return home with recollections and narratives (or put them on blog sites). According to their blogs, many of those narratives include a renewed or revised patriotism.

'A confrontation with one's own emotions may transform the very structures of thinking', writes Askjellerud, perhaps optimistically (2006: 9). Many bloggers referred to their own raised consciousnesses about the futility of war, and love of their homeland. One observer described the ANZAC tourism experience as a 'blubfest', a 'sobfest'.[6] Hundreds of blogs present momentary 'shock-horror' responses to historical events at Gallipoli. As Kelly reminds us, 'it is difficult to find anyone who is opposed to peace' (Kelly 2006: 3).

But I did not find blogs in which the writer expressed any developed sense of pacifism, as a consequence of their touristic experience. Perhaps blogs are not the site for such pronouncements? Tourists expressed awe rather than outrage. They appeared ensnared in an official jingoism, rather than becoming critics of those events. The ANZAC legend appears to have been co-opted as soft patriotism, inviting shallow emotional response. That old hopeful 1960s mantra 'make love, not war' appears forgotten.

I suggest that tourism itself is a conservative activity. It is not one that generally fosters radical activism. Tourism has no solid history of equating *seeing* with *thinking*, *politicizing* or *taking action*.[7] The tourist experience at Gallipoli, like anywhere else, is ephemeral: just a glimpse or gaze. Touristic practices encourage tourists to be passive consumers, not active cultural critics. The inherently conventional character of tourism itself could be a fertile focal point for the liberal scholars at the Academy of Hope.

Notes

1 This has been well documented by numerous historians, including detailed accounts in Gallipoli: the New Zealand story by C. Pugsley; New Zealand, Reed, 1998; and R. Kyle (2004), *An Anzac's Story*, Australia: Penguin.
2 *Te Ara Encyclopaedia of New Zealand* is just one official document that uses the 'coming of age' term.
3 *Gallipoli*, Australian Film, 1981, directed by Peter Weir, starring Mel Gibson. It is about young men from rural Australia, sent to Turkey in the First World War. The climax takes place on the battlefield at Gallipoli, ending with the futile, savage attack at The Nek. The film is constructed with the assumption of empathy for the Australian soldiers.
4 Numerous travel websites advertising tours to this site offer partying as part of the package.
5 For New Zealanders, drinking after a funeral may be a residue of the tradition of the Irish wake. Many of the early settlers to New Zealand were Irish. Today it would be unusual for any funeral to be alcohol-free.
6 Personal communication, Auckland, March 2009.
7 Some recent advances on this include opportunities for volunteerism through tourism. However, this may not be the most effective way to deliver aid, and might also be 'fraught with potential inequalities and challenges', as explained by K.D. Lyon and S. Wearing (2008) *Journey of Discovery in Voluntary Tourism*, USA: CABI.

References

Alaszewski, A. (2006) *Using Diaries for Social Research*, London: Sage.

Askjellerud, S. (2006) *Tourism and Peace: The traveller*, IIPT Occasional Paper No 4. Global Educators Network for the International Institute for Peace through Tourism.

Ateljevic, I., Morgan, N. and Pritchard, A. (2007) 'Editors' introduction: Promoting an Academy of Hope in Tourism Enquiry', in *The Critical Turn in Tourism Studies: Innovative Research Methodologies*, UK: Elsevier.

Barlow, Aaron (2008) *Blogging America: The new public sphere*, Westport, CT and London: Praeger.

Barry, M. (2007) 'At peace with the past', *New Zealand Listener*, 208 (3494).

Bell, C. (2001) 'How to be a global citizen: Constructing self identity through tourist consumption', *Anglos-Saxonica. Revista do Centro de Estudos Anglisticos da Universidade de Lisboa*, Series 11(14 and 15): 15–24.

Bell, C. (2002) 'The big OE: Young New Zealand travelers as secular pilgrims', *Tourist Studies*, 2 (2): 143–158.

Billig, M. (1995) *Banal Nationalism*, London: Sage.

Bruns, A. and Jacobs, J. (2006) *Uses of Blogs*, New York: Peter Lang.

Coleman, S. and Elsner, J. (1995) *Pilgrimages Past and Present in the World Religions*, London: British Museum Press.

Featherstone, S. (2009) *Englishness: Twentieth-century popular culture and the forming of English identity*, Edinburgh: Edinburgh University Press.

Graham, J. (2008) 'Young New Zealanders and the Great War: Exploring the impact and legacy of the First World War, 1914–2014', *Paedagogica Historica*, 44 (4), August 2008: 429–444.

Griffin, L. J. and Hargis, P. G. (2008) 'Surveying memory: The past in black and white', *The Southern Literary Journal*, 40 (2).

Grodach, C. (2002) 'Reconstituting identity and history in post-war Mostar, Bosnia-Herzegovina', in *City*, 6 (1 April): 61–82.

Harding, Nina (2008) *Composing the War: Nation and self in narratives of the Royal New Zealand Air Force's deployment to the 1991 Gulf conflict*, Christchurch, New Zealand, M.A. Thesis, University of Canterbury.

Jones, M. and Alony, I. (2008) 'Blogs: The new source of data analysis', *Journal of Issues Informing Science and Information Technology*, 5: 433–446.

Kelly, I. (2006) *The Peace Proposition: Tourism as a tool for attitude change*, IIPT Occasional Paper No. 9, Global Educators Network for the International Institute for Peace through Tourism.

Kyle, R. (2003) *An ANZAC'S Story*, Australia: Penguin.

Lennon, J. and Foley, M. (2000) *Dark Tourism*, London: Continuum.

Lyon, K. D. and Wearing, S. (2008) *Journey of Discovery in Voluntary Tourism*, USA: CABI.

Maffesoli, M. (1996) *The Time of the Tribes: The decline of individualism in mass society* (trans. Don Smith), London: Sage.

Meuller, A. (1998) *Rock and Hard Places: Travels to backstages, frontlines and assorted sideshows*, USA: Forulli Classics.

Nardi, B. A., Schiano, D. J. and Gumbrecht, M. (2004) 'Blogging as social activity, or, would you let 900 million people read your diary?' CSW'04, November 6–10, Chicago, IL.

Nguyen, V. T. (2009) 'Remembering war, dreaming peace: On cosmopolitanism, compassion, and literature', *The Japanese Journal of American Studies*, 20.

Pugsley, C. (1998) *Gallipoli: The New Zealand Story*, New Zealand: Reed.

Ross, M., Blatz, C. W. and Schryer, E. (2008) 'Learning and memory: A comprehensive reference', in H. L. Roediger III (ed.), *Social Memory Processes*, New York: Elsevier, pp. 911–926.

Scates, B. (2006) *Return to Gallipoli: Walking the battlefields of the Great War.* Cambridge, New York; Cambridge University Press.

West, B. (2008) 'Enchanting pasts: The role of international civil religious pilgrimage in reimagining national collective memory', *Sociological Theory*, 26 (3): 258–270.

Wilson, J., Fisher, D. and Moore, K. (2009) 'Reverse diaspora and the evolution of a cultural tradition: The case of the New Zealand 'Overseas Experience'', *Mobilities*, 4 (1): 159–175.

Winter, C. (2009) 'Tourism, social memory and the Great War', *Annals of Tourism Research*, 36 (4), October: 607–626.

Blogs

www. blogs.brisbanetimes.com.au/bluntinstrument/archives/2008/04/the_smell_of_th.html

www.Blogs/nzherald.co.nz/blog/escapism/2008/6/26/emotional-jounrey-gallipoli

www. inastrangeland.wordpress.com/2008/04/24/anzac-day atheist

www.masey.com.au/tag/travel

www.masey.com.au/2001/04/anzac-day-gallipoli/-

www.myway2go.com.au/.../166998,anzac-day--gallipoli-2009.aspx

www. realtravel.com/e-205748-gallipoli_entry-anzac_day_the_dawn_service – 63k

www.smh.com.au/news/Letters/Modern-values-demean-

www.stuartwright.wordpress.com/2007/04/

www.stuff.co.nz/national/anzac-day.../Poignant-visit-to-Gallipoli-for-Kiwis

www.travel.msn.co.nz/.../lonely-planet-stay-away-from-anzac-service –

www.travelpod.com/travel-blog-entries/pollies/1/.../tpod.html

www.43things.com/persomn/wakelpa

13 Diverse economies and alternative economic practices in tourism

Jan Mosedale

Introduction

Research on tourism economies still lags behind contemporary research in the wider economic social sciences (mainly in anthropology, geography and sociology). It is dominated by quantitative, universalistic survey methods framed by studies of consumer behaviour and to date largely ignores the cultural meanings of exchange relationships. The bulk of research on tourism economies either fails to mention alternative economies or simply views them as minor distortions of a capitalist system. The inherent difficulty of quantifying and measuring alternative exchanges and thus incorporating or addressing alternative economic practices in national accounts or official accounting systems offers governments and researchers a pretext to disregard, ignore or trivialize these economies.

In this chapter, I claim that critical tourism scholars should engage with and think critically about the representations of 'the economy'. I aim to challenge a capitalocentric understanding of tourism and argue for an economy that is constituted of complex and dynamic relationships between a variety of economic practices at multiple sites and spaces. In making this argument, I primarily draw on literature on diverse economies (Gibson-Graham 1996, 2006, Leyshon *et al.* 2003) and alternative economic practices in varied cultural and socio-economic contexts (Smith and Stenning 2006, Pavlovskaya 2004, Amin *et al.* 2002) and use examples of economic practices from the tourism literature.

First the chapter will discuss and deconstruct the representations of 'the economy' to unlock diverse economies; second, practices are briefly contextualized as a new epistemological strategy to analyse the meeting point of structure and agency in respect to economic actions; finally, the diverse economies of tourism are separated into economic practices according to market, alternative market and non-market exchanges following the diverse economies framework by Gibson-Graham (2006).

(Re)thinking economies

The dominant discourse in most societies elevates the economic to an entity that ultimately controls society. This meta-narrative is widely presumed to be following an inescapable economic logic (Williams 2005): economic transactions are performed according to 'free' market exchange (unrestrained by social or political impediments). Prices are determined by the laws of supply and demand and labour is sold to producers in order to transform raw materials into products to be sold for a surplus. The labourers' wage allows for the purchase of the necessities of life and additional luxuries.

In this narrative, there is no room for differences or alternatives. Yet although this myth of a single and pervasive capitalist market economy is uttered by many academics, politicians and capitalists (see Williams 2005), there are multifarious social exchanges that *do not* follow the 'rules' of a capitalist market economy (Williams and Nadin 2010, Gibson-Graham 1996, 2006, Leyshon *et al.* 2003, Williams 2005). Yet, 'the economy' has been elevated to a mythical status beyond the control of society, leading Gibson-Graham (2006: 53) to question its common usage: 'Why has Economy become an everyday term that denotes a force to be reckoned with existing outside of politics and society – a force that constitutes the ultimate arbiter of possibility?' The capitalist market economy is generally considered to be 'the economy', but is merely one aspect of a bundle of different social practices that together constitute a set of diverse economies.

This representation of 'the economy' as a singular and all-encompassing abstract entity reduces the economy to mere monetary values and stifles possible alternatives and parallel economies (Gibson-Graham 2006). Yet, the term is itself socially constructed and therefore open to a de-construction in order to reach a pluralist understanding of economies (Massey 1997, Mosedale 2011). The problem is not that there is a dominant, capitalist discourse but that this representation of the economy has become extradiscursive (beyond discourse) and thus hegemonic, that it does not permit any alternatives. We have come to accept the singular and pervasive nature of 'the economy' and do not question its meaning (the meaning has been fixed in our collective imagination). This leads to the 'economistic fallacy' (Polanyi 2002) where 'the practice of analyzing all economic systems through the theoretical gaze that presumes that the horizons of the economy are fully comprehended by a map that includes only market exchange and the calculative behavior couplet' (Adaman and Madra 2002: 1046). The dominant discourse should not diminish the diverse nature of our economic practices. In order to understand the diverse economies in tourism, we need to go beyond a capitalocentric understanding of the tourism economy and use a map or ontology that makes it possible to include different economies. Then the economic subject is shaped, formed and constituted by social structures, as well as agency and the local context.

Critical scholars should 'unfix' or deconstruct the meanings of 'the economy' in order to reconstruct diverse economies that are inclusive of economic difference (economies that differ from the dominant capitalist economy). Once we start to (re)think the artificial and socially constructed boundaries of 'the economy' and view it in a more pluralistic manner, 'new economic imaginaries' (Gibson-Graham 2002: 2) can emerge and become discursively viable: 'Then a whole new world moves into view' (Thrift and Olds 1996: 311).

The Cultural Turn and its effect on the economic social sciences was the first major turning point for a deconstruction of 'the economy'. In their seminal volume Lee and Wills (1997), for instance, offer an analysis of different approaches towards the economic subject and promote the widening of economic research to include culture as a key constituent. The Cultural Turn led to a significant shift from seeing 'the economy' as transactions which are somehow separate from social and cultural spheres to understanding the economic subject as a fluid economic landscape consisting of multiple economies embedded in place-specific cultural, as well as historic, contexts and social relations (see Mosedale 2011 for a more detailed discussion of the relationship of culture and economies following the Cultural Turn and how it relates to tourism research).

Poststructural political economists take a slightly different approach to diverse economies in that they do not merely see the analysis of the multiple natures of economic practices that constitute diverse and pluralist economies as a new research agenda, but also as a political project to prepare the ground for a multifaceted, flexible and open-ended economy of non-capitalist practices that is able to overcome the grand narrative of capitalism: the myth of a singular, pervasive economy (Gibson-Graham 1996, 2006). Recognizing that discourses about the economy are contested may lead to wider representations of frictions within the capitalist economy and offer opportunities to embed the term within every-day practices influenced by specific geographical and historical contexts. For a critical analysis of economies it is necessary to reconnect economies with wider society, as they are constantly reproduced via social practices (Mosedale 2011).

Practices

The economy is not an abstract notion but something that people *do* in everyday life as people create livelihoods. By analysing practices and concentrating not just on the social structures but also on human agency it becomes possible to view individuals not as mere subjects of the economy, or 'anticapitalist subject, with its negative and stymied positioning' (Gibson-Graham 2006: xxxv), but as actors that are engaged in shaping and (re)producing economies. Focusing on practices offers an opportunity to transcend debates on structure and agency (Mosedale 2011). Both structure and agency meet and become visible in practices (Giddens 1979), which can be employed as tactics or strategies to resist structures and yet may also result from these structures. Hence, de Certeau (1984) views everyday practices as individual tactical decisions either to conform to a social order or to resist or subvert the dominant structure via the expression of individuality. In this context, economic practices provide 'ways of knowing the world through action, but also form – through action – the materiality of the world through the creation, reproduction and unfolding of material social relations' (Smith and Stenning 2006: 192–193). Practices can be helpful in analysing how overarching phenomena such as class, gender, networks etc. are enacted, (re)produced and potentially transformed in everyday practices by individuals who themselves embody these phenomena. The analysis of practices and actions then become an epistemological strategy as everyday practices become the object of analysis for the interpretation of socioeconomic processes (Jones and Murphy forthcoming). This new focus on seemingly mundane or ordinary practices can inform our understanding of economies as constituted of multitudes of practices, social structures, materials and meanings.

Alternative economic practices in tourism

Economic practices as individual strategies influenced by structure and agency form the focus for the following discussion of diverse economies in tourism. Gibson-Graham (2006) demonstrates the diversity of economic practices by highlighting the difference in transactions (the mode of exchange), labour and the configuration of production, ownership and distribution of surpluses (organizational form). Table 13.1 presents an overview of diverse economies with examples of different economic practices occurring in tourism.

This section will follow Gibson-Graham's (2006) categorization of economic practices in order to explore the varied forms that economic practices may take in tourism and how they are embedded in specific social, cultural and political contexts. The confines of this chapter do not permit a discussion of the full range of economic practices in tourism, but the aim is to provide selected examples in order to convey the diverse nature of social economic relations.

Organizational form

One aspect of economic diversity is the general configuration of production, ownership and the distribution of surpluses (i.e. different ways and structures of accumulating and distributing wealth). The economic organization in capitalism is centered around privately owned capital and social relations of material transformation are negotiated by means of wage-based labour. The price of goods and services is determined via the rules of supply and demand and the resulting surplus is distributed to the owners of capital. However, there are other forms of economic organization that differ in the distribution of surplus as profit maximization is not always the only underlying reason for engaging in exchange transactions. Alternative forms of capitalism are influenced by ethical values, e.g. social justice, equality and sustainability. While the accumulation of capital still plays a role in alternative capitalism, some surplus is also distributed to non-producers. Firms increasingly recognize that their responsibilities extend beyond the search for profits and that their operations should benefit the wider economy, society and the environment. Corporate social responsibility (CSR) is a clear example of alternative capitalism, as part of the surplus is distributed to wider stakeholders rather than to the owners and investors. Henderson (2007) analysed the CSR of hotels in Phuket, Thailand after the 2004 Indian Ocean tsunami. She highlights the complex interplay between philanthropy and capitalist interest especially with the notion of the triple bottom line, which combines social, environmental and economic returns.

Table 13.1 Examples of diverse economies in tourism

Organizational form	Transactions	Labour
Capitalist Surplus appropriated by owners	*Market exchange* Ruled according to supply and demand, also includes 'illegal' economies	*Wage labour* Labour that is remunerated with money according to a labour market (demand and supply of labour)
Alternative capitalist Maximization of profit is not the only contributing factor for exchange transactions as some of the surplus is distributed to non-producers *Ethical tourism* *State enterprise* *Green capitalist* *Corporate social responsibility* *Non-profit*	*Alternative market exchange* Exchange is socially negotiated rather than exclusively subject to supply and demand *Home exchange* *Voluntary contributions* *Couch surfing*	*Alternative paid* Labour that is remunerated (not always monetary) outside of a labour market *Self-employed* *Cooperative* *Reciprocal labour* *In kind*
Non-capitalist Surplus is appropriated by non-producers *Communal* *Independent* *Feudal* *Slave*	*Non-market transaction* No rules of commensurability or equivalence, i.e. the transaction does not require a balanced exchange *Gift giving* *State funding* *Charity* *Deviant transactions (e.g. theft, embezzlement, begging)*	*Unpaid* Labour that is not remunerated with money, goods or services, yet usually not uncompensated *Family work* *Volunteer tourism* *Slave labour (e.g. prostitution for sex tourism in some cases)*

Source: adapted from Gibson-Graham (2006: 71).

Non-capitalist forms of organization include communal ownership of resources, in which labour surplus is appropriated by the wider community even though it might not have been involved in production. While truly communal ownership is rare in tourism, Ying and Zhou (2007) offer insights into communal tourism development in Xidi, Anhui Province, China. The village committee (elected by local villagers) set up a corporation to develop and manage tourism and to distribute the economic gains. While the households that welcome tourists into their homes receive a wage, a portion of the profit is distributed to the rest of the village regardless of their involvement in tourism and some profit is spent on community welfare projects. Forms of organizations like the 'Xidi Tourism Service' are organized around an ethic of solidarity, as some of the labour surplus is distributed to individuals that are not engaged in the production process.

The organization of production, ownership and the distribution of labour surplus is just one factor that can be used to categorize economic practices, yet often the form of organization is most influenced by social structures. The next section will discuss the specific exchange relations within capitalist, alternative capitalist and non-capitalist forms of organization.

Transactions

Goods and services are circulated via exchange relationships, and these transactions are varied in nature and not necessarily confined to capitalist market exchange following the relationship between supply and demand. In alternative markets, for instance, the equivalence of the exchange is socially negotiated rather than purely subject to supply and demand.

Home exchange is one such economic practice in which the exchange is negotiated between the two parties although elements of demand and supply do still play a role in the exchange. Home exchange can be organized individually but is often mediated by companies who charge a fee to include ads in an online database. The databases offer a marketplace to view and evaluate house exchanges and for interested partners to exchange details. More often than not this is a direct exchange between two parties but may involve more parties, e.g. in a three-way exchange where A stays in B's house, B stays in C's house and C stays in A's house.

Demand and supply clearly is a factor in home exchange as home owners who live in locations that are undesirable for others find it more of a challenge to find possible exchange partners: 'An appealing self-made marketing of the overall destination (including overcoming seasonality issues), the location, the neighborhood and the house itself is often crucial [in] "wooing" the partners' (Arente and Kiiski 2006: 86). The houses do not necessarily need to be of equal value (in terms of housing market or in terms of standard), as location (country, proximity to tourist destinations or urban centres) plays an important role in the exchange as evident in the following quote from an interviewee:

But if we want to exchange with a family from the south of France ...
maybe we would accept a two bedroom's [*sic*] apartment. We can't expect a
big villa with the swimming pool. And it will be all right, because the south
of France is more appealing to us.

(cited in Arente and Kiiski 2006: 58)

As the exchange is not regulated, trust is paramount and is often created via
communications prior to the exchange (Arente and Kiiski 2006, De Croote and
Nicasi 1994). Queries such as insurance cover for the house, usage of the car,
telephone charges, etc. need to be addressed in advance to steer clear of potential
disputes but also to build up a level of trust between exchange partners before
the exchange. Our homes can be quite personal and 'one has to get used to the
fact that other people sleep in one's bed, cook in one's kitchen, live in one's
house' (de Croote and Nicasi 1994: 23).

The home exchange experience can become more than just an exchange of
houses. Arente and Kiiski (2006) talk about 'emotionally bonded communities'
between the exchange partners but also with the communities that are
'exchanged': 'We were a part of the local society, community where we lived,
and that you really can't buy. You can't buy that!' (Interviewees cited in Arente
and Kiiski 2006: 64). These bonds may last beyond the duration of the initial
transaction.

The equivalence of transactions is usually negotiated directly between the
parties (as in the example of house exchange), but there are numerous examples
of alternative transactions where the price of exchange is left to the discretion of
the tourist or visitor. Some museums and national parks, for instance, either ask
for any amount of voluntary contributions, suggest a range for voluntary contributions, or insist on a contribution but leave the amount to the visitor. In the
current context of decreased government funding for cultural and natural public
goods and services, publically funded institutions increasingly have to generate
additional income (White and Lovett 1999). Many have turned to alternative
market exchange in order to be able to continue to provide an easily accessible –
essentially still *public* – good or service.

At the same time, the traditional roles of cultural institutions in particular
(conservation and education) have changed with more emphasis being placed on
their role in regional and urban economic development. Thus Tufts and Milne
(1999) offer interesting insights into the relationship between cultural institutions and urban economies by not reducing museums to purely economic actors.
Yet the tourism literature has focused primarily on assigning monetary values to
public goods and services by concentrating on the willingness-to-pay of tourists
and visitors (Reynisdottir *et al.* 2008, Chung *et al.* forthcoming), rather than analysing the social relationships and factors involved in the transaction.

These examples are a mixture of alternative market transactions (via the voluntary contribution) and non-market transactions in the case of visitors that
choose not to contribute anything. In most museums and national parks that use
voluntary contributions by visitors, these complement public funding (mostly

because of reductions in or generally inadequate public funding). So if the voluntary contribution does not cover the cost, the non-market exchange makes up the difference. In addition, visitors may choose not to pay or their contributions may not reflect the true value/cost of the museum. Similarly most publically funded cultural institutions offer reduced and sometimes staggered pricing for seniors, retirees, students, unemployed people, etc. In this case, socio-economic factors are taken into account in addition to supply and demand when determining the cost of transaction.

In contrast to alternative market exchange, non-market transactions do not require a balanced exchange. There are numerous examples of non-market transactions in tourism including some deviant transactions like theft (Botterill and Jones 2010) or embezzlement. Another example of non-market exchange is state involvement in tourism by funding education and training, tourism development to ensure economic regeneration of cities or regions, or tourism promotion, etc. This state funding operates outside of market environments with no relation to supply and demand dynamics or balanced exchange, as capital may be redistributed to areas of need either by funding tourism development directly or indirectly (via the provision of associated infrastructure or subsidies) (Hall 2008).

Gift-giving is another example of non-market transactions. Gifts are a symbol of social relationships between the donor and the recipient. Gift-giving is therefore dependent on the cultural context of role status and role expectations. The gift is decoded by the recipient in terms of the finances, time and effort that the donor has invested in the gift (Clarke 2008). Gift giving is not inherently – in reality seldom – altruistic as there may be expectations of non-material returns such as friendship, etc. and egotistic motivations behind the giving of gifts such as an increase of power and status for the donor (Sherry 1983). Gift-giving may form part of a system of exchange in which the value of countergifts are augmented in each round of giving in order to convey social prestige and power (Bourdieu 1970, 1977).

The essential elements in gift exchange are the social ties or obligations that are created or reinforced between the donor and the recipient via the symbolism of the gift. In Chinese *guangxi* networks gifts are the mediators of obligation and reciprocity. The exchange and circulation of gifts in *guangxi* networks are calculated means to gain social capital (Yang 1989, Lew and Wong 2004). Part of the *guangxi* obligations of Chinese tourists is to purchase souvenirs as gifts to maintain or increase their social capital (Guo *et al.* 2009), whereas expatriate ethnic Chinese are expected to occasionally return to China in order to fulfil their *guangxi* obligations, which inevitably involves gift-giving (Lew and Wong 2002).

Of course gift-giving is also important in the West, as Ateljevic and Doorne (2003) demonstrate in their analysis of tie-dyed fabric commodities as gifts from New Zealand tourists. The gifts were used as a strategy for self-identity and social positioning, while at the same time they connected 'the other' (in terms of the context of production) with the values and lifestyles of the 'life worlds of consumers' (Ateljevic and Doorne 2003: 138). The meaning of gifts therefore may extend across geographic and social distance with the associated differences and inequalities and thus create value in a specific context of social relationships.

Charity is a specific form of gift-giving which acts as redistribution of personal capital, as the donor is conscious of socio-economic inequalities and gives charity to contribute to mitigating and addressing these inequalities. Turner *et al.* (2001) distinguish between three types of charities in tourism: 1. charities that work outside the industry and use tourism as a means to raise further funds for their charitable projects not involving tourism, 2. charities working 'above' the tourism industry which seek to influence decision-making on overarching issues such as social justice and sustainable labour conditions, and 3. charities working within tourism, i.e. which have charitable tourism projects.

North South Travel, for instance, is an example of a charity that uses tourism as a means to generate funds. As a non-profit UK travel agency, it donates all net profits to development projects in the global South. The UK-based charity Tourism Concern can be classified under the second type of charity in that it aims to influence public policy on such issues as displacement of locals by tourism development, exploitation of workers and environmental damage. It has received considerable attention for its campaign to improve porters' working conditions in the Himalayas, on the Inca Trail in Peru and at Mount Kilimanjaro, Tanzania.

Yet charity in itself is not unproblematic as charities are 'deeply embedded in local social networks of access and exclusion. Indeed, it is impossible to consider these organizations without reference to their position in local social networks' (Bryson *et al.* 2002: 55). In her study of Buddhist charity and merit in northern Thailand, Bowie (1998) argues that uni-directional transactions such as charity 'may be important in mediating the processes of hegemony and resistance in the sociopolitical constitution of complex societies' (Bowie 1998: 469).

Critical voices argue that charity does not change the structural inequalities that are inherent in mainly capitalist systems, but merely addresses its symptoms:

> In the modern world, according to its apologists, there is, on the one hand, the world of money, which pretends it has nothing to do with social obligation, and another separate antithetical world, the world of charity where those who have benefited from commerce salve their consciences by 'free gifts' to inferiors, an act which they see as in no way caused by an obligation on their part but merely as due to the internal prompting of their consciences.

(Bloch 1989: 168)

As demonstrated by the quote above, charity may not be free of egotistical meanings, which leads Kosansky (2002: 362–363) to critically assess the 'facile oppositions between altruism and hierarchy, generosity and self-interest, charity and profit'. In a study on charity in Moroccan Jewish pilgrimage, Kosansky

(2002) reveals that the ritual exchange of bidding for candles as charity to honour Jewish saints are performances of wealth and honour involving 'sacred' strategies to gain profits in the capitalist economy.

Labour

The analysis of labour in economic exchange systems takes a prime position in political economy, especially as 'capitalist societies are underpinned by the antagonistic relationship between capital and labour' and the ensuing distribution of surplus to the capitalist class (Bianchi 2011: 18). Yet, labour is performed and compensated in different ways, resulting in diverse relationships between labour and capital (Gibson-Graham 2006). While the term labour has become almost synonymous with wage labour, there are numerous forms of alternative paid or unpaid labour in tourism. Labour that is 'paid' but not compensated according to the labour market is deemed to be alternative pay. Examples include self-employed business people that pay themselves below or above market value, cooperatives that receive capital payments due to the ownership of production, in-kind payments or reciprocal labour.

World Wide Opportunities on Organic Farms (Wwoof) uses in-kind compensation for labour as the wwoofer supplies four to six hours (this depends on negotiations with the host) labour per day in exchange for food and accommodation. This is an increasingly popular phenomenon for backpackers in some countries who either want to gain experience and knowledge of organic growing methods, different lifestyles and/or to maximize their travel budget (see McIntosh and Campbell 2001, McIntosh and Bonnemann 2006, Mosedale 2009). Wwoofing is straightforward, as backpackers join the local wwoof organization (this involves a small fee), get access to the database of hosts and contact the host to determine whether there is any work at any given time. Although the simplified exchange is labour for food and accommodation, the success of the exchange relationship depends on the social interaction between host and wwoofers. Wwoofing is usually a short-term exchange between strangers, so there is an element of uncertainty for both hosts (who are welcoming a stranger into their home) and the wwoofer (who is thrust into someone else's home). While this uncertainty is challenging for many, the complex interplay of unpredictability, alternative lifestyles, being embedded in local culture and cheapness is also part of the attraction. As opposed to formal monetarized transactions (such as staying in youth hostels) or waged labour relations, wwoofing offers a sense of adventure and new and unexpected social experiences (Mosedale 2010).

Examples of unpaid work in tourism include family labour within family-owned SMEs (Shaw and Williams 1990), and voluntary work. While unpaid labour receives no monetary compensation, it is usually compensated via social relations (e.g. friendship, love, etc.) or an increased sense of self and achievement. In some cases, such as slave labour, which regrettably is still occurring in the sex tourism trade (see Jhappan 2005), labour is not compensated.

Volunteer tourism (often referred to as voluntourism) is one aspect of unpaid labour that has received increased attention in the tourism literature (Campbell and Smith 2006, Halpenny and Caissie 2003, McGehee and Santos 2004, McIntosh and Zahra 2007, Stoddart and Rogerson 2004, Wearing 2001). Although unpaid labour is at the core of voluntourism, it is far from decommodified as it is often facilitated by fee-charging organizations: 'Some of the most exciting conservation work in Africa from €950–€1700 (2–4 weeks) ex flights' (responsibletravel.com n.d.). These companies create 'a space populated by the existence of consumable experiences of "the other", which is the central commodity for sale' (Simpson 2004: 683).

The idea that tourism should bring positive impacts to local communities in the destination lies at the heart of voluntourism, yet most academic research in the field focuses on the volunteer experience as multifarious associations between the motivations for engaging in voluntourism (e.g. a means to travelling, a challenge, to gain knowledge and experience or to contribute to the community), the context of the volunteer work, and the relationship with the local community and with fellow volunteers. To date, little regard has been given to power relationships associated with this type of labour. For instance, the relationships between the voluntourists and the local community or between the voluntourist organization (whether a charity or a commercial business) and their local partners, and the meanings that the local community ascribe to the volunteer labour remain unexplored (Sin 2009).

Conclusion: practicing economies in tourism

In this chapter I have attempted to critique the hegemonic capitalist discourse of a single pervasive capitalist economy and to offer a different view of our economies as open, plural and consisting of a variety of economic practices set in particular social, cultural and political contexts. A focus on practices offers a way to move research on diverse economies forward as practices are the result of individual strategies in the face of social structures and human agency. Unfortunately, a detailed critical analysis of the varied economic practices in tourism was beyond the confines of this chapter, but the examples provided hopefully demonstrate the diverse economic practices that individuals and institutions engage in and how they actively shape our economies.

The study of alternative economic practices is a promising research area for critical scholars of tourism, hospitality and mobility. Research on alternative economies is largely focused on place-based economies (as geographically fixed communities facilitate the development of trust and reciprocity) and critical tourism scholars could contribute to the wider debates on diverse economies and economic practices in the social science by focusing on alternative economic practices and exchange spaces situated within contemporary mobilities such as wwoofing (Mosedale 2010), house exchanges (Arente and Kiiski 2006) and couch surfing (Germann Molz 2007). Of course, alternative mobile practices are also of interest with reference to empowerment, activism, and resistance to the hegemony of the dominant capitalist economy. At the same time, it is necessary to extend critical questions to and problematize concerns of exploitation and inequality in alternative economic practices.

References

Adaman, F. and Madra, Y. M. (2002) 'Theorizing the "third sphere": A critique of the persistence of the "economistic fallacy"', *Journal of Economic Issues*, 36(4): 1045–1078.

Amin, A., Cameron, A. and Hudson, R. (2002) *Placing the Social Economy*, London: Routledge.

Arente, H. and Kiiski, V. (2006) *Tourist Identity Expression through Postmodern Consumption: A focus on the home-exchange phenomenon*, Master thesis No 2005:78, Göteborg University.

Ateljevic, I. and Doorne, S. (2003) 'Culture, economy and tourism commodities: Social relations of production and consumption', *Tourist Studies* 3 (2): 123–141.

Bianchi, R. V. (2011) 'Tourism, capitalism and Marxist political economy', in J. T. Mosedale (ed.), *Political Economy and Tourism: A critical perspective*, Abingdon: Routledge.

Bloch, M. (1989) 'The symbolism of money in Imerina', in J. Parry and M. Bloch (eds), *Money and the Morality of Exchange*, Cambridge: Cambridge University Press, pp. 165–190.

Botterill, D. and Jones, T. (2010) *Tourism and Crime: Key themes*, Woodeaton: Goodfellow.

Bourdieu, P. (1970) 'The sentiment of honour in Kabyle society', in J. G. Peristiany (ed.), *Honour and Shame: The Values of Mediterranean Society*, Chicago: University of Chicago Press, pp. 193–241.

Bourdieu, P. (1977) *Outline of a Theory of Practice*, Cambridge: Cambridge University Press.

Bowie, K. A. (1998) 'The alchemy of charity: Of class and Buddhism in northern Thailand', *American Anthropologist*, 100 (2): 469–481.

Bryson, J. R., McGuiness, M. and Ford, R. G. (2002) 'Chasing a "loose and baggy monster": Almshouses and the geography of charity', *Area*, 34 (1): 48–58.

Campbell, L. M. and Smith, C. (2006) 'What makes them pay? Values of volunteer tourists working for sea turtle conservation', *Environmental Management*, 38: 84–98.

Chung, J. Y., Kyle, G. T., Petrick, J. F. and Absher, J. D. (forthcoming) 'Fairness of prices, user fee policy and willingness to pay among visitors to a national forest', *Tourism Management*.

Clarke, J. (2008) 'Gifts of tourism: Insights to consumer behavior', *Annals of Tourism Research*, 35 (2): 529–550.

De Certeau, M. (1984) *The Practice of Everyday Life*, Berkeley, CA: University of California Press.

De Croote: and Nicasi, F. (1994) 'Home exchange: An alternative form of tourism and case study of the Belgian market', *The Tourist Review*, 49: 22–26.

Germann Molz, J. (2007) 'Cosmopolitans on the couch: Mobile hospitality and the Internet', in J. Germann Molz and S. Gibson (eds), *Mobilizing Hospitality: The ethics of social relations in a mobile world*, Aldershot: Ashgate.

Gibson-Graham, J. K. (1996) *The End of Capitalism (As We Knew It): A feminist critique of political economy*, Oxford: Blackwell.

Gibson-Graham, J. K. (2002) 'A diverse economy: Rethinking economy and economic representation'. Retrieved from: www.communityeconomies.org (accessed May 2003).

Gibson-Graham, J. K. (2006) *Postcapitalist Politics*, London: University of Minnesota Press.

Giddens, A. (1979) *Central Problems in Social Theory: Action, structure and contradiction in social analysis*, Berkeley, CA: University of California Press.

Guo, Y., Pei, Y., Ye, Y., Chen, Y., Wang, K.-C. and Chan, H.-C. (2009) 'Tourist shopping behavior: A case of Shanghai outbound tourists', *Journal of Tourism, Hospitality & Culinary Arts*, 1 (2): 49–66.

Hall, C. M. (2008) *Tourism Planning: Policies, processes and relationships*, Harlow: Pearson Education.

Halpenny, E. A. and Caissie, L. T. (2003) 'Volunteering on nature conservation projects: Volunteer experience, attitudes and values', *Tourism Recreation Research*, 28: 25–33.

Henderson, J. C. (2007) 'Corporate social responsibility and tourism: Hotel companies in Phuket, Thailand, after the Indian Ocean tsunami', *Hospitality Management*, 26 (1): 228–239.

Jhappan, R. (2005) 'Of tsunamis and child sexual exploitation: The political economy of supply and demand in the sex tourism and trafficking trades', *Asian Women*, 20: 137–174.

Jones, A. and Murphy, J. T. (forthcoming) 'Theorizing practice in economic geography: Foundations, challenges, and possibilities', *Progress in Human Geography*.

Kosansky, O. (2002) 'Tourism, charity, and profit: The movement of money in Moroccan Jewish pilgrimage', *Cultural Anthropology*, 17 (3): 359–400.

Lee, R. and Wills, J. (1997) *Geographies of Economies*, London: Arnold.

Lew, A. A. and Wong, A. (2002) 'Tourism and the Chinese diaspora', in C. M. Hall and A. M. Williams (eds), *Tourism and Migration: New relationships between production and consumption*, London: CABI, pp. 205–219.

Lew, A. A. and Wong, A. (2004) 'Sojourners, *Gangxi* and clan associations: Social capital and overseas Chinese tourism to China', in D. Timothy and T. Coles (eds), *Tourism, Diasporas and Space*, London: Routledge, pp. 202–214.

Leyshon, A., Lee, R. and Williams, C. C. (2003) *Alternative Economic Spaces*, London: Sage.

McGehee, N. G. and Santos, C. A. (2004) 'Social change, discourse and volunteer tourism', *Annals of Tourism Research*, 32: 760–779.

McIntosh, A. and Bonnemann, S. (2006) 'Willing Workers on Organic Farms (WWOOF): The alternative farm stay experience?' *Journal of Sustainable Tourism*, 14 (1): 82–99.

McIntosh, A. and Campbell, T. (2001) 'Willing Workers on Organic Farms (WWOOF): A neglected aspect of farm tourism in New Zealand', *Journal of Sustainable Tourism*, 9 (2): 111–127.

McIntosh, A. J., and Zahra, A. (2007) 'A cultural encounter through volunteer tourism: Towards ideals of sustainable tourism?' *Journal of Sustainable Tourism*, 15: 541–556.

Massey, D. (1997) 'Economic/non-economic', in R. Lee and J. Wills (eds), *Geographies of Economies*, London: Arnold, pp. 27–36.

Mosedale, J. T. (2009) 'Wwoofing in New Zealand as alternative mobility and lifestyle,' *Pacific News*, 32: 25–27.

Mosedale, J. T. (2010) 'Being mobile off the grid: Experiencing mobility and alternative economic practices', Presentation at the Annual Meeting of the Association of American Geographers, Washington, D.C., April 14–18.

Mosedale, J. T. (2011) 'Thinking outside the box: Alternative political economies in tourism', in J. T. Mosedale (ed.), *Political Economy and Tourism: A critical perspective*, Abingdon: Routledge.

Pavlovskaya, M. (2004) 'Other transitions: Multiple economies of Moscow households in the 1990s', *Annals of the Association of American Geographers*, 94 (2): 329–351.

Polanyi, K. (2002) 'The great transformation', in N. W. Biggart (ed.), *Readings in Economic Sociology*, Oxford: Blackwell, pp. 38–61.

responsibletravel.com (n.d.) 'A better way to see the world'. Rerieved from: www. responsibletravel.com/TripSearch/Volunteer%20travel/ActivityCategory100011.htm?g clid=COnRmsqqj6UCFYE14woddncaOQ. Accessed November 7th 2010.

Reynisdottir, M., Song, H. and Agrusa, J. (2008) 'Willingness to pay entrance fees to natural attractions: An Icelandic case study', *Tourism Management*, 29 (6): 1076–1083.

Shaw, G. and Williams, A. M. (1990) 'Tourism, economic development and the role of entrepreneurial activity', in C. Cooper and A. Lockwood (eds), *Progress in Tourism Recreation and Hospitality Management*, London: Belhaven Press, pp. 67–81.

Sherry, J. (1983) 'Gift giving in anthropological perspective', *Journal of Consumer Research*, 10: 157–168.

Simpson, K. (2004) '"Doing development": The gap year, volunteer-tourists and a popular practice of development', *Journal of International Development*, 16: 681–692.

Sin, H. L. (2009) 'Volunteer tourism: "Involve me and I will learn"?', *Annals of Tourism Research*, 36 (3): 480–501.

Smith, A. and Stenning, A. (2006) 'Beyond household economies: Articulations and spaces of economic practice in postsocialism', *Progress in Human Geography*, 30 (2): 190–213.

Stoddart, H. and Rogerson, C. M. (2004) 'Volunteer tourism: The case of Habitat for Humanity South Africa', *GeoJournal*, 60: 311–318.

Thrift, N. and Olds, K. (1996) 'Refiguring the economic in economic geography', *Progress in Human Geography*, 20 (3): 311–337.

Tufts, S. and Milne, S. (1999) 'Museums: A supply-side perspective', *Annals of Tourism Research*, 26 (3): 613–631.

Wearing, S. (2001) *Volunteer Tourism: Experiences that make a difference*, Wallingford: CABI International.

White, C. L. and Lovett, J. C. (1999) 'Public preferences and willingness-to-pay for nature conservation in the North York Moors National Park, UK', *Journal of Environmental Management*, 55 (1): 1–13.

Williams, C. C. (2005) *A Commodified World? Mapping the limits of capitalism*, London: Zed Books.

Williams, C. C. and Nadin, S. (2010) 'Rethinking the commercialization of everyday life: A "whole economy" perspective', *Foresight*, 12 (6): 55–68.

Yang, M. M.-H. (1989) 'The gift economy and state power in China', *Comparative Studies in Society and History*, 31 (1): 25–54.

Ying, T. and Zhou, Y. (2007) 'Community, governments and external capitals in China's rural cultural tourism: A comparative study of two adjacent villages', *Tourism Management*, 28 (1): 96–107.

14 Hotel Transvaal and molar lines as a tool to open up spaces of hospitality

Alexander Grit and Paul Lynch[1]

Resistance is possible only through a creative act: Artists, filmmakers, musicians, mathematicians, philosophers, all resist.

(Deleuze 1988: 1)

In this article Hotel Transvaal (www.hoteltransvaal.com) is used as a case study to add to the discussion: 'How can hospitality practices lead to spaces of difference?' In the case study of Hotel Transvaal, artists apply 'hospitality' principles to draw attention to massive state interventions in a so-called 'problem neighbourhood'. The artists invite others to experience this transformation through a stay in Hotel Transvaal. Hotel Transvaal is unlike any other hotel, since it is not fixed in one building, but includes an entire neighbourhood. A neighbourhood houses residents and Hotel Transvaal turns these residents into hosts and guests. Hotel Transvaal is a case study in which the authors indicate how Hotel Transvaal, by playing with the organising principles of hospitality, evokes unexpected becomings and intensities and hence Hotel Transvaal facilitates difference. This article is structured as follows: First, the transformation process of the Transvaal neighbourhood is described; the neighbourhood forms the context for Hotel Transvaal. Second, the setting of the daily operations of Hotel Transvaal is conceptualised as a space of hospitality which can be regarded as a Deleuzian assemblage with a certain amount of organisation. This conceptualisation clears the road for the third part, a spotlight on the becomings and intensities that are 'produced' by the assemblage Hotel Transvaal. The last, fourth, part discusses the becomings and intensities within a larger context of art, new space and cultural laboratories.

The Transvaal neighbourhood

During its existence the Transvaal neighbourhood in The Hague, The Netherlands, has undergone several transformations due to increased human mobility and the associated processes of globalisation. Transvaal is situated south-west of the city centre in The Hague. Before the Transvaal neighbourhood was built, the area housed a castle and a large farm. The Transvaal neighbourhood was built at the beginning of the twentieth century. During that century, the inhabitants of Transvaal became more diverse throughout the history of the neighbourhood and the amenities had changed character accordingly. On 1 January 2007, Transvaal hosted 190 different nationalities in 16,033 houses. Since then, the neighbourhood has attracted many businesses, such as restaurants, including many ethnic cuisines from, for example, Turkey, Morocco and Suriname, (Ayurvedic) massage salons, barbers and Internet cafes. The Ministry of VROM (the Dutch housing and environmental department) considers the Transvaal neighbourhood as one of 40 problem neighbourhoods (*De 40 wijken van Vogelaar*) (VROM 2007), which were categorised as such on the basis of a clustering of social, physical and economic problems. Subsequently, these 40 neighbourhoods were redefined as 'Power neighbourhoods' (*Krachtwijken*) (VROM 2007).

At the time of this study, in 2008, the Transvaal neighbourhood was undergoing a large-scale transformation process. Three thousand social rented houses had been demolished and 1,600 new houses were being built. These large-scale transformations of neighbourhoods are not rare in the Netherlands. Governments at various levels and housing cooperations in large cities must manage deteriorating neighbourhoods, and the policy towards addressing this deterioration is that of demolition and rebuilding. The consequences for the inhabitants of the neighbourhoods were that they were being reallocated to other parts of the city and might have the option of moving back. A proportion of the homes that were being newly built were intended for sale and not to rent out, unlike the previous situation where all the homes were rented through housing co-operatives. The people who live in the houses that would remain in the neighbourhood were experiencing a complete makeover of the urban space, including nailed-up windows, the creation of open fields and the start of building activities.

Hotel Transvaal conceptualised as a space of hospitality and machinic assemblage

Friese (2004), philosopher at the Goethe Universität in Germany, argues for more hospitality and it is argued here, in line with others (for example, Kant, Derrida and indirectly Kafka) that healthy societies need spaces of hospitality that are open for difference. Statements about locating hospitality within the broader social issue of diversity and integration could be made. By healthy societies, we mean societies that are open for difference and where the minority becomes a voice. We would like to argue in favour of opening up spaces of hospitality, for having new experiences, bringing about difference, and to open up spaces of social relationships.

We argue for a welcoming of the stranger, as put forth by Friese (2004). She theorises the guest as a stranger, who holds a special position within society. Friese questions this tendency to 'reduce' the guests' role to that of the stranger. According to her, the stranger embodies the encounter with the unknown, dubious, incomprehensible and uncanny. We contend that by 'destabilising' hospitality spaces, the guests can become 'other', instead of the stranger. According to Friese

[t]he fine art of hospitality avoids the destabilization of a fragile equilibrium, it certifies esteem and consideration which is exceptional but not challenging or insulting, as does the clear rule to depart at the right time, so as not to interrupt the daily routine and rhythm of the house and become a burden or a nuisance.

(2004: 70)

The term 'spaces of hospitality' needs explanation. It refers to spaces where 'others are invited'. The notion of space adopted in this article is that of glue, holding matter and ideas together. Thrift (2006: 149) indicates that '[t]he world is made up of all kinds of things brought in to relation with one another by this universe of spaces through a continuous and largely involuntary process of encounter and the often violent training that the encounter forces'. Spaces of hospitality are created or opened up by inviting the other to participate. However, is the guest invited to become glue as well? In other words, is the guest being treated as a stabilised, singular identity or as someone who could evoke difference?

Hospitality has been seen so far as a response to the arrival of an 'other' and a demand inevitably always already implies a form of reciprocity. In this sense, hospitality intervenes as a regulatory factor in the obligation of the guest towards the host; and the mutual pact created between the one who receives, or the host, and the one who gives him/herself to the host, or the guest. This mutual pact, though promising negotiation and agreement, cannot be considered to be guaranteed or assured by hospitality (Friese 2004: 73). Through this, Dikeç (2002) implies that 'conditional and controlled hospitality' from a host perspective may not be hospitable at all, considering the political and legal implications of a hospitality transaction, and as it is perceived by the guest. Instead, the 'hospitableness' within a hospitality encounter, based on the dynamics in the host–guest relationship, may evolve into a different space. Dikeç argues that thinking about hospitality should involve thinking about openings and recognition, and acknowledges the inherent nature of boundaries in the notion of hospitality. He implies a 'mutuality of recognition', and argues that boundaries need to be opened, without being totally abolished, and the stranger needs to be given space, thus providing for recognition on both sides of the boundary (2002: 229).

Concerning hospitality, both Dikeç and Friese want to open up spaces of hospitality to difference. We agree with Dikeç and Friese, that the notion of hospitality is one that needs critical reflection and investigation, and re-conceptualisation. It may not always be liberating or emancipatory, for both the host and guest, but may on the other hand hide an unjust aspect beneath its welcoming surface (Dikeç 2002: 228; Robinson and Lynch 2007). We develop this argument and search for initiatives which organise hospitality interactions differently and consequently may open up space for new 'becomings'.

Conceptualisation of spaces of hospitality as a machinic assemblage

The Deleuzian concepts of 'assemblage', and 'organisational lines' facilitate the analysis of Hotel Transvaal. As these terms are not widely known, a brief explanation of the terms is given as well as a short introduction to the philosophers behind the concepts.

Philosopher Gilles Deleuze, together with French psychoanalyst Felix Guattari invented the concept of assemblage. In the 1970s their cooperation resulted in far less predictable modes of philosophical writing (including references to mathematics, biology, geology, sociology, physics, literature and music). Colebrook argues that

> More than any other thinker of this time, Deleuze's work is not so much a series of self-contained arguments as it is the formation of a whole new way of thinking and writing. For this reason he created an array of new terms and borrowed specialist terms from previous philosophers.
>
> (2002: xviii)

These terms form a sort of philosophical toolbox for analyzing change. Malins (2004: 92) indicates that this toolbox can be used 'to open up space to new becomings and to enable thought to move away from essences and internal truths and toward multiplicities, affects and machinic potentials.' According to Deleuze and Guattari (1987), it is not relevant to ask what a body 'means' or signifies; but rather, to what extent it has the capacity to 'become' different and to communicate intensities when it connects to another body, thus forming an assemblage. Deleuze and Guattari state very clearly that an assemblage should be measured for what it does in relationship with other assemblages. In their book *A Thousand Plateaus: Capitalism and schizophrenia* (1987: 4), Deleuze and Guattari ask, referring to the concept of assemblage, 'what it functions with, in connection with what other things it does or does not transmit intensities, in which other multiplicities its own are inserted and metamorphosed'. Malins (2004) argues that 'a body should, ultimately, be valued for what it can do (rather than what it essentially 'is'), and that assemblages should be assessed in relation to their enabling, or blocking, of a body's potential to become other'.

An 'assemblage' is one of these terms that can be found in the toolbox, that is, any number of 'things' or 'pieces' gathered into a single context. An example of an assemblage is a snowman, where a snowman is an arrangement of snow, broom, carrot and perhaps coal. Another example of an assemblage is an office, which gathers paper-clips, coffee and morning talks. An assemblage can bring about any number of 'effects' – aesthetic, productive, destructive, consumptive, informative and so on. Marcus and Saka (2006: 101) state that 'an assemblage is a sort of anti-organisational structural concept that permits the researcher to speak of emergence, heterogeneity, the decentred and the ephemeral in nonetheless ordered social life'. The concept of an assemblage can be seen as a reaction against 'structure'. Structure in the natural and social sciences grounds causal determination within a logic of stability and linear causality. Basically this means that assumptions towards action and reaction are drawn. An example of such an action and reaction assumption in a hospitality setting is the term 'McDonaldisation'. The sociologist Ritzer (1996), author of the book *The McDonaldization of Society*, states that efficiency, calculability, predictability, standardised control, etc. lead to predictable and homogeneous hospitality venues. Common sense knowledge underwrites this: visitors can perceive cities with hospitality venues which look all the same. However, by evaluating the McDonaldisation nature in venues at a local level, a radical alternative picture could be drawn. Although the menus and the physical appearance may be standardised, a hospitality venue can produce different and/or specific, and vital and vibrant spaces at a local level. This example indicates the limitations of approaches based on notions of determination which fail to explain change, resistance, or give insight into the unexpected or unpredictable.

Concluding this section, a space of hospitality, considered as an assemblage, is a space where the other is invited and welcomed to participate. The actualisation of this welcoming becomes the space of hospitality itself.

Hotel Transvaal as assemblage

Hotel Transvaal was initiated in 2005 when the artists' organisation *Mobiel projectbureau OpTrek* asked the architects Jan Konings and Duzan Doepel united in Ral2005 to visualise the transformation of the Transvaal neighbourhood. The concept of a hotel was chosen for this visualisation, not a common hotel but a place in which, according to the artists, the whole neighbourhood became the hotel and all inhabitants became hosts. The hotel rooms are situated in those houses that are ready for demolition. As hospitality scholars, it is an interesting challenge to analyze such a venue, since it forces one to rethink the notion of 'hospitality' when a combination of the concepts of 'hotel', 'hospitality', 'neighbourhood' and 'renewal' become entwined.

Harvey and Verwijnen (1999) indicate that public art has become a part of urban regeneration schemes such as waterfronts, and is increasingly used to raise the value of real estate property and large-scale projects. They argue that in order to avoid a superficial decorative role, artists will increasingly have to operate as facilitators of local civic participation. Hotel Transvaal clearly qualifies for this category, since the local is the assemblage.

By accepting the concept of an 'assemblage' to analyse Hotel Transvaal, causal relationships become useless and room is made to focus on potentialities. So much for what Hotel Transvaal is – now let us look at what Hotel Transvaal enables. When focusing on Hotel Transvaal from an assemblage point of view, the emphasis is not so much on what Hotel Transvaal 'is', but rather on what Hotel Transvaal 'does'. Questions which are relevant in this respect include: what connections are being made by the production of the assemblage Hotel Transvaal? What encounters and spaces do the assemblage Hotel Transvaal produce? What consequences are produced by its encounters?

The organisational lines of the machinic assemblage Hotel Transvaal

Organisational lines indicate how the constructive parts of the assemblage are connected with one another. Although Deleuze and Guattari do not explicitly write about hospitality and space, their ideas about space and movement, and the ethics of space and movement, are relevant since these are present in spaces of hospitality. In *A Thousand Plateaus* (1987), Deleuze and Guattari develop a set of concepts which can illuminate the organisation/movements in spaces. They mention 'lines' which express or effectuate different kinds of organisation of space. These lines are molar lines, molecular lines and lines of flight. Woodward indicates that 'molar lines organise by drawing strict boundaries, creating binary oppositions and dividing space into rigid segments with a hierarchical structure' (2007: 69). As a result, the space of hospitality characterised by its organisation through molar lines becomes highly organised and as a result the host-guest roles become strictly defined and predictable (Robinson and Lynch 2007). Molecular lines organise space in a subtle way, interlacing segments in a non-hierarchical way (Deleuze and Guattari 1987). The line of flight on the other hand does not organise space in a fixed fashion. According to Woodward, '[t]he line of flight is a pure movement of change which breaks out of one form of organization and moves towards another' (2007: 69–70). As a result, the space of hospitality becomes highly unpredictable and the host–guest roles can even become undone and the space of hospitality may cease to exist. Furthermore, Woodward argues that the line of flight is the privileged line for Deleuze and Guattari since it is the line of metamorphosis and change, and that a line of flight breaks with tradition (2007: 69).

Various complex combinations of these lines in particular assemblages express varying tendencies towards different kinds of organisation. Many spaces in contemporary society are organised through molar lines, the most obvious example being a prison. In a prison organisation the distinction, for example between staff and inmates is very much defined, and is visible in the design of the building and in clothing. A hotel is also organised along molar lines: the transactions in a hotel setting are usually very predictable; the distinction between host and guest is clear and the financial consequences calculable, secured through procedures, rules and rigid places. The creators/artists of Hotel Transvaal chose the molar line of organisation to 'build' Hotel Transvaal, to connect the fragments together. A residence/host/guest is an example of such a fragment.

The molar lines, which the creators implemented in the Transvaal neighbour-hood, can be explained through the Quintessence model (Zwaal 2003: 25): In traditional hospitality management, 'the Quintessence model can be applied in conducting an organizational diagnosis for any company in the service business sector.' Zwaal (2003) refers to five perspectives, known as the service pentagon, covering the quintessence of service management. These perspectives are the HRM perspective (*all people involved*), technological perspective (*efficient and effective systems*), operational perspective (*to create and deliver, efficient, effective*), customer and marketing perspective (*a valuable and satisfying experience*) and, finally, a financial perspective (*efficient, effective*). It is this way of organising hospitality space which leads to molar hospitality spaces, dividing the host and guest into separated roles. HRM is purely for the host; marketing attracts the guests, while finance objectifies the relationship between host and guest and also between organisation and employees. Furthermore, technology optimises the processes of dividing the host and guest and operations ensure a smooth separation between host and guest. Hotel Transvaal reinforced its existence by printing its name on the bathroom towels. The model functions to show how a service provider functions, and it is useful to see which molar lines are used to construct Hotel Transvaal. However, such an analysis would not convey its special features. From a hospitality management standpoint the unique aspects of the hotel will be hidden underneath the balanced scorecards and income statements.

Apart from the use of Molar lines by the creators/artists of Hotel Transvaal, they also applied lines of flight to organise Hotel Transvaal. The neighbourhood is transformed into a hotel through molar lines which inevitably evokes lines of flight since it transforms residents into a mixture of hosts and guests and pulled streets, together with its cats, dogs, residents and so on, into spaces of hospitality. By transforming residential spaces into spaces of hospitality, the creators/artists applied lines of organisation which broke with the tradition of homes and transformed these houses into hotel rooms.

Becomings and intensities 'produced' by the assemblage Hotel Transvaal

Hotel Transvaal is an interesting case since it creates many different spaces of hospitality within one assemblage, with different bodies and other assemblages. It illustrates the different power relationships in spaces of hospitality and the separation of the creator and the creation of the assemblage. The creator-artists, who embody the creative side and take up the entrepreneurial role of hotel manager, at the same time construct an assemblage which hosts different spaces of hospitality.

The unique aspect of the hotel is that it is created out of fragments. These fragments are 'assemblaged' into a single context, namely Hotel Transvaal. To illustrate, a blackberry bush, once part of a garden, becomes wild and becomes a part of the landscape of the hotel; a child playing with a bicycle on the street becomes a local attraction. A 'Wham' poster, from the 1980s pop group, at one time featured in the context of a teen's room within the context of a family life; the artist, who (re)decorated the room, incorporated the poster into the design of the room and this fragment becomes part of the interior design. Local shopkeepers and restaurant owners become 'amenities' in the context of the hotel. The massive revitalising of the neighbourhood becomes the 'theme' for the hotel, just as the Disney Company applies a 'Wild West theme' to Disney's Davy Crockett Ranch. Fragments which formally belonged in other contexts or still form the context in other contexts are forged into a hotel concept.

Hotel Transvaal has several of these spaces, such as the space where the artist is invited to design the rooms (a building which is ready for demolition); the space where the guest is invited to rest (bedroom); the space where the employee is invited to welcome the guest (reception, bedrooms); the space where the guest can experience food and entertainment (restaurant and other amenities); the space where journalists and social scholars are invited to produce materials regarding spaces of hospitality; and the space where other artists are invited to participate. Spaces all have their nature as to how the encounter between things, people and ideas become organised (Lynch 2005). These encounters generate effects which in the Deleuzian sense can be linked to embodied sensations. Merleau-Ponty (1964) defined embodiment in a way that reflects how we live in and experience the world through our bodies, especially through perception, emotion, language, movement in space, time, and sexuality. He spoke of existence as known only in and through the body.

One of the authors remembers Hotel Transvaal for the effects that were produced in the silence of the night. The researcher stood in front of the open window on the chilly floor. It was two o'clock and the author looked out at nailed windows illuminated by the moonlight, the long shadows created by the trees, the uncontrolled rose bushes scattered around the window, the sweet smell of wilderness of the garden, the big yellow container to collect wood for recycling, the sight of graffiti and a sense of the overwhelming power of the government. The sight of the uncontrolled roses reminded him of the fairytale sleeping beauty. She slept a hundred years. If this had happened in Transvaal, sleeping beauty would have been awoken by a destruction hammer ... or perhaps not.... The spindle would have ended up for sure in the yellow container. Moreover, Hotel Transvaal helped the authors to create and sharpen their ideas of spaces of hospitality. The encounter of one of the authors with the hostess Sabrina, who was also a part of the assemblage then, brought him in contact with other scholars, Bollywood DVDs from the local market and with you, the reader of this chapter. The guest of the hotel becomes part of a slice of history of the Netherlands. How the Netherlands copes with urban forces of the twentieth century is made sensible through Hotel Transvaal, which through the concept of a hotel, connected fragments into a Deleuzian assemblage. These fragments, which formally belonged in other contexts, or still indeed form the context, are forged into a hotel concept. The inhabitants of the Transvaal neighbourhood become hosts and the streets become the hallways and the houses are turned into rooms. Connections between former seemingly unconnected entities are made by the designers. Fragments are linked, marked and redefined and put into context. In short, Hotel Transvaal connected the unconnected within one context and this assemblage as space of hospitality created more spaces in which the stranger is invited to participate.

Hospitality space within a larger context

New space

In many ways, this chapter serves as a valuable basis for critiquing theory on traditional conceptions of tourism space. In the case of Hotel Transvaal, a space of hospitality is assembled, which produces several other spaces of hospitality within the neighbourhood. These are the interactions of the Hotel Transvaal guests with the different 'fragments', which lead to new becomings in the form of spaces of hospitality. The creators/artists of Hotel Transvaal have created a paradox using a rigid (Hotel) organisation in order to create 'becomings'. These new becomings are aesthetic and ideological. The ideological part is to show an insight into a 'deterritorialisation' of the neighbourhood by the government, in the sense that governments at various levels are reallocating inhabitants, and changing social and physical structures. It can be seen through this chapter, the significance of an assemblage constituted by molar lines connecting fragments together, and its role in facilitating lines of flight, produced new spaces of hospitality.

Looking at the nature of the interactions within the new spaces of hospitality produced by Hotel Transvaal, the authors argue for the label 'smooth space'. This is a Deleuzian post-structuralist notion for open-ended spaces; in other words, spaces which are not defined by a path between fixed and identifiable points (Massumi 1987: xiii). This can be linked to the notion of opening spaces of hospitality proposed by Dikeç (2002); being hospitable or extending the notion of hospitality does not imply the sovereign power of the host over the guest, but the recognition that we play shifting roles in our engagements, both as hosts and guests. It is further argued that 'hospitality is not about rules of stay being implied or predefined through power relations between hosts and guests, but about recognition that we are hosts and guests at the same time in multiple and shifting ways' (Lashley, *et al.* 2007: 239). In this aspect the roles of the host and the guest, are not to be pre-conceived but are mutually constitutive of each other and are relational in nature.

Space of hospitality as cultural laboratory

Hotel Transvaal challenges the guest's existing ideas and facilitates cultural laboratories. Löfgren (1999: 7) indicates that 'in a cultural laboratory, people are able to experiment with new aspects of their identities, their social relations, or their interaction with nature and also to use the important cultural skills of daydreaming and mind-travelling'. Hotel Transvaal has facilitated true cultural laboratories, which are based on hospitality principles. Moreover, Hotel Transvaal re-engages and develops hospitality theory, and suggests an alternative way of thinking about the exchange of hospitality, where there is an inviting of the 'other' and a diffusion of host and guest roles into one another. Hotel Transvaal clearly involved the shifting of roles and opening up spaces of hospitality through gluing different spaces within the neighbourhood together into one assemblage which produces new hospitality spaces; hence, society and its inter-actions themselves became more hospitable. Furthermore, this paper endeavours broader implications for the production of new hospitality and tourism space as well; or, for example, the development of hospitable socio-organisational space, which includes innovative ideas about the regeneration of urban space for hospi-tality and tourism. For Deleuze, art has a distinctive role of resisting fixed repre-sentations, 'to create,' is 'to resist.' It means 'it's effective, positive; the world would not be what it is if not for art, people could not hold on any more' (Deleuze 1988: 9). For Deleuze, resistance is possible only through a creative act: 'whenever one creates, one resists' (Deleuze 1988: 1). Hotel Transvaal is such a creative act. Hotel Transvaal resists 'problem neighbourhoods' and its molar tendencies of including and excluding. By creating one assemblage which produces many other spaces of hospitality, Hotel Transvaal resists hostility.

Note

1 The authors would like to thank Dr Donald Craig, Sabrina Lindeman, Bram Heijkers and Maaike de Jong for their valuable contributions.

References

Colebrook, C. (2002) *Understanding Deleuze*, Australia: Allen & Unwin.

Deleuze, G. (1988) *Bergsonism* (trans. H. Tomlinson), New York: Zone Books.

Deleuze, G. and Guattari, F. (1987) *A Thousand Plateaus: Capitalism and schizophrenia* (trans. B. Massumi), London: Continuum.

Dikeç, M. (2002) 'Pera peras poros: Longings for spaces of hospitality', *Theory, Culture & Society*, 19 (1–2): 227–247.

Friese, H. (2004) 'Spaces of hospitality', *Journal of the Theoretical Humanities*, 9 (2): 67–79.

Harvey, D. and Verwijnen, J. (1999), *Public Art and Urban Development*. Retrieved from: www.eliaartschools.org/_downloads/publications/EJAE/2000/economy/Harvey__Verwijnen.pdf (accessed 28 March 2009).

Lashley, C., Lynch, A. and Morrison, A. (2007) 'Conclusions and research agenda', in C. Lashley, A. Lynch and A. Morrison (eds), *Hospitality: A social lens*, Oxford: Elsevier, pp. 173–192.

Löfgren, O. (1999) *On Holiday: A history of vacationing*, Berkeley, CA: University of California Press.

Lynch, A. (2005) 'Sociological impressionism in a hospitality context', *Annals of Tourism Research*, 32 (3): 527–548.

Marcus, G. E. and Saka, E. (2006) 'Assemblage', *Theory, Culture & Society*, 23: 101–109.

Malins, P. (2004) 'Machinic assemblages: Deleuze, Guattari and an ethico-aesthetics of drug use', *Janus Head*, 7: 84–104.

MacCannell, D. (1999) *The Tourist: A New Theory of the Leisure Class*, Berkeley: University of California Press.

Massumi, B. (1987) 'Foreword', in G. Deleuze and F. Guattari, *A Thousand Plateaus* (trans. B. Massumi), London: Continuum.

Merleau-Ponty, M. (1964) 'Eye and mind' (trans. C. Dallery), in J. M. Edie (ed.), *The Primacy of Perception and Other Essays*, Evanston, IL: Northwestern University Press, pp. 159–190.

Pasquinelli, M. (2008) 'Beyond the ruins of the creative city: Berlin's factory of culture and the sabotage of rent', *Consistory Talk I: The Artist and Urban Development*. Retrieved from: www.rekombinant.org/mat (accessed 28 March 2009).

Pine, B. J. and Gilmore, J. H. (1998) 'Welcome to the experience economy', *Harvard Business Review*, 76 (4): 97–105.

Pine, B. J. and Gilmore, J. H. (1999) *The Experience Economy Work is Theatre and Every Business a Stage*, Boston: Harvard Business School Press.

Ritzer, G. (1996) *The McDonaldization of Society* (revised edition), Thousand Oaks, CA: Pine Forge Press.

Robinson, M. Lynch, A. (2007) 'Hospitality through poetry: Control, fake solidarity and breakdown', *International Journal of Culture, Hospitality and Tourism*, 1 (3): 237–246.

Thrift, N. (2006) 'Space', *Theory, Culture & Society*, 23: 139–155.

Woodward, A. (2007) 'Deleuze and suicide' in A. Hickey-Moody and P. Malins (eds), *Deleuzian Encounters*,Hampshire: Palgrave, pp. 62–76.

VROM (2007) *Wonen, wijken en integratie: Actieplan krachtwijken – van aandachtswijk naar krachtwijk.* Retrieved from: www.vrom.nl/pagina.html?id=2706&sp=2&dn=7376 (accessed 28 March 2009).

Zwaal, W. (2003) *Models for Graduate Students*, CHN School of Graduate Studies. Limited publication.

Epilogue

Hopeful tourism: an unfolding perspective

Nigel Morgan, Annette Pritchard and Irena Ateljevic

Hopeful tourism's new story

We introduced this book by suggesting that now is an appropriate time to reflect on our ways of understanding and being in the tourism world since humankind seems at a tipping point environmentally, economically and socially. Such conceptual reflection is also pertinent as many conventions and orthodoxies appear increasingly stressed and new perspectives are emerging across all kinds of disciplines and research fields (Rifkin 2009). As one such emerging perspective, we have seen here how hopeful tourism can shape research (from ontological-through to methods-level decisions), offer broader philosophical understanding of how we know our multiple, entwined worlds *and* produce specific, attainable, transformative acts, whether through education or activism. We have also seen how the perspective draws on an enquiry–learning–action nexus – the three entwined elements of knowledge-based radical critiques of social settings and institutions, the nurturing of reflexive, ethical tourism researchers, practitioners and policy-makers and advocacy of and activism for human rights, dignity and just societies in tourism arenas.

Hopeful tourism remains an as yet evolving vision which offers an alternative to the dominant way of understanding and being in the tourism world not by dismissing it but by engaging it to demonstrate that it offers but one perspective. It seeks to disturb and shake up tourism's hegemonic ontologies, methodologies and practices and reduce the isolation experienced by interpretive and critical researchers in a field where objectivity, generalisation and distance are the norm. As a field of study, tourism has certainly experienced exponential growth in recent decades, seeing a considerable rise in the numbers of higher education institutions offering undergraduate and postgraduate programmes, a tremendous expansion of its doctoral, post-doctoral and professoriate communities and a significant increase in the number of tourism-related journals and book series. In many ways these indicators suggest a field which is thriving and in rude health. Yet if we probe a little deeper and ask some more profound questions, we find a field of study which lacks balance, philosophical depth and intellectual maturity.

A number of scholars have commented on the lamentable lack of theoretical development in tourism, including John Tribe (2000, 2009), Julio Aramberri

(2010) and Adrian Franklin (2004) to name just three. Certainly, tourism knowledge-building is overly incremental and additive and dominated by scholars who, Keith Hollinshead suggests, prefer 'the comfortable sureties of the old and largely empirical conventional scientific objectivities to the emergent and plainly messy irregular social discourses which are involved in the new interpretivist/postmodern ways of knowing' (2004: 78). It remains the case that critical tourism-oriented reflections on the market economy and its performance continue to be marginal as many researchers eschew difficult social, political and ethical questions in favour of technical problem-solving and profit augmenting research; for too many such scholars 'markets are all they know and they marvel that people might even question their very raison d'être' (Aramberri 2010: 23). Julio Aramberri goes further to suggest that tourism research is in crisis, beset by an every growing 'chasm' of 'Mutually Accepted Disinterest' whereby researchers are divided between the '*How tos* [who] feel secure that the markets they probe are here to stay' and the '*whys* [who] profess a complete distaste for the framework their opponents take for granted and hope that … it may be done away with' (2010: 24).

This impasse in which tourism now finds itself suggests a range of future scenarios. In the first, the field becomes even more closely aligned to the needs of industry and tourism education blurs into training (although recognition of the recent excesses of the global financial markets may militate against this). In the second, the cultural critics or the *whys* gain further ground (but if the intention is to dismantle what has been established as orthodoxy in the academy, the task may be too great). In either of these two scenarios, the status quo prevails and Aramberri's chasm of mutual disregard remains or splits the field. There may however be a third *both/and* rather than an *either/or* scenario; one that starts with hope and depends on harnessing the abilities of all tourism's knowledge networks to create a more hopeful future (Ren *et al.* 2010). The essence of hope is that it looks forwards not backwards; it seeks to imagine possible potentialities rather than rely on the certitudes of the past; it aims to build a future for the tourism industry guided by principles of mindful not mindless development. In hope, tourism can be linked to the pursuit of justice and human rights; in hope, tourism has the potential to spur syncretic growth, engage reflexive and ethically aware consumers, operators and employees and thereby build fairer neighbourhoods, communities and societies. As bell hooks (2003: xiv) reminds us:

> Hope stretches the limits of what is possible. It is linked with that basic trust in life without which we could not get from one day to the next.… To live by hope is to believe that it is worth taking the next step.

Hopes, transformations and realizations

The contributors to this collection have shown that as a perspective hopeful tourism offers a compelling new story. Across the three parts of the book we have seen that more hopeful tourism futures are possible and just how the perspective can shape research decisions and designs, offer more profound onto-logical understanding of how we know our multiple, entwined worlds and produce definite, achievable transformation, whether through education or activ-ism. The scholars here and others (more and less) associated with the Academy of Hope are confronting 'the opportunities and obligations inherent in interven-ing to foster change' (Mair, this volume) and while some only share aspects of the hopeful tourism perspective as fellow-travellers, others hold close its tenets (Pritchard *et al.*, this volume). But such interventions are not without personal, intellectual or professional risk and here again, it is instructive to quote bell hooks (2003: 22) reflecting on how difficult it is to work on the art of being and loving in the current context of rationalized economic, political and academic structures:

> As an intellectual working as an academic I often felt that my commitment to radical openness and devotion to critical thinking, to seeking after truth, was at odds with the demands that I uphold the status quos if I want to be rewarded.... While much lip service is given to the notion of free speech in academic settings, in actuality constant censorship – often self-imposed – takes place. Teachers fear they will not receive promotions or that in worst-case scenarios they will lose their jobs.

We have underlined that hopeful tourism is focused on co-transformation and it seems that a key prerequisite of transformative social shift is a transformation of self (Schwarzin, this volume). To become hopeful scholars Peter McLaren (2009) urges us as academics and teachers to ask ourselves: (1) what has society has made of us that we don't want to be? (2) where am I? (the ethical question) and (3) who am I (the epistemological question)? He suggests that we need to take both the language of critique and the language of hope into the spaces of our knowledge production, our classrooms and our activism. He defines praxis not only as a theory translated into practice but also as a process of our efforts to change society through which we change ourselves. Thus we need to develop self-awareness and create inner and outer liberation if we are to truly engage with the development of social change.

Yet in order to do so we need to work on further developing methods and experiential learning that help us to learn the art of being and living in terms of developing our human capacity qualities: vitality, passion, coherence and align-ment (between mind, spirit and body). While the corporate world has been quick to recognize the importance of this form of experiential learning to develop human capacities, their absence in mainstream academic thinking is surprising given the global urgency to change our deeply embedded ways of doing, think-ing and conceptualizing (Senge *et al.* 2005; Rifkin 2005; 2009). We need to develop innovative pedagogical methods that will liberate ourselves and our stu-dents and help us cultivate a mindful way of being (Fromm 1993) that leads us to a mindful future. As Peter McLaren and Nathalia Jaramillo argue in their fore-word, 'a transformative pedagogy for a critical tourism studies must attempt to create an explicit connection with a philosophy of liberation that projects the path to a totally new society. It must, in other words, not simply exist at the plane of immanence, but also possess a Promethean side that points towards a transcendence of the given.'

Having outlined this 'manifesto' we invite you to engage in all those critical spaces of potential activism that structure this book – critical tourism research, critical tourism education and critical action in the (tourism) world. Only time will reveal how hopeful tourism will evolve as a perspective and whether more researchers will find value in its aims of co-transformative learning and syncretic growth. Who can tell how an idea will develop, whether it will chime with others' aspirations or not? Hopeful tourism scholars are by no means lone (or the first) voices in the tourism academy to call for a greater engagement with long-term planetary goals. We join a growing group of academics who argue that our field needs to break free of the performance-led, industry-driven intellectual straightjacket which binds it to a narrow, present-focused empirical research agenda. Tourism needs to engage with more profound ways of being and knowing and maybe what we sow now may grow into something nurturing and sheltering in the future:

> An old woman in the Middle East planted a date and described the process: When you plant a date, you know you'll never eat from the date tree because it takes about eighty years to grow roots deep enough to go to the scarce water. The date tree gets so buffeted in that time by windstorms and droughts that for the most part, the tree looks like it's dying. If you didn't understand its process, you could easily cut it down. But if you understand the process, you can make the commitment. You have to have an image of what will happen. Once you do, it makes all the difference.
>
> (Ray and Anderson 2000: 64)

We planted an olive tree to mark the closing of the third Critical Tourism Studies Conference in Zadar in 2009 (Figure 15.1) and that continues to thrive. We trust

Figure 15.1 The Zadar Conference olive tree.

that hopeful tourism offers an agenda which will in part resonate with research-ers engaged in critical and interpretive practice *and* with the wider tourism academy. It is not a finished intellectual product nor is it a template for social justice. As it stands, it is an unfolding vision, a perspective and a way of knowing which is values-led, which embraces the oneness and integration of mind, body and spirit found in non-western wisdom traditions and which is empowering and participant-driven. If we can fold these values into tourism learning, then we may develop a broader philosophical understanding of the ways in which social relations structure institutions of power in our multiple, entwined tourism worlds. In this, maybe hopeful tourism enquiry has something to offer which is worth holding out for, since 'The hopes of today are the realisa-tions of tomorrow' (Mirra Alfassa 2004: 73).

References

Alfassa, M. (2004) *Words of the Mother III*, Pondicherry, India: Sri Aurobindo Ashram Publication Department.

Aramberri, J. (2010) 'The real scissors crisis in tourism research', in D. G. Pearce and R. W. Butler (eds), *Tourism Research: A 20–20 Vision*, Oxford: Goodfellow Publishers, pp. 15–27.

Franklin, A. (2007) 'The problem with tourism theory', in I. Ateljevic, A. Pritchard and N. Morgan (eds), *The Critical Turn in Tourism Studies: Innovative research methodol-ogies*, Oxford: Elsevier, pp. 131–148.

Fromm, E. (1993) *The Art of Being,* London: Constable and Robinson Ltd.

Hollinshead, K. (2004) 'A primer in ontological craft', in J. Phillimore and L. Goodson. (eds), *Qualitative Research in Tourism: Ontologies, epistemologies and methodologies*, London: Routledge, pp. 63–82.

hooks, b. (2003) *Teaching Community: A pedagogy of hope*, New York: Routledge.

McLaren, P. (2009) *Critical Pedagogy for a Post-Capitalist Future*, a keynote address at the 3rd Critical Tourism Studies Conference 'Connecting Academies of Hope: Critical actions and Creative vistas', Zadar, Croatia, 21–24 June.

Pritchard, A. Morgan, N. and Ateljevic, I. (2011) 'Hopeful tourism: A new transformative perspective', *Annals of Tourism Research*, in press.

Ray, H. P. and Anderson, S. R. (2000) *The Cultural Creatives: How 50 million people are changing the world*, New York: Harmony Books.

Ren, C., Pritchard, A. and Morgan, N. (2010) 'Constructing tourism research: A critical enquiry', *The Annals of Tourism Research*, 37 (4): 885–904.

Rifkin, J. (2005) *The European Dream: How Europe's vision of the future is quietly eclipsing the American dream*, New York: Penguin Group.

Rifkin, J. (2009) *The Empathic Civilization: The race to global consciousness in a world in crisis*, Los Angeles: Tarcher.

Senge, P., Sharmer, O., Jaworski, J. and Flowers, B. S. (2005) *Presence: An exploration of profound change in people, organizations, and society*, New York: DoubleDay.

Tribe, J. (2009) 'Philosophical issues in tourism', in J. Tribe (ed.), *Philosophical Issues in Tourism*, Bristol: Channel View, pp. 3–25.

Tribe, J. (2004) 'Knowing about tourism: Epistemological issues', in J. Phillimore and L. Goodson (eds), *Qualitative Research in Tourism: Ontologies, epistemologies, and methodologies*, London: Routledge, pp. 46–62.

Index

Page numbers in *italics* denote tables.